THE TWICE-BORN

THE TWICE-BORN

A Study of a Community of High-Caste Hindus

G. MORRIS CARSTAIRS

with a Preface by
MARGARET MEAD

1961
INDIANA UNIVERSITY PRESS
BLOOMINGTON

All Rights Reserved
*
Library of Congress
Catalog Card number 58-9003

First Published 1957
Second Impression 1961

Manufactured in Great Britain

PREFACE

ADVANCES in the application of scientific knowledge to our understanding of man have been dependent on two developments, methods of observing other human beings and methods of observing ourselves, as observers. Articulateness about the observed, unrelieved by articulateness about the biases and blindnesses of the observer gives us arid material, either devoid of all meaning or so heavily weighted with unacknowledged emotions that they are meaningful only to those who share the same biases.

Dr. Carstairs' book is a notable contribution to those studies which include the observer. An unusually felicitous set of circumstances, chief among them his childhood spent in India with Hindustani as a first language, has made it possible for him to treat his own motives as gently and thoroughly as those he is studying. An unusually full training which has added work in cultural anthropology to training and practice in psychiatry provided him with methods of field work. His own remembrances, feeling for the people, and sensitive respect for their values, have provided the book with a humaneness which is extraordinarily rare and difficult to achieve. He has called the book *The Twice-Born*, and as appropriately one might describe his field work as the " twice experienced ".

The Twice-Born is a study of the differences in character which characterise three Indian castes, in a remote and only recently modernised community in the state of Rajasthan. Through intensive study of individuals, we are given a picture of the way in which caste position in India expands the imagination and limits the possibilities of the members of each independent caste. The details are vivid, moving and strange. This study should not only enrich our materials on national character and caste character and India, but enrich our sense of the strangely contrasting fates which human cultures offer to human beings.

MARGARET MEAD

May 21, 1956

CONTENTS

Preface, by Margaret Mead — page 5
Acknowledgements — 8
Introduction — 10

PART I

Chapter
1. The Village of Deoli — 19
2. Dramatis Personae — 28
3. Inter-personal Relations — 39
4. Family Relationships — 63
5. The Hindu Body-image — 77
6. Religion and Phantasy — 89
7. Traits shared and not-shared by each Caste — 106
8. The Reverse of the Medal — 125
9. Hindu Personality Formation—Conscious Processes — 137
10. Hindu Personality Formation—Unconscious Processes — 152
11. Summary and Conclusions — 170

PART II

Three Hindu Self-portraits

1. Shri Rajendra Singh, Rajput — 175
2. Shri Shankar Lal, Brahmin — 216
3. Shri Puranmal Mehta, Bania — 260

Appendix I. Census of Deoli, February, 1951 — 316
Appendix II. Formal Psychological Tests Employed — 318
Appendix III. Glossary of Hindustani Words — 326
Bibliography — 335
Index — 339

ACKNOWLEDGEMENTS

THIS book, and the field work in India upon which it is based, represent the fulfilment of a long-standing ambition. It is not uncommon for psychiatrists to read the accounts given by anthropologists of remote peoples, and to envy these travellers their exotic experiences ; but it rarely happens that they are given the opportunity themselves to carry out research of this kind. The author owes debts of gratitude to those who encouraged and directed his studies in social anthropology, namely Professors E. Evans-Pritchard, Meyer Fortes, Alexander Leighton and Morris Opler, and Drs. Abram Kardiner and Margaret Mead: to the last-named an especial debt is due, owing to the inspiring example of her own similar studies. Mrs. G. P. Steed not only contributed invaluable theoretical and practical instruction in methodology but also made possible his first field work in India by inviting him, in 1949-50, to participate in the Columbia University sociological research project which she directed. The field work in 1951 and 1952, during which the material for this study was collected, was made possible by a Rockefeller Foundation grant, and by the award of a Henderson Research Fellowship in social aspects of psychiatry. It was carried out under the supervision of Professor Fortes of Cambridge.

In India, generous co-operation was received from the Council of the Church of Scotland mission in Rajputana, and from the administrative offices of Mewar Division, at Udaipur. Among the many individuals whose help contributed to the carrying through of the research, mention should be made in particular of H.H. Sri Bhagwat Singh, Maharana of Udaipur, Major Manohar Singh of Bedla and Raj Rana Khuman Singh of Delwara; of Dr. Dhanda of the Udaipur Public Health Service and of Sri Kalu Lal Shrimali, then Principal of the Vidya Bhavan Teachers' Training College, and of Mr. Moti Lal Agarwal and Mr. Mohan Lal Vyas. Above all, thanks are due to the anonymous citizens of " Deoli ", contributors of the information on which the work is based.

In the preparation and revision of the text the writer has profited by advice from several readers. He owes especial debts in this regard to Miss Pearl King, Mr. David Sutherland Graeme, Mrs. Gitel Steed and above all to Dr. Margaret Mead;

and he is grateful to Miss Rosemary Gordon for her interpretations of informants' Rorschach tests. Not least is he indebted to Vera Carstairs who both shared the rigours of fieldwork and sustained him in the task of authorship, and finally undertook the checking of the text and the preparation of the index and glossary.

To all these helpers, the author offers his heartfelt thanks.

INTRODUCTION

THERE are many rich sources to be tapped by anyone who is curious to learn about Indian psychology. The classics of Hindu religion, literature and philosophy have been made accessible to the West by generations of scholars—but these works, it might be objected, are concerned almost exclusively with " life as it ought to be ". It is in the legacy of realistic imaginative writing to which the long association with Britain gave rise, that one can find projections of Indian " life as it is ".

In their several ways Kipling and E. M. Forster, C. F. Andrews, Leonard Myers and a host of other writers have presented their portrait groups of Britons and Indians (who often reveal themselves most eloquently in their mutual misunderstandings). There are many Indians also who, writing in English, have vividly expressed their own experience and outlook—the names of Tagore, Mahatma Gandhi and Pandit Nehru, and of contemporary novelists like Mulk Raj Anand, R. K. Narayan and Sudhin Ghose come at once to mind.

Thanks to this literature the characteristic features of the Hindu attitude to life are widely recognised and have even won Western proselytes. Consequently, any study which professes to identify and to analyse some of the basic features of Hindu personality must be prepared to meet the scrutiny of an audience already to some extent familiar with the subject. In order to justify its appearance such a study must add something new, in respect either of definition or of interpretation, to what is already known. As yet, however, there have been few attempts to explore the essential differences between Indian and Western personality structure by means of planned, systematic psychological observations.

This book records such an attempt; but it was not originally conceived as a study in national character. It was undertaken with a view to solving a rather different problem.

When confronted with a case of neurotic illness a psychiatrist tries to explain how it has come about. He commonly inquires into what happened to that patient in his earliest, most formative years and relates those experiences to the ultimate breakdown. Sometimes the relationship is clear; often it remains ambiguous, and the doubt arises: " Suppose he had

INTRODUCTION

not been treated in this way by his father, or in that way by his mother; would he necessarily be a very different person now?"

This question often occurred to me when I began to study psychological medicine. That it did so was due, no doubt, to a personal bias against " enthusiasm " in psychological theory —to use the word in the pejorative sense imparted to it by Scottish theologians. I had learned from the philosophy of David Hume some of his distrust of speculation that cannot be submitted to the test of experience; and this was subsequently reinforced by the example of Sir David Henderson's matter-of-fact approach to clinical problems during my apprenticeship in psychiatry under him.

" The test of experience "—but where could this be found? Already, as an immature House Physician my imagination had been stimulated by reading William McDougall's observations on the Dyaks of Borneo, and W. H. R. Rivers' accounts of his several field studies among the Todas and the Melanesians. It was these two doctors-turned-ethnologists who introduced me to the study of anthropology, and kindled the interest which led ultimately to this present study. The plan which eventually matured was this: to select a community whose values, culture and social customs were consistently different from those with which we middle-class Westerners are familiar; to learn their language and live among them, and in so doing, to try to observe on the one hand those formative experiences peculiar to their society, and on the other any personality characteristics common to their adult members and differing from my own conceptions of the normal.

Having done this, I should be in a position to see whether my concepts of personality development were adequate to explain the relationship between these adult traits and these formative experiences. The personality theory with which I was equipped was basically that of Adolphe Meyer's psycho-biology, to which I had added extensive readings (but not as yet first-hand experience) in Freudian psycho-analysis. If I succeeded, this would still offer only presumptive evidence in favour of the greater or less " rightness of fit " of these theories; but at least the experiment should provide me with a wealth of test cases, such as I could not hope to accumulate in years of psychiatric work in my own society.

Studies of this kind have been carried out in several cultures, with varying degrees of thoroughness and expertise, since Margaret Mead blazed the trail with her justly famous studies of personality formation in seven different societies in Melanesia and the South Seas; * but field studies by psychiatrists have been comparatively rare.†

The Community selected for study was to be one of high-caste Hindu villagers: villagers, because the traditional ways of life are more tenaciously retained in the country districts of India than in the cities; and high-caste, because these are the communities in which education is most common, and in which Brahminical teachings are deliberately inculcated. I proposed to make Udaipur, the chief town of the former Princely state of Mewar, my point of departure in looking for the village in which I should work. I chose the State of Rajasthan for two reasons: it was there that I spent the greater part of my first nine years, with Indian children as my playmates and Hindustani as my mother-tongue; and in the first half of 1950, while living in a village in northern Mewar, I had succeeded in recapturing at least a halting fluency in the language, coloured with idioms and pronunciations peculiar to that State. Udaipur commended itself as being the seat of the oldest, and most conservative, of the former Rajput dynasties.

Of all the former principalities of Rajasthan, the State of Mewar (of which Udaipur is the capital) comes first in precedence. It has been governed since the ninth century by the same line, Rajputs of the Sheshodia clan; but its claim to precedence dates from the Moghul empire. When every other prince in India had submitted to the authority of Akbar, Mewar alone remained defiant; its ruling house was the only one which refused to give a princess in marriage to the conquerors. The ruler of that time, Rana Partab, was the Robert the Bruce of Rajasthan. His entire reign was spent in the guerilla warfare of a resistance movement. The most famous of his battles was that of Haldi Ghat, in which his war-horse, Chetak, was fatally wounded but yet carried him to safety. To this day, the whitewashed walls of houses in Mewar are often decorated with paintings of Rana Partab and his steed.

In the early years of the nineteenth century, the state was again devastated by prolonged warfare, its towns and villages looted by the Mahratta armies of the Sindhias. In 1817, however, the ruler signed a treaty with the British and entered into an alliance which survived even the Indian mutiny. Up to the end of the Rajahs' autocracy, in 1948, the coins of Mewar

* M. Mead (1939).
† Outstanding examples are: G. Roheim (1932) and E. H. Erikson (1950)

commemorated this alliance with the legend in Hindi letters: " Dosti Landhan—The Friendship of London ".

Under the terms of this treaty, the Rana of Mewar accepted military support and acknowledged the sovereignty of the British crown. A British " Resident " acted as adviser to the ruler of the state. His function was to encourage social and economic progress, but not to interfere (except in emergencies) with the internal conduct of administration. To some extent, the latter part of his duties effectively cancelled out the former. Udaipur retained an intensely conservative autocratic régime. Education and public health services were on a very limited scale. Even the material advantages of a proposed railway link with the main lines were long viewed with suspicion. When at last the Maharana consented to its construction he stipulated that the station must remain at a distance of three miles from the sacred precincts of his capital city. Another consequence of the preservation through this alliance of the Rana's mediaeval rule was that in Mewar (as in other Rajahs' States) the spread of the democratic " liberation " propaganda of the Indian National Congress was vigorously suppressed.

A token force of the Indian Army was stationed in Udaipur, and the Bhil Corps, which was established in 1844 to maintain order among the warlike tribesmen in the mountainous western part of the state, was staffed by British officers. These troops were engaged in police, rather than military activities.

Major warfare has not been known in Rajasthan for over a century, but local brigandage was not easily eradicated, and still occurs, especially in the hilly western part of the state. This history of violence and social disruption is still alive in the memory of the country folk. On several occasions villagers described to me dreams in which they had to take refuge in the hills while their homes were plundered by a passing warrior band.

In choosing my village, I was guided by three criteria: (i) that it should be a large one, of at least 1,000 inhabitants; (ii) that it should not be on the railway line, nor show obvious signs of modern influence (such as a small factory, or a public wireless set, or electric light, as are found in many of the larger villages in Bombay Province, to the south of Rajasthan); (iii) that it should contain adequate numbers of each of the three top caste-groups, represented here by the Rajputs, Brahmins and Banias, who are respectively warrior-landlords, priests and merchants. Members of these three castes form a conscious élite in Hindu society, distinguished from lowlier castes (although nowadays the distinction is being challenged) by their prerogatives of wearing the sacred thread and of assuming the epithet " twice-born ".

After considering a series of possible villages, and visiting the likeliest of them, my wife and I finally settled upon one which I shall call Deoli, situated in the foothills of the Aravallis in the vicinity of Udaipur, with which it is linked by a broken road, winding across a mountain pass. For the next year this village and its citizens became the focus of my inquiries into the personality of high-caste Hindus, and into the formative experiences of their early years. These inquiries were carried out in face-to-face interviews with a succession of informants, all of whom were youths or men. In this locality the segregation of women is still strictly enforced, at least among high-caste families. As a doctor, I was frequently invited to pass through the purdah barrier in order to visit the sick; but for me to hold long private conversations with their women-folk would have been quite unacceptable.

With each informant, I began by discussing the aim of my study. I presented this as an attempt to understand what sort of people the Rajputs and Brahmins and Banias were. To members of each caste I said: " I am trying to learn what sort of a man I should be now if I had been born in your family, and been brought up as one of your community. This is why I should like you to tell me all you can remember about your own life, from your earliest years." Then I would ask some factual questions about the composition of the household in which the informant grew up. Thereafter, in each interview I encouraged him to talk about his life in whatever way he pleased. When his conversation flagged I would introduce themes which others had raised, and wait to see if he would elaborate upon them. Occasionally, also, I intervened to change the subject if, as sometimes happened, he embarked upon a recital of purely factual information of an impersonal character. Later in the sequence of interviews, I enquired about dreams, and asked for associations to those which were reported. Each informant performed a non-verbal intelligence test (Raven's Progressive Matrices) and a Rorschach Test for me. Each was also given a word-association test, in which twenty words believed to be potentially charged with emotional significance were interspersed with forty others of a neutral character. Where the response was delayed, or of an unusual character, further associations to the stimulus word were

INTRODUCTION 15

sought, or else it was introduced as a cue in the course of interviews.*

With four exceptions, all conversations were carried on in Hindustani. The exceptions were two Rajputs, a Brahmin and a Bania,† all of whom had had two or more years of college education after passing their matriculation examination at the age of seventeen or eighteen. There were three others (two Rajputs, one Brahmin) who knew a little English and liked to practise it; but in their cases the interviews were conducted in Hindustani with only occasional interpolations in English. My aim was to spend twenty hours with each informant. This was exceeded in a number of cases, but in the rest the number of hours of " fruitful " interviewing varied between ten and twenty.

In all, a total of 45 case-histories was compiled,‡ being distributed as follows: Rajputs 13; Brahmins 11; Banias 12; Moslems 9. In addition, there were eight abortive case-histories which stopped short after one or two interviews for various reasons: three were young men visiting home, who decided on second thoughts not to let me monopolise so much of their holiday time; three were Banias whose illnesses made them too atypical for inclusion—one had contracted leprosy and lived in semi-retirement, another proved to be a paranoid schizophrenic, and a third was a high-grade mental defective who was also very paranoid. One Brahmin, who was the village *vaid* or doctor, showed himself unable to co-operate in the work: he devoted the whole of our interviews to giving me instruction in *ayurvedic* medicine, or retailing myths from the Sanskrit epics, until I despaired. The last was a prosperous, retired Bania, who was so intensely suspicious of my motives that he devoted his first two interviews to ecstatic eulogies of the British Raj, and thereafter became so anxious and confused whenever I suggested that we resume our talks, that I thought it better to leave him alone. These unfinished histories went to swell my day-to-day observations, notes on relationships within the families whose houses I visited in order to treat the sick, notes on child-handling and children's behaviour, and incidents in the life of the village.

The forty-six shorthand notebooks and diaries which I brought back after my ten months' stay in Deoli have provided the raw data from which the present study is compiled. It is

---
* Analyses of the results of these tests are given in Appendix III
† This educated Bania was not, however, a native of Deoli—see p. 260
‡ Brief details of each of the Hindu informants are given in Chap. II

from the subsequent analysis of the topics which emerged in some hundreds of interviews and informal encounters, that the observations on Hindu character traits contained in the next five chapters are derived. Chapter VIII is devoted to a consideration of another community in Mewar, members of the Bhil tribe, who live in jungle valleys of the Aravalli Hills, in the Western part of the state. These tribes-people, although near neighbours of the Hindus in Deoli, present the most striking contrast to them in many respects—in character traits, in conduct, and in their system of child-rearing. I found a three-months' stay among them rewarding, not only for the stimulus of encountering a new and unique conception of normal personality, but also for the fresh light which their contrasting behaviour-patterns threw upon those of the high-caste Hindus who had been my companions during the previous ten months.

The next two chapters contain my analysis of the significant " formative influences " which can be identified in the early experience of my informants. In order to illustrate the type of source-material on which this analysis has been based, I have presented, in Part II, three of the case histories *in extenso*. Some readers may prefer to study these first, before reading chapters IX and X, in order to form their own conclusions; others may find it preferable to read them afterwards, as a check upon the validity of my generalisations.

Throughout this work, when I refer to " Hindu ", it must be understood that I am dealing only with the high-caste groups of a country district in Rajasthan. Hindu society is vast and widely differentiated: there are great differences of customs and of social organisation in different parts of that country, which must be reflected in modifications of the social character.

A variation peculiar to this particular locality lies in the fact that here the merchant caste, or Banias, belong almost without exception to the Jain sect, whereas elsewhere the majority are orthodox Hindus. Yet it is still true that Banias and Vaisyas (as the merchant caste is elsewhere usually termed) are identical not only in their economic role and in the relationship to members of other castes but also in their emphasis upon non-violence and vegetarianism and their concern about not taking life.

It need hardly be emphasised that the majority of these Rajasthani villagers are, superficially at least, profoundly unlike the educated Hindus of the great modern cities of India, and bear little resemblance to the cultured Indian students who

INTRODUCTION

are to be found in the Universities of Europe and America. A contemporary of Shakespeare and a present-day Londoner would scarcely be more dissimilar in dress and in sophistication; and yet both Englishmen might find that they shared many fundamental attitudes in common, and the same may be true of Indians of the city and of the village. Wherever high-caste Hindus adhere to their traditional beliefs, there must also be a certain uniformity of formative experiences. For this reason I hope that my observations will prove to have some relevance for Hindu society in areas other than Rajasthan—but as to the degree of relevance, I must wait to be advised by others whose experience of Hindu communities has been more extensive than has mine.

Throughout this book, first personal pronouns will be much in evidence. This is deliberate, if not inevitable; because the bulk of my data consists in the record of conversations with my informants; and what emerged in these exchanges was a function of my personality as well as theirs. In these circumstances, to claim impersonal objectivity of observation would be unwarranted. It becomes relevant to know that the observer was a Scotsman, born in India of parents who were both missionaries, that the Rajasthan dialect of Hindustani was literally my native language and was more familiar to me than English until at the age of 9 I began my formal education in Edinburgh; that I was a theist and a lapsed Presbyterian; that I had practised for over ten years as physician and psychiatrist, and that I had received instruction in the theory and field methods of social anthropology in successive years at Oxford, in the United States of America (at Cornell, and subsequently at Columbia) and finally at Cambridge University. For six months, during 1949-50, I had had the privilege of working in another village in Rajasthan, as a member of the Columbia University sociological research team led by Mrs. G. P. Steed. In the conduct of the present research my aim was something other than merely fact-finding; or rather many of the facts which I sought could be recognised only in the context of my interpersonal relationship with my informants; hence it was necessary for me (as it will be for my readers) to bear in mind my own idiosyncrasies, skills—and limitations—in interpreting my data.

The study would not have been possible at all, were it not for the generous help given me by my village collaborators, most of whom gave me their time without any reward except the knowledge that I was ready to help them with medical attention whenever called upon—I did in fact have occasion to treat the informant himself, or members of his family, in every case, in the course of the year. In nine cases I persuaded them to accept a small gift of money in return for their help; but in no case did financial reward act as the inducement to elicit their co-operation.

My helpers were aware, with varying degrees of understanding, of the purpose of my study, and contributed generously towards it with their own personal histories, knowing that one day this information would go into the making of a book. In order to respect their anonymity at least to some degree, I have rechristened their village, and have exchanged each person's name for another appropriate to his caste. In so doing, I have taken a certain licence with the prevailing nomenclature. All Rajputs have the suffix *Singh* to their names; and for ease of identification, I have made each Brahmin's name end with *Lal*, and each Bania's end in *-mal*, although these common usages were not so universal in their respective castes.

Part One

CHAPTER I

THE VILLAGE OF DEOLI

FOR centuries the state of Mewar has been ruled on feudal lines, with the Maharana at the apex of a pyramid of authority. His leading noblemen owed him services, which included a period of personal attendance at his court, the supply of a body of armed men in time of war and an annual contribution to his revenue. The etiquette of the Maharana's court was strict, and intensely conservative, even down to the details of court dress (which is the same today as in sixteenth-century Rajput paintings) and this set a model of princely behaviour which was copied in each Rajput landlord's domain.

As in England in Norman times, the homes of the Rajput nobles were built on military lines, surrounded by battlements, embrasures and gun-emplacements. They were fortresses rather than mansions, and their sites were chosen with a view to military rather than domestic convenience. So it was with Deoli, which had been until 1948 the centre of government of a *Tikhana* (a sort of dukedom) ruled by a prominent Rajput family for some hundreds of years. The village is dominated by a towering fortress-palace built like Edinburgh Castle on a prominent rock.

From the walls of the fortress there is a commanding view over the roof-tops of the village, and over the valley in which it stands—a narrow valley, beset on all sides by ridges of stony hills covered with sparse jungle. To the east there is a gap in the hills, leading to the part of the Tikhana which lies in the plains. There, the villages have more extensive fields; here in the *magra* (the foothills) only the valley bottoms and the lower slopes of the hills can be cultivated; but both regions are equally dependent upon the capricious monsoon. When the rains are abundant the summer crop of maize needs no irrigation and the wells, which will water the winter crops of wheat and barley, are replenished; but when they fail, as happens every three or four years, one or both of these crops will suffer. Reserves of grain are never plentiful, so there is a recurrent threat of famine.

On nearby hill slopes can be seen two stone towers, shooting-boxes from which the Ruler and his guests could hunt deer, wild boar and panther driven towards them by lines of beaters. Game is less plentiful now, but panthers are still common in the hills. News of their kills of domestic cattle is sent at once to the fortress because panther- and tiger-hunting is an aristocratic privilege of the Rajputs, a last relic of their warlike functions. The summons is responded to with alacrity: Rajputs of every rank enjoy big-game hunting and pride themselves upon the number of their trophies.

In past years the Rajput aristocracy and British officers (both military and civilian) found common ground in their enthusiasm for blood sports—which are abhorred in principle by most Hindus—and for horses. Thus it came about that in Deoli the commonest occasion for a European's presence was as a guest of the Ruler on a hunting expedition. On one occasion, some nineteen years previously, an English official had adjudicated in a memorable dispute concerning land tenure in the vicinity of Deoli. In general, European influences were transmitted to the village at second-hand from the city of Udaipur which in turn had been brought nearer by the gradual introduction of country bus services.

From the fortress gate a dusty lane runs to join a metalled road which passes near the outskirts of the village. This lane has become the main street of a community of over two thousand persons. It is lined on either side with the shops of merchants who deal in cloth and grain and money-lending. In Deoli the Bania or merchant caste is the most numerous and, after the Ruler's family, the most influential social group.

The large size of this village and the busy commerce of its bazaar could both be attributed to the former traffic of the Ruler's subjects and adherents who had business to transact in the fortress. The seat of formal power lay in his court, but the merchants came to exercise a very widespread influence both through their purveying of important commodities, and through their money-lending. Everyone, even including the Ruler, was in debt to the Banias at one time or another. Since the abrogation of the Ruler's powers, traffic in the bazaar has somewhat diminished, but on the other hand it has become, in succession to the fortress, the most important focus of social life in the entire Tikhana.

On either side of the bazaar narrow alley-ways lead off into clusters of close-packed little houses with mud-plastered stone walls and loose tiled roofs, which fill in the spaces between the more spacious buildings of the high-caste families. The former are the homes of members of the humbler communities, each of which congregates in its own sector of the village with its own temple or open-air shrine; but the bazaar is the common meeting ground and centre of gossip for the whole village.

Throughout our stay, the ex-Ruler of Deoli generously allowed us to make our quarters in some empty rooms in the lower reaches of his fortress. This arrangement had much to commend it from the point of view of our personal comfort and hygiene, but it was obvious that to identify myself exclusively with the palace would effectively prevent my gaining the confidence of many of the villagers. Accordingly, during the first few days, which we spent exploring the village and becoming acquainted with its principal citizens, I succeeded in hiring an empty room in the centre of the bazaar and let it be known that this was my office, where I could be found throughout the day.

We soon came to appreciate that Deoli was dominated socially, no less than physically, by the fortress that towered over it. Until 1948, it had contained a court of law, a police station and a jail, revenue offices—all the business of administration for a Tikhana encompassing sixty smaller villages. The Ruler was always attended by a number of his subordinate Rajput *Jagirdars* (holders of hereditary grants of land, called *jagirs*) and by a retinue of 200 servants, including hereditary elephant-trainers to look after his two elephants, and grooms to keep the stable of thirty horses. The courtyards and stairs were alive with people in those days, officials and tenants, litigants, and petitioners waiting for an audience with the Ruler. This affluence of people was responsible for the flourishing little bazaar, the nearest shopping centre for all these sixty villages.

In the approaches to the fortress, armed sentries kept watch at three successive gateways which gave access to the uppermost courtyard. They would turn back anyone who was not dressed formally, according to his station, as this was taken as a mark of disrespect for the Ruler; and when the latter went through the village mounted on his elephant, or on horseback, or in a car (but never on foot) everyone was required to bow deeply as he passed, calling out " Andata! "—" Giver of Grain ".

Inside the palace, a sundial told the time, and it was one of the duties of the watchmen at the innermost post to strike the hour on a brass gong. This would be repeated by the sentry at the gate, and again by a servant in a temple in the village bazaar. This custom is still maintained in Deoli, as it is in Udaipur, so that people speak of " palace time " in contradistinction to " railway time ". I was reminded of the practice which continued during the reign of George V, of keeping " Sandringham Time " which was at variance with that observed by the rest of England.

Deoli not only took its time from the palace; its whole social life revolved about it. The few *pakka* houses, with cemented walls and flat roofs of stone, belonged either to Rajputs, junior members of the Ruler's lineage, or to the wealthier merchants, who owed their prominence to being officials of the Tikhana—one being the keeper of the treasury; another, supervisor of the revenue-collectors; another, controller of the granary, etc. Even those merchants who were not in his employ were expected to consult the Ruler before they embarked on any major business transaction, or built a new house, or opened a shop in the bazaar.

The Brahmin families, who occupied houses less impressive than those of the prosperous Banias, provided a number of priests whose whole time was devoted to the service of the several temples within the palace walls. It was the same with the crowd of artisans—members of the potters', weavers', oil-pressers', masons', cobblers', washermen's and other similar castes. Each trade had some members who served " by appointment " in the palace, and these were the leaders of their respective castes.*

The main street of Deoli, with its rows of open-fronted shops, presented an appearance of leisure if not of indolence. There was always a number of men idling and gossiping and the shop-keepers themselves lolled on cushions waiting for their next customer. Gangs of children played in the dust, always ready to form a noisy crowd at any untoward occurrence such as the arrival of a stranger, or the outbreak of an altercation in the bazaar. Cattle and goats strayed through the lanes on their way to graze on the slopes of the surrounding hills, and often camels would be ridden through, or would be tethered while their owners stopped for a smoke and a talk.

This was the life of the bazaar, but all around, each in its adjacent group of households, the thirty-six caste-communities led their separate family-centred existences. It has to be remembered that although research inquiries were focused upon members of the three highest castes, in Deoli, as throughout India, they formed only a minority of the population.

* Caste Census of Deoli is given in Appendix I

Whenever one stepped aside from the roadway to enter a *teli's* courtyard, where a blindfolded ox circled all day round the oil-press, or to call upon the potter squatting before his wheel, one was aware of entering a separate little world; and this impression was heightened when one was invited to witness religious ceremonies or to take part in a feast within the closed circle of their community.

Since caste has been for centuries a cardinal feature of the social structure of the Hindu world, and remains so still in villages like Deoli, it may be advisable to summarise what it is, and what it is not.

In the *Encyclopaedia of the Social Sciences*, Professor A. L. Kroeber has written: " A caste may be defined as an endogamous and hereditary subdivision of an ethnic unit occupying a position of superior or inferior rank or social esteem in comparison with other subdivisions." Caste is distinguished from class in that in the former social mobility from one group to another is virtually impossible.

During the nineteen-thirties and nineteen-forties a series of challenging studies showed that the race problem in the southern States of America could be viewed as an instance of a " class and caste system ".*

These studies clearly showed the economic, social and above all sexual restrictions which impose an inferior status upon coloured people in the deep South. Their use of the term " caste " to describe this phenomenon deliberately ignored the ethnic differences on which the discrimination was supposedly based in order to highlight the purely social prejudices which in fact perpetuate it.

In India the major division between the élite (the " twice-born " members of the High Castes) and the lower-caste majority has also been rationalised as having an ethnic basis. In theory, the High Castes are descended from fair-skinned Aryan invaders, the others from darker indigenous peoples, and this gives rise to a popular prejudice in favour of fairness of complexion. In fact, however, there has been a very thorough intermingling of ethnic stock during the thirty-five centuries since the Aryans first came to India.

Caste in Hindu society is distinguished by its antiquity, its formalisation and its close integration into religious and

* This was first stated in an article, " American Caste and Class ", by W. Lloyd Warner (1936) and subsequently elaborated in works by John Dollard (1937), Davis and Dollard (1940) and Davis and the Gardners (1941)

economic life. Each hereditary sub-caste (of which there are literally thousands of separate endogamous units) is traditionally associated with a distinctive occupation, and each has acquired its own strict conventions of dress, behaviour and ritual. These rules are enforced by caste courts or *panchayats;* and none are enjoined more strictly than the rules concerning marriage and commensality which give clear expression to the relative status of adjacent castes. Marriage is strictly confined to the sub-caste or *jati*, which forms an endogamous group. This group in turn is composed of extended lineages (called *gotra*) within which intermarriage is prohibited.

Although assertively conscious of their separate identities (which are given visible expression in Deoli by the grouping together of the houses of each caste) the castes are yet interdependent, linked by mutual services and obligations which are reciprocated by members of the same families over many generations. Caste thus has a cohesive as well as a separating function. Nor are the relative positions of castes immutably fixed. Accidents of history, deliberate changes of occupation, or Sanskritisation * of their rituals may cause a sub-caste to move up or down the religious-social scale. Thus there can be found low-caste Brahmins and royal Sudras (generally the labouring caste) in different parts of India. In Deoli there are sub-castes of Rajputs who have fallen so low that other Rajputs will no longer eat with them, and at least one Sudra caste (the Yadows) who have risen a long way in the last five generations. Here, also, a local variation on the theme of caste hierarchies was introduced by the influence of Palace patronage.

This way of life continued unchanged until 1948, and then, without warning, the mainstay of village life was removed. The Congress Government pressed home its democratic reforms, abruptly relieving the Ruler of all his former administrative powers. In order to emphasise the change, the new magistrates' court, revenue office, and civil administration, were centred in different towns and villages, each more than twelve miles away.

In 1951 the Palace was an empty shell. The elephants and most of the horses were gone; nine-tenths of the retainers had been turned away, and the stairs and courtyards were deserted. Only the inner and outer sentinels remained, ringing the hours on their brass gongs. Visitors were few, even the *Jagirdars* only putting in a perfunctory appearance; many of them had commuted with a cash payment the duty of attending upon

---

* The writer owes this term to M. N. Srinivas (1952), p. 30

their Ruler, which once had seemed a privilege. The Rao Sahib himself sat at his upstairs window, dressed informally because formal audiences had become infrequent. He would brood for hours over the village lanes and roofs, far below, and would at times sink into a mood of utter depression, at other times busy himself for days on end with spiritual exercises, or toy with the idea of entering into politics.

The village, too, seemed stunned by the pace of events. Hitherto, one's standing in the Palace had been the universal yardstick, and this habit of mind persisted, especially among the older men. Gradually, however, it was coming to be realised that the Ruler's day was over. Congress officials came and addressed meetings in the bazaar, condemning the old régime in language which, before 1948, would have earned them rough handling and a sentence in the Palace jail—but they were unopposed. Power had gone elsewhere; but the citizens of Deoli were still uncertain who, or what authority, would take the Ruler's place. This indecision was made apparent when the Ruler drove through the bazaar. Now, it was only the Rajputs and the older Banias who bowed low and cried " Andata ". Of the lower castes, a few did so, and these were the ones who were still in palace employment. The rest looked on sullenly, vaguely resentful of the change which had thrown so many families out of work.

In addition to its hereditary trade, every family except the poorest had one or two fields, in which to grow maize in summer, and wheat or barley during the winter season. These grains were their staple diet. The wealthier families owned land but employed others to till it for them; yet there were instances of Rajput and Brahmin families who cultivated their own fields.

In one corner of the village, just outside the palace gate, was a section of poor houses occupied by Mohammedans, all of whom had formerly been in the service of the Ruler. This group had built a little mosque. Elsewhere in the village were four Jain and thirty-five Hindu temples. Some of the latter were frequented by members of all the castes except the untouchables (sweepers, leatherworkers and butchers), but the majority were the property of individual caste-groups, and served as their community *nohera* or meeting place.

The four Jain temples were frequented almost exclusively by a section of the Banias who were *mandirmargi* (temple-worshippers). In Deoli, as is the case throughout southern Rajasthan, almost all of the Banias were Jains, only two families being *Vaishnavi* or orthodox Hindus; but they all took part in the festivals of the Hindu religious year, and worshipped at Hindu temples both in Deoli and at pilgrimage-places nearby. These Jains, who could boast of more schooling than the majority of their neighbours in the bazaar, were more familiar than those with the stories of the Gita, the Mahabharata and the Ramayana, which contain so much of the inspiration of popular Hinduism. This eclectic attitude influenced even the relations between Moslems and Hindus in the village. Though neither community would enter the other's temple or mosque, there was considerable sharing in communal and family religious festivals. Thus the Moslems would dress well and give feasts like their neighbours on the Hindu high holidays, and prominent Brahmins and Banias followed the procession of the Tazia at Moharram, the most important celebration of the local Moslems' year.

Apart from the temples to recognised gods and goddesses of the Hindu pantheon, there was a multitude of open-air shrines to lesser gods, whom the Brahmins dismissed as mere ghosts, or demons; yet it was round these shrines that the day-to-day religious life of the mass of lower-caste villagers was centred. They all had in common this feature: that the spirit would manifest himself (or herself) by entering into the body of the attendant of the shrine. The man thus "possessed" lost consciousness for minutes or hours, during which time the god spoke through his mouth. Such priests were known as *bhopas* and they were regularly consulted to diagnose and cure witchcraft and sickness (which were generally synonymous) and to answer any and every vexing problem. Members of the superior castes poured scorn upon these bhopas except for some of the humbler Rajput families, who shared the prejudices of their farmer-tenants. Even Banias admitted to me: "Of course, our caste does not believe in all that rubbish: but when someone is sick, you can't help it, you have to go and consult them".

This willingness to try other peoples' remedies gave me an admirable opening. I said that I was a doctor, and that I had brought some European medicines. I dispensed these free to the poorest villagers, and for a small charge (which inspired confidence) to the richer ones. My early fears that I would be embarrassed by continual demands for medical attention were not realised. I seldom had more than a dozen patients coming to my office during the day; the vast majority preferred to wait until they saw me pass their door, and would then call me in with every sign of urgency.

At first, I announced that I would see patients during the first half-hour of my day in the " office "—which began at 7.30 in the cold weather, an hour earlier in the hot months—and again for half an hour after the mid-day meal. At the same time I enlisted the help of a number of informants and proposed that they should visit me for interviews lasting from one to two hours, at appointed times. Both of these arrangements gradually lapsed. They would have been abandoned sooner had I been quicker to appreciate that this orderly time-table was my own cultural importation, and quite alien to the experience of my village neighbours.

Gradually, a compromise evolved. I learned not to be surprised when an informant failed to appear at a given hour in spite of the most fulsome promises. Instead, I kept a series of informants simultaneously " on the go ", reaching for each one's individual notebook when he presented himself; and if our interview was interrupted, as often happened, by a visitor arriving, greeting us and squatting nearby, I would attend to the newcomer's request and then usher him out with due formality so that our conversation could continue.

In the course of successive interviews, as each informant's notebook became filled, I acquired a more or less detailed account of his upbringing, of his personality and outlook; and as the number of the individual case-histories increased, it was possible to recognise some patterns which recurred in them all, and others which were characteristic of their several sub-communities. It was, however, only in the course of the subsequent two years, after my return to England, that I was able to complete the systematic analysis of all the recorded notes and interviews, upon which are based the generalisations about the personality of the high-caste citizens of Deoli contained in subsequent chapters of this book.

CHAPTER II

DRAMATIS PERSONAE

THE following are the informants whose conversations and life-histories provided the major part of the data on which this book is based. After each one's description is given his level of schooling (S.1, 2, 3 or 4); his amount of experience of Western institutions (W. I, II or III), and his score in the Raven's Progressive Matrices test (R). The maximum possible score in this test was 60. (See Appendix II.) When sufficient information had been acquired about each informant to make the assessment possible, he was assigned one of three " prestige levels ". This was an estimate of whether in the eyes of his caste-fellows he rated as socially prominent, as an average citizen, or as socially inferior. This rating has also been given at the end of each short annotation.

RAJPUTS

1. *Rao Sahib Rajendra Singh*, aged 33. Married, has three children. Inherited the Rs. 100,000 a year tikhana of Deoli on the death of his father, when he was 20 years old. Deprived of his ruling powers, of privileges, and of much of his income by governmental reforms of 1948. Talks good English; has had considerable experience of social contact with Europeans. (S. 1; W. I; R. 27. Prestige level one.)

2. *Thakur Devi Singh*, aged 29. Younger brother of Rajendra Singh. Married, with two children. Is landlord of a small village, but prefers to live in Deoli or at the Deoli mansion in Udaipur where he and his elder brother spent their early years. Dislikes hunting and athletic pursuits, prefers city pleasures. Speaks halting English; has had several European contacts. (S. 1; W. I; R.—declined. Prestige level one.)

3. *Vikram Singh*, aged 29. Married, one daughter. Third son of a small landowner. An athletic, vigorous, vehement man, ardently religious, belligerently patriotic and traditionalist. Divides his time between husbandry and religious

devotions. Some years ago, championed the poorest peasants in a dispute with landlords, earning the hostility of his fellow-Rajputs. Identifies himself with his pious, energetic, highly-respected father, who died when he was " 9-10-11 years old ". (S. 2; W. II; R. 23. Prestige level two.)

4. *Hira Singh*, aged 24. Married, one son. Younger brother of Vikram Singh. A slightly-built, anxious young man, who has studied very hard. Passed Matric but failed B.A. at his first attempt. Now headmaster of Deoli village school. Intellectually critical of many Rajput traditions, but emotionally attached to them. Interested in history, religion, politics, but hesitates to commit himself in any direction. Harbours frustrated ambition for a military career. (S. 1; W. I; R. 21. Prestige level two.)

5. *Latchman Singh*, aged 40. Married, three children. Eldest son of a retainer of the Rao Sahib, to whose family he is distantly related. Owns and farms a small plot of land. Sceptical, irreligious, possesses a pawky sense of humour; quarrelsome, unambitious, but proud. Parents were strict; mother died when he was 10, father soon re-married. Unlike most Rajputs, includes several men of other castes among his closest associates. (S. 4; W. III; R. 13. Prestige level three.)

6. *Amar Singh*, aged 35. Married, four children. Brother of Latchman Singh. Suffers from congenital clubbed foot. Although lame, is adept at hunting. As personal attendant to the Rao Sahib has shared his interest in religious teachings and in Rajput epic verse. Fiercely traditionalist and communally bigoted; in all things, more ardent, less sceptical than his elder brother. (S. 3; W. II; R. 25. Prestige level three.)

7. *Partab Singh*, aged 21. Unmarried; college student. Only son of a village landlord, a subordinate jagirdar in the territory of Deoli. Strongly attached to Rajput ideas of prestige, and proud of the traditions of his own family and clan, as contained in verses of their minstrels. Idealistic; torn between traditionalism and pride in the " new India ". Self-conscious, well-mannered, ambitious. Loyal to superiors, likes discipline, quick to notice lack of deference from social inferiors. Understands some English, but is diffident about trying to speak it. (S. 1; W. I; R. 39. Prestige level one.)

8. *Nathu Singh*, aged 39. Married, four children. A retainer of the Rao Sahib and holder of a small hereditary jagir. Family was impoverished in his youth because his father was mentally unbalanced and incapable. This subject was interviewed in jail, where he was serving a twenty-four-year sentence for the murder of his brother and sister-in-law as a result of a quarrel over their patrimony of land, in December 1948. Previously used to alternate between excessive drinking and religious zeal, now very devout. (S. 3; W. II; R. 29. Prestige level three.)

9. *Bhagwat Singh*, aged 25. Unmarried. Only surviving brother of Nathu Singh. Busily engaged in administering and farming the family lands. Has had several years' experience of work for contractors to army camps in large towns of central India. Professes pro-Congress sentiments, cultivates non-Rajput acquaintances, but is aware that he is barely tolerated by " respectable " upper-caste villagers, because of the disgrace of fratricide in his family, and his own bouts of aggressive drunkenness. (S. 3; W. II; R. 26. Prestige level two.)

10. *Mal Singh*, aged *c.* 45. Married, two children. Younger son of a small rural landlord, orphaned at the age of 10. Employed as household servant of local Thakur; then adopted by a childless retainer of the Ruler of Deoli. Served for several years in State Police; in last ten years as Palace guard in Deoli. A touchy, aggressive, fearless, quarrelsome man, jealous of his caste prestige. Twice dismissed his post for insubordination; later placated the Rao Sahib and was re-instated. (S. 4; W. II; R. 18. Prestige level two.)

11. *Bheru Singh*, aged 62. Unmarried. Eldest son of an impoverished small-landlord and palace servant. Inherited his father's role as bhopa of a Goddess-shrine in the outskirts of Deoli, but becomes possessed only on rare occasions. Served in the Udaipur State Army (chief functions, mounting guards at city palace and acting as beaters in big-game hunts). Too poor to get married himself, he succeeded in getting his younger brother married; still is head of their joint household. (S. 4; W. III; R. 14. Prestige level three.)

12. *Puran Singh*, aged 22. Married, one daughter. Eldest son of retired sub-inspector of police. Has served in Indian army; now studying at home, ambitious to make a career in

one of the Services, or in the Police. Critical of diehard traditionalism, guardedly pro-Congress in outlook, sceptical in religious matters, but conformist. (S. 2; W. I; R. 37. Prestige level two.)

13. *Nar Singh*, aged 23. Married, one daughter. Eldest son of a small-landlord. Helps father supervise their fields and also works as debt-collector for a wealthy money-lender. Familiar with the jungle districts, fond of hunting. Has unquestioning faith in local deities—he attends the Vijayshan-Mata shrine regularly to decapitate goat-sacrifices with his sword—but is unversed in the niceties of Brahminical Hinduism. Loyal to the old régime, but not interested in politics. Sturdy, fearless, usually good-humoured but aggressive when provoked. (S. 3; W. III; R. 25. Prestige level three.)

BRAHMINS

1. *Shankar Lal*, aged 36. Married, four children. Eldest son of a clerk in Deoli administration, who died when he was a child. Although always poor, applied himself unsparingly to study, qualified as teacher. Now is second senior in a large school in the town of Nathdwara; but maintains his home in Deoli. Earnest, serious, deliberate in speech and gesture. Progressive in politics, conservative in religion, to which he devotes much attention. (S. 1; W. I; R. 33. Prestige level one.)

2. *Moti Lal*, aged 60. Married, five children. Is hereditary priestly officiant to a nearby hamlet, where he has some fields. Also is employed as caretaker of a Jain temple in Deoli. Has seldom travelled more than a few miles from the village. Deplores modern times. Untutored and incurious about religion and politics, seeks only to follow a familiar, simple routine. (S. 4; W. III; R. 13. Prestige level three.)

3. *Devi Lal*, aged 36. Married, six children. Eldest son of Moti Lal, lives in his father's joint household. Never robust, afflicted with severe squint. Earns a modest living as astrologer and priest, and by teaching a junior grade in the village school. Conservative in religion and in social outlook but keenly aware of contemporary changes, feels he will have to modify some of his cherished taboos. Observant of his

fellow-villagers, teasingly critical of their shortcomings. Has few regular associates, one of whom is his neighbour, Latchman Singh. (S. 2; W. III; R. 11. Prestige level two.)

4. *Rup Lal*, aged 30. Married, one son. The robust younger brother of Devi Lal. Untrained in priestly rituals, has sought employment in towns. Recently has worked as servant of a milk-seller in Bombay, living apart from his family when so employed. His ambition is to save enough money to be able to buy some land near Deoli, and farm it himself. Association with a self-contained " expatriate " community of caste-fellows in Bombay has tended to make him more, rather than less, orthodox in observing social and religious taboos. (S. 3; W. II; R.—declined. Prestige level two.)

5. *Kalu Lal*, aged 50. Married, four children. The eldest son of a priest employed in the palace, he inherited his father's duties there and in a hamlet where he officiates on ritual occasions. Lived through years of great hardship after father's death, when he was 16: family was poor, numerous, and ostracised. His widowed mother was accused of being a witch, and one sister was out-casted for immorality. Now better-off and well-regarded, he shuns company other than that of his family; devotes his time to farm work, temple worship, and private religious exercises. (S. 3; W. III; R. 19. Prestige level two.)

6. *Gopi Lal*, aged 40. Married, two children. Younger brother of Kalu Lal. It is due to Gopi Lal's strenuous efforts that the family's prosperity has been restored: he earned the money for his own and his two younger brothers' marriages. Now has a busy and widespread practice as pleader in rustic litigation. His ambition is to accumulate enough capital to be able to set up as a money-lender. Was elected Sirpanch of Deoli in 1951. Orthodox in religion but discreetly pro-Congress in politics. Always immaculately dressed, punctilious in exchange of courtesies, intimate with none. (S. 1; W. II; R. 28. Prestige level one.)

7. *Hari Lal*, aged 71. Unmarried, lives alone. Younger son of a priest with an official position in the palace. From the age of 14 was employed as personal servant to wealthy Brahmins in towns elsewhere in Rajasthan: for twenty years was employed by a peripatetic lawyer, seeing most large cities

in India. In recent years was priest in the temple of Eklingji. Now is frail, bronchitic and has failing eyesight, lives by begging from families who still count it a pious act to feed a Brahmin. (S. 3; W. II; R. 14. Prestige level two.)

8. *Girdari Lal*, aged *c.* 65. Married, six children. Priest and religious instructor to the Ruler's household. Officiates as Brahmin, is widely consulted as astrologer. Very well versed in religious teachings and legends. An excitable, voluble, eloquent talker, but always relapses into blunt, often coarse, village idiom to illustrate his pious dissertations. Himself strictly observant of social and religious traditions, he is a heated and vituperative opponent of advocates of social change. (S. 2; W. II; R. 25. Prestige level two.)

9. *Roshan Lal*, aged 20. Married, no children. Elder son of Girdari Lal. Educated in Udaipur, now working as school teacher but with ambition to go on with College and study law. An elegant, rather aloof young man, admired by his contemporaries and sure of his own intellectual superiority. An ardent idealistic nationalist, composes patriotic poems: admires Gandhism in politics, is intellectually persuaded of the need for social reform, but never criticises his father's contrary views. (S. 1; W. I; R. 42. Prestige level one.)

10. *Himat Lal*, aged 23. Married, two children. The pampered only son of a well-to-do priest and landowner. Until his father died, when he was 18, Himat Lal was obliged to conform strictly to old-fashioned prejudices in respect of dress, religious study and social behaviour. Since then, he has become a "new man", wearing semi-European dress and flouting many of the old taboos. He is an enthusiastic Congress propagandist. Having spent most of his patrimony, he now earns his living as ticket-seller for the local bus; also officiates occasionally as Brahmin at rituals in the village hereditarily associated with his family. (S. 2; W. II; R. 25. Prestige level three.)

11. *Kripa Lal*, aged 28. Married, two children. The elder son of a wealthy Brahmin who owned a score of houses in Deoli. When Kripa Lal was a child his parents often quarrelled, his father accusing his mother of immorality, and beating her frequently. When he was 7, his mother absconded with a lover and was not seen again. The two boys were brought up

by an uncle, and trained as magistrates' court pleaders. On the death of his father in 1944, Kripa Lal rapidly squandered the bulk of his estate. He now earns his living as a vakil, and aspires to a political career, being an eloquent and active supporter of Congress. He is separated from his wife, and lives with a concubine of low-caste origin. Being aware of the censure of the village elders, Kripa Lal courts the admiration of the adolescent and young adult groups, and is the recognised leader of the "new men". (S. 2; W. II; R. 21. Prestige level three.)

BANIAS

1. *Birmal*, aged 28. Unmarried, second oldest of six brothers and two sisters; son of a small shopkeeper. Lived with parents in Udaipur for most of his early years: went to school to age of 14. Thereafter, worked in merchants' shops in a number of distant cities. Now divides his time between working for a few months as shop manager, and living for long periods on his savings and on his parents' support while he devotes himself to voluntary public service and preaching Gandhian principles, which he does with pithy eloquence. Has day-dreams of being a famous national religious leader, but is held in derision in the village as an idle busybody. (S. 3; W. II; R. 18. Prestige level three.)

2. *Chauthmal*, aged 23. Married, one child. Only son of one of the wealthiest merchants in Deoli. Keenly enjoys his work (cloth-selling and money-lending) and is also interested in Congressite politics—visiting Congress organisers are usually entertained at his father's house. Chauthmal sympathises with the socially unorthodox views of the "new men", but is too much under the influence of his father to flout conventions in his behaviour while in the village. Is keenly engaged in factional disputes with rival groups of merchants. (S. 3; W. II; R. 29. Prestige level one.)

3. *Shrimal*, aged *c.* 30. Unmarried. Son of a small trader who died when he was a child. Relatives misappropriated his patrimony so that he, his mother and sister were left very badly off. While he was in his teens, both women became wandering nuns (dhundias). He is lame as a result of infantile paralysis, very slight and thin. Makes a pittance by selling glass bangles. Is the bhopa of a Bheruji shrine frequented by the Banias. A

humble, retiring, obsequious, but spry and cheerful man. (S. 4; W. III; R. 17. Prestige level three.)

4. *Bhurmal*, aged 33. Married, three children. Third son of a rich and influential merchant; but adopted when aged 24 by widow of another (also prosperous) kinsman. Like his elder brother, a former Sirpanch, he takes an active part in the Congress-sponsored village council, but remains conservative in social behaviour and conformist, though largely indifferent, in religious matters. Conducts his own cloth-selling and money-lending business. (S. 3; W. II; R. 24. Prestige level two.)

5. *Surajmal*, aged 25. Unmarried. Third son of a moderately successful village cloth-merchant. His mother died when he was 5 years old, since when he has been brought up by his father and a servant woman. Unlike his one younger and two older brothers, who all have jobs in Ahmedabad mills, Surajmal professes to enjoy shopkeeping, and village life. He is conservative in outlook, leads a very domesticated life with his father, taking turns at cooking their meals. Hopes to acquire a wife when the family has put aside enough money. A village Babbitt, with no rebellious tendencies. (S. 3; W. II; R. 28. Prestige level two.)

6. *Rajmal*, aged 33. Widower, with one child. Son of the wealthiest merchant in Deoli but formally adopted into an heirless household. Stout, cheerful, a successful and avowed racketeer. Besides money-lending, is believed to organise robberies, and to extort money from criminals in return for suborning members of the police. Notoriously libertine, flouts social etiquette which his brothers still obey. Has twice been imprisoned for theft. Indifferent to religion and cynical about politics. (S. 3; W. II; R.—declined. Prestige level one.)

7. *Chandmal*, aged 27. Married, childless. Son of an elderly, invalid Raj-guru, formerly tutor to the Ruler of Deoli. Chandmal has taught in Jain schools in Jaipur and in Calcutta; now teaches in Deoli village school. Although officiously eager to be an informant on Bania matters at the outset of the research, he became very suspicious of concealed political motives behind it, and politely evaded later interviews—hence, his record was not completed. (S. 2; W. II; R. 45. Prestige level two.)

8. *Daulmal*, aged 41. Married, one child. A tall, cadaverous, consumptive individual. His father died when he was 5, mother when he was 7. Blames an uncle for misappropriating his patrimony; but adds that what was left of it he squandered in his 20s, on drink and women. Now makes a meagre living at tailoring. Has a lugubrious, sceptical outlook on contemporary events and on the motives of his fellow-men. (S. 4; W. II; R.—record lost. Prestige level three.)

9. *Attarmal*, aged 71. Orphaned in childhood. Father was a well-to-do merchant. Accuses his uncles of robbing him of his inheritance. From earliest years has been a pedlar of bottles of scent, always poor, yet with a reputation for having been an opium addict and heavy drinker of bhang, which he still takes twice daily. Given to ostentatious display of piety, which does not prevent his having the reputation of a broken-down old rake. (S. 3; W. III; R. 17. Prestige level three.)

10. *Bhagmal*, aged 18. Unmarried. Youngest of four children of a deceased pedlar (who still benignly haunts his household, speaking in his widow's mouth as a purbaj). Has worked as mill labourer in Ahmedabad; plans to resume similar town employment. Restless, lacking in application, often accused of being a thief. Left the village hurriedly in mid-1951 leaving a number of indignant creditors, chief of whom was Surajmal. Bhagmal is an ardent nationalist, active member of the R.S.S. (Hindu right-wing youth movement) when in town. (S. 2; W. II; R.—record lost. Prestige level three.)

11. *Chenmal*, aged 64. Married but childless. Lives in a joint household with an elder brother. Acts as estate-manager for the widow of a former Ruler of Deoli, whose assiduous, devoted and ever-grumbling servant he remains. He is especially well versed in the history of his own and his mistress's family; in the teachings of Jain and Hindu holy men whom he entertains on the Rani's behalf, and in indigenous medicine which he practises for charity. Conservative in outlook, observant but critical of contemporary events. (S. 3; W. II; R. 22. Prestige level one.)

12. *Puranmal*, aged 25. Married, two children. Only son of a city shopkeeper, in whose cramped household he still lives. Torn between affection and resentment towards his

over-solicitous parents. Alternately sceptical and devout in religious matters. Idealistic Gandhi follower, with soaring philanthropic ideals which tend to founder in the realisation. A clever student, now making a career in the executive branch of the state civil service. (S. 1; W. I; R. 45. Prestige level one.)

13. *Jaimal*, aged *c*. 35. Son of a small shopkeeper. Both parents died when he was a child. He was grudgingly cared for by uncles until the age of 12, since when he has fended for himself. Makes a very meagre living as a tinsmith. Is too poor to have any hope of marrying, but prides himself on his independence. Although solitary, touchy and quarrelsome he was noticeably good with small children and popular among them. (S. 4; W. III; R.—declined. Prestige level three.)

NOTE ON THE SELECTION OF INFORMANTS

In drawing up plans for this research, my intention was to try to obtain prolonged interviews with twenty-seven informants, nine from each caste. In each case, three were to be relatively eminent and highly-regarded members of their community, three average, and three unquestionably low in their caste-fellows' esteem. Further, my ambition was to try to find one elderly, one middle-aged and one young man in each group of three.

This schematic grouping can be represented diagrammatically thus:

Prestige Level	*Rajputs*				*Brahmins*				*Banias*			
	I	II	III	Total	I	II	III	Total	I	II	III	Total
Elderly	1	1	1	3	1	1	1	3	1	1	1	3
Middle-aged	1	1	1	3	1	1	1	3	1	1	1	3
Young	1	1	1	3	1	1	1	3	1	1	1	3
Total	3	3	3	9	3	3	3	9	3	3	3	9

Grand Total—27

In practice, this orderly scheme was not fulfilled, even though in the endeavour to find a subject to occupy each compartment of the diagram, the total number of informants was increased from twenty-seven to thirty-seven. The actual distribution of the informants, in respect of age and community-prestige level, was as shown below:

Prestige level	Rajputs				Brahmins				Banias			
	I	II	III	Total	I	II	III	Total	I	II	III	Total
Elderly (40 and over)	–	1	2	3	1	3	1	5	1	–	2	3
Middle-aged (25–40)	2	2	2	6	1	2	1	4	1	2	3	6
Young (18–25)	1	2	1	4	1	–	1	2	2	1	1	4
Total	3	5	5	13	3	5	3	11	4	3	6	13

Grand Total—37

An attempt was also made to keep a balance between the number of informants who were eldest sons and those who were younger sons. These were finally represented in the following ratios; Rajputs 7:6; Brahmins 7:4; Banias 6:7. Two other factors, which were not foreseen, became apparent in the analysis of the life histories. These were respectively, bereavement during childhood, and marital state.

It was found that no fewer than eighteen of the thirty-seven informants had lost one or both parents before reaching the age of puberty. Since there was no reason to believe that the selection of subjects had been biased in this respect, this finding served to emphasise the physical and emotional hazards associated with living under conditions of primitive hygiene in a rigorous climate.* The emotional deprivation of these orphans would be mitigated to some extent by the diffusion of family ties through the members of the large Hindu joint families; but some consequence of the loss may be presumed, if only a reinforcement of the protective withdrawal into the self which is described in subsequent chapters. The disparity between the number of unmarried men in the Bania group (six bachelors, as compared with three Rajputs and one Brahmin in the same state) could be attributed to the high wedding settlement which had to be paid to the bride's father in that caste.

* Dr. A. Geddes, an authority on human geography, has indicated the social, economic and psychological consequences of living in what he terms a " recurrent crisis area " (of which Rajasthan is an example) in his paper: " The Social and Psychological Significance of Variability in Population Change, with examples from India, 1871-1941 ", *Human Relations*, vol. i, No. 2, 1947

CHAPTER III

INTER-PERSONAL RELATIONS

It is a perplexing business, trying to learn the nuances of social intercourse in an unfamiliar community. At one stage, when I still felt keenly aware of my ignorance and awkwardness, I reflected that the experience was not unlike that of one's first flights in a light aeroplane—everything is going steadily, one begins to gain confidence; and then there is a lurch, the 'plane tilts over, the engine cuts out or roars louder. One's enjoyment gives way to a sudden access of misgiving. It is only with practice that one learns to be familiar with each manoeuvre. In social life, as in flying, confidence is greatest when one knows what is going to happen next.

This initial gaucherie, however, is a valuable aid to observation; it can signal the occurrence of unobtrusive differences in what the visitor and his hosts regard as the " proper " social response. One is never so perceptive of the quiddity of a foreign scene as during the first few weeks of one's stay. My work in Deoli therefore called for a complex adaptation; on the one hand, I must quickly master sufficient *savoir-faire* to avoid offending the susceptibilities of my informants. I must encourage a good rapport with them, but on the other hand I had to resist the temptation to relax my awareness-of-difference, by feeling too much at home in their environment. I found a helpful stimulus lay in alternating my contacts among Brahmins, Rajputs and Banias (and, in later months, among Moslem informants as well), because it required a constant effort of attention to appreciate the different emphases which members of these groups placed upon the same subjects. There were, of course, many elements of reaction-pattern and of belief which they shared in common.

My first impression of the people of Deoli, before I had come to know them as individuals, was of their ebullient, Latin quality. They were friendly, welcoming, showering hospitality and questions upon us with cheerful exuberance. I was gratified to receive many promises of help, of all the information I cared to ask—but the eager helpers failed to appear next day, and for many days afterwards. As months went by, I came to recognise a pattern in this; again and again I would find myself in a friendly group, in which good humour and fellow-feeling would mount rapidly like a blaze of straw. We would make plans for the future and be united in mutual confidence and goodwill as we did so; yet no sooner had we dispersed than the glow of this enthusiasm would dwindle and die out. Within an hour or two, one of the group would warn me that someone else was only in the scheme for his own advantage; that the proposer could not be trusted with our subscriptions, and so on. Next day, the plan would be tacitly set aside.

This meant that the most successful instances of communal activity in the village were impromptu affairs. On several occasions we were summoned to elaborate feasts, at a few hours' or minutes' notice. Even the celebrations of great festivals of the Hindu calendar began haphazardly and worked up during the day to a hectic climax.

Perhaps the most enjoyable event of my stay came near the end, when pupils of the village school organised a moonlight picnic, to be held that same evening, in honour of their headmaster who was leaving. It was a thoroughly successful excursion, masters and children overflowing with camaraderie. The new headmaster paid a moving tribute to his predecessor, the boys cheered him, and sang patriotic songs. Yet, even as we dispersed, the fellow-feeling ebbed away: " That new man is very clever," said one of the village masters in my ear: " but it wasn't right of him to pull strings, the way he did, to have Hira Singh sent away."

When finally we left the village, it was the same. There had been spurts of interest, short-lived plans to " do something about it " for several days before, but nothing was done. At the very last moment, enthusiasm kindled again; the children ran to and fro collecting flowers to make garlands for us; friends insistently called us into their houses so that their women-folk could look at our new baby, on whom they pressed gifts; a band appeared and a minstrel, who sang extempore verses about our stay in Deoli: there were speeches and presentations, and we drove off in a spate of goodwill and flower petals.

This fitful spontaneity was one of the most agreeable aspects of life in the village, but it had its obverse side. From the beginning to the end of my stay, my notebooks record instances of suspicion and mutual distrust.

That the villagers should be suspicious of me was only to be expected. In previous years, European visitors had been rare indeed. Those who came were either guests of the Ruler, invited for a day's shooting, or senior government officials: no one could recall any visit by a missionary. It was therefore a complete novelty to see a " Doctor Sahib " who spent his days in the bazaar and showed an insatiable curiosity about their private lives. Everyone who spoke with me was cross-examined afterwards, and at night long discussions were held on the steps of shops in the main street. The general opinion was that I must be connected with the C.I.D., perhaps sent to spy upon the black-market in grain and rationed cloth; minority views were expressed that I was a spy of Pakistan, or of the British Government. Soon the rumour ran that hundreds of European spies, like me, had appeared in villages all over Rajasthan.

At the end of a fortnight I felt that I must make an effort to counteract these fears, and so I invited all of the twelve members of the village *panchayat* to come to my office in order that I might explain the nature of my work, and answer any questions. They agreed very politely—and none of them came. Next day I took my cue from an impromptu village gathering which I had since observed, and sent a crier through the lanes to invite everyone to a meeting that evening. This time, a large crowd appeared, and listened with interest to my talk, which emphasised that I was not connected in any way with authority, neither that of the late Rajahs' rule, nor that of the British, nor of the Congress government. Many questions were asked, and one in particular was remembered in conversation for months afterwards. A member of the *panchayat* said: " That is all very well, but suppose you are attacked and beaten in this village, what will happen then; who will come to your aid? "

I replied: " If I am attacked, I hope that I shall have found friends in Deoli who will help me, because no one else is going to do so. Besides, I come here as your friend, and my work can only proceed if I succeed in making friends among you—and so far, it has seemed to me that you people are more ready to be friendly than to beat me."

The meeting caught fire in a blaze of goodwill, and there were renewed promises of assistance, but next day, and at intervals throughout my stay, I continued to be told of suspicions and doubts as to what my real motives might be.

Much later, I remembered this experience, when Rajmal told me of the Ruler's brief incursion into politics, in 1948, when he addressed meetings of peasants in favour of the Maharana's rule. He spoke well, and roused his audiences to a pitch of enthusiasm—" But as soon as they broke up, they said: ' The man's no use, he's a fool, nobody trusts him.' "

For some weeks, I assumed that it was simply as a foreigner that I excited so much suspicion. Gradually, however, the evidence accumulated that my informants were also distrustful of each other. Several of them warned me not to leave any belongings in my room, as the others would be sure to steal them. They insistently reminded me that the door leading to the flat roof of my office had no lock, and must be secured. It never was, and yet nothing was ever taken from the room. The instances continued to multiply. In April, Birmal was still warning me: "These people are not to be trusted, they will be sure to rob you.... You should not trust me either. How can you know what is really in my heart?"

Birmal did not as a rule accept this prevailing distrust with such resignation. He wanted more than anything to be the sort of man whom everyone would trust, and to whom people would turn for help and advice; but instead he found himself a laughing-stock, nicknamed "Netaji" ("Saviour of the Country") after the patriot-hero, Subhas Chandra Bhose. ("But", said Kripa Lal, "Subhas Chandra died in an airplane crash, and our Netaji will be killed falling from a bullock-cart.") In another conversation, Birmal told me how he once visited a strange village and as he sat there in his spotless *khadi* cloth and Gandhi-cap, he heard the villagers whispering about him, wondering if he were a government spy. At this, he went and spoke to them, and before long he won their applause with a glowing account of the social and moral ideals of Mahatma Gandhi. "If people suspected me of being a spy, can you wonder that they are suspicious of you, a foreigner? There is too much distrust in their hearts."

To the end of my stay, informants continued to report rumours and conjectures in the bazaar as to what might be my real, undisclosed purpose; and this was always pictured as threatening and inimical. This suspicion was usually ascribed to others, and disclaimed by my interlocutors, but in one of our last meetings, when we had drunk each other's health in *daru*, Amar Singh let slip: "So you've been here, I don't know for what—all right, pardon me, pay no attention."

Birmal insisted that there was no one in the world whom he could really trust, and he quoted an incident of the previous year, when his best friend in the village, one Mohan Lal, had turned upon him and accused him unjustly of embezzling *panchayat* funds. His theme was echoed by every one of my informants. Some took it for granted—only a fool would trust people, and expect not to be let down. Others spoke bitterly of their personal experiences: Daulmal, Rup Lal and Bhagwat Singh in particular, denounced Deoli as a place where people were notoriously untrustworthy. Even in the Palace, the subject cropped up one night, when the Rao Sahib was talking with a lawyer from Udaipur, the organising secretary of the Rajputs' political party. This lawyer said that his party committee had had a long debate over which candidate they should select for an Udaipur constituency, and found there was no one in whose honesty they had any confidence. The Rao laughed, and agreed: "We are all like that—I am included in it too."

A further indication of reluctance to trust one's neighbours, or even one's nearest kin, was given by frequent references to the practice of making a secret cache of one's gold and jewellery, or savings in coin. It was taken for granted that every man did this, keeping the secret even from his wife and family. After a man's death his relatives often probed the walls of his house, or excavated likely-looking corners of his courtyard, and sometimes they were rewarded by finding a pot full of valuables.

Distrust extended also towards the wandering holy men, whose claim to have renounced all worldly desires was often suspect. Hari Lal said: "In this age, there are few real devotees. How can anyone tell if a man practises devotion truly or not? That's a thing you can't tell by looking at him, he keeps that to himself. A true *bhagat* will not show all his neighbours that he is a devotee; he will be more likely to leave his fellows and live alone in the jungle."

In contrast to this all-pervading distrust was a group of young men, including members of all three castes—Bhagwat Singh, Birmal, Chauthmal, Himat Lal and one or two others—who seemed fast friends. They were all "Naya Admi"—"New Men", who approved of the Congress government and its plans for social reform. Almost every day they met to drink tea at a stall run by one of them, or descended in a body upon my office and called for tea to be brought there. This was in March; but by the end of May Bhagwat Singh began to leave the group, telling me that under a cloak of Congress activity they were promoting a deal in black-market cloth. In June, this faction came into open conflict with their rivals in the bazaar, and Birmal began to wash his hands of their concerns. Two months later, Himat Lal led a mob of youths armed with sticks to drive out Chauthmal from a shop which rightly belonged, he said, to one of the village temples. At the end of my stay, these two were friends again, but by now I had learned that this was a constant process in the village's life: there was a continual re-forming and shifting of alliances, none of which persisted for long.

It is necessary to emphasise that these repeated disillusionments never seemed to destroy my informants' belief that each new encounter might provide the experience of complete mutual trust for which they longed, but which seemed always to elude them. In their initial enthusiasm over a new project or a new acquaintanceship there was an infectious warmth and cordiality: they made extravagant promises and uttered professions of the deepest regard—and for the moment they really meant it. These outpourings of goodwill were no less genuine because they proved so ephemeral. They could last only so long as each could believe in his partner's sympathy being still wholly and unreservedly committed; and they were doomed to disappointment because too much was hoped from them.

In time I came to recognise, in my own social gaucherie, a pattern of misunderstanding which seems often to have frustrated the desire for good relations between Indians and Westerners. When confronted with a prompt, generous, idealistic response to a friendly overture, I would be embarrassed. I found myself regarding my new friend's protestations as exaggerated and sentimental, if not insincere; and he must have found me cold, calculating and unresponsive. Slowly I learned to respond with fitting appreciation to these explosions of goodwill, recognising (even when I could not share) the amiable phantasy engendered by such occasions. Few Europeans have been able to respond with complete spontaneity to the quicksilver moods and the insistent boundless claims of Indian friendship. In his book *The Hill of Devi*, Mr. E. M. Forster has shown that he is such a one.

When I introduced the theme of friendship into my interviews, the responses, though various, were unanimous on one point: none of my informants could say he had ever had a *true* friend. The ideal standard of " true friendship " proved unattainable. They would assess their best friends as " 60 per cent. true ", even as much as " fourteen annas in the rupee ", but never wholly to be relied upon. Significantly, their definition of a friend was very much akin to their description of the *Guru*, or religious guide. As Gopi Lal put it: " The first mark of a true friend is to tell you when you do wrong, and help you when you need help." Birmal said: " Most friendship is feigned; only one friend in a thousand is the kind who is ready to forget his own interests entirely out of regard for you. There are no true friends in this village—I stand alone."

When I asked, could a wife not be a friend, I was reminded politely of the facts of life in a Hindu joint family. A man's wife is chosen by his elders and the wedding usually takes place before, or soon after, she reaches puberty. Marriage is patrilocal, but for some years the young wife will come and go between her home village and that of her husband, spending a few weeks or months at each in turn, and while at the latter she must efface herself as much as possible in the presence of her in-laws. Out of respect for his parents, the bridegroom must act towards her with formal indifference. If she even wishes to hand him something while her mother-in-law is in the room, she must give it to her mother-in-law, who gives it to her son. Only years later, when she has had several children, and when they have established a separate hearth, can this constraint be fully relaxed; and even then, the best that my informants expected from their wives was that they should carry out their domestic responsibilities without complaining. To talk of " true friendship " with one's wife seemed irrelevant.

Within the family circle, only the mother and the sister seemed to fill the role of this devoted, self-denying-friend. My informants made it plain that it is only in relation to these figures that one can feel completely secure of support and affection.* Towards the father, one could have none of this depth of feeling: relations with him were based upon a strict observance of mutual obligations. In this he stood in contrast to the guru, who was often referred to as a second father. The guru was seen as a figure possessing magical powers, imparting not only knowledge, but also more tangible blessings. Rajendra Singh said one day: " Ah Sahib, I wish if my guru came and simply put his hand on the head of my son—then he would not suffer any more illness the whole of his life." Towards this beneficent figure one could feel, and express, a rare warmth of affection and trust. If he is to be regarded as a parent-figure, it should be as an ideal, good parent—or parents, because the guru, like any other powerful person from whom there is an expectation of help, is commonly addressed as " Ap hamara man-bap hain "—" You are my father and my mother ".

Although mutual distrust seemed to underlie most relationships in the village, it only infrequently was expressed in open conflict. On the surface, there was a deceptive show of cordiality and esteem. For example, within two weeks of our arrival in the village, there was an evening meeting in the

* In phantasy, however, as will be shown later, the mother is regarded with feelings of ambivalence

bazaar to elect a new chairman of the panchayat. Gopi Lal was unanimously appointed, and made a touching speech in praise of his predecessor's work, promising that he would devote himself unsparingly to this public service. He was warmly applauded, but as we dispersed, my neighbour in the crowd shook his head: "No good will come of this," he said, "he was only elected because that crowd of Brahmins forced the other to resign; and he's a mean, grasping man, Gopi Lal: only last week he was beaten with shoes by a poor man from whom he was demanding too much interest on a loan."

When feelings of ill-will *did* find open expression, as happened in a number of explosive quarrels during my stay in the village, two features were especially remarkable. Firstly, the utter collapse of self-control, all the more remarkable for its contrast with the formality of normal exchanges. During a quarrel, the participants' faces were contorted with hatred, their eyes bloodshot, their whole bodies quivering. They abandoned themselves to anger with a completeness which previously had been familiar to me only in the temper-tantrums of young children. Looking at these changed features, of men who were usually so polite and affable, I was able to understand for the first time the epidemic of massacre and counter-massacre which had swept over this "non-violent" country only a few years before. Himat Lal told me, one day in May: "I get angry very quickly if I hear people tell lies about me or abuse me; but if I hear them abuse my mother, then I get beside myself—if ten people come at me then, I'll think nothing of taking them on, I get so carried away with rage that I tremble all over, and I'm ready to do anything." At the time, I thought he must be exaggerating because he had always shown himself good-humoured and diplomatic, but a month later when the rivalry between two factions of cloth-sellers came to a head, he was the centre of an impassioned brawl, screaming obscene abuse and trying to belabour his opponents' heads with his shoes. With Bhagwat Singh, it was less surprising; although usually amiable, he was reputed to be quarrelsome when he was drunk. One evening in April, a group of young Banias jeered at him. One called out: "He's been drinking piss again"—and at that he went for them in such a frenzy of rage that one suffered a broken nose and two others were badly hurt. For this he was summoned before the panchayat. He was fined, and made profuse apologies before the elders of the village.

In any quarrel, but especially where a man's sexual jealousy was aroused, the recognised extreme sanction was to cut off one's opponent's nose. This symbolic castration had the merit of being conspicuous. The victim was obliged to display his humiliating injury for the rest of his life.

The second consistent feature of village quarrels was the presence of peace-makers, who intervened between the disputants, reminding them how wrong it was to give way to anger, urging self-control and compromise. In turn I saw Birmal, Bhagwat Singh, Shankar Lal and others play the role of mediator; and as I listened I was reminded again of references to one's guru, or one's father, telling one how to behave.

So constantly is the intervention of a third party associated with quarrels, that it occurs also in dreams. Thus Rup Lal told me of a dream in which he and Birmal nearly came to blows because they both wanted to take the front seat in a country bus. A small boy of eight rebuked them, told them not to quarrel; so they made it up. During the stress of their several feuds, Chauthmal, Birmal and Himat Lal each described dreams in which, having seen their opponents being ill-treated by police or by angry peasants, they intervened to put a stop to the violence. This suggested that it was felt to be better to be the " third party " to a dispute than to be the victor—if any of them could be said to have a victor. In time, the verb *samjhana* (to impart instruction) became recognisable as an element in everyone's experience, providing a counterpoint to the prevailing distrust. The role of moral adviser, counselling moderation and control of one's passions, is one which compels an impulse to obey, and at the same time, a surrender, however temporary, of one's customary suspiciousness. In this context, the mediator is allied with something very deep-rooted in the personality, the super-ego itself. In the end, he always is obeyed; the disputants regain their composure and the dam through which these strong passions burst for a time is reconstituted; the enmity goes underground once more.

These two basic patterns, the impossibility of reposing trust in anyone, and the supreme virtue of self-restraint, were recognisable in many other contexts besides that of quarrelling. It began to be apparent to me that not only people, but also things and ideas, were felt to be shifting and unreliable. Not only were there two kinds of time in the village, there were also two scales of weights, using different multiples of one rupee-weight to constitute a *ser* and a *maund*. There were different versions of the Hindu calendar, with various definitions of when was the New Year, and when the Season of the Rains officially began. Numbers were usually quoted in this way: " It was 5-7-10 years ago " or " We walked for 10-12-15 miles " or " There will be Laxmi-puja tonight at 7-8-9 o'clock ". Punctuality and precision were wholly foreign to village life. One or two, who had seen Europeanised cities, where trains and businesses are run by the clock, used to make fun of the village way. " The ceremony will be at 9 o'clock, Mewari time," said Devi Lal one day: " that is, it will be some time tonight, and probably a couple of hours later than you expect it."

This imprecision of detail was most conspicuous in versions of stories from Hindu mythology, and accounts of celebrated local temples. " I went to Kailashpuri yesterday ", said Chandmal, " and had a *darshan* of the God there. There's a very big Vaishnavi temple there, did you know ? "

" Is there really ? I thought it was a Shivite temple."

" It's all the same, it's Hindu religion, Vishnu and Shiv."

On another occasion, Kalu Lal embarked on a complicated story, in which successive gods became inextricably confused. When I tried to disentangle these, he waved my questions aside: " *All* Gods are Sath-Narayan ", he said; and at another time, " Whatever exists, that is Ishwar: he is in everything ". It was he also, who described his daily ritual of washing down an image with Ganges-water, and when I asked about this, he explained: " All water is Ganges-water, here too."

It was well summed up by Shankar Lal, who answered my bewilderment at a transposition of gods in his narrative: " Mahadev, Vishnu, wuh ekhi maya hai—they are all the one illusion." The entire, seemingly diverse, world is an illusion, and so is the apparent multiplicity of gods and goddesses: the single, underlying reality is God, Parmatma. In this mirage of deceptive appearances, the only thing one can be sure of is one's own self. This had important consequences in my informants' approach towards religion, which will be discussed in a later chapter; but it had also a bearing on their everyday life.

Formality of demeanour was highly esteemed. The exchange of courtesies of speech and gesture appropriate to each other's age and caste was a habitual and enjoyable activity. At such times people spoke with confidence and dignity as if good manners had power to neutralise all that was uncertain and inimical in a shifting world.

One of the earliest marginal comments in my Deoli diaries reads: " Apparent lack of sympathy: detached view of each other's personalities ". My informants continued to impress me with their lack of emotional involvement in each other's concerns. On the one hand, there was a striking lack of indignation in describing other people's failings. For example, Bheru Singh told me about His Holiness, the high priest of a nearby pilgrimage centre, who spent his days in a palatial house in Bombay, drinking whisky and squandering money on film stars: his father before him had kept a Moslem concubine —" What if he did? It's his own choice, they're wealthy people." This last phrase, " Rais hain ", might be better translated as: " They are the lordly ones ." It was invoked as an explanation for every eccentricity on the part of one's rulers. On one occasion, the Rao Sahib described how for a whim, the Maharana of Udaipur had caused a wolf, a deer, a wild buffalo, a panther and a donkey all to be made drunk with alcohol, and then released into a common arena. The result was disappointing; most of them lay down and slept, while the donkey staggered about kicking the others impartially. " Next time, he says he will put a tiger in as well. I do not know how he came to have this idea—he is a rich man, can do as he likes." The same attitude tended to blunt the villagers' resentment when they described flagrant instances of injustice and misrule by the Rajahs: if they chose to act like that, it was their affair —" Rais hain ".

A similarly dispassionate attitude was shown in discussing the failings of lesser men. There were two notorious thieves in the village (both of whom were among my informants), but no one expressed indignation against them. It was frequently explained to me: " Stealing is like a bad habit: when you once get in the way of it, it's hard to stop." Discussing a fellow-Rajput who had shown cowardice on a panther-shoot, Mal Singh said: " God gives it to some to act bravely—it is his will."

This attitude of unconcern over the sins of others was summarised in a much-quoted couplet:

> Kabir ah teri jhompri, galkation ke pas
> Karega so bharega, tu kyun rah udas.

(Oh Kabir, whose hut is nigh to the cutters of throats, As a man sows, so shall he reap; why should you be sad?)

Another manifestation of this emotional detachment was apparent in my medical practice: onlookers would interrupt a patient to discuss his symptoms, and often his private life, with a seeming disregard for his feelings. It seemed to me that the patients were sometimes quite painfully embarrassed by this, although they did their best to appear indifferent. Girdari Lal asked me one day to give an opinion upon his grandson: " See, he's an imbecile ", he said, " He's fourteen years old, and still he's in the second class at school. He isn't fit for anything, is he? " The boy looked on with a rather anxious smile. There was the same apparent disregard for others' physical as well as emotional sensitivity: several helpers would roughly demonstrate a patient's ulcer or abscess for my inspection. Whenever anyone accidentally stumbled, or injured himself, this invariably provoked laughter, but of a constrained " social " kind, as if to cover up the lapse from dignified behaviour.

Other instances of seeming indifference to the feelings of one's fellows were met with when joining with villagers in social visits. There was always an elaborate show of hospitality, but this seemed at times more calculated to display the host's generosity to the best advantage, rather than to consult the desires of his guest. Many times I was the witness of mock disputes, in which a guest insisted with apparent sincerity that he did not wish anything more, and the host over-ruled his objections and made him take another helping. On these domestic occasions, there was no concealment of the fact that it was the host who was the happier man.* This was made explicit one day when a wealthy Rajah's car broke down near Deoli, and he was entertained by the Rao Sahib. Telling me about this afterwards, Rajendra Singh enumerated all the items of food and drink, the expensive cigarettes, the bottles of liquor with which he had supplied his guest, as if they were so many minor victories. He said: " Thanks to the bounty of God, the Rajah has been here and has eaten my salt: so I have the whip hand."

* Officious hospitality of this sort has its counterpart in Scottish social history. In 1625 the Town Council of Aberdeen ordained that no person should, at any public or private meeting, presume to compel his neighbour at table to drink more wine or beer than he pleased, under penalty of forty pounds. This edict was useful, since for many years prior to its being passed compulsory drinking was rampant. To prevent " shirking " or reluctance to drink, a rule obtained in Perthshire that if the glass was not emptied the offending guest was compelled to drink to the same toast a second time from a full glass. Some hosts had the feet struck off their wine-glasses. Mr. William Maule of Panmure, late in the eighteenth century, locked the door upon his guests and then passed round bottles so constructed that they could not stand. Dean Ramsay, in his *Reminiscences of Scottish Life*, describes how a London merchant turned upon his Forfarshire host (who was following him to his bedroom with a bottle and a glass) with the remark that " his hospitality bordered upon brutality "

A further evidence of insensitivity towards each other was observed in conversation with groups of Hindu friends. Usually, two or three people would be talking at once, and talking in intermittent monologues: no one troubled to listen to his fellows' points of view, but interrupted impatiently to assert his own.

Girdari Lal was one of the first to impress upon me the connection between this solipsism and the Hindu religious life. "When she dies," he said, pointing to his elderly wife while three of his children listened respectfully, "I'll become a wandering *saddhu*."

"But, these sons and daughters, won't they miss you?"

"Why should they miss me? I am on my way to God, that's all."

Daulmal also spoke of becoming a wandering holy man, undeterred by the fact that he had a wife and a young child, and many debts: "You don't think of anything else at all, you think of God only: you just feel assured that your family will get whatever is fated for them."

The rationalisation for this supremely self-centred attitude to life is that each man carries within him an *atma*, a spark of God-stuff, and that his highest duty is to tend this atma with such diligence that it swells into flame, and ultimately merges with the light of the divine soul, the Parmatma. Echoes of this religious teaching are met with in everyday life. More than one of my informants told me how they were accustomed to consult "the God within" before embarking on any day's work. Nar Singh was one of these, and his inner voice was particularly fickle. Although we were, I thought, on very cordial terms with each other, I learned never to rely on his appearing at an agreed time, no matter how insistently he had promised. He would return a day or two later, and explain that that morning he "just knew" that he must attend to some other business first, out in the jungle.

One way in which a man can consult the God within him, is by taking omens, and this is understandable as an indirect, and correspondingly more candid, way of discovering one's real wishes. For example, I have known Bhurmal to postpone a journey because he stumbled as he crossed his threshold; and Latchman Singh to turn back from a jungle path because he heard a partridge cry on the right as he set out. Another Rajput, not one of my informants, told me that before any important task, he would breathe through his nose against the back of his hand. Like others here, he believed that one normally breathes out through one nostril at a time, alternating every few hours. In his case, he could only start work at a time when the right nostril was in operation. In their different ways, all of my informants were constantly pausing to see if their current course of action "felt right" to themselves. Very often, apparently, it did not: hence the uncertainty which attended all arrangements. My host would decide one evening that we would go out shooting next day; and next morning the excursion might be postponed, counter-manded and re-affirmed in the space of a few hours. It was the same with all his plans, which were continually being announced, elaborated, and suffering kaleidoscopic change. The same was true of my friends in the bazaar. Ultimately I learned, like them, to enjoy the zest of making plans without placing too much reliance on their being carried out.

With the initial premise of this self-centred view of the world, the Hindus' unshakeable belief in astrology became more comprehensible. As each man is the hub of his private universe, it is only natural that the stars and planets bear a unique relationship to the events of his life. Everyone knows that this is so, yet no one, least of all the busy astrologer, is surprised if the horoscope is wrong. This is an infinitely complicated science, and a village horoscope cannot be expected to correspond as faithfully to the client's destiny as would a really careful one, which would be most expensive. My rational mind kept prompting another excuse which Girdari Lal himself eventually quoted: "And then, these village people, how are they to know just when they were born? And the exact time is essential if the horoscope is to be quite true." It was not necessary for the prophecy to be confirmed by events: everyone was emotionally predisposed to believe in it, regardless of the evidence.

If, as I suggest, my village informants found nothing sure and reliable except their inmost selves, it would be quite misleading to think that the promptings of the self were consistent. On the contrary, they were vacillating in the extreme. My informants showed a keen appreciation of the contradictory elements to be found in any statement or situation. It is common enough in Western society to find that our patients (and we ourselves) hold logically incompatible views without being aware of the fact; but when they are forced upon our attention, we feel that we must sacrifice one or the other. The Hindus of Deoli, on the other hand, were not at all disconcerted by the juxtaposition of opposites. Thus, Nar Singh told me emphatically: " I never see ghosts, I'm not that kind of man ", and almost in the same breath he went on to tell me how he saw a ghost in the jungle, quite recently, which appeared at first as a flame, and then as a crying child: " If I had been on a camel, I'm sure it would have leapt up behind and attacked me, but I was on horseback, and the horse is a godlike animal so I was saved."

This particular contradiction was illustrated by many others. Everyone claimed to be *Dev-gun* by birth, as opposed to *Rakshas-gun* and it is only the latter, born under an evil star, who can see ghosts: and yet everyone, with the single exception of Shankar Lal, had ghost stories to tell. For a time I thought I was guilty of an error of translation, in taking " Ham bhut-palit ko nahin mante hain " as " I don't believe in ghosts ", instead of " I don't acknowledge the power of ghosts "; but still the contradictions continued: " I *never* see them—I remember seeing one once." " That Khub Chand was killed by sorcery, I'm sure of that—perhaps, though, he got a chill after being overheated."

The Ruler: " All my people love me . . . some of them are opposed, just 20 or 30 of these Banias and Brahmins."

Shankar Lal : " There is a serious competitive exam. . . . it is nothing, it is farce only."

Amar Singh: " I hate all Mussulmans, they are not to be trusted . . . that Moslem driver is my good friend."

Shankar Lal, describing Shiv's lingam : " It is invariably black, generally black; sometimes it is also white or yellow."

Rajmal, on bhopas: " They are all nonsense, nothing but lies "—then he goes on to describe the miraculous bhopa-cure of a sick member of his family.

In time, whenever a particularly emphatic statement was made to me, I learned to expect it to be qualified by another which seemed to contradict it; and I found that if I intervened, pointing out the illogicality of the two statements, my informants were pained and distressed. For them, it was no less provocative of anxiety to be asked to choose between two incompatible alternatives than it is for us to tolerate our own inconsistency.

During the summer of 1951, this reluctance to commit oneself was, observed also in the sphere of Indian politics. When Mr. Nehru, in June, submitted his resignation to the Working Committee of the Congress Party, the Secretary exclaimed in consternation: " It is absolutely impossible for me either to accept or to refuse his resignation." For many months, too, Mr. Acharya Kripalani occupied an equivocal position as a radical critic of Congress, and yet a member of its government: it was only after a protracted agony of vacillation that he ultimately acknowledged that he was no longer a Congressite, and formed his own opposition party. More recently, in January 1954, the Western powers were perplexed by a seeming ambiguity in the attitude of the Indian Government over the question of the Korean prisoners of war. As *The Times* put it: " General Thimayya appears to wish both to eat his cake and have it."

Life in Deoli was replete with paradoxes; or perhaps it would be truer to say that living among its citizens I learned a new awareness of the contradictory aspects of things.*

All of these paradoxes, it now seems to me, have one element in common: an inner sense of instability and insecurity —nothing and nobody, can be relied upon, not even one's own self. One indication of this inner doubt was my informants' seeming inability to tolerate a bad prognosis. Their own priests and physicians invariably say " He will get better ", and in time I realised that it is incumbent upon them to do so even if they think the case is hopeless. On one occasion, when I went to see a patient in the village who was dying of cancer of the liver, and was now in coma, his son asked me: " Will he live? " and I explained that he could not be expected to live much longer. Afterwards I was reproached for this. Birmal told me: " Even if you think he is going to die, you should say to them—' If it is God's will, he will live '."

On a less tragic level, I was frequently struck by the compulsive optimism shown by examination candidates and supporters of an electoral campaign: " Oh yes, of course I must pass "; " No doubt I shall be the best "; " Most certainly we shall win." Students in India await their examination results in a state of passionate anxiety. (Hira Singh was able to tell me a number of nightmares he had had while waiting for the result of his " B.A. previous ".) If they look forward to the results with a precarious optimism, they react to failure by abandoning themselves to despair, or at times to indignant protests. I was struck by the contrast between this impersonal, Western examination system, which weighs a man

* Recognition of the contradictory elements in human experience has never been wholly lacking in Western thought since Heraclitus enunciated the principle of *enantiodromia*—" the contrariness of things ". Two modern re-emphases of this insight are seen in the Freudian concept of ambivalence as a necessary feature of emotional life, and Jung's stress on the interplay of opposite tendencies in the personality; but such views are at variance with the belief in material causality which is implicit in our daily lives

and finds him wanting, and the old tradition of receiving instruction from father and guru. In the latter case, if the pupil only performed the act of complete submission and supplication, he was never turned away, but could be sure of acceptance and support. The displeasure of the examiners must be felt to be as terrible as the anger of a father, which is all the more threatening because it is known chiefly in phantasy, seldom or never provoked in real life.

This basic, elemental uncertainty is given its clearest expression in the two antidotes which are called into use in order to appease it, namely the bhopa's prophecies, and the ideal of the religious life. The former derived its efficacy from the immanence of a divine power. I was more than once told, when talking with a bhopa: " It is not I who make them better, it is Her work", indicating the Goddess of the shrine. Whether the possessing deity were a mother-goddess, or the male Bheruji or Ragliaji, the pattern was always the same; the supplicant prostrates himself in an attitude of helplessness and suffering, and the deity intervenes to ease his pain. " It's all rubbish, all lies ", said Birmal: " They just repeat ' Hau vejay —It will get better ' over and over again; and yet, if people have full faith in it, they will get better—it is faith that heals." (Birmal, it may be remembered, was one of the most eloquent expounders of the prevailing distrust.)

That aspect of the individual religious life which was most insistently stressed by my informants, was the assurance, and the utter constancy of purpose, of the advanced ascetic. This was expressed with many illustrations, but one was so general as to be clearly an established item of folk-knowledge, namely that a profoundly religious man will have fore-knowledge of future events, including the hour of his own death, and will meet them unperturbed. This calm and steadfast ideal figure embodied those very elements which my Hindu informants felt lacking in themselves.

There are in fact two contexts in which Hindus show prolonged and unremitting application to a task. The first of these is the self-dedication of the sannyasi. In some cases the original religious inspiration seems to flag, so that they become mere charlatans and professional beggars. My informants frequently warned me against such spurious holy men. On the other hand there are many genuine saddhus, who show themselves capable of persevering in their vocation. These are truly " unworldly " characters: and in this epithet perhaps lies the key to understanding their position. They are able to escape from their fellows' recurring crises of doubt and mistrust because they have renounced the attempt to form personal ties with anyone at all. This renunciation (with the accompanying renunciation of all sensual appetites) gives them an enviable serenity and detachment.

The other context in village life where sustained *engagé* activity is shown is in the accumulation of wealth through trade. This was exemplified by many of the Banias. Here serenity and detachment were conspicuous by their absence, and yet there was a link with the sannyasis' attitude in that the most rapacious Banias succeeded in business by virtue of renouncing all sentimental ties and obligations towards their fellow-men. Others among them vacillated, like their fellow caste-Hindus, between being wholly self-absorbed, and showing sudden bursts of generosity and short-lived trustfulness towards each other. For all their reputed avarice, it was the Banias who contributed most generously (if fitfully) to beggars and to plans for village betterment.

There was one element in village social life which I was at first inclined to discount as being of superficial importance only, a stereotype derived from religious teaching: but in time, I came to see that it also had a strong personal significance—as perhaps all such stereotypes must have, which are kept alive in action and not merely by lip-service. This was the attitude towards begging. Begging was often mentioned in the conversation of Brahmins, whose traditional right it was in former times to expect alms from members of the other castes. Their constant complaint was that nowadays people give only grudgingly, so that Brahmins are increasingly compelled to neglect their sacred duties, turning to the professions and even to trade for a means of livelihood. It was never challenged, however, by any of my informants, that a person who is in need has a right to beg what he requires from others who are more fortunate: on the other hand, there is a clear obligation upon the donor to give what is begged of him. Failure to do so will have evil consequences. This was brought out most clearly in the accepted account of witchcraft, to which were attributed the vast majority of illnesses, especially those affecting women and children.

The description of witchcraft given me by Devi Lal was repeated in similar terms by many other informants: " Witches, they're like this: suppose there's a witch and she asks you for something—you're a woman, you understand—and you refuse. Then she goes away, and after a while you get a fit of yawning, or of weeping, and then it comes on you and then some look one way or another, some do various things, often they cry out. People come and some use charms to drive out the spirit; and some beat the woman with slippers, beat her good and hard, and she doesn't seem to feel it. Until the witch leaves her, she won't feel it—and then, when it does, she will cry out, ' Oh, you're hurting me '."

In most cases the supposed witch was a woman (not necessarily old) who had been refused something she had asked for—" You must give, when someone begs ; it is a duty ", said Hari Lal. In two instances, men described how women had importuned them to make love, and on being rejected, had struck them with witchcraft.

The usual Western attitude towards beggary is one of guilt at the spectacle of sheer destitution, often expressing itself in indignant disapproval. In theory, one or two of the younger men of Deoli disapproved of one class of beggars, the spurious holy men who made a profession of their mendicacy: but in practice, they all shared in this inability to refuse when approached with supplication, and felt uneasy if they ever did so.

In the background of all my informants' references to personal intercourse was the system of caste. The traditional pattern of caste inter-relationships seemed indeed to be the most stable feature of village social life. It was bound up with religion: the caste into which one was born was determined by the accumulated sins and virtues shown in one's previous existence, that was one's *karma;* and one of the aspects of Hindu *dharm* (right behaviour) consisted in the acceptance of one's lot, and the observance both of the restrictions and the prerogatives peculiar to one's caste. Among the three communities from whom my informants were drawn, there was no lack of mutual criticism and recrimination; but the idea that one might prefer to have been born in another caste was never expressed. One's own caste role was taken for granted, and so were those of one's social superiors, and those of the menial groups which were linked to each other and to the high-caste families by a formally recognised, hereditary association. Acceptance of these impersonal, universal obligations could be seen as the counterpart, in society, of the individual's need to subordinate his own spontaneous impulses in conforming to an ideal of formal, restrained demeanour.

Each Rajput, Brahmin and Bania household had been served by the same families of washermen, barber, potter and priest for generations, and the latter looked to their social superiors not only for a part of their livelihood (there were few families which did not own or cultivate some land), but also for advice and support in their dealings with the outside world. To the conservative-minded, any other way of ordering society was impious: " This Congress government is bound to be inefficient ", said Vikram Singh, " because it is run by tradesmen, who were not born to rule." Mol Singh put it more strongly: " When a eunuch is able to serve a woman, then this government will be able to rule with authority, and not before."

In one sense, the supposed hierarchy of castes, each fixed for ever in its proper station, was a fiction. It might hold true for the major divisions, as described by Amar Singh: " The Brahmins come first, they're made from God's head; and then we come, the Rajputs, made from God's arms; and then the Banias, made of his belly; and then there are several varieties of Sudras who work for us—*Nais* shave us and cut our hair, *Kumhars* draw water for us, and so on, and when there's food in the house we feed them. That's always been their duty."

Where this traditional relationship was still observed and respected, as was the case in the majority of households in Deoli, it carried with it a certainty of one's own social role, and that of one's near neighbours. The vacillation and uncertainty which I have stressed earlier in this chapter were least apparent in the performance of familiar caste roles; but unfortunately, the younger members of every caste were beginning to find that they could no longer earn a subsistence in their hereditary occupation, and in their new employments as bus-drivers, or mechanics, shop assistants or government servants, they had lost this moral support of fulfilling a familiar, time-honoured role.

Even before the recent economic changes, within the major caste divisions there was a constant straining towards social betterment. Some Rajput clans were *asli* (the real thing) whereas others were to a greater or less degree *halki* (below par) and in consequence, were at a disadvantage in making marriage alliances. The same was true of sub-divisions within the other major groups. Among Sudra castes, the process of climbing the ladder of respectability was sometimes very evident; thus in Deoli there was a large colony of *Yadows*, formerly workers in cow-hide, and untouchable. Now, for five generations, they had given up this work in favour of stone-masonry and general labouring, and hoped in time to cease to be regarded as untouchable. In Mewar, as in many other parts of India, many of the menial castes are beginning to assume the style of Rajput, and to apply the suffix " Singh " to their names. This was demonstrated to me one day when I happened to ask a countryman what was his caste: " Rajput ", he said. " And of which clan? " " A potter-Rajput."

This tendency was bitterly resented by the real Rajputs, and indeed by members of all the three top communities. The old men's constant lament was that caste rules were being widely flouted, that the authority of the caste-meeting had gone, and that a visible sign of this demoralised state of society was the willingness of young Brahmins, Rajputs and Banias to sit with their social inferiors, drinking tea in public tea-shops. The young " New Men " on the other hand, welcomed the loosening of old caste restrictions: but everyone, old and young alike, described the internal distress which they experienced at the thought of having to sit and eat or drink with members of the lowest " untouchable " castes: the more conservative among them prided themselves on the fact that so far, they had never done so.

When expressed in terms of what it meant to them personally, caste was found to be related intimately to the idea of bodily purity and defilement, and will be discussed in the context of the Hindu body image. Often, talk of caste tended to lead to a recital of bygone rules of behaviour, already honoured more in the breach than the observance, and at such times the emotional tone of an interview could be felt to relax. It was very different if my informants were faced with a sudden personal challenge, such as whether or not they should sit to eat with me and with other guests whose caste status was questionable: this dilemma could make them acutely uncomfortable. These scruples about commensality had become so nearly second-nature to me, also, that I was quite moved when I observed one night that my two guests (both young Jhala Rajputs and so distant cousins) were drinking *daru* from the same brass dish: the gesture was symbolic of an intimate family solidarity, which was all the more striking in contrast to the demonstrative avoidance-of-pollution which underlies so much of Hindu social etiquette.

In talking about caste, my friends frequently used the expression " all the twelve-and-a-half communities " (*sarhe bara quam*) to denote the whole society of their world. The " half-quam ", I was told, referred to the class of *hinjras* or male prostitutes who are found in Rajasthan. These hinjras are transvestites, men who dress as women, but in a crude parody of female costume. They derive from any caste, but are invariably out-casted and live alone. They are known to be passive homosexuals, and to make a living by selling their services secretly for this purpose. Two hinjras were met with in Deoli, one of whom, called Latchman, lived in a hut near the palace gate. He had formerly belonged to the *Rawat* community of unskilled labourers, and had been a married man before he adopted the role of hinjra. He was reputed to have his regular patrons, but this topic was so scandalous that it was discussed with great reluctance by my informants. Besides Latchman, there was another hinjra who visited Deoli periodically, spending most of his time wandering from one village to another in the surrounding countryside. There was said to be one in every group of villages, and several were to be seen in the streets of Udaipur.

Homosexuality was considered a very shameful aberration, one which was known to be fairly common, but which could be condoned only if practised in secret. What made the hinjras an abomination in the sight of respectable people was their shamelessness in parading their perversion before the public gaze; and yet, although detested, these hinjras had a recognised social role. Each had a territory in which he was known, and would appear at weddings in that area, either alone or with another of his kind, in order to claim the alms due to him. They would perform travesties of women's songs and dances, and when, as invariably happened, they were abused and threatened, they would utter obscenities and expose themselves in a grossly indecent manner until the wedding party flung coins to them in order to be rid of them. In their normal begging, the same course of events was followed; their " turn " would be derisively cheered by a gang of village children, until the adults threw them small coins in order to put a stop to the repulsive and disturbing spectacle.

Hinjras were among the poorest of the several varieties of mendicants, and they seemed to lead a wretched existence, despised by everyone. On the other hand, they had the security of knowing that they had no vestige of dignity or social position to maintain; and their shamelessness made people reluctant to provoke their obscene retaliation in a public quarrel. Even the Ruler's servants were unable to silence an opponent who recognised none of the restraints of decency, and the Rao Sahib himself was liable to be taunted and pestered for alms if he was confronted by the hinjra. By their very persistence and their adherence to a common pattern of dress and behaviour it was clear that this "half-quam" also played a significant part in the social life of the wider community.

It is noteworthy that this extra group is perceived as occurring at the bottom of the caste scale, and so adding to the implicit awareness that caste is not so static and rigid as it is verbally depicted but that it is subject to a constant upward pressure from the inferior communities. The hinjra demonstrates in extreme form the way in which the lower castes can at times even coerce their social superiors.

From the point of view of the aberrant or exceptional individual, however, the accident of birth into a particular caste presents him with only one approved role and one permitted set of values out of the many which he sees exemplified in the other castes: the rest are designated as "not for you". In the face of this constraint one means of escape is to become a holy man, to whom caste rules no longer apply. Another is to become a hinjra and be outcasted. The dilemma of being confronted with a number of for-ever-inaccessible roles may also contribute to the Hindu's constant striving after essences, and towards a state of absolute certainty. In practice, a Hindu youth almost invariably accepts his lot, repudiating all possible roles except that into which he was born. This stoical acceptance is made easier by the high valuation of emotional restraint and moderation which he learns in other contexts of behaviour.

SUMMARY

A review of all the references to social relationships in the informants' interviews reveals a striking antithesis between those occurring in personal and those in formal contexts. The latter were by far the more numerous. The hierarchies of caste-groupings in society, of status within the extended family were clearly defined. So, too, was the behaviour of each member towards each other in these hierarchies. In the repetition of such formal behaviour, informants displayed poise and calm assurance. In contrast, all those relationships between individuals which were dependent upon spontaneous feelings and emotional exchanges were precarious and shifting. Emotional insecurity coloured each individual's experience of the world, as well as his private contacts with his fellows. It could be held in abeyance by concentrating upon his formal caste and family role, but finally overcome only by the religious technique of complete renunciation of all material and personal ties. In a few instances, aberrant individuals appeared to find it intolerable either to come to terms with the social expectations of their family and caste-fellows or to adopt the religious life. For them an alternative social role was available, that of the transvestite, which catered not only for the individual temperamental misfits but also for disavowed and yet persisting needs of the community as a whole.

CHAPTER IV

FAMILY RELATIONSHIPS

My informants were unanimous in declaring that it is a child's mother who plays the greatest part in determining what he will be like. Her influence is at work throughout the period of gestation, when she should take rich food and indulge in rhythmical exercise such as churning butter and grinding corn in order to make him strong. The Rajputs would have her take alcohol, " to give the baby flashing eyes "; and Girdari Lal prescribed an elaborate course of music and religious verse, so that the child would be born already equipped with some classical knowledge. " If the mother gives way to bad temper while she is pregnant ", said Chandmal, " her child will be bad-tempered too."

During the first days after birth, mother and child remain secluded in an inner room. The mother is ritually impure, as she is during menstruation, and must avoid all contact with the other members of the family, but especially with the hearth and cooking utensils. After six days or so there is a ceremony called *Suraj ki puja* (Worship of the Sun) conducted by the family Brahmin, who tells the parents five names which will accord with the child's horoscope, and they choose one. At this time the house is cleansed, and all soiled clothes are either destroyed or taken to be washed. The mother does not resume her full activities until forty days have passed, when she will worship the water of the well, bathe and change her clothes and shed her state of impurity.

High-caste Hindus regard the colostrum as unhealthy, and like to express it before giving the child the breast; but not all remember to do this. It is important for a mother to suckle her own child—" Jaisa than vaisa shan " is the customary saying: " It takes its nature from the breast ". Devi Singh attributed his own low resistance to infections to his mother's having been in poor health while he was a baby: " It was because she was sick that her milk did not nourish me properly. . . . In everything, I am generally weak from my childhood because we take our strength from our mother's milk—isn't that so, Sahib? " Suckling is moderately prolonged, weaning taking place usually at about two and a half years. By this time, the child is eating quite a generous diet, and the surrender of the breast might not seem too violent a wrench. Still, I was told, it usually provokes many days' crying and anger, because the child has not been accustomed to being thwarted. The mother may cover her nipples with a bitter paste until weaning is established; or rarely she may leave the child for two or three days.

The parents are supposed to abstain from intercourse during the last four months of pregnancy and for some months (variously given as 1, 3, 4, 6 and 9) after a child is born. If a second pregnancy soon follows, the previous child will be weaned early, and fed with ass's * or goat's milk, as it is thought injurious to the foetus for a mother to continue suckling while she is pregnant. On the other hand, the youngest child of a family may have a prolonged suckling period. The mother of one of my informants (Bhagmal) told me that he still occasionally took the breast when he was six years old.

When a Hindu mother carries a small infant, she holds it with its back reclining against her left upper arm, her fore-arm supporting its buttocks and legs. This leaves her right arm free, and also keeps the baby in a position where it can readily take the breast. At an early age—in many cases, before the infant is six months old—it is transferred to sit astride its mother's left hip. Quite small children soon learn to grip with their knees in order to help sustain this position. In later childhood it is a common sight to see older children, particularly girls, with a younger brother or sister perched astride their left hip and held with a supporting arm round their back.

During the first two years of life, a child is seldom separated from its mother, and it is never allowed to cry for long. Crying, it is said, will make it weak, will make its eyes become infected. A good mother will pick the child up at once and let it have her breast whenever it complains: " Balak aur badsha barabar hain "—" a child is equal to a king ", said Jaimal; and he went on to emphasise how a mother will uncomplainingly clean up her infant's mess, and how at night, if it wets the bedclothes, she will lie on the damp place rather than let her baby suffer discomfort.

When not in its mother's, or another relative's arms, the baby lies in a cradle consisting of a shallow wickerwork basket which is hung from the rafters, or from the branch of a tree. To prevent his fretting when he wakes, the basket is kept gently

* The ass, in India as in the West, is a symbol for stupidity; but its milk is paradoxically believed to impart wisdom

swinging. This swinging cradle is called a *jhula*. Here, again, a baby has something in common with a king. A regal form of luxury (which is emulated in many prosperous households) consists in reclining upon a swinging couch, hung from the roof. This also is called a jhula. In the hot weather the movement of air caused by this gentle swinging is refreshing. Daily, during the hot season the village Gods, or their small replicas, were also set upon miniature jhulas and swung for some hours in the forecourt of their temples.

At first it seemed to me that the sensuous pleasure of being " swung " was greatly exaggerated. Its peculiar attraction becomes more understandable when one reflects upon its emotional associations. Reclining passively upon this swinging cradle, the adult can recapture an echo of that early omnipotent state when all his desires were satisfied as soon as expressed: when he was assured of an attentive, ever-present minister to his wants.

Understandably, the word *mata* (mother) carries a very strong affective charge. It is invariably linked with the sacred cow, *gau-mata;* and it is as a symbol of motherhood, succouring, gentle and the antithesis of violence * that the cow is liable to be worshipped with a show of feeling which leaves non-Hindus embarrassed and bewildered. *Mataji*, also, is the generic name for the Mother-goddesses, whose shrines are to be found in every village in Rajasthan. In Deoli, there were several Matajis, the principal one being called *Vijayshan-Mata;* and Hindus of every caste consulted her when they were in distress. Even the Rao, who scoffed at bhopas as relics of superstition—" Though it may be that *some* of them are genuine article "—consulted her in 1944 about his Rani's barrenness; and when an heir was born in the following year, he had a handsome temple built to replace her former dilapidated hut.

During its prolonged suckling, the child sleeps with its mother who is separated from it only when she has intercourse with her husband; and then only temporarily. In principle, Hindu parents are enjoined to abstain from intercourse as long as the mother is suckling, but in practice it is quite uncommon for this abstinence to be prolonged for more than six months. Husband and wife, in households such as those of my informants, sleep on adjacent beds, with the youngest child either in its mother's bed or in a cot at her side. Small children are

* In historical accounts of battles in Rajasthan, the defeated side is sometimes reported to have come forward with grass in their mouths, signifying " We are as cows ", in token of surrender

considered too young to be aware of adult sexuality, so no attempt is made to prevent their being witnesses of their parents' intercourse. From the dawn of his ability to distinguish between persons in his immediate world, the Hindu child is confronted with this recurrent experience which cannot fail to be profoundly moving although imperfectly understood. Here it encounters a new aspect of its hitherto exclusively attentive mother, and sees in its father an overwhelming rival claimant for her love.

In the joint-family household, the child's grandparents supplement the mother's "spoiling" (as we would say) of the child. The earliest recollections of many of my informants were of receiving presents, especially sweetmeats, from their grandmothers. As Roshan Lal put it: "She would wake me every day with *laddus*, and I'd drink fresh cow's milk."

As will be seen below, the presence of the grandparents in the joint household profoundly modifies the behaviour of the child's own parents. Neither father nor mother may fondle their own child in their elders' presence. Tension is acute between mother-in-law and daughter-in-law. The latter is obliged by strict custom to defer in all things and to obey her mother-in-law's orders without question. She must look on impassively while the grandmother makes much of her child—unless the child begins to cry. Only then is she entitled to assert her first claim to "mother" her baby, by clasping it in her arms and giving it the breast.

In this setting the pattern becomes established that a mother is an attentive but pre-occupied person, whose feelings only become apparent when the child cries to her in distress—and then she hurries to supply all his wants.

Until the age of 2 to $2\frac{1}{2}$, when the child can walk and is "beginning to understand", it is seldom reproved in any way, although mention was made of a mother's giving her child an affectionate slap to warn it not to crawl too near the fire. Till this age, it performs its toilet function as and where it pleases: the mother wipes up after it with no reproach. After two, however, it begins to be told to go out to the yard. At any time after twenty months, the child will learn to indicate to its mother its need to go to stool. It will be led to a corner of the yard, and afterwards the mother (or a sister, or grandmother) will cleanse it with water. From the age of 5 or so, children learn to imitate their parents, walking out into the surrounding fields at dawn or dusk, carrying a *lota* of water with which to bathe themselves after defaecation. Throughout the later years of childhood the ritual as well as the physical importance of bathing is constantly reiterated.

The idea of slapping a small child because it soils within the house was rejected by all who discussed this with me—" How can it know, before it is old enough to understand? "—but it was agreed that children of 3 and 4 were often reminded of their duty to go outside, with threats: " The Babaji will carry you off! " or, " The tiger will get you! " and not infrequently with slaps given by its mother, who is now distinctly less indulgent than is its grandmother. It is a stereotype of domestic behaviour in these households for the grandmother to scold her daughter-in-law for being too harsh towards her grandchild; and my informants suggested that she secretly welcomed these scoldings, as evidence of the grandmother's concern for the child of the house.

Indian children are not discouraged from playing in the nude or very scantily dressed until they are 6 or 7 years old. This effectively prevents morbid curiosity about the physical difference between the sexes and enables adult Hindus to discuss the physical aspects of sexuality without false embarrassment.

As the child learned to accept responsibility for its own bodily cleanliness, it was also taught the importance of avoiding the invisible pollution conferred by the touch of members of the lowest castes. The mother or grandmother would call him in, and make him bathe and change his clothes if this should happen, until his repugnance for a low-caste person's touch became as involuntary as his disgust for the smell and touch of faeces. Children are seldom excluded from any of the adult activities of village life: indeed there is an absence of the Western emphasis on the separate role of childhood. In Deoli, children were never sent to bed at a fixed hour: they were present at midnight weddings and at protracted ceremonies. Sometimes they would fall asleep, and an older person would pick them up and wrap them in a blanket. Dr. Lois B. Murphy quotes a very apt remark made by an Indian friend, in this connection: " You bring up your children—we live with ours." *

In striking contrast to all this attentive mothering, the child's father is an aloof, seemingly unwelcoming figure. The reason for this is that a man, so long as he remains under his own father's roof, must keep up the fiction of denying that he leads an active sexual life of his own. Not to do so is to be

* G. and L. B. Murphy (1953), p. 51

disrespectful. Consequently, a man and his wife can never talk to each other naturally, in his parents' presence; nor is it proper for either of them to show affection for their own children in front of their elders. This obligatory suppression of any overt show of tender feelings is relaxed only when the child cries; then his needs take precedence even over the grandparents' authority, so that he will be handed over to his mother, often with the command " Give him the breast ". A father, however, experiences no such exception to the demand that he remain impassive and detached. Even if his wife or child falls ill he must contain his feelings and surrender the responsibility of tending them to his own parents. This taboo perpetuates in each generation the tension which exists between father and son; and it is very strong. Young Chauthmal, who lived in his father Bhurmal's house, had a boy of eighteen months, and often the grandfather could be seen carrying this child in his arms, or dandling him while they sat at their shop—but never Chauthmal: " I don't like to fondle him, even when we are alone in our room," he said: " if I did, he might get into the habit of running to my knee in the bazaar, and that would not look right."

Men of all three castes described the same attitude in their own families and commended it. On the other hand, there were three among my younger informants (Daulmal, Puranmal and Himat Lal) who disregarded the rule, and openly fondled their young children. They were able to do so because in each case their fathers were dead, and they were the heads of their several households: but still the consensus of opinion (as they were well aware) condemned their unashamed display of affection.

The usual father-child relationship, then, was drained of spontaneous warmth of feeling. Instead, it was governed by strict obligations on either side. It was Shankar Lal who first made it clear to me that in one respect a father is dependent on his son, quoting a Sanskrit *slok:* " This is the real definition of a son: Punnamna naraka trayate tat putr—The son is he who rescues a man from hell (because only a man's own son can perform the funeral rites and without those rites he cannot attain *nirvana*)."

The obligations of each to the other, of financial support and instruction on the one hand, and dutiful service throughout one's father's life (and after his death) on the other, were constantly emphasised, but personal intimacy was conspicuously absent. Puran Singh spoke for most of the others when he said: " My father was very stern when I was small, but now he sometimes even speaks nicely to me." The very marked insistence upon the need to submit oneself unreservedly to one's father's authority, to treat him as a god, suggested that the relationship was not an effortless one: but if it was maintained only with a struggle, the alternative of defying one's father's command was generally regarded as unthinkable. Two of my informants did mention occasions when they had challenged a father's decision. Himat Lal refused to conform to the usual village custom of *banola* (ceremonial processions, with bands playing) during the days preceding his wedding: he said that practice was old-fashioned and should be dropped. His father had a high reputation as a Brahmin, thanks to his prolonged daily exercises of prayer, but he was known to be excessively lenient towards Himat Lal, his only son, and in this case he let the boy have his own way. During 1951, Amar Singh disagreed with his father's decision to sell corn from the family fields for a price which could have been bettered, and they quarrelled over this. Here, the father was old and ought to have surrendered the management of his affairs to his sons, who were exasperated by his interference. Both Amar Singh and Himat Lal, however, were among those who assured me that a man must always defer unhesitatingly to his father's word.

In principle, the same subservience was postulated in relation to one's elder brother. As Rajmal put it: " If my father or my elder brother tells me to stand in one place, I'll stand there, dammit, all day if need be, until they tell me I can move." He was exaggerating, because he was in fact a man of very independent spirit; and like some other younger sons in the village, he went his own way, seldom bothering to consult his elder brother. In general, however, elder brothers were accorded, at least in public, the deference due to their position in the family; and the same restraint was observed by a younger brother in suppressing all show of affection towards his wife and children before an elder brother, as before his father. As Hira Singh put it: " Even if she is sick, I would not like to say this to my elder brother—but if younger brother is there, I can tell him and ask him to go for medicine." Hari Lal extended this category further saying: " Every man has got five fathers, and it is his duty to obey them without question, whatever they ask him to do. They are, his father, his elder brother, his king, his guru and his friend."

The formal distance interposed between each man and his father is clearly shown in the customary forms of speech.

A Hindu youth invariably addresses his father and elder brother as "Ap", which is the honorific, deferential mode of address, and he will use the polite form of an imperative, such as "berajie—pray be seated"; whereas in talking to his mother he will generally use the more familiar "Tum" and the brusquer expression "baitho—sit down". Custom therefore "allows" him to come that much nearer to a personal relationship with his mother than with his father.

The Hindu's relationship with his sisters is a very special one. It is based upon a far-reaching concept of incest. All the young women of one's own lineage are regarded as sisters, and as such are ineligible as marriage partners; but the prohibited degrees of kinship include also the lineages of one's mother and one's father's mother. The two latter lineages usually live in distant towns or villages and are met only in the exchange of formal visits. Those whom one addresses as "sister", however, probably live in the same village. So secure is the force of the ban upon their intermarriage that these "brothers" and "sisters" can meet and talk without the strict restraints which weigh heavily upon normal social intercourse between the sexes. This difference is epitomised in a village saying: "Gaon men chori, pargaon men to ladi"—"At her own village she's a girl, at her in-law's she's a bride." The words "chori" and "ladi" denote two quite different types of behaviour. Within each household, daughters of the family could easily be distinguished from daughters-in-law by their greater freedom of speech and bearing, and their comparative disregard for the niceties of purdah.

A man has a nebulous family tie with all those whom he addresses as sister; but he is bound to his "real" sister by lifelong obligations of support on his side and of grateful solicitude on hers. It is to her brothers that a married woman turns in time of trouble. Whenever a man visits the village where his married sister lives, he offers gifts to her and to her children, and he is entertained by them with respectful attentions. His presence is expected, as *Mama* or mother's brother, at the wedding of her children, to which he contributes a generous gift.

Each year at the festival of *rakhi-bandan*, sisters visit their brothers, tie a *rakhi* or ornamental bracelet on to their wrists, and wait upon them respectfully. In return, the brother gives her a present of apparel. The festival recapitulates their mutual interchange of affection and support.

This brother-sister bond is idealised in popular imagination. The custom still obtains in Rajasthan of adopting an honorary brother-sister relationship (dharm-bhai and dharm-bahin) with for example, the wife of one's friend or neighbour. This permits the man and woman to relax the scrupulous formality which would otherwise attend all their meetings. It is generally assumed that this institution safeguards the proprieties as effectively as the incest ban itself. Some, such as Shankar Lal * believe that it is frequently abused as a cloak for promiscuous affairs, but theirs is decidedly a minority opinion. As one informant put it: " Anyone can address a woman as bahinji, that means very little; but if he has accepted her rakhi that is different—then he must always treat her like a sister."

Elder sisters are expected, from an early age, to take a share in looking after their younger brothers and sisters. It is perhaps significant that they are not, like their mothers, obliged to refrain from fondling these infants when the grand-parents are present. Hence the growing child experiences in his relationship with his sisters a *continuity* of physical and emotional contact which is necessarily denied to him by his parents. This may explain why in later life the relationship with one's sister is not only uniformly idealised, but is charged with agreeable emotional tone—in contrast to the ambivalent feelings which are aroused by mother- and father-figures. The brother reciprocates by accepting responsibility for his sister's welfare and she comes to regard him as her protector. When her father dies, it is to her brother's house that she repairs on her periodical return visits to her natal village.

A son looks to his father for instruction in his adult role in life, and he learns as much by imitation as by precept. Thus, Kalu Lal: " My father taught me most of these verses that you say at weddings and the like; but much of this work can only be learned by watching." While living in the village, I saw instances of this deliberate instruction going on. Chauthmal and Surajmal each had a cloth-shop of his own, but each was still jealously supervised by his father; Moti Lal and Girdari Lal had taught their respective sons, Devi Lal and Roshan Lal as much as they knew of astrology and of Brahminical ritual, and had sent them on to have higher education.

Already, mention has been made of a parallelism between the attitude of a man towards his religious guide, or Guru, and that towards his father. In both cases, there is an unqualified self-abasement, a willingness to accept what he is told as being

* See page 236

infallible, and a confidence that by thus subordinating his will to that of the father-figure, he will be set on the true path. A father's teaching and example is invariably idealised. He stands for self-control, disciplining of the passions and the emotions; for everything that is formal, restrained and correct. In the measure to which one can adhere to his austere standard of behaviour, one has the assurance of one's father's acceptance and support. On the other hand, to yield to spontaneous emotion or to sensual appetite is felt to be both wrong and dangerous: this is especially the case with sexual satisfaction, which is always felt to be illicit and somehow impious.

With the sole exception of the annual saturnalia, the Holi festival, a youth may never use obscene words or refer to sexual matters in the presence of his elders. It is also unbecoming, and will attract rebukes, if he gives way to anger or laughs unrestrainedly: this is described as " behaving like an animal ". The most scandalous conduct of all, which was discussed only in hypothetical clauses, would be for a young man and a girl to exchange smiling glances in public. If this were seen by an older relative, they would receive a beating, said Bhagwat Singh, Chauthmal, Himat Lal and Nar Singh, who all hinted that this had been their experience.

It is not surprising that in these Hindu families, sex is never discussed between parents and children. The latter learn the facts of sex, and the pleasures of erotic stimulation, from each other at an early age. My informants agreed that most children masturbate, and indulge in heterosexual and homosexual play for years before puberty: but they know that this is disapproved of by their elders, so it is done secretly. Masturbation and homosexual practices among children were condemned as " weakening " (although Birmal maintained that the passive partner would thrive, being enriched by the other's semen) but they did not give rise to strong feelings of antipathy. On one occasion, Rajendra Singh told me that some holy men were advised to masturbate as a means of relieving their minds of sexual thoughts: " That is the best thing ", he said, and absent-mindedly made a masturbatory gesture of the right hand as he spoke. In general, however, masturbation in later childhood or in adult life was vehemently condemned.

As children approach puberty, they begin to invest sex with attributes of danger and fascination, taking their cue from older brothers and friends. One recurrent experience of early years, whose importance was brought to my attention by Dr. Kathleen

Gough, is the periodic seclusion of the child's mother during her menses. At such times, the mother withdraws from the normal life of the household, into an inner room; she is dangerous and somehow defiling to touch—although the defilement does not apply to her infant—and she sheds blood. (The association of seclusion and blood brings to mind accounts of the *dakan*, or witch. She also is said periodically to shut herself in a darkened room and abandon herself to her hostile desires, drinking the blood of some, eating the livers of others of those who have slighted her.) The need for the child to practise avoidance of his temporarily " unclean " mother does not begin until after he is weaned. As he grows older, and learns that all this has to do with sex, it cannot fail to add to the fearfulness, as well as to the mystery of that function.

Those of my informants who discussed sexual matters freely (and that most of them were able to do so may have been due to my role as a physician) were agreed that women, like men, varied among themselves as to the intensity of their sexual appetite; but in general, their need for sex was felt to be the more imperative and they were described as taking the initiative in suggesting intercourse. The need to procreate a son and the need to satisfy one's wife were felt as two major impediments to leading a good life. Girdari Lal mentioned, as a rider to his description of the virtues of celibacy, that a well-instructed man will satisfy his wife twice in a night, when she shows that she desires it. Birmal reminded me that every woman needs sexual satisfaction at least once a month; if she is not given it within the ten days following her period, she is bound to go astray. Many people told me instances of the cunning with which adulterous women seduced their lovers. Promiscuity, it was generally agreed, is more women's fault than men's. Hari Lal said: " Even God himself doesn't know a woman's hidden intentions." Daulmal summed it up with: " Sexual intercourse was given by God in order to keep us from being good too easily."

The guilt and longing for restraint which attended sexual life were not quite universal. Rajputs were able to indulge in occasional drunken parties, in which sexual licence could be enjoyed with their social inferiors, low-caste girls and prostitutes; but this was quite divorced from their behaviour within their own families. Among the others, young Kripa Lal, Himat Lal and Chauthmal, liked to boast of their sexual adventures when in Udaipur, freed from the censure of the elders of the village; but only Rajmal was bold enough to admit that he loved women and liquor, and indulged himself without restraint. This was generally known, but it was such scandalous conduct in a Bania, and of a rich family at that, that it was never mentioned except in whispers.

A man's wife comes to him as a stranger, chosen for him as a result of negotiations in which he and she have had little say. She is, moreover, an emissary of the race of women and as such, she stands for carnal temptation, for seduction from the ideal values represented by his father and his *guru*. It is as the mother of his children, and as a faithful housekeeper that a Hindu wife comes nearest to a personal relationship with her spouse; and yet the formal obligations between them are reciprocal, although at first sight the wife seems to have an overwhelming disadvantage. Most of my informants, who were all male, stressed a wife's duty to tend her husband as a god. The Rajputs in particular were gratified when in September 1951 a Rajput widow in the village Kundela, in Rajasthan, let herself be burned alive on her husband's funeral pyre as a mark of her devotion. This rite of suttee is not the monopoly of any one caste, although it is commonest among Rajputs. In the village cremation ground there were four memorials to past suttees, two of whom had belonged to Sudra castes, one to a Rajput and one to a Bania family. This last was held in especially high regard because the girl was still a virgin, married to her husband but not yet old enough to have lived with him, when he died, and she committed suttee. Memorials to past suttees in the Ruler's family stood in their separate cremation ground. In each case, it was the husband's name, and not that of his wife, which was commemorated on the monument, although at the time of the event it is the dutiful wife who is venerated, to the point of deification.

There were, nevertheless, some indications that the wives, although pent up within their *zenanas*, also claimed their due. Thus Gopi Lal said: " If my wife knew that I had gone with another woman, she'd bar the door and refuse to allow me in my house "; and Girdari Lal: " My mother and my wife were always quarrelling, and it was my mother's fault; she could not control her temper. In the end my father told me to take this house and live apart from them, and we have lived here ever since." Unkind critics of the Ruler asserted that he was not the master of his own house: " She rides him like a donkey ", said Rajmal.

One aspect of Hindu family life which impresses Western observers, is the emphasis upon the extended family group, and the relative playing-down of the nuclear, biological family. It is true that children are usually brought up in an extended household, containing several families, with a grandfather or uncle as its head. The dispersal of family roles is underlined by the classificatory terms of kinship which extend the range of persons who are called brother, sister, uncle and aunt to all fellow-members of the *gotra* * of the same generation. A father's elder brother is referred to with respect as " Bara bap " or " Dataji " whereas the class of father's-younger-brothers are addressed by the term " Kakaji " which has less intimidating associations. At periodical re-unions of the extended family, such as occur after a death, or at a wedding, there is a formalised demonstration of the ties of mutual obligation which link together the separate branches, and it is at such times that the family group can express its corporate disapproval of aberrant members. A sense of dependence and expectation of support colours a child's relationship with the gotra of his mother's brothers, and this association persists throughout life. In Deoli, Shrimal was indulgently treated as a nephew by the older Chenmal, who happened to belong to the same gotra as his mother, although their relationship was a very distant one.

Similarly, there is a relationship of a peculiar (less intimate and more ambivalent) character with the gotra of one's in-laws; and beyond this, there is a diminishing sense of kinship with other members of one's sub-caste, and caste, which is given expression in the ability to eat, drink and smoke together, like members of one family. Beyond this, the social barriers against commensality interpose like a warning of the limits beyond which intimacy cannot proceed.

This consciousness of an extended kinship bond modifies, but does not by any means replace, the influence of a child's own biological family: on the contrary, for the small child it serves to emphasise his unique relationship with his own mother, who is the source of all his early gratifications, and who behaves like his devoted servant. When an informant wished to illustrate the difference between brothers and cousins (both termed *bhai*) he would commonly say: " Ekhi man ka " (of one and the same mother) or " Ekhi dudh ka bhai " (of one and the same milk). The father, in the wider family setting, is lessened as a person in his own right, being seen as one of a hierarchy of male figures of authority; but he remains intimately related to his child as the rival for his mother's attention, and an overwhelming rival, to whom the

* Exogamous subdivision of the endogamous caste unit

mother must be surrendered from time to time, in circumstances calculated to heighten his awesomeness in phantasy.

In summary, then, the aspect most consistently stressed in the relations between children and their parents is that of observing dutifully one's mutual obligations. In the earliest years, the mother is the one person from whom there is an assurance of affection and unquestioning support; in time, however, she has to repulse the child in order to resume her sexual relations with the father, and with her sexuality is associated the mysterious and dangerous phenomenon of her periodic menstrual seclusion. The father, on the other hand, is one of a number of remote disciplinary male figures, who ultimately intervenes to take possession of one's mother. He is all-powerful, and must be approached in an attitude of complete submission; and it is in relation to him that one learns the imperative social duty of suppressing one's appetites, and desires, and every demonstration of emotion.

CHAPTER V

THE HINDU BODY-IMAGE

A WESTERNER living for the first time among Hindus is soon made conscious of the fact that his hosts have certain culturally ingrained concepts relating to the human body, which he must learn if he is to avoid committing solecisms. Most of these concepts relate to purity and defilement; perhaps the chief exception being the special ideas associated with the head—" Because all this part above the neck belongs to God ", said Kalu Lal: " The head is the root of a man's body—he is like a tree walking upside down. Just as, if you tend the roots of a tree well and water them plentifully, so it will grow and have branches and leaves and bear fruit, so it is with a man's head. If it catches cold, or becomes feverish, his whole body dries up. That's why you ought to take special care of your head, and anoint the hair with good oils."

Kalu Lal's own head was always well-groomed, with handsome beard and whiskers dressed in the Mewari style; and his observations caused me to be aware of the care with which every high-caste villager anointed his head regularly with oil. I found that the medicine which my patients prized most highly of all my stock was an aromatic ointment containing menthol and wintergreen. They would use this to anoint their foreheads and claim immediate relief from headaches and other troubles.

The importance of head-dresses could never be overlooked in Rajasthan, where turbans of distinctive local styles are the most striking feature of male attire. In fact, head-dress has become symbolic of political affiliation, Congressites asserting themselves by wearing the white " Gandhi-cap " (which contrasts with the Rajputs' colourful *safa*), while people of progressive opinions who are not members of the Congress party go bare-headed or wear a hat of European style.

A humble reflection of this cherishing of the head could be seen in any crowd of peasants, on a winter's morning. Whether sleeping or squatting waiting for the sun to rise, they would muffle their heads with the coarse cotton cloths which serve them as a wrap: one was reminded of the sleeping forms which can be seen on any large Indian railway platform at night, their heads buried beneath their blanket.

Girdari Lal gave another reason for the importance of the head: " There's a sun inside your belly, that keeps your body warm, and there is nectar in your head. It drips down your throat from that point (the uvula) and is caught by the sun inside your umbilicus. . . . There are some holy men who learn the trick of stopping the falling nectar with their tongues; and as long as they do that, they cannot die."

Linked with this especial concern for the head is the importance which Hindus attach to the *choti* or pigtail growing from the vertex of the head. This must never be cut, even though the rest of the scalp may be regularly shaved by the village barber. Young men who affected a European haircut would assure me that the choti was still there, among the rest of the hair: a complete crew-cut would be unacceptable. The preservation of the choti seemed symbolic of a man's social existence within the Hindu community: when a holy *saddhu* renounced his caste, along with all other worldly ties, his choti was cut off. In phantasy, loss of the choti was represented as robbing the victim, like Samson, of all his strength and independence as the following legend shows.

Several informants had spoken in passing of " the ghostie's well " near Shankar Lal's house before Himat Lal told me its history: " You know Jaggan Lal, the Brahmin? His grandfather once was going past the burning-ghat on his horse. It was at night. A ghost took the form of a baby and began to cry. He said: ' The child's crying, it must have been left here by mistake.' So he put it on his horse and went on. It was a ghost though, d'you see: so all at once it grew big, like a huge man. So he said to himself: ' This must be a ghost.' So he took a dagger that he had in his belt and cut off the ghost's choti—when you do that a ghost loses all its power to harm and becomes your slave. So he came back home, and the ghost came with him and lived here. He built a house for himself, and built that well. That Brahmin tied up the choti with a thread, tied it in a knot; and as long as it was like that he couldn't run away. Then one day the ghost went to that Brahmin's wife and said ' He wants some string ', and she gave him the bundle of string with the choti in it—and he made off."

Later, I was to hear of the head in other contexts, as the reservoir in which is stored semen, the " Lord and Master of the body " (Rajmal), and as the place into which a devotee's life is concentrated when he goes into a contemplative trance. In telling of their mastery of the technique of contemplation, informants would describe a progressive loss of awareness of the limbs, then of the abdomen and chest, until finally, the whole of one's consciousness seems confined in a small space within the skull, inside the forehead.

In contrast, the feet are considered to be the lowliest part of one's anatomy. Ordinarily people take great care not to come in contact with each other's feet, even in the press of a seated, barefooted crowd. On the other hand it is a mark of profound respect to clasp the feet of one's elders: and the greatest self-abasement of all (reserved for persons of god-like holiness) consists in placing the other's foot upon one's own bowed head.*

It was not the fact of this discrimination between the head and the feet which was unfamiliar; to some extent Westerners share in this evaluation. The difference lies in the intensity of feeling which Hindus invest in this subject. Only gradually did I come to appreciate to the full the potential defilement attaching to feet and shoes, or the profound shock which would be caused by treating a man's head with disrespect. In time I recognised the unobtrusive tact with which these threats to each other's dignity were daily averted, and realised the importance of conforming to these courtesies if I did not wish to cause offence.

My appreciation of the Hindus' emotional involvement in these bodily conventions was quickened by the recognition, in myself and in other Europeans, of a quite irrational resistance to the Eastern etiquette of taking off one's shoes on entering a temple or a private house. At first, to conform to this custom seemed to us to imply an obscure affront against our personal dignity. This was forgotten as soon as one came to share the feelings of one's hosts, and to realise that a neglect of this custom would indeed be felt as a personal affront by them, because of the offensive associations of footwear in this culture. No one would willingly touch another's shoes. If they needed to be moved, they would be grasped and carried with one's toes. Shoes were often invoked, and sometimes threateningly raised in the course of village quarrels. To be struck on the head by another's shoe conveyed a humiliation out of all proportion to the physical hurt.

It was not difficult to follow my neighbours' example with regard to footwear; but they found me slow to learn the importance of hair-oil and of head-dresses. To be thus negligent of one's head was felt to be indecorous. More than

* St. John i, 27: "He . . . whose shoe's latchet I am not worthy to unloose"

once, I was reminded by village friends that it was unseemly for me to appear bareheaded at a public meeting. On formal occasions, even in the middle of the night, it was necessary for me to wear my sun-helmet.

What was more imperative, however, was to learn new rules about cleanliness. The first of these was to emulate the practice of cleansing oneself with water after defaecation. This act has ritual as well as merely hygienic significance, and its omission is a serious obstacle against gaining the confidence of a conservative Hindu. The left hand is employed in this operation, and the right, or *jiman hath* is alone used for eating —all meals being eaten with the fingers. On watching closely, however, I observed that there was no strict taboo against handling food with the left hand, which might be employed for example in lifting *chapattis* from a central dish on to one's own tray; but the ban was absolute against bringing the fingers of the left hand into contact with one's lips. On the other hand any food which had touched one's lips itself became *jutha*—leavings—and the thought of its being eaten by anyone else was regarded as disgusting. This applied also to pipes and to cigarettes, which were never applied directly to the lips, but held between the fingers of the cupped right hand. Thus protected against defilement, they could be passed from one to another of a group.

There were, however, two conspicuous exceptions to this rule of the untouchability of jutha. A man's children, and his wife, might be invited to finish off a part of the meal which he had left on his tray, and this was regarded as a mark of benevolence on his part. Also, in every temple there were periodical distributions of *prashad*, which is food which had been offered to the god and then shared out among the worshippers, his children. The identification of prashad as the jutha of the god was made plain to me when I visited a hermit in the jungle seven miles from Deoli. This holy man was the priest of a celebrated image of Shiva with horns, known as Singhirasi Mahadev, which lay in a cave. He wished to offer me refreshment and so he placed a bowl of milk inside the cave, lowering a curtain across its mouth, and blew on a conch shell while another attendant beat a gong. Then he withdrew the milk, saying: " Maheshwar has fed; now have some of his prashad." *

* The same word also denotes the leavings of one's Guru's repast, of which it is a privilege to partake. Dr. Kathleen Gough has informed me that in south India the word equivalent to *prashad* means " the spittle of the god "

A polite Hindu would not take bites out of a large piece of chapatti but would tear small portions off, and swallow then entire: similarly, the polite way to eat roast corn on the cob is not to raise it to the mouth and bite it, but to shell off the grains with the fingers of the right hand, and swallow a mouthful at a time. Our custom of putting our lips to a glass of water, and then setting it back on the table, is distasteful to them, and so is our custom of washing the hands by immersing them in water in a container.

At the end of an Indian meal, one goes to a place apart, and water is brought and poured over one's fingers, while one washes them. Next, it is proper to wash out one's mouth several times with water, rubbing the teeth with one's right forefinger: then one leans forward holding the cupped right hand palm upward against one's chin in order to drink a few swallows of water poured into one's hand—this gesture, and the quick tilt of the head which means " Enough ", become second nature when one lives or travels in company with Hindus. Finally, the fingers are washed once more. It is made clear, in this cleansing ritual, that whatever has been in contact with the lips or the inside of the mouth, is defiling. The Hindu's daily early-morning bath further illustrates this concept.

Every informant who was asked to describe the happenings of a day in his life began by mentioning his going to stool, and then his bathing, as being two of the most significant events of the day. During these morning ablutions, he would pay especial attention to washing out his ears, eyes and nostrils, as well as his mouth. Any secretion from the inside of the body is defiling, but the most defiling of all is human excrement. " To do it properly ", said Devi Lal, " a man should cleanse himself with earth and then with water twelve times after going to stool, and three times after making water—but few are so particular nowadays." It was still a common measure of a man's piety to remark upon the size of the *lota* of water which he carried when he went to stool.

Another illustration of the relative degrees of defilement associated with the processes of elimination is given by the rule that the sacred thread (worn by all Brahmins and Rajputs and by some of the Banias in Deoli) must be wound round one ear on micturition, and round both ears on defaecation: but no such precaution need be taken with the *janoi* during sexual intercourse.

The threat of faecal, and to a lesser extent urinary contamination pervades much of Hindu social and religious etiquette: and cleanliness with them is a *sine qua non* of godliness. Members of all three castes, but especially the Brahmins, emphasised the need to bathe at once, and change one's clothes if one came into contact with a member of the untouchable castes. The rationalisation for this abhorrence was that they were befouled by excrement in the course of their daily duties: and that they neglected to bathe scrupulously as would a caste Hindu. In the same context, informants would tell me of the need to bathe if one came into contact with a menstruating woman; and after taking part in a cremation, in order to remove the ritual pollution of death. Shankar Lal, a very conscientious Brahmin, said scrupulous bathing was necessary: " Because we make water, we go to latrine—and intercourse also—there are so many sources of impurity—and touching an impure thing. But everything is washed away—and after bath we feel some sort of inspiration and alertness. It is both physical and spiritual cleansing."

In the course of my medical practice in the village I was introduced to a number of concepts about the body and its workings, some of which were known to all of my informants, others to only a few. The fullest account of the ayurvedic humoral system was that given to me by Bhagwati Lal, the village physician, and by other Brahmins, Shankar Lal, Girdari Lal and Hari Lal, who all professed a certain knowledge of medicine. Of the three bodily humours which they cited, two were most commonly invoked to account for current illnesses, namely *kaf* (phlegm) and *vayu*, which was generally described as a sort of gas, trapped within the bodily tissues, which moved from place to place giving rise to swellings, aches and pains. Daulmal, whom I considered to be suffering from phthisis, complained of both *kaf* and *vayu*, but he, sometimes at least, attributed his illness to having been affected by bad air while living in the slums of Udaipur. In his description, the bad air turned into a sort of evil miasma, called *garab:* " Sometimes you can see the garab in the house, sometimes you can't. All sorts of illnesses get worse when it is about. . . . It's like radio currents which come from the sky and cause music to come out of a wireless set: so too, when garab is about, it enters your body and gives rise to illnesses." Here, Daulmal was quoting a fragment of a complex theory of illness which was evidently beyond his comprehension. It is noticeable, however, that the explanation which he has confusedly derived from ayurvedic teachings is one which reflects a strikingly paranoid concept of the world about him.

It was typical that Daulmal described his *garab* illness to me in terms of dogmatic assurance; and yet he turned to me, to the bhopa, to a man who drew off bad blood by branding him with red-hot irons, and also to other would-be healers for treatment. In this he was like most of my patients. Occasionally it happened that one of my medicines (quinine, or aspirin, or a pill for worms) produced a dramatic result within a few hours, and then the patient would come back gratefully for more; but more often than not he would lose confidence and go on to other remedies, returning perhaps at irregular intervals.

While they were sick, my patients felt themselves to be invaded by something evil. This might be expressed in physical terms, as bad air, bad blood or phlegm; but still more often it was personified, as the invasion of one's body by a witch or an evil spirit. The crisis of a cure always coincided with the summoning of this spirit, and its being exorcised with bribes or threats. Once this was done, the patient might feel weak, but he knew that his life was saved; from now on he could look forward to recovery.

The more educated of my informants tried hard to divest themselves of this animistic view of sickness, in favour of ideas of infection and hygiene: as Puranmal said: " Nowadays, educated people say they don't believe in it, but if a witch strikes one of their household, then they have to believe in it." Those who tried to achieve a scientific understanding of disease were hampered by their insistence upon the supernatural power of faith. To a certain extent I could agree with them that faith in the outcome, and confidence in one's physician, were both conducive to cure; but they were caught in a familiar dilemma. For them, faith must be absolute and unqualified, or it would lose its efficacy; and they knew from experience how hard it was to persevere in trustfulness towards anyone. In sickness, therefore, the body became the focus of that alternation of paranoid anxiety and momentary flashes of trustfulness which characterised most personal relationships.

In health, on the other hand, phantasies about bodily functioning revealed one system of beliefs to which all my informants subscribed. This concerned the making, storing and expenditure of a man's semen (*viriya*) in which resides his strength. Everyone knew that semen was not easily formed; it takes forty days, and forty drops of blood, to make one drop of semen; but the process was variously described. Hari Lal said: " There is a fire in your stomach, whose heat warms the body, and everything you eat goes into two stomachs, solid food into one and liquids into another, and there they are cooked until they yield *ras*, and this in turn gives blood, and blood in time forms semen."

Rajmal described four stomachs, in series, in which food is progressively digested until first blood, and then semen, is formed. Everyone was agreed on one point, that the semen is ultimately stored in a reservoir in the head, whose capacity is twenty *tolas* (6·8 ounces). Semen of good quality is rich and viscous, like the cream of unadulterated milk. A man who possesses a store of such good semen becomes a super-man. "He glows with radiant health", said Shankar Lal. He excels all normal men in strength and stamina, both moral and physical. As an example, I was always told of idealised holy men, unlike those imperfect exemplars we had actually seen, whose life of celibacy and piety had brought them to this peak of condition.

Celibacy was the first requirement of true fitness, because every sexual orgasm meant the loss of a quantity of semen, laboriously formed. Here was another inescapable dilemma, because one's sons must be procreated, one's wife satisfied—hence the need to compromise, to restrict sex to a defined number of occasions. In order to make good the depredations of sex life, certain rules must be obeyed. "Cool foods" should be eaten, among them milk, butter, wheat flour, rice, sugar and most fruits; " hot " foods, such as vegetable oil, maize and millet flour, unrefined sugar and strong spices should be abjured. It was noticeable that the "cool" foods were the more expensive ones, whereas the "hot" substances formed the staple diet of the indigent, low-caste majority of the population. Opinion was divided about meat, eggs and wine. All Brahmins and Banias (except Rajmal and Daulmal), and some pious Rajputs, declared liquor to be "hot" and to be abjured, but the majority of Rajputs considered it fortifying if taken in small quantities, regularly. Rajputs recommended meat and eggs, which the others would not touch; but Rajmal again was an exception. Being, as he claimed, the most sexually active man in the locality, he had given a lot of thought to this matter, and concluded that the quickest way to restore lost semen was to drink raw eggs and honey, beaten up in milk.

It was not considered sufficient, however, merely to eat the appropriate diet in order to restore one's semen; nor was the sexual act regarded as the only way of losing it. "Two things give rise to the loss of a man's semen", said Amar Singh:

"*Badparhez* and *badpheli*—that is, eating what is wrong, and doing what is wrong." Under the latter head he included not only sexual promiscuity, but every sort of violation of Hindu *dharm*, such as, mixing and eating with people of inferior caste; acting disrespectfully towards one's elders ; drinking to excess; giving way to anger or to lustful thoughts, to fear or to excessive worrying. In all these cases, what happens is that a man's semen curdles and goes bad and can no longer be retained, issuing from him in the form of a thin, evil-smelling fluid. Consequently, any purulent discharge which seemed to come from inside the body was held to be " spoiled semen ", whether it came from the ears, eyes or nose, in the sputum or in the stool. Especial concern was directed to any discharge coming from the penis, which was invariably identified as semen; and yet there was at the same time a fairly general appreciation of the nature of venereal disease, both syphilis (*garmi*) and urethritis (*sujak*), being known by name although often confused. Venereal disease was considered to be both an infection *and* an evidence of deterioration of one's semen.

What was much more striking than the cases of venereal disease (of which I had occasion to treat only sixteen during ten months in Deoli), was the pre-occupation which many seemingly healthy men showed with a real or imagined spermatorrhoea (*jiryan*). Again and again patients would ask me for some good strength-giving medicine, or injection, and I would look for signs of chronic infection, of malaria, or tuberculosis, or amoebiasis, or secondary anaemia to account for their lassitude, and treat them accordingly. At last, confronted with the same complaint from brawny, well-fed farmers, it dawned upon me to ask: " *Why* are you so weak? "—and then would come the familiar account of *jiryan*. On reviewing the notes of my thirty-six principal Hindu informants, I find that twenty-five of them either believed that they suffered from *jiryan* or else described special measures which they adopted to counteract it. The same was true of six out of my nine Moslem informants.

I found a reflection of this pre-occupation in a pharmacopoeia of Ayurvedic medicines presented to me by the village *Vaid*. Out of thirty-nine proprietary medicines advertised in the end-pages of this book, fourteen were recommended for spermatorrhoea. In Western medical practice this condition is a rarity; on the other hand anxiety centring upon impotence, nocturnal emission, or fear of venereal disease, is a common presenting syndrome in a psychiatrist's out-patient clinic—but this anxiety is shown by a few neurotic individuals, burdened with the disproportionate guilt of an unresolved oedipus complex, not by the majority of the male population.

In order to understand these very real complaints of weakness, of wasting-away of the bodily tissues (which looked unchanged to the corporeal eye) it was necessary that my patients should communicate their sense of guilt at having broken the rules, with regard to sex, and commensality, and control of their feelings. As they did so, I was made aware of another dilemma; these rules were so uncompromisingly strict that anyone whose personality resisted the complete surrender of instinctive spontaneity, must sooner or later infringe them. My informants acknowledged this by describing two types of ideal person, the unworldly religious devotee, and the practical man. Only the former could rise to the acme of physical and spiritual perfection. To the *yogi's* undoubted ability to endure physical privation with indifference were added magical powers, such as the ability to practise levitation, to become invisible, to be present in the flesh in two places at once.

Several informants told me this story of Kalyan Singh, a Ruler of Deoli two centuries ago, who was an exalted worshipper of God, an " arrived one ": Kalyan Singh was performing his annual duty of attendance on the Rana in Udaipur when the day came on which he was accustomed to make a prolonged puja before the image of Ranchor-Raiji in his castle in Deoli: and the Rana would not give him leave to go. He remained at court, lost in meditation, and suddenly his hands were seen to be stained with *sindur*, though he had brought none with him. The Runa sent a messenger to Deoli on a racing camel, and there he found a " double " of the same Kalyan Singh, with *sindur* on his hands, intent upon the worship of his God.

Holy men are believed to have power over animals, and to converse with them in the jungle; and even the elements are subordinated to them. When a saddhu called Govind Guru visited Deoli, I was one of a crowd of villagers who sat at his feet during a shower of rain. " Did you see? " said Hari Lal to me afterwards, " on Govind himself, and on his sitting-place, no drops fell." But that had not been my observation.

The " arrived " worshipper of God acquires these supernatural powers by virtue of the increase of god-like qualities in him, and their physical counterpart is the intact store of rich, uncurdled semen in his head.

The ordinary man, involved in worldly commitments which

he cannot bring himself to disregard, cannot aspire to this ideal unless in his old age. As Hari Lal said: "Most people have to work and earn their food and keep their passions alive." The best they can hope for is to order their lives so that their acts of piety suffice to compensate for the inevitable wastage of soul-stuff and of semen.

The clue to this compromise lies in the words *niyam se*—" in proper measure ". Appetites may be indulged, feelings given an outlet, sexual relations experienced, provided always that they be subjected to a strict voluntary control: if that is observed, this situation is not too threatening, but the problem is to know what *is* the correct *niyam*. In the case of sexuality, everyone referred wistfully to the ideal of unbroken celibacy; or failing that, of sleeping with one's wife only once in a lifetime, as the father of the mighty Hanuman was said to have done. If you have sexual intercourse only once or twice in a lifetime, your children will be correspondingly robust. The due *niyam* for sex was variously quoted. Four informants (Hari Lal, Girdari Lal, Vikram Singh and Birmal) claimed to have abjured sex altogether; the rest indicated their conception of the proper measure, and then complained how hard it was for human frailty to adhere to this ideal. As a mechanism of defence against anxiety, this attempt to confine sensuality " niyam se " too often let them down—hence the widespread pre-occupation with jiryan, which I would claim to be the commonest expression of anxiety neurosis among the Hindu communities of Rajasthan, and perhaps elsewhere as well.

Sexuality was taken by my informants to stand for the instinctive life in general: thus, while discussing the topic of abstinence, Hira Singh said: " There are only a few Rajputs who give up taking meat and wine, for the sake of religion: most of them eat, drink and remain *must* " (the word *must* is used of elephants on heat, and also of vigorous, libidinous young men). This discussion led us at once to talk of local concepts of the religious life from which, as will have been observed, ideas about physical health and prowess cannot be entirely dissociated.

SUMMARY

My informants' references to ideas about the human body and its functions were principally concerned with two topics, both charged with feeling. The first was the paramount need to restrain one's instinctual impulses, if they could not be suppressed altogether. This applied with especial force to the sexual impulses, whose gratification was believed to lead to physical and spiritual degeneration. These attitudes found expression in the complex of ideas relating to the creation, preservation and loss of semen.

The second dominant topic was that of defilement. Many sources of defilement—such as various bodily secretions, the leavings of a meal, or any utensil which had touched another's lips, or the person of an outcast—were found to be associated with the carrier of the profoundest defilement of all: human excrement. Many features of social etiquette could be recognised as means of safeguarding oneself against this arch-contaminant.

CHAPTER VI

RELIGION AND PHANTASY

In Deoli, as perhaps in most Indian villages, there is an inextricable confusion of Brahminical Hinduism and primitive animism, of magical phantasy and superstition. To the newcomer, it is the latter elements which are immediately apparent: the multitude of wayside shrines, the stories of ghost-afflictions, of witchcraft and of sorcery. The very houses are congested with spirits; three of my informants described how, whenever they slept on a certain part of the floor of their house, an angry spirit troubled their dreams, so that they had to move. The open countryside is scarcely less haunted: several patients informed me that their sickness was brought on them by a ghost which was angered because they had urinated on its territory. Ghosts and demons are protean, taking the form of animals, or snakes, or even of a crying child: a wise man was always on his guard against being thus deceived.

Gods, as well as demons, may at any time appear in human form, and this was advanced by Girdari Lal as the reason for the Hindu rule of hospitality: "You should always treat a stranger with respect, give him a place to sit, and offer him food and drink, because we know that God can assume any form at will; for all we know, this stranger may be a God." *

A phantasy often met with in dreams, was that one's especial deity should appear, giving a *darshan* (an enriching vision) of his or her person. This happened to several of my informants, at times when they were anxious about some personal crisis, and they invariably derived fresh confidence from the event.

In a community where mutual distrust was so prevalent, it was not surprising to hear many accounts of black magic. I was told in whispers about charms which could kill, charms which had to be " ripened " at midnight at the burning-ground, with the help of the dead. Hindus ascribed these evil charms especially to Bhils and to Moslems, while Moslems attributed them above all to Brahmins and to Hindu saddhus. There

* Cf. the Gaelic rune: " Set food in the eating place, and drink in the drinking place, and a place by the fire. Often, often, often goes the Christ in stranger's guise "

were several men in Deoli who were known to possess beneficent charms, which would cure snakebite, or fever, or drive out a witch: but the same individuals were suspected of secretly dealing in the malevolent type of magic. In every case of sickness in the village, the possibility of sorcery, ghost-affliction, or witchcraft was first considered; and whatever other remedy was adopted, this influence had also to be exorcised.

A typical illustration of phantasy about each other's powers was given me by Hari Lal, Bhagmal and Shrimal, who all warned me to beware of my near neighbour in the bazaar, a Moslem tailor called Mahommed Pinara, reputedly a possessor of supernatural powers. Bhagmal said: " What he does is, he puts a little of a fine scent on his thumbnail and then he puts some lampblack over that, and then he looks at it intently, near his eyes like this: and in a moment or two he sees a wide scene, like a plain; and then a sweeper comes and sweeps the ground; and then a *bhishti* comes and waters it: and then a *chaprassi* comes and sets up a table and a chair and a blackboard; and last of all, a Sahib comes and sits down. And then, any question that he puts, the Sahib gets up and writes the answer on the blackboard, plain, so that he can see it. And if he doesn't know the answer at once, he sends a servant off, and he soon comes back and gives the true answer."

Bhagmal described illnesses in his family which were diagnosed as due to sorcery: " There's a lot of this sorcery goes on round here—but don't you learn it, it isn't good. And besides, people won't tell you about any magic that they have; it loses its strength if they let out the secret of it, and such magic isn't easily made."

The phantasy of acquiring sudden unexpected wealth was common in Deoli, as it is in the Western world; but here it presented itself in a peculiar form: the characteristic daydream (or actual dream) took the form of meeting a benevolent holy man, or a god-like stranger who would impart the secret of how to become rich, and who would remain an aloof, all-powerful, but beatific figure, disappearing from the scene as abruptly as he came. Most often his instructions would be to go to such and such a place and dig, and treasure would be found. Rumours spread from time to time that this had actually happened to other people, and my informants all believed that this, or something like it, might happen to them one day.

Every individual in the village carries with him what seems to a Western observer a heightened awareness of immanent spirits and powers, mostly inimical; but this familiarity with

RELIGION AND PHANTASY

the supernatural is also institutionalised in many sacred shrines, and in legends associated with them. Typical of these were the numerous Bherujis, and the stones representing Radaji, the protector of the crops, which were to be found beside each plot of land.

Hindu mythology is baffling in its profusion. If this is true of the voluminous written texts, it is no less true of the multitude of local legends which are to be found in every village, because these villagers have a gift for myth-making, and a keen appetite for the miraculous. Even educated Indians do not like to reject the most improbable stories without the saving clause—" And yet there may be something in it."

In the village, no statement, and no narrative was ever felt to be entirely right or wrong, and so none was discarded. Contradictory, incompatible explanations were allowed to co-exist, as in the case of illnesses, which might be attributed to three different sorts of agency, and treated in three ways at once.

In the last week of October, 1951, after a spell of exceptionally hot weather, the women-folk of Deoli all began to make offerings at the local temple of Sitala-Mata, the goddess of small-pox. Asked why this happened, Hari Lal said: " You heard about the village where there was a suttee lately? The gossip has reached here that she said, before she died, that Suttee, that every household should offer worship to Sitala-Mata. If they didn't, she said, everyone in their family would die."

Next day, Nar Singh told me, with equal conviction, the following story: " Not many days ago, in a village over towards Chitor, a small boy died and was buried; and that same night his sister, a child of only five or six, woke up and cried: 'Where's my brother,' They said: 'He's dead.' She said: 'No, I tell you he's alive.' And then she got up and went out, and they followed her. She did not know where he had been buried, but she led them straight to the place and said: 'Dig here', and they dug, and found the boy alive. And when they brought him out from the ground he told them a great sickness would fall upon the children unless every house worshipped Sitala-Mata—and that's why they are doing it now."

Others in the village shrugged their shoulders at both these stories, but sent their wives to worship with the rest, in case there might be something in them. This episode struck me as typical of the villagers' attitude towards the multitude of minor gods and goddesses whose shrines were found in every field and in every corner of the village. These little gods, although superhuman, were still earthbound, still part of *maya*, the illusory world of the senses. Like fellow human beings, they could never wholly be trusted or relied upon: they had to be flattered and propitiated in order to ensure their goodwill.

In turn, and for a varying span of years, one or other of these little gods would acquire a favourable reputation, and then crowds of people would come to his or her worship, and prostrate themselves, and cry for help. They were able to communicate directly with these gods, through the medium of the bhopa, or priest, who became possessed by the spirit of the god. In 1951, the shrine of Vijayshan Mata was the most favoured in Deoli; but in and around the village there were literally scores of others, each with a few followers and each occasionally the scene of offerings and of " possession " by the god.

The link was close between these *devata* and the spirits of the recently dead (also called devata) which were known sometimes to haunt the earth, inhabiting a vague limbo until their next rebirth. In several families these " ghosts " were accustomed from time to time to " possess " the body of one of their survivors, causing him or her to shake and gasp in the same way as do the bhopas in their trance, and then these *purbaj*, as they are called, would communicate with their families. The father of Bhagmal used to do so, speaking through his widow; and Bhagmal explained: " Not all people remain behind after death. Some die thinking ' There's no one to look after my wife ', and some die thinking of their money. That kind of man becomes a kind of ghost, a purbaj; and soon after he dies, someone becomes possessed and he speaks through them." In every case, the visitant had been a father, and head of a family. Purbaj were mentioned in families of every caste, although Hari Lal maintained that they were not found in Brahmin families because they performed expensive after-death ceremonies to speed the soul on his way, unlike the Banias who merely sat in mourning for a few days and then gave a feast.

I was told that anyone might become a bhopa—just as any near relative might become the host of a purbaj—it was the will of the devata. In practice, the spirit of the god would come to one or more of a group of devoted worshippers, and having come once, would tend to come again whenever he made offerings, and bowed before the god and then waited in an expectant frame of mind. I noticed, too, that those of my informants who were themselves bhopas (Shrimal and Bheru Singh) were both poor and socially insignificant. This was true of the other bhopas whom I came to know personally: their brief authority, while possessed by the god, was in marked contrast to their usual inconspicuous role. It was implied, though never openly stated, that " possession " would never come to a rich and important citizen: that would be incongruous, because the bhopa is like a humble servant to his master, the god. Similarly, a prosperous man would not consult the bhopa's god unless he were in trouble, or had just escaped from danger—for example, on the night of the 16th of July 1951 the wealthy Bania, Bhurmal, made a generous offering to Ragliaji Bheru through his bhopa, Shrimal, in gratitude for a successful deal in black-market cloth which he had carried off unscathed.

Many persons of the three top castes professed to scorn these petty gods as mere superstitions. " They are all right for illiterate people ", said Hira Singh, " because they do not understand properly how to worship God, but these bhopas they can talk to and ask them for advice."

Rajendra Singh said : " Only one in a thousand of them is the genuine thing. People who are educated do not believe in these ghosts, witches, purbaj and such things. Even if they do exist, such things cannot harm a man who worships God."

Some devata were known to require only sweet offerings, others demanded meat and wine. Brahmins and Banias agreed in condemning all shrines where the latter sacrifices were made; but it was a young Rajput, Nar Singh, who acted as executioner at the Vijayshan-Mata shrine, decapitating goats one after the other with one cut of his sword. On such occasions, some of the blood was caught as it spurted from the severed arteries; it was mixed with alcohol and drunk by the goddess, in the person of the bhopa who was still " possessed ".

The generic term for all these shrines where a bhopa became possessed was " Bheruji "; because even where the chief deity was a goddess, a snake-god, or a locally-worshipped minor incarnation of Vishnu, such as the non-meat-eating Dharm-raj, there was always a Bheruji in attendance as well. Bhairava is defined by Dowson * as: " The Terrible—the Bhairavas are eight inferior forms or manifestations of Shiva, all of them of a terrible character." He lists Kala Bhairava as the name of one of these eight forms. In Deoli, two varieties of Bheruji were described; Kala, the commoner, received offerings of meat and wine, whereas Gora Bheruji abhorred blood-sacrifices. None of my village informants volunteered a clear-cut description of

* J. Dowson (1950)

what the Bheruji stood for, but Bheru Singh (himself a bhopa of Bheruji) came nearest to associating it with Bhairava when he said: "Bherujis all issue from Mahadev; they are the masters of ghosts, witches, demons—all that kind of thing."

The element common to all these *bhut-whut, Bheruji vagera* (ghosts and Bherujis and so on) as Gopi Lal scornfully described them, is the nearness to everyday experience. In these little gods, the villagers sought a helpful ally, as they might hope to win the favour of a government official or other person who might exercise an influence on their lives. (Conversely, villagers' mode of address towards a visitor whom they take to be a *Bara Sahib* is often embarrassingly like that with which they approach their gods.) In their supplications to these little gods, they were concerned with practical matters—sicknesses of man or beast, decisions to be taken, the outcome of the next harvest.

Another level of religious life, still open to those who were illiterate, was represented by the various forms of *bhakti-marg* or devotional worship. In these, groups of people would gather to sing hymns, sometimes the verses of Kabir Das or of Mirabai, often others of recent composition. These meetings might take place in one or other of the temples of the great Gods of the Hindu pantheon (there was a much-frequented Hanuman temple in the palace gardens, and several varieties of Vishnu-temple in the village) or they might consist of groups of zealous singers of *bhajans* (hymns couched in the popular idiom) meeting in each other's houses. The hymn-singing served a didactic as well as a devotional purpose, because the singers would often pause to point the ethical moral of their verses, every such exposition being saluted with cries of *Jai Guru Maharaj!* or *Bolo Sath-Narain ki jai!* * strongly reminiscent of the ecstatic "Hallelujahs" which punctuate a Western revivalist meeting.

Although respectable enough, this cult of bhajan-singing was seldom patronised by high-caste Hindus, to whom there was something repugnant about so public a display of emotion, even in a religious cause. They were content to be spectators, silent members of the audience. Rajput Thakurs were frequently the patrons of individuals famous for their bhajan-singing; one such performed for us one evening in the palace, singing hymns and sentimental love-songs from Indian films with equal fervour.

* "Hail to the Supreme Teacher", and "Cry, Victory to Sath-Narain"

RELIGION AND PHANTASY

During our stay in Deoli, a travelling cinema came to the village for the first time, its apparatus loaded on two bullock-carts. The film was " Mirabai ", the life of a famous Rajput saint, and it was noticeable here, as in Udaipur, that it was the singing and dancing which most powerfully gripped the audience's attention: and both of these were at once religious and sensual, like the language of the Song of Songs. On the third showing of " Mirabai " (and many of the villagers went each night to see the three-hour film over again) the projectionist interpolated a reel with a dance sequence from a purely secular film. Bhagmal said of it: " What a fine dance it was! Even the old men began to get randy and to look about them lecherously! "

This rapid transfer of associations from devotional fervour to sexuality served to underline the high-caste Hindus' distrust of all forms of overt emotionalism. One Rajput, who claimed to have reached an advanced stage in the practice of yoga, referred scornfully to a group of bhajan-singers: " Listen to them, getting all worked up and baying like animals! "

With the single exception of Rajmal, a defiant sensualist, all of my informants were eager to impart to me their conception of the religious life, although in time I came to appreciate that only sixteen out of the thirty-six were at all assiduous in attempting to practise it. They talked in terms varying widely in their sophistication, but certain underlying elements were always there.

Firstly, the aim of the religious life: this was directed to the goal of liberation from *karma*, from the need to be reborn in successive incarnations. Liberation, or *moksh*, came when a man had succeeded in purging his nature of all that was terrestrial and carnal, so that the god-element in him increased until finally he was all god and then his expanded *atma* (spirit) took leave of his body to become one with *parmatma*, the spirit of the universe. This apotheosis could be reached only as a result of prolonged effort, the culmination of many former incarnations; and the essential preliminary to advance towards this goal was to submit oneself to the discipline of *dharma*, the Brahminical version of the good life.

Shankar Lal's initial formulation of the religious life was: " One should make it one's first duty always to remember God." *

---

* This was reminiscent of the first clause in the Calvinists' Shorter Catechism, " What is man's chief end?—Man's chief end is to glorify God and to enjoy him for ever "

Generally, however, the first essential to a religious life was stated in more practical terms. In describing the daily routine of a pious man, many of my informants stressed his early rising, his defaecation and his scrupulous bathing as essential preliminaries to the serious work of prayer. These were daily duties, but there were other requirements to be met in one's conduct of life before one could hope to make any progress in religion. To begin with, it was essential to have a guru, a spiritual guide. Among serious thinkers in Deoli, even the miracle-working Saddhu Govind was suspect: "He is a *daung* (a fraud)" said Kalu Lal: "He is *na-guru;* he tries to force his way unaided into God's presence, and that cannot be done: a man must be told his way step by step like a boy learning his father's trade."

"A guru", said Vikram Singh, "is like one who sows a seed: but before the seed is sown you have to work hard, ploughing and manuring the earth to make it ready." He went on to describe some of the disciplines to which he submitted himself. First, scrupulous cleanliness and observance of *achar-bichar* (avoidance of touch or association with the lowest castes); next, cultivation of the ability to go without sleep, the practice of physical methods of yoga, abstention from meat and wine, and from sexual intercourse. Here again, the concept "niyam se" was constantly invoked: a man must sleep and eat, and sometimes satisfy his wife, but he should do it in conformity with a strict measure.

Some of the better-educated informants (Rajendra Singh, Hira Singh, Vikram Singh, Partab Singh, Shankar Lal, Gopi Lal, Hari Lal, Girdari Lal, Birmal, Chaudmal and Chenmal) showed that they were vaguely familiar with the classical Hindu stages of life, the *varnashrama*.* As Vikram Singh put it: "Properly speaking, our Hindu teaching is that a man's first twenty-five years should be a time of learning; and then he should marry a girl of sixteen to eighteen years, and they should live as man and wife till he is forty, having children. After forty, if they are right-thinking people, they will remain celibate, although together, until he is sixty years old. After that he should renounce the world and his family altogether,

---

* These are: (i) *Brahmacharya*, a student apprenticed to a *Guru*, living in his *ashram* under conditions ensuring the absence of sexual stimulation. (ii) *Grihastha*, life as an active member of society, married and raising a family. (iii) *Vanaprastha*, forest-hermit, again celibate although he may be accompanied in this state by his wife. (iv) *Sannyasi* or *bhiksha*, one who has severed all social ties

becoming a sannyasi. Of course, that is a way of life that few can aspire to, and nowadays especially it is very rare to find anyone who does it—but they do exist." Vikram Singh himself, so his brother Hira Singh told me, had forsworn sex altogether and put aside his wife since he began to devote himself seriously to religion six years before. " Such a man tries to keep himself aloof, because this kind of thing is quite contrary to worship of God." He went on to say how Vikram Singh, once his mind was set upon religion, no longer allowed himself to care about his family, never fondled his only daughter, and did not even seem concerned to have a son. Hira Singh praised his austerity, but could not emulate it: " I can't bring myself to such sacrifice yet. I have ideals too—I do want never to deceive anyone, or to take bribes—but all this about simple food and plain clothes, that I can't do. But I admire his way of living."

Girdari Lal professed himself to be impatient to leave his family (his youngest son was now thirteen, and his betrothal had been arranged), but the others were content to search for a compromise which would enable them to meet their family responsibilities while still advancing in their religious life. As Shankar Lal said: " A religious man acts in the world like a drop of water on a lotus leaf, which runs about, but is not absorbed. . . . For my own part, I say that living in the world one should live a life of awareness of God."

The point was reiterated in another talk with Vikram Singh, who reminded me that this teaching was contained in the Bhagavad-Gita: " The essential thing is to act without attaching yourself to the fruits of that action; to live in the world and yet avoid being caught up in it, knowing that the world of the senses and of desires is all illusion." Both of these informants stressed the need to steel oneself against emotional involvement with other persons; both used the illustration that if a man were told of his child's death, he would respond with a measured sorrow, and not be overwhelmed with grief. I was reminded of Horace's " Si fractus illabatur orbis, impavidum ferient ruinae ". *

There was some disagreement as to the extent of the concessions which could be made to mundane things without endangering one's spiritual advancement. Sex was accepted as a necessary evil, to be indulged in as restricted a manner as possible, but the taking of meat and alcohol was generally

* " If the round sky should crack and fall upon him, the wreck will strike him fearless still "

condemned, as being both a violation of *ahinsa* and an incitement of the flesh. Amar Singh protested that they too were permissible, " niyam se "; and in this he followed the example of his master, the Rao Sahib, but they were condemned by all the other *bhagats*,* usually with indignant emphasis. As Shankar Lal put it: " He is all wrong, he is bogus lecher. Always busy with drink and dancing girls, what can he know of this stony and thorny path? "

In general, however, it was only over the issue of alcohol and meat-eating that complete abstinence was obligatory. In other respects, it was conceded that during his active life a man must have some emotional and sexual commitments; that he must have contact with people of inferior caste, and that he cannot avoid eating some of the cheaper, " heating " foods. These impediments to the spiritual life are recognisably the same things which were cited in the previous chapter as destructive to a man's semen. As in the former context, too, their harmful effect can be minimised by attention to the principles of control—the niyam, the measured extent to which they might be indulged in—and of compensation, by means of strenuous austerities, for their deleterious influence.

If the details of these penitential disciplines were sometimes in dispute, there was general agreement about the aim of the spiritual exercises to which they were the preliminaries. These were designed to develop one's powers of concentration, so that the whole of one's attention became absorbed in one desire: " I long to meet with God." In the early stages, this must be practised alone, because distraction is the great enemy of contemplation; and much of a guru's teaching is designed to circumvent distracting influences. " Only in concentration ", said Shankar Lal, " is there true devotion."

Hari Lal put it: " The hardest thing is to concentrate. You try, but your thoughts keep straying off—to Bombay, or Calcutta. A man's thoughts are as hard to control as a *must* elephant."

Several informants gave first place among distracting influences to " the clash of anklets as a woman passes by ". Hari Lal, an old bachelor, was particularly insistent upon this theme, regarding women as the chief source of sacrilege. He quoted with approval the example of the devotee, Surdas: " He put out his own eyes, saying 'Damnation, they lead me into sin'."

One aid to concentration used by all of my informants, and recommended by every guru, was the repetition of one name of

* The term bhagat is applied to a man who devotes serious attention to religion

God over and over again, during the period of *sandhya*. This might be performed before a representation of the God (upasana-marg), or with only a mental image in one's mind (nirakarpur): " You have to fill your mind with the thought of God, of the God you are addressing " (Hari Lal).

No less important than this mechanical narrowing of attention to the single theme, was its emotional accompaniment. A man must experience a sustained longing for union with God, for without this his austerities and his concentration will remain unrewarded. Birmal told a story of two men, one of whom sat before God's image and prayed for many hours a day, but could not disengage his thoughts from dwelling lecherously upon the memory of a beautiful young harlot; the other fell into sin, and went with the harlot, but even in the act his mind dwelt upon its real desire, to have a vision of God: and it was the second man that God rewarded with a *darshan* of his presence.

Both Rajendra Singh and Kalu Lal likened the devotee's animadversion towards God to the cry of a child for its mother, a cry which compels a favourable response.

The ultimate reward of a prayerful life was often described as the experiencing of a darshan of God. This meant, to the less sophisticated, that God would appear before them in human form. Hari Lal said: " Some very great bhagats have seen God; but you can't do that unless you have banished petty thoughts from your mind, like thoughts of women, and low things. It is like a curtain that stands between us and God; by constant devotions that curtain is made thinner and thinner until at last you can see him plainly." Others, less literally minded, described the ultimate experience as a wordless, formless intuition of God's presence. Vikram Singh described it in this way: " When you advance to the high stages of *sandhya* you experience real bliss, a pleasure unlike any ordinary pleasure, stronger even than the pleasure of sex."

Intimations of this ultimate reward might be experienced by anyone who applied himself to spiritual exercises with sufficient zeal; and at the same time, the bhagat would begin to acquire superhuman powers: he would be able to perform miracles by simply willing things to happen. Rajendra Singh claimed that he was already so far advanced in holiness that he had only to concentrate his will-power and inanimate objects would move across the room; but he did not think that so trivial a demonstration merited the unleashing of his powers. In his conversation, he made it plain that in taking up a discipline of prayer and meditation, since his wealth and privileges were rudely curtailed in 1948, he had turned away from worldly things. Yet he remained keenly aware of the practical, as well as spiritual, advantages of a magical increase in will-power, and envisaged a time when he would have so far advanced in holiness that not only the Rajputs, but all India would turn to him for leadership and guidance.

The more literal-minded informants tended to describe a holy man's powers in concrete illustrations. Thus Girdari Lal gave an instance of a saddhu, one far advanced in " spiritual rise ", who could strike people dumb with a glance: once, as a demonstration of his capabilities, he was believed to have stopped an express train in its tracks, simply by willing it. Rajendra Singh insisted that a guru could cause an aeroplane to fall from the sky, by the power of thought alone. Miracles attributed to these " arrived ones " were accepted unquestioningly, because it was quite in accord with the listeners' expectations that they should have supernatural powers; and characteristically, it was feared that these superhuman powers might readily be used to harm people. Thus Jaimal told me that Sardarmal, a blind old Bania, had once as a young man offended a saddhu by bathing his feet at the well where the latter came to drink. Instead of prostrating himself with apologies, he had grumbled that he had a right to use the water too—and at that, the saddhu smote him with blindness. There was an element of fear in the zeal with which villagers brought offerings of food to these wandering holy-men; and it was reflected in the standard threat to erring small children: " The Babaji will get you! "

This belief in the acquisition of god-like powers through the practice of mortification recurs frequently both in local legends, and in the epic narratives of the Mahabharata and Ramayana. When the hero is faced with insuperable difficulties, he is advised: " *Tapassya karo!* Mortify yourself ", and then he will sit cross-legged, intent upon his inner supplication until his devotion is rewarded. So compelling is the spiritual force generated by prolonged *tapassya* that sometimes, as in the story of Vishwamitra, the Gods themselves become alarmed and beseech him to stop.

On a humbler plane the practice of withdrawal from the world in an exercise of devotion could be used in order to restore confidence to a mind disturbed by calamity or misfortune. Rajendra Singh, Nathu Singh, Hira Singh, Birmal, Chenmal, Gopi Lal and Shankar Lal all described this in their several ways. As the last-named put it: "When I was in trouble I would always call on His name, and due to His inspiration I have always been able to surmount my troubles."

The aim of all religious endeavour was to attain *moksh*, release from the chain of re-births. In most cases this goal was felt to be still many incarnations in the future, and yet its reality was kept fresh in mind by the recital of celebrated instances in which a bhagat had been known to attain this highest peak of religious endeavour. The process was described to me on numerous occasions. As the holy man's devotions approach their climax, his already superhuman faculties enable him to predict the day and hour of his release from human bondage. He would be attended throughout the last few days by a throng of worshippers and disciples, relaying each other in singing bhajans. By now, the bhagat's withdrawal into concentration is so intense that he sits oblivious to his surroundings scarcely seeming to breathe. At this time, I was told, all the life in his body is withdrawn from the limbs and trunk, to be concentrated in the vertex of his head, the *brahmanand*, where it gathers, straining for the last effort of self-surrender which will release it to join the universal spirit. At the appointed moment, the bhagat's disciples lower him, still sitting cross-legged, into a pit and bury him with earth, then build a sacred *chattri* to mark the spot. This is the act known as taking *samadhi*.

My informants repudiated the idea that the bhagat was buried alive. On the contrary, at the moment of samadhi the spirit had left his body, and this in its turn became possessed of miraculous properties. Amar Singh assured me that if one were to dig beneath such a chattri, one would come upon the body of the saint, still in perfect condition, even though he might have taken samadhi hundreds of years ago.

Such an event is comparatively rare, yet it does occur. In January 1950 I was a participant, in a village in the north of Udaipur state, in an all-night *satsang*, a *bhajan*-singing in honour of one Maharamji Regar who had taken samadhi only four months before, not far from the town of Beawar. The event had been attended by 7,000 devotees, followers of *Kabirpanth* like himself, and two from this village had been present. Later, I was shown the new marble chattri at the place where this had happened.

Commoner than samadhi, and related to it, is the ritual whereby a celibate holy man, or *brahmachari*, formally renounces the last ties which bind him to family and to caste. Hari Lal was able to describe this with reference to Shri Premananda, the chief priest of a neighbouring Shiva temple: "He used to be called Panna Lal Sirohi, and they are very high-caste Brahmins. He was still in that group while he was a brahmachari, but now that he is a sannyasi he is out of caste, and they don't even let him into their houses."

G. M. C. "How does he come to be treated like that?"

H. L. "When a man decides to become a sannyasi, he does it like this: he gets four Brahmins to come, so that with him they are five, and for a whole night they sing hymns and say prayers and repeat verses from the Vedas and they keep a sacrifice of incense going all night. And then those four, they take off all his clothes, and they take off his sacred thread and burn it and he eats the ashes, and they cut off his *choti* and give him saffron robes to wear. That is why we cannot eat with him—because he has given up the *choti* and the *janoi*, he is no longer a Brahmin."

When a sannyasi dies, he also is buried, not burned as are most Hindus. He is lowered into the grave in a cross-legged sitting position, similar to that of the man who takes samadhi. He is, in fact, thought to be assured of moksh when he dies, so thorough has been his renunciation of the flesh while in this life. A Brahmin will bow down and clasp such a man's foot; and yet he will not sit to eat with him, even if he was of the highest caste before becoming a sannyasi; because by leaving taboos behind and associating with persons of the lowest castes, he carries a threat of pollution for one who is still committed to the dialectic of pious observance versus defilement which is inescapable in everyday life.

The term "he took samadhi" is customarily used to describe the death by natural causes of a sannyasi, and it is also used as a flattering euphemism in respect of the death of ordinary persons who could not be expected to have reached these spiritual heights. It remains the ambition of every serious-minded person that one day, in this or a subsequent incarnation, it should be true for him.

There was one other aspect of religion in Deoli which was so conspicuously the antithesis of samadhi and of the values associated with that concept, that I have reserved its discussion to the end of this chapter. This is the prevalence of a number of secret religious cults known by the generic title of *Laja-Dharm*. Varieties described to me by various informants were the *Kanchli-panth* and *Kunda-panth*, the *Bij-marg* and *Jot-marg*. In so far as they were related to normal religious practice, it was to the *bhakti* forms of worship; and indeed their characteristic gatherings (*mandli*) always began with the singing of bhajans. As the devotional fervour mounted, however, non-members of the panth would be asked to leave because the crowning act of worship could only be performed by initiates; and in each case, this act involved the sexual union of the celebrants, two by two —in these panths men and women joined on equal terms. It was believed that the deity to whom their devotions were addressed made itself manifest in the climax of the sexual act, and in the " male and female semen ", of which the celebrants jointly partook at the end of the ceremony: this was their prashad.

This form of worship was known to every one of my informants, and rejected as a travesty of all they held most sacred. Three of them (Rajmal, Puran Singh and Nar Singh) claimed to have witnessed mandlis, at some risk to themselves as the participants jealously guard their secrecy. If a stranger tried to enter into their ceremony, they would first ask the name of of his guru, to ensure that he was of the same panth and they would further test him with cryptic sentences, to which only initiates knew the correct response. For the most part the active members come from the lowest sudra castes, but this was not invariably the case. Among known members of these panths there were one or two Banias. The father of my informant Partab Singh, a highly respected Thakur of a remote country village, was reputed to be both a bhagat in the normal sense and an active member of one of these sects. When I stayed a night as his guest we discussed these practices. His farmer tenants made no concealment of the fact that mandlis were regularly held in the precincts of one of their temples (a temple of Ram-Devji, a Marwari Rajput incarnation of Vishnu, who, with his dharm-bahin, was believed to have been a zealous member of the laja-dharm). The Thakur himself commented that for those who believed, this too was one way of reaching towards God.

The great majority of the informants mentioned these panths only to condemn them vehemently. To Hari Lal, who often referred to them, their most revolting aspect was the indiscriminate commingling of castes; it was he also who described the Kundapanthis' unhallowed feast, after the ceremony, in which not only did high and low castes sit eating from a common dish, but they served food which should not be eaten —even, it was said, cow's flesh. Other informants were more appalled by the sexual element, and especially by the threat of incest: " In those mandlis they go and lie together with whomsoever they chance to be paired off—mother, sister, it is all one to them."

Hari Lal and Shankar Lal pointed out that these panths showed this in common with the reputable sects of bhakti-worship, that each group had its gurus, well-versed in the cult, who would induct a series of disciples into the esoteric knowledge of their several panths: but this only revealed a fresh horror, because every man should look upon his guru as a father, and his guru's wife as a mother; yet it was common knowledge that a candidate, in order to gain acceptance as a member of the panth must have intercourse with the wife of his guru. Thus, the dreaded incest was realised in a ritual act.

The laja-dharm is a stubborn and active cult, which has survived many attempts at suppression by scandalised Rajput rulers; and it flourishes in secret still, although proscribed by civil law. Another phenomenon, to which five informants referred is that of the *Augur-Babas*, or *aghoris*. These are a class of begging holy men who practise *virodh-panth*, the way of contradiction. They try to compel God's acceptance of their souls by breaking all the laws of nature and of propriety, living in filth, eating excrement and drinking urine, gnawing dead men's bones and even eating mud (hence their popular name of *mithi-maharaj*). It was not possible for me to decide whether such persons really were dedicated worshippers, as Shankar Lal would have me believe, and not mere lunatics or imbeciles, living in squalor from necessity and not from choice. The few whom I saw seemed to belong more to the latter category.

In their horrified, and yet fascinated, accounts of these practices of the laja-dharm and the aghoris (as before, of the behaviour of hinjras) my informants were portraying the direct antithesis of their own religious values; and the very vehemence of their condemnation seemed to carry an undertone of relief that someone else should have acted out their most strongly repressed urges. By describing these atrocities in others' behaviour, they seemed to experience a vicarious release of the same impulses in themselves.

SUMMARY

Several levels were apparent in the villagers' conceptions of the supernatural. The first consisted of an attribution of magical powers, beneficent or harmful—or both—to certain

RELIGION AND PHANTASY

individuals. Associated with this was the unquestioned belief in malevolent witchcraft. Next, came the belief in minor local gods, described in anthropomorphic terms. These petty gods were peculiarly accessible, themselves entering into the body of their bhopa or priest and speaking face to face with their worshippers. The spirits of the recently dead might also haunt one spot, and could communicate with the living in the same manner.

High-caste Hindus tended verbally to scorn these beliefs, although conforming to them in fact.

Their avowed beliefs were on a third level, that of formal Hindu religious teachings. They were able to describe orthodox religious practices, consisting of various " Ways " towards the common goal of liberation from the cycle of rebirth. Devotional exercises, and the observance of ritually correct behaviour were the first steps on all these ways. Serious application to religion invariably demanded in addition, first, severe restraints, and eventually the complete suppression of sexual and emotional desires. The accomplishment of this rigorous suppression of sensuality was believed to impart supernatural powers, leading eventually to release from human existence. In contrast, a secret, ostensibly abhorred, and yet persistent religious cult represented the violent antithesis of all pious Hindu values. In this cult, sexuality was regarded as divine, the sexual act as an act of worship: its initiates committed ritual incest with the wife of their guru.

None of my informants belonged to the above cult, although the father of Partab Singh was said to do so. All subscribed to the first level of supernatural beliefs; and all acknowledged the existence of the local gods, although the Brahmins and the wealthier Rajput and Bania families considered it beneath their dignity to be seen among the crowds of low-caste members who attended their worship regularly. All subscribed in principle to the precepts of Hindu dharm, but the degree to which they actually concerned themselves with religious exercises varied from individual to individual. Only one (Vikram Singh) made it his major concern; fifteen others (four Rajputs, eight Brahmins and three Banias) practised prayer and meditation daily. One Rajput (Devi Singh) and one Bania (Rajmal) were the only informants who openly expressed indifference to religious matters. Kripa Lal was the only Brahmin who openly flouted the religious code: yet even he gave it his verbal adherence.

CHAPTER VII

TRAITS SHARED AND NOT-SHARED BY EACH CASTE

Looking back over the previous chapters, it is now possible to state very briefly those respects in which the personalities of my Deoli acquaintances differed consistently from my conception of the Western norm. I found them quick, alert and responsive to new encounters, eager to plan and to initiate projects but generally failing to carry them through if they required sustained application. They were vacillating and inconstant though great admirers of constancy. For them the world was a place in which nothing could be regarded as fixed or sure: the co-existence of contradictions was accepted as part of the order of things. Although persuaded of all-pervading uncertainty they showed a seemingly compulsive optimism, as if they were unable to tolerate a grim prospect.

They displayed an apparent lack of empathy with regard to each other's feelings; and their fellows' motives seemed to them ever arbitrary, inscrutable and suspect. As a result, association among peers was frustrated by the occurrence of paranoid reactions of mutual distrust. Interpersonal relations tended to be on a superficial level, with a display of goodwill and flattery in face-to-face encounters, followed always by dubious after-thoughts. They seldom openly quarrelled but when this did occur their usual composure would be torn aside by gales of uncontrolled aggression.

In contrast to this, they acted with the greatest self-assurance when observing the formalities of an elaborate social etiquette, or when impersonally executing the duties associated with their respective caste roles; and they were capable of reposing blind faith in one class of persons—those whom they regarded as their guru. In speaking of the guru and of the religious life to which he was their guide they were able to express warm feelings and to allow themselves to be carried away by emotion, whereas in all other contexts emotionalism was played down.

Sensual appetites were deprecated. Where they could not be suppressed altogether, they were indulged cautiously under strict controls. Hindu propriety demanded a denial of expression of strong feelings, replacing them even in intimate conjugal and family life with formal relationships and mutual obligations. They aspired towards a complete detachment from sensuality and were haunted by a fear of physical and moral decay because they failed to achieve that ideal. Their ultimate religious aim was one of severance from all emotional ties and ultimately from all physical appetites in an inward-looking withdrawal from the world. The performance of self-mortification was believed to enhance an individual's power to such an extent that miracles would happen at his wish.

In every-day life there was a marked scrupulousness in avoiding personal contamination, both physical and ritual, but this was not associated with obsessional traits in the Western sense, such as concern over punctuality or meticulous care in matters of detail. Beneath the concern about defilement lay a pre-occupation with the noxious properties of human faeces, the arch-contaminant, which was associated with personal and social degradation. That this anxiety was of greater emotional than rational significance was shown by their relative indifference to unhygienic surroundings. The physical cleanliness of their persons and their surroundings was important to them but still more so was ritual cleansing, which was felt to be effective in warding off supernatural dangers even if perfunctorily carried out.

Besides these shared characteristics my informants presented many purely individual traits. Each was a personality in his own right; and yet each also exhibited certain other traits which could be recognised as reflecting the values emphasised by the caste to which he belonged. These caste emphases will therefore be described in turn.

1. RAJPUTS

The term Rajput means "Lord's Son"; and the suffix Singh, which every Rajput adds to his name, means "Lion". These two words epitomise the attributes peculiar to this community. Their traditional duties are to rule, and to fight —but with qualifications in each case. In describing them as rulers, speakers of all three castes preferred to talk about ideal rulers, in the past. The present Ruler of Deoli was seldom praised, although every Rajput insisted on his loyalty to him: if it came to fighting, even those families which were out of favour would claim the privilege of carrying arms in his support.

His forefathers, on the other hand, were well remembered. As Bhagwat Singh put it: " They were fine people, and very well liked. They used to be on good terms with all the country folk round here. When they went abroad, people would line the road to salute them, and they'd stop their car or their elephant or horse, and talk to people . . . and when they went hunting, if they called for Bhils to act as beaters for them, for every one they summoned, two would come." Bhagwat Singh's regard for these former rulers was unshaken by the fact that one of them had, so he told me, caused his own grandfather to be murdered and thrown into a well. In general, stories of past rulers' ruthless and arbitrary acts in no way lessened their esteem: these were regarded as the Rajah's prerogative. The Rao Sahib himself described how he had once been challenged by a keeper of the Maharana's private forest, on which he was trespassing, and replied: " ' If you come one pace towards me, I shall put a bullet in your head.' . . . I should have shot him just like a black buck—a man or a black buck, it is all one to me." In fact, the keeper realised who he was, and on approaching him with proper deference was rewarded with some money.

The reigning Maharana of Udaipur was also compared unfavourably with his heroic forebears, although there was no lack of local patriotism. Amar Singh said: " Mewar is the best land in all India, the *Vir-bhumi*, of India. . . . We are proud to be men of the Vir-bhumi, and I'm ready to fight for religion and for my country—who knows when the need may arise? I'm ready, and all Rajputs are the same. Panthers and tigers don't eat grass and that's what Rajputs are, a carnivorous race."

The most unstinting praise, however, was reserved for rulers of antiquity, for Rana Partab and Rajah Vikram, about whom Nar Singh told the following story: " They say of Rajah Vikram that once he went riding through a field of standing corn, and trampled it, and a farmer came and said: ' Get off that horse. What do you mean by spoiling my crops? ' And the farmer beat him, and he let him do it, because the fault was his in spoiling his corn. That's the sort of king he was. Those great Rajputs they regarded it their duty to protect their subjects and treat them well."

This veneration of past rulers embraced Queen Victoria, to whom was given the credit for all the public works, roads, reservoirs and railways, constructed by the British throughout India during her reign. " When Queen Victoria ruled ", said

Amar Singh (who was born about 1915), " Those were the days! Then justice ruled. Criminals were severely punished and the just were rewarded." His younger brother who was listening, asked " Was she a Rajput? "

" No."

" A Mussulman? "

" No, one of his caste, a Belaiti."

If the rulers tended to be idealised, so also was the Rajputs' role as warriors. They professed to be slow to anger, but formidable when roused. Vikram Singh described it thus: " A Rajput should fight not only for the cause of religion, but also in self-defence, to protect his fields or his life or possessions. He should not fight on slight provocation if someone abuses him, for example, he should be patient and ask the person why he is abusive; but if he persists, then punish him."

Amar Singh gave a similar instance: " Suppose I'm lying in my house and you throw a stone at me. The first time, I may not notice; the second time I may look up to see if you are having a game with me, or what; but the third time, I'll pick it up and fling it straight in your face. That's what we believe: not to be easily provoked, but ready to fight once we are."

In defining this duty, Vikram Singh was careful to point out the Brahmins' different role: " It is no part of a Brahmin's duty to take life, even if he is attacked. If he is thwarted or insulted, he should not falter; he should be ready to persist in what is right, even to his death, but he should not resort to violence. What he should do is to tell his Rajput protectors, because it is their duty to fight to defend the Right." As a *bhagat*, Vikram Singh insisted that " The exercise of religion helps you to have peace of mind and strength of body: when you are afraid or anxious, you are incapable of decisive action—your *virya*, and so your strength, gets dissipated ".

Others, less educated and less imbued with religious values, were content to insist upon Rajput heroism in battle, their berserk fury when crossed; and upon the privileges associated with their caste—the right to drink alcohol (in the form of *daru*, a spirit distilled from the flowers of the *mahwa* tree) and to eat meat. These substances, if taken in strict measure, were believed to add to the warrior's virility by helping him acquire semen, and with it the qualities of courage and strength which its possession conveyed; and yet there was always the uncomfortable knowledge that meat and wine were abjured by the Brahmins, in the name of the religion which they were bound to protect. Rajputs who became seriously intent upon religion might forswear meat and *daru* altogether, as did Vikram Singh, but it was more usual to compromise, to insist that one took them only in medicinal doses—*niyam se*—which could do no harm.

In real life, however, this decorous restraint was not always maintained. "Of course, once you're in a drinking party", said Puran Singh, "there's no talk of *niyam!*" and Latchman Singh asked: "Hasn't Bhagwat Singh called you to a party yet? You should see one—they sit eating and drinking heartily till they become senseless; and then they talk loudly and make fools of themselves, and spill their food down the front of their shirts, and summon the drummer-girls, and some of them become unconscious. Oh, it's a fine sight; it's good fun!"

No Rajput ever admitted to having a weak head for alcohol. Mal Singh boasted of his furious temper when he was in his cups, and others boasted of their sexual prowess. This reckless departure from customary restraints was encouraged by the songs of the drummer-girl prostitutes, whose presence was essential to a good party. They would begin with songs flattering to Rajput esteem, with the refrain: "*Pi lo, pi lo manna Rajah*—Drink on, drink on oh my King." "You see", said Rajendra Singh, as he interpreted the songs to me, "they know our psychology. They know that when we drink we get very lusty, and then we are ready to call them to spend the whole night with us. . . . Ah, Sahib, I used to be very fond of dancing-girls and all such things, but since I have come on the right path—or the wrong path?—I don't have anything to do with them. I only listen to them, there is no harm in that. See, now they are singing: 'The bed is spread, and I am waiting; oh, my Lord do not be long!'"

Often guests would be inspired to recite *dohitas*, rhymed couplets composed by the hereditary minstrels of important Rajput families—"You are the right Lord of all intoxications, oh Twice-distilled. . . . When the war-drum beats he will not feel afraid. . . . It makes the eyes red, it keeps the pleasure going between the pair; how shall I praise you enough, oh *Dobaro!*"

Rajendra Singh recalled especially fine parties at princes' wedding-feasts. "They will call the dancing-girl to sit on their lap, then they will get stirred and take her into a room and bar the doors—and the others will beat upon the door and say: 'Eh, Rao Sahib, we also want to see this girl'—but pay no attention! Poor girl, where can she go, all doors are locked.

Enjoy till morning, she must do what you want. Then give her Rs. 100/-, she goes away happy. That is what Rajputs are like, Sahib; uneducated, uncivilised, lusty men."

On that occasion, the Rao Sahib spoke ironically, enjoying his Rabelesian memories; but at other times he felt uncomfortably aware of the contradiction between his spiritual aspirations and his regal pleasures. Then, he would repeat his belief that *daru*, taken *niyam se*, need not hinder the practice of concentration, but might actually help it; and he would for a time apply himself with extra zeal to his programme of self-discipline.

The same ambivalence towards alcohol was shown by Hira Singh: " As for drinking, we Rajput people if we once start drinking, we go on to excess, not caring. Many Rajputs have ruined themselves through drinking too much. In our fighting days, Rajputs took *daru* in order to forget their love of family and fears for themselves; but now the fighting days are gone, yet still they take wine and are ruined by it. My father used to drink a fixed quantity of wine, from a very small measure, every night: it was his *niyam*, his rule."

There were songs other than drinking-songs which were familiar to the Rajputs' ears. The *Charans* or bards, who periodically visited the great houses, kept alive a tradition of ballads, many of them in the poets' dialect known as *dingalbasha*, and it was by listening to these that young Rajputs were instructed in their history, and in the heroic virtues of their clan. In these ballads, courage and desperation go hand in hand—as in British history, victories may be overshadowed by tales of glorious defeat. Often in these ballads, Rajput warriors assume the saffron robes of the *sannyasi*, to show that their lives are committed unreservedly to the fight: and there is a recurrent pride in the *johar*, the rite in which Rajput widows immolated themselves in a communal funeral pyre, on learning that their husbands had died fighting.

This suicidal desperation seemed the counterpart to the Rajputs' valiant boastfulness: it was expressed by several of my informants, even the mildest-mannered of them all, Hira Singh, sharing this mood in the course of violent phantasies: " My intention was, I shall be killed no doubt but if they capture me, they will hurt and insult me, so I shall kill myself instead."

Usually, these excesses of desperation were confined to the phantasies of an evil mood, but there were several instances of outbursts of homicidal rage in the recent histories of these

Rajput families. Significantly, the provocation of such rage was usually ascribed to an "insult", and on inquiry this was found to mean that a Rajput's authority had been challenged by his inferior. In the latest such instance, which occurred in December 1947, Nathu Singh lost all control of himself when he was defied by his younger brother: in a fit of anger he killed him, then killed his pregnant wife. In analysing the circumstances of this crime,* I have concluded that it caused less revulsion among his caste-fellows than might have been expected, because it expressed the Rajputs' firmest conviction—that of the unlimited, unchallengeable authority of the ruler, or the father, or his substitute, the elder brother.

Coupled with this fierce assertion of authority was its antidote: anger could not be sustained in the face of demonstrative submission, as in the case of the Rao Sahib's father, who became furious if anyone displayed insubordination—" He had him slapped, shoe-beaten: but if he confessed that he had done a mistake, clasped his feet and asked forgiveness, then he would forgive him." (Dr. Lorenz, the naturalist, has described a similar phenomenon in wolves' fighting: when the loser assumes an attitude of helplessness, exposing its vital parts to attack, the victor finds itself compelled by a strong instinct to suspend the attack and spare the other's life. In contrast, he points out that the supposedly meek and harmless turtle-dove has no such restraining instinct, and will peck away at a defeated rival until it is dead. Rajputs would be quick to identify the latter with the Bania caste, who profess non-violence and practise ostentatious humility, but drain one's blood with their usury: " Their way is to kill you by slow degrees ", said Bheru Singh.)

A Rajput child's upbringing differs from that of other castes in certain respects. There is an explicit stress upon patterns of authority and submission. In early infancy, the child enjoys the customary generous mothering, but owing to the Rajputs' strict observance of *purdah* there is a sharper differentiation between the woman's world, where the child is king, and the man's world, where the head of the household rules dictatorially. As soon as he can walk, the boy spends much of his time in the male side of the house, the *mardana*, where he is looked after by Rajput or servant-caste attendants; and these male nurses instruct him in his future role. From their example and teaching, he learns to address his elders with proper deference, and to demand the subservience of members

* Carstairs, G. M. (1953)

of the lower castes; and they teach him how to ride and shoot, and how to wield a sword.

In Mewar, as in most of Rajasthan, Rajput families observe the law of primogeniture. To the eldest son goes the *Jagir*, with its titles and the bulk of its revenue, while younger sons are granted only a twentieth part of their father's estate. As a consequence of this, a Rajput elder son grows up into awareness of tension between himself and his father on the one hand, and his younger brother on the other. Fathers were noticeably more indulgent towards their younger sons, whereas they were at once stricter, less spontaneous and more demanding in relation to their heirs. This was illustrated by a conversation with Rajendra Singh on his return to Deoli after having spent some weeks in his town house at Udaipur. The Rao Sahib asked his five year old son, Prithur Singh, which he preferred, the city or the village, and the boy replied: " 'Daipur." " He likes the town best, because he has driving every day. Here he does not get to go drives, see the animals in the gardens. Ask *him* which he prefers "—indicating Fateh Singh, his elder son. Fateh Singh sat, small and still in a big armchair, his eyes fixed on his father. After a pause, he said: " Deoli." " You see," said Rajendra Singh, " he is learning. He says what he thinks will please his father. He really prefers the town, but he says Deoli in order to please me." As he spoke, he stared thoughtfully and unaffectionately at his elder son.

One cultural reflection of this father-son tension was the recurrence in history of conflict between a ruler and his impatient heir. This was not expressed as armed rebellion, but as a fear on the father's part that he would be poisoned, in order to be put out of his son's way. I was told that the reigning Maharana of Udaipur required that every meal should be tasted by a reliable courtier, half an hour before he ate, in case of poisoning by the faction of his adopted heir. This story was unsubstantiated, but what was significant was that my Rajput acquaintances accepted it as a reasonable assumption. Another institutionalised expression of this situation was seen in the circumstance that every former Rajput nobleman has a memorial built in his honour, in the family cremation ground: but this memorial is built by his grandson, not by his immediate successor.

Tension between brothers was often evident. It might be denied, by idealising the relationship as did Amur Singh: " My big brother, I have to respect him like a father; and he has to take care of his younger brothers, just like Ram Chandarji did with Latchman." * Yet in their family, to my knowledge, quarrels were frequent; and in every family the elder brother seemed to be impelled to keep on asserting his superiority, as if only the repeated display of his brother's subservience could keep in check his anxiety on this score. This process was nowhere more conspicuous than in the palace of Deoli. The Rao Sahib constantly ordered his younger brother about, over-ruled his wishes, and emphasised his subordinate position. One evening, this brother's children, Kamalini and Ragunath Singh, were present. Rajendra Singh explained to me that they addressed their own father as "Papa" and himself as "Data". He called the little girl to his side and said: "Which is better, Papa or Data?" Falteringly she said: "Data". Then he called to five year old Ragunath Singh, who was standing by his father's chair: "Which is better, Papa or Data?" The boy looked anxious, and said: "Data." "You see," said Rajendra Singh, "they love me best."

His brother, as always, sat in silence, showing no emotion whatever. At other times, however, when alone with me, Devi Singh expressed himself quite strongly on the subject of Rajput elder-brothers: "Their great fault is this: they think of themselves as lords, and they think all those like younger brothers as inferior, very mean-type fellows." Other younger brothers also guardedly expressed their resentment of this system.

If Rajput families thus had their internal stresses, they were united in their attitude towards other castes. Brahmins were accorded their formal respect, as was shown in the traditional exchange of courtesies, the Brahmin saying: "May you live long and protect the Brahmins and the cows" and the Rajput replying: "I clasp your feet." In order to command this respect, however, a Brahmin must keep to his priestly role, and accord the Rajput the deference due to his temporal position: those who entered politics or business, and had the temerity to dispute the Rajputs' ascendency, were intemperately abused.

For the caste of Banias, on the other hand, no Rajput had a good word. They were described as unclean, cowardly, underhand and grasping, and were accused of having perverted true Hinduism with their exaggerated scruples against taking any form of life. Rajputs were obliged, like every other caste, to have recourse to the Banias in their capacity as money-lenders, and they liked to preserve at least an appearance of

* These are the brother-heroes of the Ramayana legend

good relations with those with whom they had business dealings; but with the single exception of Bhagwat Singh (and that only temporarily) none of my Rajput informants included any Banias among their personal friends.

II. BRAHMINS

Brahmins share with Rajputs an unshakeable belief that their own caste is the most desirable one in which to be born, but with this difference, that a Rajput's role demands qualities of aggression and self-assertion if he is to win his proper place in the hierarchy of temporal power and individual prestige, whereas a Brahmin's pre-eminence is accepted by his fellow-men simply by virtue of his birth and his observance of the religious obligations incumbent on his caste. So long as he adheres to these rules, no Hindu will dispute a Brahmin's inherent godliness, which places him in a category separate from the rest of mankind, and earns him the formal greeting: " *Maharaj* "—Great Lord.

I was often reminded that a Brahmin whose conduct did not conform to Hindu *dharm* forfeited the claim to be revered. Kripa Lal told me: " It is a man's mode of life that shows his caste: a Brahmin who goes in for promiscuity and drunkenness is no true Brahmin, but should be classed among the sweepers." In saying this, he was expressing his own sense of guilt, because he had squandered his patrimony on drink and prostitutes, and even now kept a low-caste concubine in Udaipur. His name was constantly cited by other informants as one who would certainly be outcasted, if the caste-panchayats had not lost their former power. The older people spoke of this with regret but not so Himat Lal, who admired Kripa Lal and envied his emancipation. He said: " It's got now so that no one is ever put out of caste, not in our caste—the Banias still do that. If a Brahmin has committed a grave offence, we come and give him some Ganges-water, and purify him: sometimes there's a fine to be paid, but that's not usual."

On the positive side, every Brahmin felt it incumbent on him to display his piety, and the chief stress was upon formal observances. " A Brahmin's first duty ", said Hari Lal, " is *achar-bichar* "—that is, to avoid contamination by touch, or by sitting down to partake of food or tobacco in low-caste company. Each one, in enumerating the events of his daily routine, laid particular emphasis upon early-morning defaecation, followed by careful bathing. Only after this was mention made of the spiritual exercises, although eight out of eleven Brahmins (as compared with five out of twelve Rajputs, and three out of thirteen Banias) did practise daily meditation; two of these aspired to do this at all three times—early morning, noon and evening—but had to admit that they failed to do so regularly. Still, everyone knew that this was an important part of his caste duties. In Girdari Lal's words: " Man's life is not for getting rich, it is in order to get union with God. Release is what everyone wants; and there are innumerable Ways to gain Release. One way is to be a Brahmin and do *sandhya*, three times a day, with *gaitri-mantar* (holy texts) and offerings of fire, and worship of the Gods."

By common consent, one of the most highly-esteemed Brahmins to live in Deoli for many years had been the father of Himat Lal, of whom it was said that he knew by heart all the four Vedas. His daily routine, for years before his death, was to sit engrossed in contemplation from 7 a.m. till 2 p.m., then to take some *bhang* or other cold drink, and a little fruit. For two hours he would talk with his family, and rest, and then resume his prayers until nightfall, taking his only meal of the day after dark so that each day counted as a religious fast. Although he was generally admired for this zeal, there were some who urged him to share his wisdom by helping in caste and village affairs; but he declined to do so. His son told me: " When my father died, it was just before my wedding, so I might have been expected to feel it badly, but I didn't: I only wept one day . . . but when our Mahatma Gandhiji died, then I wept for two whole days, then I was really wretched." Himat Lal's father made him wear a loincloth, and shave his head (all but the *choti*) and frowned on his interest in Congress politics and talk of social reform—" It's only since he died that I have really lived—I'm a post-1945 man."

In their family life, Brahmin children learned to adopt an attitude of formality and respect, rather than one of affection or indeed of intimacy of any sort, towards their fathers. The only exception to this rule was Himat Lal, who frequently carried about his infant son and made much of him: he was able to do so only because his own father had died before the son was born. In every other household I was impressed by the detached way in which a father discussed, in his son's presence, the youth's abilities and shortcomings and his plans for the future, while the son looked on, keeping a decorous silence. In spite of this formality, or perhaps because it was generally accepted without question, these Brahmin families seemed relaxed and secure in their acceptance of mutual obligations. They were free of the Rajput tensions between father and elder son, and between brothers, because in their caste each child was entitled to an equal share of the inheritance; but the ban was absolute against a youth's showing any evidence of his sexual or emotional life in his elders' presence. For that matter, it was unheard of that a father should betray warm feelings for his wife or children: to do so would not only betray grave moral weakness on his part, but would be considered most improper.

Sex was never discussed directly between the generations, but it could be talked about quite candidly by an older man while his son looked on. It was in such discussions with heads of families that I learned the Brahmins' views on sexual morality. They deplored all forms of extra-marital relationships as inimical to godliness (though the younger men, when alone, would boast of sowing their wild oats) but insisted that an instructed person should go regularly with his wife, during the span of their reproductive years. More than any, it was the Brahmins who stressed that it is women who demand sexual intercourse: the older men described it as the chief among worldly distractions, impeding the soul's progress towards Release, but the younger ones (Devi Lal, Rup Lal, Himat Lal and Kripa Lal), did not deny their furtive enjoyment of sexuality. Himat Lal said there was a great deal more promiscuity in the village now than in former years: " Women have grown more desirous, and men too; because they eat more than they used to do, and eat hot things like *pan*. . . . In the old days, people were very strict about what they ate, and who touched it—now they eat whatever comes to hand, in hotels, and from sweetmeat sellers; and as a result their lust is greater."

Rup Lal was one of many persons who commented upon the Banias' misguided piety in treating *all* intercourse as sinful: " There are many of them who avoid sex relations altogether— *shil-vrit*, that's called. They regard it as sacrilege because so many small creatures must die every time the semen comes out, and they think that that will prevent their getting Release. Many of them take oaths—' I won't have sex for six months '; or twelve months, or for the rest of their lives. Brahmins are not like that; they copulate a great deal, all through the month —not like those Banias who say that one shouldn't copulate on certain days of the month. We copulate all the time, except when our wives are menstruating."

Perhaps it was because sex was granted a place in the life-long programme of dutiful acts which constituted a Brahmin's *dharm* that it could be discussed dispassionately; even in describing the orgiastic rites of the *laja-dharm*, Brahmins appeared less scandalised by the overt sexuality than by the commingling of high and low castes, and by the threat of incest.

Mention has been made above of the Rajputs' ambivalent attitude towards their privilege of drinking wine and eating meat. Brahmins were ready to concede these practices, and to make allowances for occasional debauchery as the natural failing of a warrior caste: but they were vehement in insisting that no Brahmin should ever take alcohol. "If we are even touched by a drop of *daru*," said Hari Lal, "we must go and wash ourselves and all our clothes"; and on another occasion: "The result of eating meat and drinking wine is that you become filled with passion, rage—and then what happens? The spirit of God flies out from you."

Not only alcohol, but all other forms of intoxication, such as tobacco and tea, were proscribed by strict Brahmins; all, that is, except one. The exception was hashish, the drug contained in the plant *cannabis indica*, which grows readily in this area. In Deoli, this was commonly prepared as a fresh infusion called *bhang*, and there was a group of Brahmins who used to meet every afternoon to drink *bhang* together and then disperse to their several houses in order to enjoy its delayed effect.

At first, seeing some of these Brahmins in a state of profound intoxication, I was at a loss to know why this drug was approved, while alcohol was condemned. There was no concealment of its use. Some informants reminded me that bhang is a sacred drink, used by Shiva himself; others pointed out that it was the favourite refreshment of Saddhus whom one often observed red-eyed and fuddled under its effects. It was not, however, until my Brahmin friends had made me drink a generous dose that I fully understood their discrimination in its favour.

The intoxication of bhang has a great deal in common with that of mescalin, so eloquently described by Aldous Huxley in his recent essay.* There is a transient phase of euphoria, in which one's appreciation of time and space is distorted, and in which visual and auditory perceptions are charged with a heightened intensity and significance. Some two hours after taking the drug, this phase of stimulation is succeeded by a profound feeling of detachment from all worldly ties, and an ecstatic trance-like state supervenes, the state known to Arabic

* Huxley, A. (1954)

hashish-takers as El Kif, the Blessed Repose. The affinity of this condition with the Brahmins' religious exercise of withdrawal from the world of sense is clear. Baudelaire described his experience of the trance as " l'apothéose de l'Homme-Dieu ", which is as near as any Western man has come to realising the concept of *samadhi*.

Mr. Huxley described mescalin intoxication as a " gratuitous grace " for those who wish for a direct mystical experience of existence. In Deoli, Hari Lal meant much the same when he said of his drug: " It is very good for *bhakti;* you get fine concentration with *bhang*." Rajputs, on the other hand, had little to say for this drink, although there was nothing to prevent their taking it. " It's not a thing I like ", said Bhagwat Singh: " It makes you very sleepy, and your throat dry . . . it makes you quite useless, unable to do anything. Daru isn't like that; you may be drunk but you can still carry on." *

I could share his feelings, because my own Western bias towards a life of action, of extraverted interests, had prevented my enjoying, or indeed fully entering into, the profoundly inward-looking, other-worldly experience which *bhang* makes accessible. On reflection, it seems unlikely that Mr. Huxley's vain hope that mescalin should replace tobacco and alcohol as Western man's drug of escape, will ever be realised, unless Western society experiences a change of values at least as great as the difference between Rajput and Brahmin ideals of behaviour.

III. BANIAS

When asked what were the distinguishing features of their caste, Banias invariably dwelt upon their strict observance of *ahinsa*, respecting and sparing all forms of life. Whereas Brahmins in Deoli were vegetarian, Banias would profess to be still more scrupulous, forswearing all tuberous vegetables, and all fruits with numerous pips, in case they were guilty of taking the life of a single seed. If this was their distinguishing characteristic on the ideal plane, there was another which was at least equally conspicuous in their everyday life: this was, their worship of money. Once a year, on the festival of *Dhan-teras*, this worship is carried out quite literally. In secret, behind closed doors, each Bania family offers *puja* to its store of coin and jewellery. Shortly after this comes *Divali*, and

---

* I have discussed the cultural attitudes to these two drugs in greater detail elsewhere—see Carstairs, G. M. (1954)

on this night Brahmins come to each Bania's shop to preside over the worship of his ledgers, pens and ink, instruments of Laxmi, Goddess of Wealth.

This concern about money was not, however, a matter of mere ceremony, but rather the lynch-pin of the Banias' life. Besides their shops, each Bania family did business as money-lenders, and it was through this business that they acquired fields, houses, and a steady income of grain from the crops of chronically indebted farmers. In their eyes, to be wealthy meant that one had received God's blessing, and they regarded the poor with a revulsion which was stronger than any impulse to pity them. The urge to become rich was certainly greater than the obligation to support their kin. The five poorest Banias in Deoli (three of whom were among my informants) all had this in common, that they had been orphaned while quite young, and had been despoiled of their inheritance by the relatives who brought them up.

It was felt as axiomatic that protection of one's own business interests took precedence over any question of loyalty to one's caste. Thus, Bhagmal described how his father had built up trade as a pedlar in jungle districts beset by robber Bhil tribesmen. He had conciliated these Bhils, and they left him alone. One day, he saw a number of them preparing an ambush, and later he met a group of Banias from Deoli carrying merchandise. They were attacked and looted; and afterwards they reproached him for not having warned them, as he could have done. His defence was that he did not want to offend these dacoits with whom he had profitably come to terms.

This unremitting attention to money-making inevitably earned them many enemies. It would be no exaggeration to say that they were the most hated community in this area; and they were reminded of this fact in the altercations which not infrequently broke out in the bazaars. Young Banias explained to me that they had to learn proficiency in swearing and giving abuse—how else would they be able to force interest out of a grudging debtor? Rajmal said quite frankly: " Lots of people here dislike me, and many of them are envious because we've got on, and are successful." He was, indeed, a merciless businessman. In recent years, besides money-lending, he had established himself as a go-between in murder cases in the surrounding areas, bribing the police and confusing the investigations, at a cost of thousands of rupees to the guilty or suspected parties concerned. He was usually attended by two Moslem bodyguards—a necessary precaution, as it turned out, because six months after I had left Deoli I received a letter from Bhagwat Singh telling me: " Rajmal has been waylaid, and had his nose cut off."

One night, during the rains, I was called out in the dark to attend to a young Bania who had been found unconscious in a field. My friends explained that he must have been attacked by one of his debtors—that seemed to them the likeliest explanation—but when he came to he was able to explain that his horse had stumbled and he had struck his head in falling to the ground.

Rajmal represented the paradigm of a ruthless Bania, but it would be misleading to suggest that their entire activities were devoted to business. Many of the Banias were officiously active in religious matters. When holy men came to Deoli, whether they were saffron-clad Hindu *saddhus* or Jain monks in white robes with a gauze mask across their mouths to prevent their killing small insects, it was usually a Bania house which sent them their food. Banias contributed to the upkeep of Hindu as well as Jain temples in the village, besides endowing the government " Middle School " with a fund of money to add to its amenities.

The Jain " saints " were former members of Bania families, who had renounced all worldly possessions. They lived on charity, devoting their lives to wandering from village to village preaching their religion of non-violence, self-control and respect for every fellow living creature. They were, in fact, Banias who had given themselves over to the direct antithesis of normal Bania behaviour; and they commanded very great respect. During the four months of the rainy season, the " saints " stayed in one place, and acted as keepers of the conscience of the Bania community who were their hosts. In 1945, one such " saint ", called Indarmalji, had stayed in Deoli. At that time the Banias were split into three fiercely antagonistic camps, but thanks to his eloquence, coupled with a threat to fast to the death if they would not amend their ways, these factions settled their quarrel during Indarmalji's stay and the community was re-united for a time. By 1951, however, passions were running so high between the group of merchants who had secured the contract for ration cloth, and those who coveted it, that there seemed urgent need for a new mediator.

Birmal was a young Bania who had been profoundly impressed by the ethical teaching of these saints, and by other idealised figures, such as Mahatma Gandhi. He seemed on the verge of becoming a holy man himself; certainly his ambition was to become renowned as a selfless philanthropist, for all that he remained unemployed, " eating twice a day in his father's house ". Most of his fellows were more realistic, and hoped to compromise between their business life, which came first, and their religious promptings. " I want a bit of both," said Chauthmal, " to make money *and* to help people." The idealistic promptings of Chauthmal, Birmal and other young men in the village, were none the less sincere because they were seldom long sustained. Several of the younger Banias were supporters of Congress plans for social reform. The older ones were more conservative, but were not slow to appreciate that power in the land seemed to have passed from the Rajputs to Congressites, the majority of whom were themselves educated Banias from the cities.

The interiors of the Banias' houses differed from those of the Brahmins in that the former were often more spacious and pretentious, and invariably less scrupulously clean. As compared with the Rajputs, their women-folk were less insistent upon observing *purdah*. Child-rearing habits were as described in Chapter IV. The father was less remote and self-controlled than in a Brahmin home; every young Bania would see his father shout and swear and threaten his debtors and would learn that in this context, at least, a show of feeling was permitted: but within the family, feelings must still be played down. Sexuality was feared. Mention has been made already of the Banias' view of it as sacrilege. " It destroys your money, and your health, and your good name ", said Surajmal, revealing which came first in his scale of values.

This formal abhorrence of intercourse was accompanied by a good deal of venal promiscuity on the part of the young men. In the Bania caste, more than in any other, there was a formidable obstacle to early marriage in the custom whereby the bride's father must be given a " dowry " of Rs. 3,000 to Rs. 6,000. As a result, there were more young bachelors among them than in the rest of the community, and some of the poorest were unable to marry at all.

Co-operation was close and seemed to come easily within the biological family, in contrast to the slight regard for other kin. In Puranmal's family, father and all three brothers pooled their earnings and economised, so that the youths could be married in their turn. Inheritance was shared equally among a man's sons. The practice of adoption was frequent, and was prompted by economic considerations. If a man died without an heir, his widow would be coerced by the nearest relations to adopt one of them as her son. When this occurred, the adopted son lost all rights to his own father's property, but continued to treat him with respect and to maintain close relations with his original family. When a Bania died, his degree of success in making money would be reflected in the size of the funeral feast, on the twelfth day, to which as many people as possible would be summoned; and if he was really wealthy, his grateful sons would continue to celebrate his name by repeating this feast on the corresponding day of the month of *Bhadrapada* for a number of years after his death.

Banias did not, as a rule, contest the stereotypes with which Rajputs and other castes described their characters: " They are a timid race ", said Vikram Singh; and Daulmal said much the same: " Bania's blood is cold—they are fearful by nature." He used the third personal pronoun, and in doing so, he drew attention to his own, and his caste-fellows' readiness to condemn other members of their own community. It was as if the Banias, aware that every man's hand was against them, were peculiarly unable to identify themselves with any except their nearest kin.

This chapter has necessarily dealt in generalisations, and it has been possible only to outline the ideal patterns of each caste, and some of the deviations from those patterns in everyday behaviour. Besides these minor deviations, it will be as well to note that even within the limited range of my informants, there were individuals in each group who differed conspicuously from its norm—thus, Vikram Singh, although of such aggressive spirit that he prayed for an opportunity to fight in a holy war against Pakistan, was unusual among Rajputs in devoting the greater part of his time to religion; Kripa Lal flouted many of the rules of Brahmin conduct, although he still clung to the prestige of his caste; and Rajmal was generally thought to be foolhardy in his defiance of Bania proprieties, and able to act with such impiety only because of his great wealth. Yet each of these " deviants " could, and did, describe to me with exceptional clarity the traditional values which they respected in principle, though not always in practice.

SUMMARY

The values given different emphasis in the three castes are related to the concept which each caste has of its hereditary role. That of the Rajputs being to rule and to fight, they stress the importance of authority and obedience, of personal fortitude, of pride and self-assertion. In this community the rule of primogeniture obtains (contrary to the practice of most Hindus, including some other Rajput clans) and causes increase of tension between elder and younger brothers, and between father and son. Stress is also laid upon the prerogatives of the Rajputs—their licence to take life, to drink alcohol and eat meat, and to keep concubines—which are contrary to the Hindu religion which it is their duty to uphold. In consequence, there is a conflict between a Rajput's caste and his religious values.

No such conflict obtains in the Brahmin caste, whose role is to devote themselves to the ritual observances of Hinduism. Their peculiarity is to over-emphasise tendencies present in every Hindu upbringing, such as the replacement of personal feeling-based relationships within the family with formal ties of mutual obligation. Whereas other castes fight a losing battle in their struggle to achieve an impossible ideal of self-restraint, the Brahmins are supported by the assurance that they are already god-like, such is the exalted religious status of their caste. With this support they are able to pursue the Hindu religious goal of moksh with the confidence that they have less far to go than other men. Irreligious Brahmins run the risk of severe condemnation from their caste-fellows, but seldom lose the assurance of still being holier by birth than their disapproving lower-caste neighbours.

Banias, on the other hand, subscribe to the same ideal values as Brahmins but are taught in practice to prize wealth above everything. They have neither the sensual privileges of the Rajput nor the birthright of sanctity of the Brahmins. As a result, they are forced to adopt a hypocritical role, protesting " non-attachment " while competing avidly in business. They are disliked and despised by the two other castes, and in defence they make a virtue of ruthless worldliness. Those of them who take Hindu religious values seriously are aware of this painful antithesis between their ideal and their real aims. Many are content to give only lip-service to the ideal values, concentrating their energies upon the serious business of getting rich. The great majority of my Bania informants, however, tried to temper their materialism with contributions of their time and money to religious and philanthropic causes, including (in eight out of the thirteen) active support for the social reforms advocated by the Congress Party.

CHAPTER VIII

THE REVERSE OF THE MEDAL

In carrying out field work of the type described in this book, one has to rely to a great extent upon subjective impressions. This has its advantages. In the emotional exchanges of a series of interviews, one is given clear indications of the importance or relative indifference of a topic to the person with whom one is talking. In fact, one's sensitivity to such pointers becomes an important part of the technique of inquiry.

It is, however, necessary that this subjective bias should be as far as possible under conscious control. There is always the danger—well known to social anthropologists—of seeing other people in one's own image, or in the light of one's own projective systems. For this reason it is desirable that the investigator should not only become aware of his involuntary reactions to people and events, but should aspire to a measure of that unclouded self-knowledge which a successful psycho-analysis is believed to impart. This combination of sensitivity and detachment in personal relationships is not sustained without effort. There are times when one begins to doubt the validity of subjective reactions which had previously been accepted with confidence.

Some six months after the beginning of my work in Deoli I began to experience just such a mood of doubt and indecision. It occurred to me that the picture of high-caste Hindu personality structure which was taking shape in my notebooks (of paranoid suspiciousness, of egocentricity and reluctance to make other than superficial and transient relationships, of ever-shifting uncertainty together with a longing for stability and assurance) might simply represent the reflection in caricature form of some of my own characteristics. What was happening here was a form of counter-transference, in which my own feelings were becoming involved in the values of the community which I was studying. An analyst learns to anticipate this tendency, and to exorcise it by analysing his own emotional involvement; but in Deoli my difficulty was resolved in a different way.

In the month of August, there appeared in the village a band of Bhil tribesmen from a hamlet in the jungle. They performed their *gawri* dance on three successive days, and everyone turned out to watch them. The gawri is essentially a religious performance. In the centre of their dancing circle is set an iron trident, the symbol of the Goddess, and from time to time they sing hymns in her name and perform dance steps which are a parody of the dance of her consort, Lord Shiva. At other times they act a crude Morality, in which masked dancers play the parts of gods and demons; but these sacred interludes are punctuated with profane scenes of comedy and farce, and with exciting dances to the rhythm of drums, cymbals and a one-stringed fiddle.

These Bhil dancers burst into the sedate leisurely tenor of village life with an explosion of noise and vigour and exuberance. I remembered that I had seen Bhils dance on two previous occasions, both in the first weeks of my stay. The first had been a wedding procession, in which the bridegroom was preceded by a whirling, leaping, singing body of young men, brandishing swords or bows and arrows as they danced. Everyone in that party appeared to be a little drunk, and in high spirits. From time to time, one of them would ram a charge of gunpowder down the barrel of his muzzle-loader and fire it into the air. Soon after that, another party of Bhil dancers came to Deoli at the Holi festival, and begged a gift of country brandy from the Ruler, after which they danced and whooped for hours in the fore-court of his palace. Their songs were tuneful, and set to exciting rhythms, and their dancing was both intricate and energetic. On this occasion their womenfolk were also present, dancing sometimes in a group apart, and sometimes in conjunction with the men's group.

Here was clearly a people whose values were strikingly different to those cherished by my Hindu informants, as the latter indeed insisted. The Bhils were boisterously demonstrative. They shouted, sang, laughed aloud and were unashamedly drunk in the public gaze. All these, I was told, were indications that they were nearer to monkeys than to men. But there was worse than this to tell: had I not seen that they would dance together, men and women? They were even so shameless that Bhil husbands and wives could be seen walking hand in hand, talking and laughing together. This open display of affection was profoundly shocking to an orthodox Hindu.

It occurred to me that the opportunity lay here at hand to counteract my gathering Hindu bias by spending some time among the Bhils in order to learn whether their values and their mode of life were really as much at variance with the Deoli pattern as it seemed. Accordingly, the last period of my stay in Udaipur was devoted first to exploring the hill jungles of Kotra Bhomat where, I was told, the real uncivilised Bhils were to be found; and then to settling for two months in the Bhil village of Khajuria.

Few of these Bhils had ever seen a European, other than the officers of a military detachment whose responsibility it was to keep down major lawlessness and to discourage the murder of parties of travellers passing through these jungles. This military force, itself manned by Bhils, was often harsh in its treatment of the villagers; and those who had had least contact with the British held dramatic phantasies about their ruthless severity—largely because of their persistence in trying to punish murderers whom the Bhils could not readily recognise to be criminals, since they had merely conformed to recognised tribal practice.

When I settled in their midst in a Moslem shop, an isolated trading-post where Bhils of several villages came to barter jungle produce for grain and spices, they concluded at first that I must be a military officer. Throughout my stay, they were unable to decide exactly what I was doing (other than offering them my medicines) but they did not harbour paranoid ideas on the subject. Having satisfied themselves that there was no danger attached to my presence, they accepted me as a stranger in their midst and made me welcome in all their activities.

This brief excursion was sufficient to illuminate the very striking antithesis between the Bhil way of life and that of the Hindus; and yet the first impression I received was one of similarity. A Bhil informant warned me in a friendly way against being robbed: " They are all thieves round here," he said, " you have to watch them closely." At first it seemed that this was an expression of the familiar pattern of paranoid suspiciousness: but soon I learned that it was in fact a perfectly realistic outlook. Thefts *were* extremely common. During my two months in Khajuria, I heard the alarm given seven times, to warn fellow-villagers of an attempted raid by Bhils from a distant village or, in two cases, from an adjacent one.

Villages in this Bhil country are quite unlike those of the plains. Bhil houses are built at some distance from each other. Sometimes a man's married sons will build their homes close to their father's but most houses are alone, built strategically on the top of a small hill, or on a jungle slope so as to command a view over the paths of approach. To a stranger these houses seem to be scattered at random all over the countryside; but stop and speak to any Bhil and he will be able to say to which village his house belongs, and who is his *Mukhi* or headman. Village names are very numerous, and refer sometimes to a group of only four or five huts in a tributary valley, but a Mukhi always belongs to a larger group, of a dozen or more households; and in some cases several smaller hamlets come under his jurisdiction. Thus Malia belongs to Mithi-bor, a hamlet of five houses, which is an offshoot of Bodi village. If he is involved in any dispute, he may consult old Ladu, the Mukhi of Bodi; but if it is a really serious matter, they will both resort to Kuma, the Mukhi of Tep, whose authority is acknowledged by all three villages.

This post of Mukhi is hereditary, with the provision that the most capable and not necessarily the eldest, son of the previous headman is accepted by the villagers as his successor. The Mukhi represents the village in all dealings with other villages or with the Ruler's representatives. His authority is unchallenged—provided that it is sensibly exercised—because all the time there is an accompaniment of discussion of each village event among the senior heads of houses and only if the Mukhi's decisions are endorsed with their approval does he command his villagers' obedience. The Bhils here are organised in exogamous patrilineal lineages, akin to the *gotra* of caste Hindus. When referring to one another by name, they quote the lineage as a surname; thus the three men mentioned above are known as Malia Bhumaria, Ladu Kheir and Kuma Dhangi respectively. If further identification is necessary, they add " of such and such a village ". The usual Hindu practice of quoting a man's name and then his father's is new to them, although they are rapidly becoming familiarised with it on ration cards and (in 1952) on the voter's roll.

Each village has a nucleus of households of the same lineage as its Mukhi who is traditionally descended from the first settlers in that area. But in almost every case other lineages are also represented. In about 10 per cent. of marriages the couple finally settle in the bride's village. Most villages also have one or two families who have settled in the course of the last few years, either bringing their cattle to new grazing, or staying to clear a strip of jungle and plant crops. Such incomers are generally related more or less distantly to some members of the village; but strangers may also come, and having obtained the Makhi's consent, build their home in the outskirts of the village area.

THE REVERSE OF THE MEDAL 129

As may be inferred from the above, there is no serious congestion in this territory. Everyone raises *makai* (maize) in the rainy season—as much as he can tend—and still a good deal of available land in the smaller valleys is left to run wild. In winter, the hill streams usually do not dry up and their waters are led by an ingeniously constructed series of earth and wooden channels, called *saran*, to irrigate fields of wheat and gram. In a year of drought, however, the streams dry up and in consequence most of the fields lie idle until the next rains.

The jungle provides good grazing all the year round and every family has a modicum of cattle and goats, whose milk they turn to *ghi* and sell at the nearest trader's shop. This, and the sale of bee's wax found in the jungle, and leaves for the wrapping of *bidis*, provide them with a few annas a day, just enough to buy the essentials of life—salt, pepper, grain and tobacco. Their diet rarely includes any vegetables; occasionally it is relieved with small game, which they hunt with bows and arrows. Their idea of luxury is a feed of *gur* and a drink of *daru*, the spirit locally distilled from *mahwa* flowers.

To a newcomer, a striking feature about these northern Bhils is that they all go about armed, carrying bows and arrows, or muskets or swords—and invariably a sharp dagger in a sheath at their waists. When they see a stranger walking in their hills, they stand with weapons at the ready, looking to see who he is; and this wariness is not misplaced, because robbery and violence are of common occurrence. At night they sleep huddled round a log fire, on the earth floor of their flimsy leaf and bamboo huts, and they sleep with one eye open, ready to rush to the attack if a raider tries to steal one of their cattle in the dark. When this happens, they cry " thief " and someone runs to beat the drum which is kept in every Mukhi's house. This brings out all the men of the village armed and ready for a fight. If the thief is caught, he is given a very thorough beating and then let go.

In an idle and hungry time, like the 1951-52 year of drought, robbery is especially rife. Thieves who get away with a valuable prize, such as a cow or a bullock, will try to drive it to a distant part of Bhomat, or southwards into Gujrat, and there sell it; but if the chase is too hot, they hide, and slaughter the cattle, and have a feast. They do not share the Hindu's abhorrence of eating beef.

If they rob each other, they are still more prone to rob strangers passing through their countryside. Wayfarers are set upon, beaten and robbed of all they have, down to the last shred of their clothing. For this reason travellers find it necessary to move in parties, carrying guns, or else to employ Bhils to give them *agwa*, that is, to provide an armed escort to protect them from the others.

When grazing is scarce in the plains of Mewar and Marwar and Sirohi, numbers of *Rebari* herdsmen come to these jungles with herds of sheep, goats, cattle and camels—and they are regarded as fair game. The Rebaris are told by the villagers in whose area they have camped, that they must sacrifice a young buffalo to the village goddess, then they can rely on the Bhils' support in case of theft. They do so, and the villagers have a feast—but still in spite of their vigilance (and here the Rebaris also carry weapons all the time) they suffer a constant toll of beasts stolen in the jungle.

Besides pre-occupation with theft, the Bhils devote a good deal of time and energy to the pursuit of love and to the feuds that break out whenever a husband discovers that he has been cuckolded. In a group of five villages it was found that 15 per cent. of all marriages were cases in which the bride had been abducted, usually with her own connivance. They call this " zai baraw " or " gis len ayo " or " tani layo " *—and always they smile with relish in recalling this gallant sport. When they describe such incidents, Bhils pantomime a bow-and-arrow combat. They take it for granted that each theft or abduction might provoke a fight; and their fights are in real earnest, with no mediator to come between the protagonists. To the Bhils, the expression of rage is as natural and acceptable in its place as is their customary cheerfulness. An abduction causes a state of hostility to break out between the villages concerned, especially if there is an aggrieved husband in the case. " My nose has been cut off ", he says, and his kinsmen often help him to avenge the insult by attacking the offender's village. In such a feud, it is not necessarily the abductor himself who is the target of attack, but the most eminent man in this village. He may be shot at or waylaid and beaten.

In the daily life of these Bhils, magic and witchcraft plays a very important part while religion occupies a minor role. It is true that they sometimes invoke Bhagwan, whom they regard as being above all other gods, but seldom intervening in the lives of ordinary mortals; and they have a smattering of knowledge of some of the Hindu deities. Indeed, every large village has its separate *devra*, a small roofless stone hut, in which

---

* Run away with ", " caught her and took her ", " brought her by force "

are placed a row of images—of Dharm Raj, Kala-Nag, Bhairav and one or other Mataji. These images are of baked clay, and brightly painted. They are made in the village of Molera, near Nathdwara, and it costs the Bhils a six-day journey on foot to bring them. They refer to them as " those Mewar gods ". Once brought, however, these handsome images are neglected, left out in all weathers, so that in most devras they lie colourless and badly worn. On one night in the year, there is a *jagaran* or Wake, at this shrine, but for the rest of the year no one bothers to visit it. Whereas in Mewar the bhopa, or priest of the shrine, is a very important person, here among the Bhils he is regarded as a figure of fun and is little respected. They turn instead to the *devalo*, or village magician for the diagnosis of all cases of sickness, and to solicit his magical remedies. Whereas the magical healers of Deoli were obliged, and expected, invariably to pronounce a hopeful prognosis, a Bhil devalo could be brutally realistic. In a case of serious illness he would sometimes say: " *Mari kari ni lagi* " —" This is not within my powers ", or else: " He will be dead within five days." If the devalo is esteemed highly, it is partly because of the universal belief in witch-craft. Not only is every adult woman believed to practise this: in addition, every head of a household keeps a *Sikotri*, that is, a demon-goddess with her attendant executive agent, the *Vir*. If appealed to with appropriate *mantars*, this Sikotri will send her Vir to strike down your enemy and when this happens, only the skill of a very clever devalo can save his life. So prevalent is this magic, that in making a betrothal, the negotiators commonly ask: " Is there a Protector in the House? " by which they mean— " Do you have a Sikotri? " and only if the answer is " Yes ", do they proceed.

Some households, instead of Sikotri keep a shrine sacred to *Kamria-path*, a fierce and jealous male god, who demands homage in the form of singing and dancing to strange, exciting traditional Bhil tunes: in turn, he frequently enters into and " possesses " the worshippers as a sign of his goodwill—and he is heartily feared by all who do not adhere to this sect.

Put briefly, then, the Bhils show a dim awareness of some aspects of Hindu worship, but their own old gods and demons still command much greater fear and respect. A similar pattern of lip service to the new and real adherence to the old ways can be seen in their mode of settling disputes.

For as long as the Bhils can remember they have lived under two different, sometimes contradictory, systems of social discipline—their own tribal customs, and the exactions of the " Raj ", by which term they denote all alien authority, whether that of the Rajahs and their soldiery or the British-officered Mewar Bhil Corps, or the new civilian administration of *Tehsildar* and Magistrate, and Forest and Revenue Officers, backed by the armed police. This Raj is always there in the background; and at times it is deliberately invoked. For example, in cases of murder or serious theft, it is becoming a recognised form of retaliation to file a complaint and so bring upon the offender's village the scourge of a rustic police investigation; but that is really irrelevant to the serious process of settling the dispute.

So long as a feud exists (and in every village there are always two or three " ubo ", i.e. " outstanding ") the parties to it " break off diplomatic relations ", that is, they will not sit nor eat nor smoke together and like sovereign powers they " reserve the right to take appropriate action " with bow and arrow or sword or muzzle-loader. It is this continuing threat of the recourse to violence which stimulates the Mukhis and the neighbours of the families concerned to work for a settlement. When tempers have cooled a little (and preferably before blood has been shed) the Mukhi of the offender's village begins to negotiate with the other Mukhi. In cases of abduction the aggrieved husband has to be paid a considerable fine —usually in the form of calves and bullocks to the value of Rs. 200/- or more. If the girl was unmarried a much more modest sum (Rs. 15/- to Rs. 30/-) is given to her father as *dhapa*, or bride-price.

A Bhil marriage is much more of a personal relationship than that of an orthodox Hindu, who is forbidden by rules of propriety from becoming acquainted with his fiancée. Bhil women work side by side with their husbands in their fields, travel with them to fairs where they also drink and dance and sometimes view other men with a roving eye. Genuinely affectionate marriage relationships are common, because each partner has the alternative of absconding with a lover should his or her spouse prove unsympathetic.

In this setting of highly valued love-relationships it was noticeable that the Hindus' prevailing concern about impotence was completely absent. Patients came in large numbers for treatment for venereal diseases, which were extremely prevalent: but not one uttered the familiar complaint of loss of strength through loss of semen. Nor was there any desire to emulate the Hindu ideal of celibacy and asceticism. No evidence of homosexuality was encountered among these Bhils, nor had they any institution of transvestism comparable with the *hinjra*.

Their own gods and goddesses were worshipped with lively celebrations, and with offerings of gur and liquor such as they themselves enjoyed; and when they persistently failed to respond to their requests, the image of the offending god and goddess was sometimes taken down and beaten and thrown into the mud " to teach it a lesson ".

This impious defiance of the gods had a counterpart in family life. The relations between members of a Bhil family depended on personal regard to a much greater extent than on considerations of duty or obligation. If a young man were chastised, and resented it, he would think nothing of retaliating and fighting with his own father. A clear indication of the degree of good feeling existing between fathers and sons was to be seen in the building of their huts. When a son first brought home a wife he would continue to sleep beside his father's fire. Soon, the desire for privacy in his married life would lead him to build a hut of his own. This would be built either within the same enclosure of thorn branches, or nearby, or a long way off, according to the state of his feelings towards his father. He might go to live in his wife's village, or both of them might migrate and build their home in a different valley altogether.

The early upbringing of Bhil children is in no less striking contrast to that of high-caste Hindus. Owing to the extreme simplicity of their huts, and the scarcity of their clothes, a Bhil child has to be hardy, if it is to survive, and this toughening process begins early. A Bhil mother observes less rigid seclusion after a birth than would a Hindu, and that only for ten to fourteen days. During this short period she and her baby are inseparable, but after this she resumes her share in the work of the family group, and temporary absences are quite the rule. There is no regularity in the amount of attention an infant receives, except that it *is* irregular. If a mother has no work to do she will keep the baby at her side all day except when it is laid to sleep in a basket hanging from a branch. On the other hand she may leave it for many hours on end, instructing an older child to give it some goat's milk from a folded leaf if it cries. Unlike Hindus, Bhils do not show immediate concern when a small child cries. They may remark: " It's crying—children do cry." Weaning is delayed until the age of 3 or longer, except where another child is born.

In a flimsy bamboo hut, where all the family sleep around the open hearth, there is little privacy. Bhils say that when they have intercourse they wait until their children are asleep and then retire to a little distance; but it must be a common occurrence for a child to witness the "primal scene".

Fathers and mothers are rough and ready in their upbringing of the children, generous with threats and beatings. From an early age, the youngsters are expected to be useful members of the family work-team. On the other hand, there is far less stress than in a Hindu family upon a formal show of submissiveness of a son towards his father. When the latter becomes senile, his most capable son—not necessarily the eldest—takes over his place and his responsibilities.

Habit training is leisurely and unforced. There is none of the Hindus' extreme abhorrence of faecal pollution—indeed one of the Hindus' taunts against the Bhils is that they are content to cleanse themselves with a leaf or a stone instead of with water (a practice as repugnant to the orthodox as is the Europeans' use of toilet paper). Nor is there any need to learn the necessity of avoiding caste pollution, because they have no castes. In the eyes of Hindus they are untouchable; and those Bhils who live in the plains, in contact with Hindu villages, have acquired something of the low-caste communities' humility and self-abasement; but here in the Bhomat they regard themselves as inferior to none, carry themselves proudly and look strangers squarely in the eye.

A young Bhil has few intricate crafts to learn as he grows up. With one exception (the manufacture of their bows and arrows) their technological skills are rudimentary. What is, however, extremely important is for a young man to show proficiency in music, singing and dancing, for these are their principal modes of self-expression. Their songs are a living tradition. As they dance, a young man will chant verses, with one hand upraised, and the rest will take them up in antiphonal repetition. These may be hymns to local deities, such as *Kali Dungri Wali*—"She of the Black Mountain"—or ballads in praise of famous brigands and their battles with the soldiery. New songs are made up each year, and a singer will often add verses, extemporising under the inspiration of his intoxication. Whereas Hindu dancing is a professional accomplishment, and conforms to rigid canons of style, this Bhil dancing is relatively unformalised, giving scope for impromptu innovations and individual self-expression.

The quality which most forcibly distinguishes between

Hindus and Bhils is the latter's zest and enjoyment of life, accepting pleasures and dangers as they come. They are as uninhibited as the Hindus are restrained. Meat, drink, love and laughter are all enjoyed without reserve. A Brahmin once remarked to me: " Look at them, dancing and enjoying themselves, although they are so poor that they often do not know whether they will have anything to eat for their next meal—isn't that a strange thing! "

Here in the jungle there existed a completely foreign way of life, which unashamedly asserted the very antithesis of Brahminical values. It was a refreshing experience to live among the Bhils for a time. Their very difference, and my ability to appreciate it, served as a reassurance to me that my reactions to the Hindu culture-pattern were not merely subjective but reflected, however imperfectly, its own specific properties.

Despite its extreme difference in emphasis, life among the Bhils had certain elements in common with Hindu village life: and especially with that of the low-caste communities who form the majority of Hindu society. During the first six months of 1950, I had lived in a small hamlet in the northern extremity of Mewar. My hosts were all peasant farmers, members of the *Rawat* caste. Until a century ago, the Rawats were a bow and arrow tribe, with many cultural features in common with the Bhils. Now they aspire to the status of Rajputs, and profess their adherence to Hindu dharm. It was not until my later experiences in Deoli and Khajuria that I came to appreciate how incomplete this conversion to caste-Hindu values still remains.

Rawat customs, beliefs and rituals are in fact an intricate mix-up of tribal and Hindu elements. They practise blood-sacrifices to their Goddess: and not so long ago the sacrifice was of a buffalo—before that, it is said, of a bull calf; and before that again, of a male child. They are hunters, and prone to fighting among themselves. Marriage by elopement is not uncommon, although now disapproved, and widow remarriage is permitted. They worship all the gods of the Hindu pantheon, but their chief pre-occupation is with earthbound local deities, who enter into the bodies of their attendant *bhopas*, causing them to " play " in a convulsive form of dance, and to speak the god's words while they do so. The old ways assert themselves at the spring festival of Holi, when the Rawat men and women join in dancing *Gher*, which is akin to the Bhils' style of communal dance. On the third day after a death, Rawat mourners take a gift of food to the cremation ground as a gift to the soul of the dead. This is common Hindu practice: but the bearer of the Rawat's *sirauni* is followed by another man who carries a toy bow and arrow, to ward off evil spirits—and this has no counterpart in Hindu ritual.

If this blend of Hindu and primitive values and beliefs was conspicuous in the Rawats' culture, it was also apparent in varying degrees in the customs observed by the low-caste communities in Deoli. They too had blood-sacrifices, worshipped demons, allowed widow-remarriage. Like the Rawats, they ate cheap " heating " foods, and relished meat and liquor when they could afford them: but they had no tradition of a former alternative mode of life. They themselves acknowledged their inferior status in Hindu society and deplored those respects in which they failed to conform to the Brahmins' rules of orthodox behaviour.

It has long been known that the religious and social practices of low-caste communities present a mixture of Hindu and of other, pre-aryan elements. A fruitful opportunity for future research in culture-and-personality would appear to be indicated here: to assess the degree to which group personality-patterns in various lower-caste communities reflect the controlled, inhibited Hindu model on the one hand, and the spontaneous, violent ebullience of the tribal peoples on the other. Each such study, however, demands time and careful observation. Reverting to the theme from which this chapter has been a digression, it remains to consider the conclusions which emerge from the present observations on the personalities of high-caste Hindus of Deoli.

CHAPTER IX

HINDU PERSONALITY FORMATION
CONSCIOUS PROCESSES

In the preceding chapters an attempt has been made to delineate certain recurring patterns of behaviour, of belief and of emotional reaction which could be identified in the notes of my interviews with informants supplemented by actual observations of domestic life in Deoli. To have presented the data in this form already implies acceptance of the view that the individuals belonging to any culture will exhibit in their personalities certain regularities which are the heritage of their particular community, and which in turn can provide a key to the understanding of the psychological characteristics of that community as a whole. This view is the basis of a branch of anthropology which has come to be known as the study of Culture and Personality or (as Margaret Mead prefers to put it) of personality in culture.*

The concept of the integration of the diverse elements which are found in any culture has long had a place—though not an undisputed acceptance—in anthropological theory. Malinowski, who inaugurated a new era of research by carrying out field work of unprecedented thoroughness in the Trobriand Islands,† was the leading exponent of the functionalist point of view. He maintained that cultures are like living organisms, in which every part is meaningfully related to the functioning of the whole. Many subsequent field studies have demonstrated the functional integration of multiple elements in a society.‡

It has remained a matter of debate whether the regularities discernible in various cultures are the relatively fortuitous result of impersonal material and social influences, or whether they are intimately related to the psychological make-up of individuals who compose each society, and reflect their personal needs and affirmations. Many eminent anthropologists have shown themselves to be wary of attributing too much importance to a factor so elusive of definition as human personality.

* Mead, M. and Metraux, R. (1953), p. 18
† Malinowski, B. (1922, 1929)
‡ Examples are: Richards, A. I. (1939); Evans-Pritchard, E. (1945, 1949); Fortes, M. (1941)

Opler speaks for them when he asserts that " to borrow terms and concepts from art, psychology and philosophy may add flexibility and sparkle to the social scientist's descriptive offerings, but it has its limitations for serious analytical work ".*

More recently David Mandelbaum has marshalled the arguments which make him sceptical of attempts to base the interpretation of social forms upon predominantly psychological theories.†

It is noticeable, however, that interest in culture and personality studies is acute even among their critics, and this may be because they do, however imperfectly, advance a consistent theory to account for the existence of culture-patterns, and for the genesis of national character. This branch of anthropology is also one which has had a very wide appeal to the educated public: the early works of its leading exponents, Ruth Benedict and Margaret Mead ‡ reached a vast circulation. Both of these writers combine analytical insight with exceptional imaginative and literary gifts. Geoffrey Gorer, the leading British exponent of culture and personality is also a stylish writer—and perhaps this is no coincidence: he himself has suggested that for success in such studies " a quasi-aesthetic ability to recognise patterns is probably a pre-requisite ".§ He goes on, however, to emphasise that this aesthetic sensibility can be exercised to advantage only upon the basis of a thorough knowledge of a people's natural environment and their social structure.

The first step in attempting to analyse the social influences at work in personality formation must be to indicate those elements which operate " in the open ", for all to see. These are the processes involved in conscious learning, and in the acquisition of overt habits of behaviour (which may be picked up through involuntary imitation as well as through explicit instruction); but as will be shown in the next chapter, they are far from being the only ways in which a people's cultural heritage is transmitted.

Personality development stems from two sources, one being the individual's biological inheritance with its potentialities and limitations the other his learning experiences. The latter in turn may be considered as of two kinds: deliberate and

* Opler, M. E. (1945)   † Mandelbaum, D. (1953)
‡ Benedict, R. (1934); Mead, M. (1928), (1930), (1935), (1939)
§ Gorer, G. (1953), p. 62

involuntary. Of these, the first concerns the mastery of facts and of techniques, both practical and social, which have been consciously formulated and are explicitly conveyed to the growing child; the second includes a number of deep-seated convictions, held on emotional and not intellectual grounds, which have been conveyed implicitly in the constant give and take of relationships with the persons who loom largest in the infant's early years. The former correspond with the ideal patterns of cultural behaviour, and with the deviant patterns which are recognised by the community. The latter relate to the dynamic complexes into which instinctual drives are channelled during each individual's slow progress from dependent babyhood to maturity, complexes which find expression in his phantasy life, in his irrational quirks of behaviour, and in their concealed influence upon his supposedly rational decisions.

From the dynamic viewpoint the formal patterns of behaviour adopted by a community can also be regarded as defences against the expression of anti-social libidinal urges. The implicit, emotionally-charged influences are taken to be the more basic ones: certainly, a description of a culture which deals solely with its articulate ideal values is bound to be misleading—but the reverse is also true.

It is, of course, the work of psycho-analysts which has in recent years emphasised the importance of the unconscious promptings of behaviour, although recognition of the dualism of passion and reason, the rider and his steed, the Appollonian and the Dionysiac aspects of man's nature, is as old as philosophy itself. Freud was well aware of this duality. Because so much of his effort was directed to pointing out the unconscious elements in what people did and said, it tends to be forgotten that he also respected the proper function of rational control. This was made explicit in his therapeutic maxim: " Where Id was, let Ego be ": and in his abundant appreciation of literature and art it was not merely the exhibition of the artists' veiled libidinous urges which he admired, but the successful harnessing of these urges to provide a communicable and eloquent statement about experience.

Some psycho-analysts, in approaching the study of cultural phenomena, tend to minimise the importance of ideal patterns, of institutions, and of historical events as against the interpretation of unconscious instinctual drives whose operation can be seen most clearly in dreams, myths and phantasies, but which can also be shown to find veiled expression in the formal customs of a society. This is to forget that the Ego is no less a part of the personality than the Id; and that communication between these sides of a person's nature is a two-way process. Just as, in considering the individual, Ego-psychology as well as the elucidation of unconscious complexes must be taken into account, so it is with the analysis of cultures. A people's history represents its attempts to control its environment, its relations with neighbouring peoples, and its own unruly tendencies. Its institutions may have originated as " mechanisms of defence " in the psycho-analytic sense, but they assume a degree of stability and relative permanence which causes them to represent also an important part of the reality situation to which each new generation must learn to adapt.

The present chapter has a restricted purpose, namely, to indicate the sources in their environment from which my informants learned the consciously formulated facts, opinions and attitudes proper to their society. In order to emphasise that these " deliberate " influences continue to operate throughout their lives, I propose to reverse the usual order by first considering those experiences which occur latest in their adult career and then retracing the consecutive types of learning situation, back through adolescence to childhood. It will be appreciated that this division into periods and " areas of influence " is an abstraction from the real situation, in which the different spheres continually overlap one another.

To start at the periphery, then, with contemporary influences: by far the most important of these is the political transformation which has been taking place in Deoli, as throughout Rajasthan, since the Rajahs surrendered their absolute powers in favour of the democratically organised Congress government in 1948. This revolution was a bloodless one, carried through on behalf of, rather than by, the common people. In outlying districts the change of ruler meant very little to the ordinary people: their chief contact with authority was through the tax-collector, and he remained unchanged although under a different employer. In Deoli, however, because of the close integration of village society with the prestige of the Ruler in his castle, the change had profound repercussions. In 1951, the villagers were still groping their way in the new situation; it was becoming apparent only gradually that the Ruler's centuries-old position of dominance had come to an end, but as yet the characteristics of the new civil authorities were not understood. Within the village community, new foci of power were beginning to be recognised, not in the official *panchayat* or village council (which had not yet succeeded in commanding popular respect) but rather in the personal influence of a few wealthy and aggressive citizens.

These contemporary changes were the subject of constant debate, and they were discussed in the light of recent local history. For example, every government-inspired public meeting excited reminiscences of the Rajahs' prolonged hostility to Congress ideas, to Indian nationalist propaganda, and to the reformist teachings of Mahatma Gandhi, a hostility which had caused the several States of Rajasthan to lag far behind the rest of India in political education. It was remembered that only since 1940 had Congress views been discussed openly in Deoli, and that their first proponents (who included Gopi Lal and Vikram Singh) had run the risk of being beaten by the Ruler's servants. A small minority of the upper-caste villagers had ventured to identify themselves with the new ideas. They had attended meetings in neighbouring towns and had brought back news of the rapid growth of Congress influence there; but even now, in Deoli itself, a political meeting carried with it an atmosphere of bravado and defiance, which appealed especially to the younger men and boys.

In the innumerable informal discussions in which these changes were deliberated, a prominent part was taken by those men who had travelled abroad to do business or to find work in advanced cities like Bombay or Ahmedabad. Hitherto, village conservatism and the paralysing hand of palace rule had prevented these returned travellers from contributing anything new to the accepted way of life—as Bhagwat Singh put it: " Too many grey-beards, that's what's wrong with this place " —but now that rapid changes were taking place they were consulted as authorities on the new ways.

There were few in Deoli who could speak English, but this ability or, to a less degree, evidence of familiarity with Western inventions—such as electrical machinery, radios, gramophones, motor cars, wrist-watches and fountain pens—was displayed proudly and recognised as a mark of social distinction.

The impact of Western material culture upon the village was much less than in the town. Perhaps the most important feature was the daily bus service, passing the outskirts of Deoli. Its fitful progress and long delays protracted the journey to Udaipur to about four hours: but this still was a great advance in communications. In Hari Lal's youth, this had been a day's journey, calling for the engagement of armed guards to see the travellers safely through a bandit-infested pass.

A conspicuous demonstration of Western technology was given to the village when the Ruler of Deoli installed an electricity plant in his palace, in order to add to the magnificence of his sister's wedding; but for some years it had lain in disuse. His was the only house in which bright lights burned at night; the others might borrow or hire a Petromax for special occasions, but were content with frugal oil-wick lamps for the rest. The only radio was in the palace, and it was usually out of order. The ruler and the Ayurvedic physician were the only persons who subscribed to periodicals. In the bazaar, a few young men liked to show off their European-style trousers, jackets and shoes, but soon found that here this dress was not admired as in the cities but rather despised. European shirts, however, worn with the tails flapping over pyjamas or a *dhoti* were now a usual form of dress. Many of the villagers had seen films in the nearby towns, and were familiar with the sound of popular Indian dance music blaring from radio loudspeakers in the bazaars there, but only the young men seemed to hanker after these novelties.

The detailed impacts of recent social, economic and political changes are too diverse to be enumerated, but they fall under two heads: those challenging the established authority of the old order, calling into question religious and caste rules of conduct; and those offering opportunities (in new occupations, in business and administration and in politics itself) for social mobility never known before.

The current political changes were a reflection of the passing of two long-established types of authority, that of the Rajahs and that of the British Raj. Each of these had made their mark in popular lore. History, as known in the village, was concerned with the rule of Rajput princes, stretching back through historical events like the storming of the village fortress, the battle of nearby Haldi Ghat and the fortunes of the ruling house of Udaipur, to become continuous with legendary anecdotes drawn from the Ramayana or Mahabharata. Informants often described stories in which the Gods entered and played an active part. They explained that this used to be a common occurrence but now, because the world has entered into *kalyug*, the era of deceit, such interventions have become rare.*

* It was a shrewd political calculation which, in 1951-52, during the first general elections ever to be held in Rajasthan, inspired the conservative Rajput Mahasabha to describe itself as the Ram-Raj Party. This conjured up an ideal picture of just and pious government, as when Ram Chandarji

The fame of some of the outstanding Ranas of Mewar lives on in popular anecdotes inspiring Rajputs and other castes alike with a vicarious pride in their chivalry and heroism. This was seen both in the palace, where Charans intoned their heroic ballads, and also in the village school where children of all castes learned locally-patriotic songs. The Mewar culture-hero is Rana Partab, whose life history is as well-known here as is that of King Robert the Bruce in Scottish villages—and in a similarly romanticised version.

In addition to their familiarity with local history and legend, my informants were aware of a community of interest with all fellow-Hindus: but this was expressed in terms of religious rather then of political values. It was made evident in shared recognition of the gods and goddesses of the Hindu pantheon. Identification with their wider community was given expression in the throngs which assembled at holy festivals; and remote parts of India were known by name because of their sacred associations. On the other hand, until the present day the concept of a single government representing and ruling the whole of India has not been part of popular history. In the epics of the past, there was no single supreme ruler, but only Rajahs contending among themselves for a temporary ascendancy. It was left to the Moghuls and subsequently the British to introduce a centralised administration. It may have been for this reason that so many country people, in 1951, still found it difficult to believe that India had really achieved self-rule. One old blind blacksmith asked me if it were true that the British had left Delhi. When told that this was so, he thought deeply and then said: " I suppose, then, the Moghuls are in power again." He remained politely incredulous of my assertion that the Government was Indian now. Others were prone to believe rumours that the British had come back, or that American or Russian troops were about to invade their country.

This indifference to politics and sense of remoteness from the " Raj ", or government, was undoubtedly accentuated in Deoli, as in other villages of Rajasthan, because of their forced isolation from the " freedom movement " so long as the Rajahs were in power. Elsewhere in India political consciousness and fervent nationalism have for long been synonymous with popular education: but in Deoli they still carry the excitement

ruled on earth. It did not, however, completely succeed in swaying the electorate although the opposition parties led by Ram-Raj held the Congress to a very narrow majority of novelty—which condemns them in the eyes of the elders of the village.

The years of remote British rule left, in Rajasthan as elsewhere in India, a legacy of improved communications, of a bureaucratically-organised civil service and educational system, and the Indian Penal Code. These Western institutions were subtly Indianised, and yet they never lost their alien quality. As a result every detail of civil, or railway or postal administration had to be carried out with rigid adherence to the written regulations. The Penal Code came nearest to being assimilated, perhaps because it lent itself to the prevailing passion for litigation. In Mewar, the expression: *Wuh pakka char-sau-bis hai*—" He's a regular 420 ", had passed into the vernacular, 420 being the Section of the Code under which people were charged with " loitering with nefarious intent ". Other Sections, such as 307 (" attempted murder ") and 336 (" aggravated assault ") were freely bandied about in village gossip.

The contemporary political and economic changes were thus being assimilated in a process of referring them constantly to what had gone before, whether in public meetings or in the daily gossip of the bazaar. They represent instances of new learning imposed upon adults and children of all castes alike. Religion also was feeling the impact of change, though a more gradual one. The older men agreed that in their lifetime they had seen a casting-off of many religious restrictions, and deplored the process, which still continues.

Religion is not taught systematically, but rather is picked up piecemeal. As in the West, most people are content to leave philosophy and theology to those who have a professional interest in those subjects, and rub along with an imprecise, unsystematised collection of beliefs. The most basic of these concern the inevitability of fate, the need to acquiesce in all that comes, calling upon God's name. This is learned from the repeated examples of older men's sayings. More specific beliefs are picked up as a result of listening to the songs in praise of particular gods and goddesses which are sung at their several feast days and to the dissertation with which they are accompanied. As an onlooker at the temple, the villager soon learns the gestures of obeisance, and the modes of address proper to these gods. Sometimes he will have an opportunity to listen to a Brahmin reading aloud from the sacred poems (which only members of the three high castes are supposed to hear); sometimes he may see incidents from the Ramayana or Mahabharata enacted in popular versions by travelling players. Part of this religious life is common to all, but much of it is conducted separately in each caste's *panchayati nohera* or meeting place. That of the Brahmins was in a Vishnu temple; the Banias had two noheras, each a miniature caravanserai with rooms to accommodate those of their wandering " saints " who elected to stay in Deoli during the four months of the rains. Rajputs met together in the Ruler's palace, and each of the lesser castes had a temple of their own which was their place of assembly.

As they showed in their conversations with me, each villager in this way came to acquire the fundamentals of Hindu belief, which are epitomised in the concepts of *karma, dharma* and *moksh*.* They knew without question that their life was only one of a long series of re-births, that they must conform to right behaviour in order to advance their spiritual progress towards the desired aim of Release; and they knew that the hierarchy of castes and the gradations of sub-human life are a reflection of the soul's progress in working out its karma. They learned to accept a time-scale, and an impersonal ordering of existence which minimised the importance of individual existences; and to regard the material world as *maya*, a shifting illusion. In this teaching morality was linked with abstinence, with celibacy, and with a disengagement from desire of sensual or emotional gratification. Selflessness and equanimity were the qualities which they came to identify with progress in the religious life. In repeated instances they were told that the way to enlist divine help is to abase oneself unreservedly before God and to call on him with faith—because such an entreaty, if it is earnest enough, never remains unanswered.

Besides these shared elements of Hindu doctrine, each caste had social and moral rules of its own. In former years, the conferences of all male members of each caste were most important. It was here that joint decisions were taken, and these meetings had the power to out-caste offenders against their accepted customs—a very potent sanction. Nowadays, however, such caste-decisions no longer have the force of law, and formal assemblies seldom take place; but still, when a crisis occurs, or when many members of a caste are assembled for a wedding or a funeral feast, matters of common interest are

* Karma: The sum of a person's actions in one of his successive incarnations, regarded as determining his fate in the next; hence ineluctable fate or destiny
Dharma: Religious Law; duty; right conduct
Moksh: Release from the cycle of rebirth

discussed, and the expression of the elders' disapproval is still something to be reckoned with. On a smaller scale every meeting of several adult members of one caste is made the occasion for reviewing current events in the light of caste values. Listening to these repeated deliberations, children and young men become familiarised with the prejudices and prerogatives of their respective caste groups.

Acceptance of one's place in the caste system was unquestioning. It was a part of the order of nature. As a consequence of this, there was little room for ambition. A Rajput might be (and generally was) proud of the reputation of his clan; but only rarely could he hope to add to it with a conspicuous feat of valour. A Bania might hope to amass a fortune and to have his death celebrated with prodigiously meritorious feasts, but he would always remain a merchant: whereas a Brahmin was born already a god, and his only ambition was to attain Release. The new non-hereditary occupations cut across these old forms, but in the village at least each person has the assurance of knowing that if he refuses to compete, preferring to conform to his traditional caste role, he will be able to perform a task which is not exacting and can rely on the approval, and ultimately the support of his fellows even though his material rewards may be pitifully small. The old system puts a premium on conformity at the expense of personal initiative: the individual achieves integration and stability in his life habits by adhering to the pattern of his enveloping society, rather than by asserting his own personality.

At the lower end of this scale, the caste-meeting becomes a conference of members of an extended family. In these family gatherings—as indeed in every kind of meeting—children are not excluded but wander in and out among the guests, sometimes sitting to listen, sometimes playing and chattering or lying down to sleep. They are expected from an early age to show respect and obedience towards their elders. Now and again, when they get in the way, they are sternly told to be quiet and behave, but for the most part they are ignored. As onlookers, they see demonstrated the proper greetings, the forms of address to be used towards each class of relation, and in the repetitious talk they learn to recognise the approved behaviour expected from each member of the family group. In contrast, and frequently in conflict with this sphere of caste is the influence of new, foreign (and therefore casteless) roles and occupations in Westernised industries and public services. Although few villagers have yet been able to enter them, these careers offer unprecedented opportunities for social mobility to members of all but the lowest castes; but they introduce new complexities at the same time—such as fixed wage rates, competition for promotion, and the envied prestige of self-made men. The mere possibility of being able to " make good " in the big cities has already destroyed much of that sense of inevitability which was formerly a mainstay of the caste system.

For the majority of men whose education will not proceed beyond a few years at the village school the most important part of their learning occurs within the extended family. Sometimes a father will personally instruct his son in his own calling. This is seen most often among the Banias, a son helping in his father's shop for several years and continuing to receive advice and supervision thereafter, if he sets up in business on his own. Among Rajputs and Brahmins, this is not the rule. The restraint between fathers and sons is such that it is found preferable to leave it to others to act as the boys' instructors, though their fathers will watch their progress jealously. The inhibition of any open expression of affection between father and son means that the former's instructions are usually negatively phrased, in terms of admonition and reproach rather than of encouragement. In particular, there is a reiteration of the demand to be controlled in behaviour, never to betray spontaneous emotions—" like animals "—until this is firmly impressed upon the growing boy. To a Western observer, high-caste Hindu children seem unnaturally well-behaved.*

In family life, as in religion, great stress is laid on submission, resignation and obedience. Emotional relationships are played down, but one's obligations towards other family members are underlined. Security consists, within the family as in the society as a whole, in an acceptance of one's limited role with the knowledge that all one's kin will participate in every crisis of one's life.

Formerly (and still to some extent), a Rajput boy's tutor in riding, use of weapons and in pride of social position, would be a Rajput feudal subordinate, or lower-caste servants of his family, and a Brahmin pandit would come to instruct him in book-learning; whereas a Brahmin boy might be sent away from home, to an uncle's house or to the *ashram* of a religious

---

* Dr. Lois Murphy, viewing Indian children with the insight of an authority upon Western child psychology, remarked upon their smiling spontaneity in infancy and their relative unresponsiveness, and lack of initiative in later childhood. (G. and L. B. Murphy, 1952, p. 48)

teacher for several years. Today, however, all castes except the lowest meet in the same class of the village school, and are equipped, if they pursue their studies long enough, for the new clerical, commercial and administrative posts which are replacing the old hereditary forms of employment.

In Deoli a public school has been in existence for some fifteen years. Here children are indirectly exposed to Western ideas, because both the principles and the content of the teaching curriculum were inspired by the example of the British educational system, upon which the Indian schools were based. This was evident in the bias in favour of practical accomplishments—still, the apparent aim of the majority of students who reach matriculation is to become government clerks—and received open expression in the fact that higher students trained for the " Cambridge entrance " examination. Even so, certain peculiarly Hindu modifications entered the system: for example children were taught to know the names, and to admire the example, not only of celebrated teachers of Hinduism, but also of the Buddha, of Mahommed and of Jesus Christ. It is open to question whether an equal degree of tolerance is inculcated in classes of religious instruction in the West. Because the school is now an institution of the Congress government, and its teachers are for the most part " new men ", the curriculum emphasises national history and new ideals of social progress and reform.

During playtime at school, and in the neighbourhood gangs of his playfellows, a boy rehearses those items of adult learning which he is in the process of making his own; and he also debates those topics which he has overheard, but which his elders will never directly discuss with him—such as sex, and childbirth, and the exciting connotations of swear words. According to several of my informants, sexual play and experimentation, both homo- and heterosexual, was common among pre-pubertal children when they were young, and is no less common now; but it is always concealed from their elders, who would not approve of it.

Although it is particularly through his participation in the adult male world of caste and family discussions that a child receives the imprint of his community's values, the process has begun even before this, during his earliest years when he spent more time in the women's side of the household than in the men's. Brahmins commonly mentioned that it was their mother, or their grandmother, who first impressed upon them the need to bathe if they touched a low-caste person, until the response became second nature to them. It is women, also, who give a boy his early toilet training, first by attending to his needs and later by teaching him how to cleanse himself. In later years he comes to see that this learning is especially related to his high-caste status. From his mother and his substitute-mothers, a boy learns also how and what to eat, how to dress, what constitutes good manners and what is to be avoided as indecent or shameful. Their example as well as their warnings impress upon him the obligation to defer unconditionally to the male head of his family. Even in families where the husbands were reputed to be bullied by their wives, the public behaviour of each member of the household always confirmed to the " proper " pattern.

From his mother, grandmothers and aunts a child learns the concrete details of religious observance at all the multitude of holy days in the calendar. Women are said to be more conservative than men, and to insist on the performance of such duties. A part of the experience of every child in Deoli is to be taken by his mother to a *bhopa* when he is sick: he is made familiar from an early age with the belief in possession by witches and evil spirits, and in their exorcism by the power of the mother-goddess. As he grows older, the possibility of such occurrences will be confirmed by the magical healers who are consulted in cases of sickness in the family. From them, as from all his older relatives, he will learn of the many supernatural dangers believed to exist in his surroundings, and how to circumvent them.

The child's sources of verbal instruction can now be viewed as a series of concentric circles, the innermost representing the women's world; then that of the extended family in which his father, if himself a younger son, may seem to play a minor part. Through the family come contacts with village neighbours, in their respective caste roles, and with religious and magical beliefs which are shared in common with them; then comes the contact with the wider network of kinsmen which becomes evident at times of family crisis such as a wedding or a death, and finally, with the interests of the caste as a whole. As he grows older, goes to school, and mingles in the life and play outside his home, he acquires the historical, religious and social knowledge and prejudices which are the common heritage of his fellow-villagers and shares their experience of having to adjust to the changing times.

Besides these " areas of influence ", the process of deliberate learning can also be considered as occurring in three temporal stages. The first is a gentle prelude, because very small children are not forced or scolded, are not held responsible for their actions until " they begin to understand ". This dawn of understanding is believed to occur when the child can speak a few words, and respond to simple instructions; and this coincides more or less with his weaning at some time between one and a half and two and a half years of age. From now on, verbal demands and social expectations become somewhat more insistent, but a small boy is still regarded as irresponsible until he begins to perform an adult role, which happens much sooner in India than in the West; children of seven or eight commence to help with adult tasks. In Brahmin and Rajput families this is formalised by the ceremony of adoption of the sacred thread, after which any breach of caste rules is regarded as a serious matter. A Bania youth demonstrates his " putting away childish things " by working long hours in the family shop and by displaying an appropriately serious attention to money matters. The final step towards adulthood consists not in his marriage, which may be arranged early or late according to the state of his family's finances, but in his becoming the father of a son.

Every aspect of orthodox Hindu society is well integrated and yet retains its conscious formal rules, so that the complex interactions of economic and ritual relationships can be demonstrated with great clarity.* Similarly, attitudes towards each other, towards the social order, and towards the supernatural are all explicitly formulated. The cumulative effect of these learned attitudes upon the adult personality was discussed some years ago by a Western scholar who had lived and worked in Madhya Pradesh, a state adjacent to Rajasthan.† Basing his analysis upon the explicit values to which high-caste Hindus subscribe, Dr. Taylor gives a penetrating account of the inter-relations of Hindu patterns of custom and belief, stressing the impersonality of a social order where status and formal obligations outweigh personal relationships. There is little in his argument with which I would quarrel, and yet I believe that it is possible to take the analysis a stage further.

Dynamic theories of development assume that adult personality structure has its roots in emotional events and relationships which precede by several years the capacity to

* As has been done for example by Opler and Singh (1948), by Srinivas (1952), by Dube (1954) and by the contributors to *Indian Village*, edited by McKim Marriott (1955)
† Taylor, W. S. (1948)

define concepts in rational terms. These emotional relationships are formed in a child's first years of life, and they determine in large part his patterns of response in his subsequent encounters with people and events. They can be recognised most clearly when he is behaving irrationally, or indulging in phantasy: and once recognised, they can be shown to underlie a great deal of his apparently rational activities and beliefs as well.

It would be absurd indeed for me to claim to have fully comprehended the emotional springs of motivation of this group of high-caste Hindus after so short and so relatively superficial an acquaintance with them and their community. Nevertheless, I believe that I did find clues to a number of deep-seated emotional complexes, shared by most if not all of my informants: and in the next chapter I shall attempt to elucidate them. I approach the task with caution, as an alien interpreter must, but emboldened by the realisation that my own personal psycho-analysis has revealed that I share not only the same mother-tongue as my informants but some at least of their characteristic unconscious phantasies as well. Before outlining these basic phantasies, however, it is necessary to discuss the theory of personality development upon which their interpretation is based.

CHAPTER X

HINDU PERSONALITY FORMATION
UNCONSCIOUS PROCESSES

A CHILD's learning begins long before it can talk. Indeed it is likely that the learning which occurs during its first two years to a large extent lays down those patterns of expectation and response by which we recognise an individual's personality. During the earliest years the child's intelligence is gradually developing—prompted, so Piaget maintains, by social stimulation—but its feelings are from the very outset intense, though at first undifferentiated. Later on, the habit of rationalisation will intervene to an increasing extent between perception and feeling and between feeling and response: the innocent eye of childhood will be dimmed, and the spontaneity of young children will be succeeded by the deliberation and self-consciousness of their elders.

This intervention of rational categories serves a protective as well as a useful purpose. It is useful because verbal concepts make possible the learning of new techniques of mastery over persons and things; and it is protective because cerebral control damps down, if it does not altogether inhibit, feelings which can be painfully strong. Nevertheless, the life of feeling continues its subterranean existence, finding expression in emotional response to people, to nature, and to works of art, and in phantasies and dreams. In adult life feeling-responses tend to be subordinated to deliberate, rational behaviour; but on closer examination this behaviour is often found to be merely a disguised expression of emotional reactions.

These irrational, emotionally determined quirks of behaviour and response are not wholly arbitrary. They are found to recur in many different contexts; and when studied carefully they reveal a pattern and an interconnectedness in which the connections are not necessarily logical but in many cases symbolical, and only subjectively meaningful. In order to interpret them correctly intellectual understanding of the facts of an informant's situation is not enough; one has in addition to empathise, to "feel with" him before one can identify his elusive patterns of emotional response. Once identified, these emotional syndromes can provide the key to the understanding of both individual and group personality.

This is the point at which students of culture and personality part company with those psychologists and anthropologists who refuse on principle to go beyond facts which can be objectively demonstrated and quantified: and yet the antithesis between these methods is not complete. The employment of aesthetic sensibility in order to recognise emotional sequences in a person's (or a people's) thinking and behaviour does not preclude the subsequent use of systematic observation and measurement in order to verify or modify predictions to which these empathically-identified concepts have given rise.

Since Ruth Benedict's pioneering work there have been several outstanding examples of the interpretation of national character. Among others might be mentioned the studies of the Balinese by Bateson and Mead, of the American Indians by Erik Erikson, of the Americans by Mead and Gorer, of the Japanese by Benedict, of the Germans by Dicks and by Schaffner, of the Russians by Dicks and Gorer, the work of Roheim and Kardiner, and the group of studies reported by Mead and Métraux.*

Although diverse in content, these works are united by certain assumptions held in common by their authors: that the key to understanding national character lies in the study of processes in the personality development of individuals; that events which occur in the earliest stages of human psychological maturation have an enduring influence throughout later life; and that dynamic psychology provides the best available theory for the elucidation of personality development. These assumptions are also basic to the interpretations of Hindu personality development advanced in the present book.

In attempting to understand the outlook of an alien people, an ever more comprehensive knowledge of the *facts* about their language, history, geography, economics, social structure and religion can take us only part of the way. Sooner or later we come up against the realisation that these facts mean something different to them and to us. In order fully to understand a people's " otherness " we must try to grasp the essence of these distortions; and this involves a recognition of subjective emotional factors in their personalities—and in our own.

* Benedict (1934); Bateson and Mead (1942); Erikson (1950); Mead (1942); Gorer (1948); Benedict (1946); Dicks (1950); Schaffner (1948); Dicks (1952); Gorer (1949); Roheim (1932, 1934); Kardiner (1939, 1945); Mead and Métraux (1953)

Each people has a characteristic " style " of thinking and of personal interaction, and this is not fortuitous: it is due to the continuance, in the unconscious mind of each member of the society, of certain emotionally significant phantasies which were formed in early infant life. Group character can be interpreted and understood only when the underlying phantasies upon which it is based are brought to consciousness. In a personal psycho-analysis the focus is upon the unique idiosyncratic elements in each patient's pattern of phantasies; in the study of national character, on the other hand, it is the communally-shared phantasies which demand attention.

Human phantasy life can be compared to an unfamiliar script which is still in the process of being interpreted. Its cryptograms have been present since the beginnings of history, in the form of myths and legends, dreams, superstitions and fairy tales. These ciphers have always been regarded as significant because they were strangely moving although no one knew why. It was Freud who first succeeded in deciphering them and spelling out what they mean. Using psycho-analytic theory as the key, it is now possible to chart the basic phantasies found in the emotional life of individuals, and of communities.

The process whereby infantile phantasies come to underlie adult personality is closely analogous to the way in which a child learns to talk. A baby's first utterances are formless cries prompted by feelings of hunger and discomfort, and the relief of his discomfort leads him to return to silence, and to sleep. Within a few weeks, however, wakefulness begins to play a larger part in the infant's life. He begins to chuckle, to burble and to crow as well as to cry. At this stage there is a very wide range of meaningless sounds (many of them rather attractive) which he can and does utter; but during his first year he becomes increasingly interested in using this gift of utterance in order to communicate with those nearest to him, particularly his mother. At first their communication is in " meaningful sounds " rather than in words, but already at this stage he finds that the great majority of the sounds which he *can* utter are useless as means of communication—because his mother-tongue, like every human language, has selected a quite restricted number of these many possible utterances and regards only these as being meaningful. These are described as phonemes, and constitute the basic elements of sound of which the language is composed.

Already in 1911 the linguist and anthropologist Franz Boas had enunciated these principles of phonetic analysis: (1) that the total number of sounds that may be found as one proceeds from language to language is unlimited; but (2) that every single language has a definite and limited group of sounds, none of which is excessively large.*

This restriction of the gamut of " available " utterances gives each language its individual cadence and imposes upon all those whose mother-tongue it is, a style of articulation which is recognisable even when they speak in another language. It is a matter of every-day experience that one can often identify a Norwegian, a Hungarian, a West African, an Indian or a Scot by the characteristic accent which each one brings to the speaking of English. By means of phonetic analysis one can identify with some precision the repertoire of sounds to which each speaker's utterances are habitually restricted, and can predict the characteristic transpositions which will occur when he talks a language other than his own.

Clearly one begins to acquire one's native phoneme-pattern even before one has learned to talk. At an equally early age, the ground-work is laid for defining the pattern of one's future style of emotional response. As with speech, so with emotional relationship: a child's earliest experiences occur in relation to his mother. In the earliest weeks, before she can be comprehended as a separate being, the infant's phantasies are dominated by what looms largest in his experience, namely his internal feelings of hunger or satiety and the physical presence of his mother's breast and supporting arms which are so closely associated with these alternating states of feeling.

More than any other psycho-analyst, Melanie Klein † has succeeded in demonstrating the importance of the child's adaptation to these, its earliest object-relationships, in determining the tenor of its later relationships and its future capacity for constructive activity and self-expression. She has shown that even in early infancy phantasy begins to operate, not in a formless manner but in rather concrete terms, endowing the first objects which the infant is able to perceive with magical powers to succour or to harm.

In principle there is no limit to the range of possible phantasies (just as there is no limit to the range of possible utterances) but in practice children reiterate a comparatively small number of phantasies over and over again. Mrs. Klein believes that certain symbols are innate in the child's unconscious mind, just as sucking and grasping reflexes are present from birth, but that the majority of sequences of phantasy are

* Boas, F. (1911), pp. 15-16   † Klein, M. (1927, 1952, 1955)

alike because they take their cues from similar sequences of events in the give-and-take of the relationship between mothers and young children.

Applying Mrs. Klein's theory of early infantile phantasy to the study of group character, I would contend that in the first and second years of life children acquire certain *nuclear phantasies* which underlie and determine their future modes of reaction to events and to people encountered in later life. In any social group these nuclear phantasies tend to remain consistent and similar because they are transmitted unconsciously from mother to child in the context of feeling and behaviour characteristic of the nursing relationship: and this is a context which, at least in non-Western communities, is extremely resistant to change.

Just as the phoneme-pattern of its mother tongue imposes on each people, and even on each regional group, a particular accent which will always be distinguishable in its speech, so the sharing of similar nuclear phantasies in infancy will give rise to common characteristics in a people's adult " style of reaction ". This is the justification for the belief that the key to an understanding of group character lies in elucidating a community's shared infantile phantasies.

The remainder of this chapter is accordingly devoted to a discussion of some of the basic phantasies which appeared to be shared by my informants in Deoli, and of their possible influence upon Hindu personality formation.

A high-caste Hindu presents a seeming triumph of deliberate self-control over spontaneous impulse. This is conspicuously the case with the religious ascetic, who learns to subordinate all sensual promptings to his deliberate aim of cultivating non-attachment; but it is also seen in the decorous, restrained behaviour to which all adults aspire. Behind this façade, however, irrational impulses are at work, betraying themselves indirectly in a number of ways—for example, in a man's attitude towards his wife, and women in general.

Ideally, woman is regarded as a wholly devoted, self-forgetful mother, or as a dutifully subservient wife, who is ready to worship her husband as her lord. In fact, however, women are regarded with an alternation of desire and revulsion. Sexual love is considered the keenest pleasure known to the senses: but it is felt to be destructive to a man's physical and spiritual well-being. Women are powerful, demanding, seductive—and ultimately destructive. On the plane of creative phantasy, everyone worships the Mataji, the Goddess, who is a protective mother to those who prostrate themselves before her in abject supplication, but who is depicted also as a sort of demon, with gnashing teeth, who stands on top of her male adversary, cuts off his head and drinks his blood. This demon-goddess has the same appearance as a witch—and that brings her nearer home, because *any* woman whose demands one has refused is liable to be feared as a witch who may exact terrible reprisals.

In endeavouring to interpret these implicit emotional reactions to women in general, one looks to the child's first relationship with a woman, with his mother: because the feelings associated with that relationship will frame the expectations with which he approaches all subsequent heterosexual relationships. What I found in Deoli was that Hindu children, almost without exception, begin life with an abundantly rewarding experience. During their first year, they are never separated from their mothers for more than a short time, and they are given the breast generously, whenever they feel hungry or upset. An infant's mother is his willing slave, and he becomes something of a tyrant. This pattern of mothering is if anything too good. Child analysis in the West suggests that infants may be alarmed by their own seeming omnipotence, fearing that the bullied mother may one day turn and rend them (like the devouring witch) in retaliation for their own momentarily intense wishes to destroy her by biting and eating her up. In the West a child experiences greater amounts of deprivation, in the cause of " training ", and is able to test out his fits of hostility towards his mother, taking reassurance from the fact that she not only survives them, but still loves him. In the Hindu family, because he experiences so little frustration, the child develops an assurance that support and succour will never be denied him—hence his constant (and even unrealistic) optimism in later life—but his aggressive phantasies remain rudimentary, imperious and unmodified by the experience of minor deprivations—until, at the age of 1½ or 2, new experiences occur with bewildering rapidity.

Already, before this, the child will have cause to notice that his mother, though devoted to his service, is unaccountably inconstant in the warmth of her contact with him. At times she caresses him affectionately while at other times owing to the presence of her parents-in-law she becomes aloof and seemingly indifferent to him. Sometimes also he will have known what it is to have this monopoly of his mother usurped by his father, when the latter begins to claim his wife again.

Hitherto he has always slept beside his mother but now his father literally takes his place. At this time, too, the child is weaned. He has for many months been given increasing amounts of adult food and drink, so that the weaning is not a physiological hardship; but it represents a withdrawal and a reversal of his mother's previous unquestioning devotion to his needs. Coming at this point it adds to the feeling of rejection by his loved and dominated mother. When his mother resumes her menstrual functions and becomes periodically " unclean " this impurity is not believed to endanger small children; but as the child grows older he has to learn to avoid his mother at such times as one who is mysteriously dangerous, like the blood-stained demon-goddess Durga (whose name means " Unapproachable "). Other sorts of learning also crowd in upon the small boy, because now that he is beginning to be able to speak and to " understand " he ceases to be the inarticulate tyrant of the household and instead becomes the recipient of numerous instructions and mock threats.

I suggest that this relatively late reversal of a previously dominating (although emotionally inconsistent) relationship with his mother has a profound effect upon the child's later development. The underlying mistrust which seems to cloud so many of my informants' adult personal relationships may well be derived from the phantasy of a fickle mother who mysteriously withholds her caresses and attentions from time to time; but at weaning the child's emotional insecurity is suddenly intensified. Earlier experience has created in his phantasy a bias in favour of the feeling that things will come right in the end (the breast will not long be withheld) but now the two most certain-seeming facts of life—the mother's constant support and the child's own omnipotence—suddenly prove unreliable. It is as if he were accustomed again and again to climb a certain step and then suddenly found the step no longer there. His confidence is shattered and from now on he mistrusts everything that pretends to constancy—his own and others' personalities, and even objects in the material world. To such a feeling the concept of all-pervading Maya seems appropriate, if not inevitable.

In contrast with the Western child whose familiarity with intermittent experiences of frustration and delayed satisfaction has enabled him to indulge his aggressive phantasies in moderation, only to be reassured by his mother's renewed affectionate attentions, this desertion on the part of his mother seems a final one. In his phantasy she becomes someone terrible, revengeful, bloodthirsty and *demanding* in the same limitless way as the formerly imperious child. As the Goddess, she is seen as a horrific figure, decapitating men and drinking their blood. In order to appease her fury she must be placated with offerings, but what is more important, she must be appealed to in an attitude of complete submission. She becomes kind and rewarding, a mother again and no longer a demon, only when one has surrendered one's manhood and become a helpless infant once again. Significantly, as will be shown below, the offering proper to the Mataji consists of the symbolic castration of a male animal, whose blood she drinks. This may be the source of the feeling that sexual intercourse represents a victory for the woman, who must be served when she demands it, and a castrating of the man—because with every issue of semen he loses virtue and manly strength at the same time.

The most widely known of all forms of the Goddess is that which depicts her as Kali the black she-demon, naked, four-armed, wearing a garland of the heads of giants, dancing on the breast of her prostrate consort, Mahakala, who is Lord Shiv. In this context, the child's father is seen as a fellow-victim of this mother-figure who is at once an object of adoration and of fear.

Hitherto his father has been a relatively unimportant figure in his life—in most families, as we have seen, fathers refrain from " making much of " their infants—but now he becomes intensely significant, sometimes as a fellow-victim, sometimes as the towering rival whose intervention has destroyed his former blissful state. From this time on his father's voice will be associated with commands which must be obeyed. The pain of defeat by the father in the oedipal situation is greatly intensified by the frequency with which the child is an involuntary witness of parental intercourse. It is not lightened, as in the West by the creation of a warm relationship between father and son. This has been prevented by the taboo upon the father's giving expression to affectionate feelings for his child. Instead, it appears to the boy that he has no choice other than that of unconditional surrender before this strong intruding stranger, his father. He must not only submit before this rival, but must deny any wish to compete with him. This is clearly reflected in the Hindu's later attitude towards his fellow men. To his father, and to figures of authority in general he owes unquestioning obedience. He is obliged in their presence to suppress all indications that he may lead an adult sexual life, and by extension he has to stifle every manifestation of his spontaneity and emotional responsiveness. In effect all those who occupy the status of sons or younger brothers are required to enact a symbolic self-castration, denying themselves the right to lead an emotional or sexual life of their own so long as the father-figures still live and dominate them. This is implicit in the Hindus' willing subservience to autocratic Rajahs, to the rich, and to important officials. " Rais hain ", they say: " They are the lordly ones", and they submit.

On the other hand he expects a similar unquestioning subservience from all who are below him in rank and authority. This self-castration is the fundamental Hindu attitude towards the father, though it is not, as I shall indicate below, the only one.

There is a corollary to this catastrophic reversal of the infant's early blissful situation. In order to recapture it in phantasy he must become a helpless child again as he does when prostrating himself before the Mother-Goddess; and this is also the essence of a Hindu's attitude towards his father and his Guru, and in his religious worship. In each of these situations he stresses on the one hand his utter helplessness, his unlimited appeal, and on the other his ruthless suppression of his own sexuality, and with it all his sensual gratifications. When confronted with this complete surrender, the deity, the father and the Guru are compelled to offer help; the tyranny of early childhood reasserts itself. This is seen also in the universal compulsion, in Hindu society, to give alms when they are begged. People give to beggars not because they enjoy giving (though for some it can be a pleasure as well as a duty) but because they feel intensely uncomfortable and guilty if they fail to do so; and this occurs not only in public, when they might be thought to be coerced by social pressure (as we feel obliged to conform with our neighbours on flag days) but also in their private thoughts.

Infants do not have a monopoly of infantile phantasy, which reveals itself in adults in similar irrational feelings. Fathers can be unwittingly jealous of their small sons, as well as sons of their fathers.

It may well be the father's guilt at his suppressed hostility to his infant rival which obliges him to overcompensate for this, in accepting his obligation to support his son, provided the latter has demonstrated his complete submission.*

* Cf. p. 179 below, Rajendra Singh's unguarded reference to wringing his child's neck

If the supplicant's self-punitive attitude can be maintained with great intensity, as in the accounts of holy men who have practised severe austerities, it is believed that a magical result is ultimately obtained. The ascetic is rewarded in three ways —with omnipotence in face of which even the Gods, the ultimate father-figures, are powerless; with a sense of bliss, which is like sexual satisfaction, but even more intense; and finally with release from separate self-hood, back into the nothingness of union with the creator-spirit of the universe. These rewards can be interpreted respectively as the regaining of infantile omnipotence, and so triumphing over the authority of one's father; as resuming possession of one's mother with the intense gratification of infantile sexuality; and as the return to the dark mindless "togetherness" of prenatal existence. In *Samadhi*, the saint has by the progressive annihilation of all external and internal distracting stimuli, achieved the feat of voluntary regression to the prenatal state before his first encounter with the outside world. He is lowered into a pit, the womb of earth, and once enclosed there he lives for ever unchanging in a timeless bliss of union with his creator: a triumph of phantasy over the reality-scene.

I have already suggested that it is in the seeming "betrayal" by a child's mother that we must seek the explanation of the lack of empathy, and the prevailing uncertainty of mind which so forcibly impressed me in Deoli; but it is in his accommodation to the stress of intense oedipal rivalry with his father, that the pattern of his adult paranoid trends can be discerned. According to Freudian theory, paranoid reactions can be traced to one type of outcome of the Oedipus situation,* namely that in which the boy assumes a passive role and in phantasy has a homosexual love-relationship with his father. But while he longs to be possessed in this way, the child also fears and repudiates his desire; hence the transition from "I love him", through "I hate him", to "He hates me", on which delusions of persecution are based.

Already in my informants' phantasies the father has been seen as a fellow-victim of the witch-goddess-mother; but there is also a powerfully-repressed homosexual fixation on the father. This is shown not only in the ever-recurring paranoid reactions, but also, in indirect and sublimated form, in a man's feelings toward his Guru—the one context in which a warm affectionate relationship (although a passive and dependent one) is given free expression. Since this occurs at the stage of

* Fenichel (1945), pp. 427 ff.

development when anal functions are the focus of keenest emotional interest, the conflict is usually expressed in anal terms. In analysis, the buttocks and other parts of the body are found to be implied when psychotic patients give free associations to their delusions about sinister machines. The theme of supernatural influence (expressed in the West as " scientific rays ", in India as death-dealing magic, and in both cultures as mysterious powers of thought-control) is similarly found to derive from infantile phantasies about the faeces, as dark autonomous goblin-like agencies, issuing from the self.

This brings to mind the remarkable place occupied by faeces in the implicit phantasy life of these Hindus. Two forms of contamination were constantly being described: that due to faeces, and that due to association with persons of lower caste and particularly to eating with them. An indication has already been given (p. 80) of the way in which these concepts coalesce. Thus, the remains of a partly-eaten dish or any food which has once been brought into contact with the lips, becomes jutha and it is abhorrent, almost unthinkable, for anyone else to eat this, though such food may be given to the untouchable sweeper-caste. Emotionally, jutha are treated with the same abhorrence as is human excrement. It was noticeable that Brahmins might be employed as cooks (and often were called in to cook, when other Brahmins were to be the guests) but the collecting and disposal of used utensils was left to menials of low caste, or to the women of the house. Exceptions to this abhorrence of jutha occur within the family and in a sacred context. A father often summons his children to partake of food which he left over. This is a privilege; and it is also a privilege to be allowed to eat prashad, the offering of food which a God has " tasted ". Symbolically, these leftovers represent the faeces of the father and the God: the act of grateful acceptance represents a submission to their authority, and is the model of the only " good " relationship with the father. In contrast, the phantasy of a good mother goes back to the early experience of generous suckling; at that infantile level, everything issuing from the mother is felt to be nourishing and beneficent. This attitude is reflected in beliefs about the sacred cow, paradigm of motherhood, whose dung and urine are felt to have healing properties, and whose " five products " are swallowed in the course of ceremonies of purification.

An interesting aspect of the deification of the cow (which represents the wholly gratifying mother of one's earliest recollection) is the way in which the role of her consort, the bull, is minimised. He is a benevolent nonentity, as is the child's father during his first year of life; and yet as Nandi, the divine bull, this mild and passive figure is always associated with Lord Shiva, the essence of maleness. Beside every phallic lingam, representing the Great God, is portrayed a sitting bull. Philosophically, Shiva stands for both the generative power and the destruction of the universe, but in the context of village experience he represents on the one hand the ideal of tapassya (the self-castration of extreme asceticism with the aim of obliterating all sensuality) and on the other, as consort of the demon-goddess, he is sometimes her victim, at others himself a still fiercer and more terrible destroyer.

Nandi and Shiva thus illustrate three aspects of the father-figure. Another no less universally encountered, is the god Vishnu, who appears in diverse forms, but always as a benign, gentle figure, succouring and sustaining, who inspires love. In Vishnu-worship, sexuality is not abhorred, but rather idealised. As Krishna, he is the great lover; but he is portrayed as an effeminate, seductive and yet divinely powerful youth. His devotees seem at times to identify with him as he makes his amorous conquests, at other times to identify themselves with the *gopis* (the girl cowherds) who are overcome with pleasurable anticipation at his approach. This particular father-figure can be recognised as revealing a thinly-veiled longing for him as a homosexual lover. The persistence of repressed homosexual urges is suggested both by their frank display in the stereotyped deviant behaviour of hinjras and in the violent feelings of disgust which they arouse. When the same theme is presented in slightly disguised and sublimated form, it is openly enjoyed. It was noticeable that when the popular rustic opera Ram-Lila was performed in Deoli, the centre of interest was the elegant young man who played the part of the heroine Sita. Everyone spoke with admiration of his good looks, and he received many encores.

Although they showed marked paranoid tendencies, my informants were far from obsessional: and this at first was puzzling. Verbally, they seemed intensely scrupulous about cleanliness and about attention to details of ritual performance; and yet in practice they were tolerant of seemingly filthy surroundings, and in practice their rituals corresponded only very approximately to the precise formulation with which they were described. Again, their indifference to unpunctuality, their easy acceptance of abrupt changes of plan and their seeming inability to carry through long-term undertakings to their conclusion—these were all unobsessional characteristics.*

The confusion in interpretation arose from their verbal insistence upon faecal cleanliness. In the West, over-strict toilet training is believed by psycho-analysts to result in accentuation of those obsessional traits of punctuality, neatness and conscientiousness which comprise the " anal character ", and which are favoured in our culture. In contrast to the Hindu pattern, Western obsessionals are seriously distressed if they are not able to carry out their routines with precision; and they cannot discuss anal topics without embarrassment. That Hindus are unobsessional and yet pre-occupied with this topic of faecal contamination is attributable to the fact that in infancy their training in cleanliness is gentle, leisurely and unemphasised: it is only after the age of two, when verbal instruction comes into play and when the oedipal conflict is at its height, that their attention is focused upon this function. From this time onwards faecal contamination becomes intimately tied up with submission to paternal authority, with religious worship, and with questions of relative caste status. It is implicit in the emphasis upon eating only with the right hand; upon eating only with caste fellows; and upon regarding other persons' leavings as if they were excrement. To be willing to sit and eat together constitutes a powerful bond; but to eat together out of one dish represents a bond of the closest intimacy, for it means at the same time " we are fed by one mother ", and " we accept the jutha (which is equivalent to the faeces) of one father ".

This act of eating together is emotionally so important that in social life it outweighs most other considerations. Thus, a sannyasi may be regarded as a holy, god-like man: and yet his former caste-fellows will not eat with him because he no longer observes their taboos against commensality. In describing the excesses of the lajadharm, Hari Lal expressed greater horror of the fact that members of all castes supped from one dish, than he did of their sexual excesses. On the other hand, careful observance of food taboos and avoidance of association with low-caste persons left a man not only in a pure state, but fortified against sensual temptation.

* It might be pointed out that unpunctuality was only natural in a community where clocks and watches were unknown. What was striking, however, was the frequent reference to precise times (e.g. of birth, death, marriage) coupled with an indifference to punctuality in practice

The pious Hindu's repugnance for alcohol is perfectly understandable, because of its notorious disinhibitory properties. Alcoholic intoxication militates against that subjection of the self which is seen to be the principal emphasis of the religious life, just as it is the accepted way of dealing with a surcharged oedipal situation. If one looks into the associations linked with wine, its use is seen to be permissible to Rajputs in order to nerve them for their aggressive role. It is also associated with the two terrible aspects of the phantasied parent-figures, the Mataji and Bhairav, who exemplify the explosive discharge of all the violent passions which a man normally keeps rigorously under control; but never with Shiva the ascetic, or Vishnu the mild sustaining ally of mankind. It is those castes, the Brahmins and the Banias, who are denied any approved aggressive outlet (such as Rajputs enjoy in hunting, concubinage and war) who condemn alcohol with especial emotional vehemence, because it presents a threat to their customary defences against their own severely repressed emotions: a threat, and perhaps also a temptation which they must at once repudiate.

The same holds true of eating meat, but with still greater force: and even Rajputs seem to feel uneasy about their indulgence in this privilege. Many who were not over-scrupulous in other respects (such as Hira Singh, Nathu Singh, Partab Singh) took pains to assure me that they were practically vegetarians.

Here again the associations to meat-eating are interesting. The one occasion of the year when meat is plentiful is at Navratri, when a series of blood sacrifices is made to the Mataji. The most usual form of sacrifice is a goat (and it must be a he-goat) which is led before the shrine and then decapitated with one blow of a sword. In Deoli, this was the only form of meat, and whether the goat were a formal offering, or simply killed by the Khatik, it would still have to be a male, and to be killed in this way.

The identification of the male goat with the male victims of the Goddess is made explicit by the *bhopa's* act of drinking the goat's warm blood, mixed with alcohol, while he is possessed by the spirit of the Mataji. The goat is sacrificed to appease her devouring rage, and then her worshippers unite in eating its meat. This act, which is felt by Brahmins and Banias to be one of grave impiety, which even Rajputs feel to be incompatible with the enlightened religious life, means symbolically that the child feasts with his demon-mother upon his father's blood. To take meat means to eat the father's penis and so acquire his virility. This makes one strong, because meat is a builder of semen, but it puts one in peril of a similar castrating attack, either from the Goddess or from her still more fearsome consort, the Bheruji; and it estranges one from the path of submission and denial of one's sexuality, which is felt to be the only way to ultimate reconciliation with one's mother and father figures. The orthodox Hindu ban on eating meat, and the stress on ahinsa (not taking life) can thus be interpreted as the conscious reaction-formations against repressed oedipal feelings of hostility against the father, feelings which are never allowed direct expression.

There are, of course, some foods which are associated not with threatening, but with gratifying phantasies. The preoccupation with loss of semen, which is a very common source of neurotic anxiety among Hindu men, can be palliated by eating certain exceptionally good, health-giving foods, namely wheat flour, rice, milk and butter, honey and white sugar. These substances have two valuable attributes: they are " cool" foods, that is to say they give nourishment without inflaming the passions, and they have the property of building pure, unspoiled semen. In fact *white sugar* (as distinct from the dark, unpurified molasses of everyday use) is used as a synonym for semen; but the constant association of all these foods with this same theme indicates that they are all, in varying degrees, equated in phantasy with rich, desirable semen.

In two social contexts this phantasy is given clear expression. At the great temple of Shiva, only a few miles from Deoli, the bi-annual festivals of that god are the occasion for libations of milk, curds, melted butter, honey and white sugar (in this order). These offerings are poured on to the upright phallic *lingam* which represents the god's creative powers, thus bringing semen and semen-foods into conjunction.

At every Hindu wedding, there is expected to be a prodigal dispensation of these exalted foods. During the feasting which attends these ceremonies, particular emphasis is placed upon the amount of *ghi* (clarified butter) which is offered to the male guests. Young men vie with each other in the amount they can consume. It is regarded as a mark of virility to be able to swallow two pounds or more at one sitting; and the boasting and teasing which attends these feasts make it clear that here ghi is being equated with semen.

All these cherished semen-equivalents have in common the properties of being fluid (even sugar can be poured) opaque and *white*. Here is the opposite pole of that strong, unreasoning prejudice against darkness which is evident in many contexts of Hindu life (from the desire to marry a light-complexioned spouse, to the use of black flags and garments as a symbol of deprecation). Earlier, it was suggested that the emotional bias against dark things is due to the strong investment of feelings concerning the threat of faecal contamination. In contrast, pure uncontaminated semen is highly esteemed, and the favourable emotional attitudes to which it gives rise are carried over to the qualities of fairness, sweetness and freedom from adulteration—qualities which are admired in one's fellow-men as well as in one's diet.

It is claimed by psychoanalysis that one indication of a person's having attained emotional maturity is his ability to have a mutually rewarding experience of intercourse with a love partner of the opposite sex. Freud himself once defined a normal man as one who was able " to work and to love "; and D. H. Lawrence considered the full life to be one in which a man alternated between " daytime purposive activity " and a deep emotional union with a sex partner. These are norms which not only the emotionally sick but many ordinary Westerners fail to achieve: and they illustrate very clearly the occidental cultural bias in favour of individual achievement and self-realisation.

In the Hindu world, sexuality is considered an impediment to the progress towards emotional maturity, which comes only with the final triumph of asceticism. Sexuality remains always something detrimental, dangerous, seductive. A young man's sex life is restrained by many factors, by his wife's being not of his own choice, by his living in his parents' house, and his having to deny his sexual life while in their presence, by his phantasies concerning women, of whom the demon-Goddess is the paradigm, and not least by his phantasy of his father as a gigantic rival threatening instant destruction if he dares to re-assert his infantile claims upon his mother. These are the circumstances in which one would expect to encounter either homosexuality or impotence. The evidence for the existence of strong repressed homosexual urges has already been discussed. The actual practice of homosexuality certainly occurred: my informants were prone to accuse each other of it, though it was not a thing which they would describe in their own experience, except as a childhood phase. Impotence was a very common occurrence, and pre-occupation with fears of impotence or of loss of virility (a form of castration-fear) seemed to be present in the majority of men.

Another pattern of sexual response was found repeatedly: This was a sharp distinction between their potency in relations with prostitutes or in promiscuous affairs with girls of an inferior caste, and with their wives. In the former instances, it was the men who took the initiative, and they described their (necessarily secret, but not strongly disapproved) adventures with pleasure; but in their own homes it was different. There, it was the wives whose appetites must be satisfied: and there the anxieties over failing strength and potency were most intense. This was clearly because married life, conducted under one's father's roof, within the extended family, excited all the terrors of childish oedipal phantasy, whereas the despised casual sex partner could be more easily dissociated from this scene except where she was found to be older than the man—in which case anxiety returned. Significantly, almost every one of my informants told me that it was advisable to have sex relations only with women younger than oneself: to sleep with a woman several years older would destroy a man's strength in a short space of time. The older woman is feared because she conjures up the repressed oedipal craving for possession of the mother, and so intensifies the castration anxieties which dog all sexual functions.

Earlier in this chapter it was suggested that it was the abrupt change from an un-frustrated infancy to the subsequent " desertion " by his mother which not only created the Hindu child's phantasy-picture of her, and her later substitutes, as witch-like figures, but also shattered his early scheme of object-relationships, so that he found it difficult in later life to trust or even to empathise with other persons. In one sense, everyone goes through life trying to find again the good relation he once had with his idealised parents as a small child. The Hindu solution to this quest is not through personal relationships, but in an acceptance of formal mutual obligations to bridge the gap. It would be an act of blindness indeed to suggest that because relations between a Hindu son and his parents, between a man and his wife, lack that warmth and spontaneity which is expected in Western society, they are necessarily inferior. Each patterning of human behaviour has its positive as well as its limiting aspects. Psychoanalysis is better equipped to demonstrate the latter than the former; but as an ordinary responsive observer one must pay a tribute to the serenity and calm which prevail in a well-adjusted Hindu family. It is perhaps a precarious calm, based on the suppressing rather than on the resolving of underlying tensions, but still it reflects a gracious and civilised way of life.

The characteristically Hindu attitudes which have been discussed in this chapter, attitudes concerning women, sensuality, authority, power, asceticism and non-violence, the Hindu view of the material world, and of their fellow-men and the ultimate values of the Hindu religious outlook—all these things become more readily intelligible when one elucidates the nuclear phantasies which give rise to them. In the present writer's opinion genuine inter-group and inter-racial understanding will only become possible to the degree that each group's covert pattern of irrational complexes is made the object of study, as well as their history and all the overt aspects of their social life.

CHAPTER XI

SUMMARY AND CONCLUSIONS

THIS book contains the findings of a study which was planned to test the adequacy of certain theories of personality development to account for the course of character formation in a non-Western society, where children would be exposed to a different type of upbringing from that considered normal in the West. The theories in question were those taught by Adolph Meyer and his followers and termed by him Psychobiology. They are essentially eclectic, emphasising the concept of multiple aetiology in personality formation. Each adult personality is regarded as the product of biological, physical, economic and social factors as well as of the material and emotional influences peculiar to his individual experience.

The Meyerian approach dominated the method of the writer's field work among his chosen community of high-caste Hindus in a village of northern India. It became his aim to explore all the possibly significant factors in this environment, and subsequently to attempt to describe, however briefly, the geographical, historical, economic and social setting in which these subjects had their being. In Chapter IX is presented a condensed account of these explicit external influences in the development of Hindu personality in this village.

Psycho-biological theory includes also the unconscious within its eclectic embrace. Accordingly, the research plan required the carrying out of extensive non-directed interviews. By observing the spontaneous sequence of associations in these interviews it was possible to identify some unconscious complexes which were commonly encountered. These could be confirmed and further elaborated by the analysis of communal phantasies, supernatural beliefs and ritual practices.

During the course of the fieldwork two facts became apparent. First, that data of objective significance were readily (if somewhat laboriously) obtainable; and secondly, that it was the other class of data, the subjectively important complexes of imperfectly formulated belief, which seemed most illuminating in interpreting the regularities of personality structure which began to emerge.

This redistribution of emphasis was less apparent in the field

SUMMARY AND CONCLUSIONS

than during the prolonged task of analysing the verbatim reports of the interviews, many months later. In the course of this analysis new insights emerged. It became apparent that the theory of multiple causality, although logically unexceptionable, was practically useless. Where so many operative factors were invoked, the effect of none could be determined in isolation. With regard to the original intention of the research, all that could be said was that in a society where many of the contributing factors were markedly different, consistent differences were observed in the prevailing pattern of adult personality—differences which would in many cases be described as " abnormal " in Western society.

At this point the material threw up a definite challenge: could these personality features, identified as characteristic of high-caste Hindus in this orthodox rural community be interpreted as the consequence of relatively few basic processes and could these in turn be identified? In response to this challenge the research changed its focus from considering psychopathological personality-distortion in general to the related topic of *identifying the means whereby group personality characteristics are transmitted.*

In so doing, the shared influences (historical, geographical, social and economic) which derived from the " reality setting " were not forgotten. It was simply that the unifying concept of the role of infantile nuclear phantasies in the shaping of adult personality was found to play a major part in the understanding of Hindu personality formation. In Chapter X there is a discussion of those nuclear phantasies whose presence could be recognised as underlying certain of the consistencies of personality which these high-caste Hindus showed.

This concept of the part played by unconscious infantile complexes in adult thinking and behaviour was one of Freud's basic discoveries; and it has been so abundantly verified that it is accepted by psycho-analysts of every school.* In his psychiatric practice, the author had had personal experience of its usefulness in clarifying the irrational elements in an individual patient's personality. The present study brought home to him the possibility of using the same concept in order to interpret the apparently arbitrary and illogical elements

---

* It has also been fundamental to analytically-oriented research in culture and personality. Its rationale has been clearly stated and its practice elegantly demonstrated in two chapters (by Gorer and Métraux respectively) in *The Study of Culture at a Distance* (Mead and Métraux, 1953)

which give its unique character to a people's mode of thought. The recognition of consistent underlying phantasies " made sense " of much that at first seemed incomprehensible in the Hindu community of Deoli.

In order that readers may judge for themselves the applicability—and the limitations—of these interpretative concepts, three of the informants' case-histories are given at some length in Part II, together with analyses of their performance of the standard psychological tests employed.

The true limitations of this analysis of some basic elements in the personality structure of high-caste Hindus will only be apparent when its relevance to the interpretation of the personalities of other Hindus, in other parts of India, has been put to the test. It is the author's hope that some elements, at least, will prove to have a more than local validity and will contribute towards a better understanding, on the part of Western observers, of the psychology of Indians in general.

There exists today a widespread interest in studies of national character. This is perhaps due to recent developments of communications and technology which have made the realisation of a " one world " community not merely desirable but an imminent possibility. The two formidable obstacles to its achievement are conflicts over material objectives (which only political action can resolve) and mutual misunderstanding. The latter is only intensified when, as is becoming increasingly the case, peoples of the East and West wear similar clothes, talk a similar technical language and use the same machines. It is neither desirable nor likely that compatibility of outlook will be achieved by the imposition everywhere of one particular ethos, whether of the Russian or the American " way of life ". The alternative is to preserve the rich diversity of cultural traditions but to facilitate communication between members of different cultures by recognising, and accepting, the deep-seated complexes which colour our own outlook as well as those of our interlocutors. Only by making this effort, which involves the renunciation of irrational sources of reassurance (such as the belief that " our way " is the only right way of looking at things) as well as an imaginative effort of insight on either side, will we be able to overcome the seemingly insuperable obstacles to understanding each other's point of view.

This is the practical aspect of carrying psycho-analytic insight into research in social anthropology. Its theoretical contribution will also be important. The prime purpose of

SUMMARY AND CONCLUSIONS

anthropology is after all " to explain and predict the ways of men " * and in this aim a theory which claims to impart an understanding of the deepest levels of motivation must play a part—indeed in this writer's opinion a most important part.

It is natural for specialists to emphasise the significance of their respective fields of inquiry, whether they be economists, archaeologists, physical anthropologists or anatomists of social structure. Even so eminent a specialist as Professor G. M. Trevelyan shows something of this partiality when he writes: " You cannot even understand your own personal opinions, prejudices and emotional reactions unless you know what is your heritage as an Englishman, and how it has come down to you. Why does an Englishman react one way to a public or private situation, a German another way, a Frenchman in a third way? History alone can tell you." †

But for the last dogmatic sentence, this paragraph reads like a continuation of the argument of the present book. In approaching the study of a subject so complex as human nature there is surely room for the deployment of not one, but many specialised techniques of inquiry.

The method of historical study described in the same essay has this in common with psycho-analytic interpretations of national character: both demand an effort of creative imagination in order to achieve insights which can subsequently be verified by objective observations. This gift of imagination, allied with his literary distinction have enabled Professor Trevelyan to present remote events and persons with dramatic immediacy. His art conceals the laborious verification of details which distinguishes scholarship from aesthetic impressionism.

In the same way, the most eloquent interpreters of culture and personality (among whom the writer would include Ruth Benedict, Erik Erikson, Margaret Mead and Geoffrey Gorer) have shown their ability not only to understand the mentality of other peoples but also to communicate this understanding. In so doing, they have enriched the experience of us all.

It is the present writer's hope that this study will contribute towards a better understanding of the Indian point of view. If it does succeed in this, most of the credit must be ascribed to his village collaborators. They taught him, among many other things, to realise that mutual understanding between persons of different races requires not merely knowledge about

---

* Professor Daryll Forde, speaking at the International Symposium of Anthropologists, New York, 1952

† Trevelyan, G. M. (1945), p. 20

each other but also tolerance and goodwill—qualities which this Hindu community displayed in high degree.

It is only fitting in conclusion to remind oneself that this study is the merest scratching at the surface of a vast mine of unexplored material. The thirty-seven caste Hindus of Rajasthan, on whose histories it is based, are only a microscopic sample and the generalisations which can be made from their cases are necessarily very limited. Nevertheless it is hoped that the findings which have emerged have at least this in common with scientific inquiries carried out under more rigorously controlled conditions, that they may lead to further explorations into an important aspect of the study of man.

Part Two

THREE HINDU SELF-PORTRAITS

CHAPTER I

SHRI RAJENDRA SINGH, RAJPUT

It would be impracticable to reproduce all of the thirty-six Hindu personality studies which I accumulated during my ten months stay in Deoli. They, together with my diaries, are the raw data from which certain generalisations about Hindu personality patterns have been derived. In the process they have been dissected and collated so that the individuals themselves have tended to disappear behind the general characteristics which they shared with their fellows.

In order to penetrate this cloud of anonymity I propose now to present three of my informants' histories at greater length, with extended quotations of their own words. I have selected one from each of the three uppermost caste divisions: and I have chosen those individuals who of their own choice talked to me in English, so that the distorting influence of translation will be minimised. Their English may not have been perfect; however, it seems to me to express with great clarity what they had to say. They are not wholly typical of their caste-fellows; indeed their idiosyncrasies are all the more pronounced because they are in each case the most highly educated representative of their group—but like the rest, they are at once unique and typical. Behind the individual experiences and predispositions can be seen many features which they share in common with their less sophisticated neighbours: and it is this recognition of such elements of consistency in a complex pattern which is the aim of this book.

Our first meeting with Rajendra Singh was on a day in January, 1951 when we travelled to Deoli by jeep in order to discuss with him possibilities of carrying out research in that village. The jeep lurched up a rough-hewn drive to enter the gate of the castle ramparts. From there, one of the sentries took a note to the Rao Sahib, while we remained in the outer courtyard, looking up at the mass of rock and white-washed buildings which towered above our heads. Soon we were invited in, and ascended through a succession of gateways, inner courtyards and stairs until we reached his living-room, which was dark and cool, stone-flagged and furnished with comfortable sofas and armchairs of Victorian design.

Rajendra Singh greeted us cordially, invited us to take tea, and talked volubly throughout our visit showing an evident (and justified) pride in his fluency and idiomatic command of English. He asked about the proposed research study, and before I had finished outlining it he had taken up the idea with enthusiasm and offered a wealth of suggestions as to how it should be carried out—he would summon members of each high caste before me here, in the palace, and command them to tell me everything I asked. At the same time he felt confident that laborious investigations would not be necessary, because he personally could tell me all I wished to know about the psychology of Rajputs, Brahmins and Banias.

This zeal was somewhat overwhelming; but he responded with a quick grasp to my explanation that a more objective and prolonged investigation was in my mind, and was able to give me an estimate of the numbers of various caste-groups in his village which later proved substantially correct. Having agreed on the appropriateness of Deoli as a centre in which to work, and having inspected the rooms which he kindly put at our disposal, I fixed the date of our arrival.

Rajendra Singh still talked with an unstinted exuberance and vivacity. It was clear that he had enjoyed the society of Udaipur's limited number of Europeans in the past. Our presence revived memories of tennis parties at the Field Club, of dinners at the Residency, and of his teachers (Public School men and athletes all) at the Princes' College in Ajmer.

Before we left, the conversation had turned to politics. He bitterly resented the social reforms of the new Congress government—" This talk of democracies and all such things! "

His own administration, he assured me, had been exemplary: " I love my tenants, and they all love me. I will take you all about the villages and you can ask them: 'What do you think of the Jagirdar?'" In the same breath he added that there were a few malcontents who bore him grudges because he had sometimes been severe in the exercise of his judiciary powers.

He felt sure that the present régime in India could not last long: "Either Princes' rule will come back, or else there may be a turn towards Communism."

I asked: "Do the Jagirdars feel that Communism is a serious threat?"

"It is not us, it is the Banias that they will attack first. If they attack me, all right, I will fight. That is what I am trained to do. I will be killed, but first I will shoot a good many of them. And then, they will not get so much from me. But they know that if they attack the Banias it will not be so dangerous, and also they will get more."

Rajendra Singh insisted that he himself would be our first informant about Rajput family life, and Rajput values; and he was as good as his word. In the early weeks of our stay in Deoli he devoted many evenings to this talk, which he evidently enjoyed. On the first of these evening meetings, we came upon him sitting crosslegged upon a sofa, telling a rosary of wooden beads. He put them away as he rose to greet us, and explained: "Beads: this is simply to count the names of God, one name on each bead. For example, if I want to pray to the sun, I have got to take the name, Surya. If I want to pray to Lord Shiv, it should be his name. Every Hindu has a sacred thread."

G.M.C. "*All* the castes?"

R.S. "No, only the three highest castes. First the Brahmins; their duty is to pray and preach. Second the Rajputs; their duties are to rule, guard, defend, fight, keep law and order, and to pray. Those are the laws of Manu. Banias' duty is shopping and business work, to be obedient to the rulers, and to pray."

G.M.C. "They pray also?"

R.S. "Yes, all Hindus pray. The law of Manu prescribes praying also for the Sudras, a different type of prayer. There are so many kinds of prayer. For example, there is one name of God which has only three letters—Soham.* When you breathe in you pronounce So-, and when you breathe out you pronounce -ham. You may do this without saying it out loud. You do this again and again until it goes on without you thinking about it. It goes to such an extent that even when you are asleep it goes with the work of the heart. If a man has acquired that, you can feel his heart saying it. I think I have achieved about two or three annas in a rupee of this.

* In Hindi this word has three letters

"It is open to every man to worship God. The love of God is like the love of a woman, but if you love women too much and have debauchery, you will go to hell; whereas if you love God you will go to heaven. If you practise prayer for many years and try very hard to see God, sometimes you may reach to that, that you may see God. There are holy men who have done this, who have seen God with their eyes. It takes the form of light. The first sight you get is the black light, all dark, then a reddish light, and then the light of the moon, then of the sun, then of the clouds, then come to Almighty's house.

"When you have practised this contemplation, saying the name of God many times, then it comes more easily. But in order to learn how to do this, you need a guide. For example, when you first came here, you had to ask the way at the outer gate and then at the inner gate and so all the way; but now you know the way you come straight up, in fact, if another stranger comes you yourself can be his guide; and in the same way, when you begin this thing you need a guide, and that guide is your *Guru*. Now the big question is, how to find your Guru.

"Let me tell you a story. It is from our teachings. Once there was a man who wanted very much to see God, but he had no Guru and he could find no Guru in whom he could have complete trust. So he made an oath, that I will go to the city in the morning, and the first man that I meet, he will be my Guru. So he went, and there were four thieves who had committed some theft, and they were coming out through the city gate—it was a walled city, like Udaipur—and he caught hold of the feet of the first of these four thieves and called out to him: ' You are my Guru, tell me how I can get to see God.' That man said: ' Let me go, I am no Guru ', but he held on to his feet and kept on saying: ' I took an oath that the first man I should meet this morning will be my Guru so tell me how I can see God.' Then the other thieves were afraid that the police would come, so they said to that man: ' All right, you are his Guru ' and they ran away and left him. Then that man, the thief, said: ' Very well, if you wish to see God, bow your head to the ground here and say this name of God and do not stop until I tell you.' So the man bent his head to the ground and said this certain name of God and the thief went away.

"Now we believe that everything that happens, everything we do, every leaf that moves, is moved by God: and He is not

careless, he knows what is going on. So he got to know that
one man is staying there with his head on the ground, saying
my name, two days and two nights without anything to eat or
to drink. So God came up to him disguised as a man, and
asked him what he was doing. The man replied: ' My Guru
told me to remain here and repeat the name of God until he
told me to stop, if I wanted to see God.' Then God said:
' I am God, look up and stop now.' But the man said, ' How
do I know that you are not deceiving me? I will not stop
until my Guru tells me to stop.' Then God summoned the
thief and told him to tell the man to stop, and then that man
saw God, and that thief also had the *darshan*, he also saw God.
That shows that you have to have a blind belief in your Guru
if you are to see God. If you lose the slightest confidence, you
have lost.

"When you pray, what that prayer should be, should never
be in your interest. The only thing you can demand from
God is, ' Oh Almighty God, grant me good conscience so that
I can go on aright ': if you have good conscience, then the
other things will come to you.

"Now it is with God as it is with a mother who has two or
three children. She has her work to do, and so she gives them
toys and tells them to go and play, and then they will leave
her to get on with her business. So also God gives us to play,
gives you good life, good friends, gives you *shikar*, and wine.
But sometimes there is a child who is obstinate and will not
leave its mother but keeps on crying and crying for her, so that
what does she do? She lifts him into her lap to make him
quiet, and gives him mother's milk. So it is that there are
some men who keep on crying for God, and so he has to hear,
and he takes them to him. The more time you devote to
calling on his name, the more you cry for him, the sooner he
takes you on his lap."

G.M.C. " That sounds as though you were forcing God
to listen!"

R.S. " It is not forcing, it is crying, as a child cries for its
mother. . . .

" There are three duties known by the name of *jannu*. One,
never to forget God; two, never to forget your ancestors, your
mother and father, who brought you up. If he wanted, he
could do this: finish! (Makes gesture of wringing a baby's
neck.) You devote a certain part of your prayers for their
good, for the sake of their souls so they will be always happy.
They shake off their sins and go in the heavens. Three, no

guest or any Hindu beggar should go without having food from your board. I myself am not entitled to take food if I have a guest, until he is fed. That is our custom.

"When a Rajput is old enough to marry, they give you this thread (shows his triple thread) and after that you have got to fulfil all these things. You can assume these obligations before marriage if you wish.

"You know we believe in *karma*, that is, in re-birth. If you have tried to get your light into the Almighty's soul, then you are never again born. If you are unsuccessful, then you are again born but in a very high position, in a good family, good house, with riches. From the praying position you left, you start from there. If you are bad, you are given the life of a dog or a snake. Any holy man can attain *moksh*, it is upon your deeds. You may get it in your second or third birth as a man.

"Our yogis have a very wonderful science, as you will see if you read about it in the books. For example, they have the theory of the rays of the sun. They say that there are several rays of the sun, and each falls upon a particular place and has a special effect. The seventh ray of the sun, by yogi calculation, has the effect that the people of India should have more belief to worship God. The ray falling in England would have a different effect. A sub-ray of the seventh ray, which falls on Mewar produces very great yogis; the same ray falling on Ahmedabad makes very great liars—didn't Mahatma Gandhi come from Gujerat? And he was a diplomat, that is, a liar. Politicians are not men of principles, they go with the winds, they are never true people, you can never believe them. For example, Gandhi said before India was divided his own body would be divided. . . . My maternal grandfather was a great yogi."

G.M.C. "Can Rajputs be yogis then too, not just warriors?"

R.S. "Oh yes, they must be both. If they have taken the name of God truly, and are great protectors, then God will protect them. The Rajputs always were great prayer-sayers, that is why they were so brave and successful. There is one family of Rajputs, the Rathors, who are the only clan in the whole world who can fight with their heads off. For this reason they are called *kamand* (headless). This is not just an ancient story, it happened again during the '14-'18 war."

He then tells a story of a Rajput charge against a Turkish battery in which some Rathors had their heads blown off, but went on charging on horseback with the rest until their swords struck the enemy's guns and they knew that they had won the victory: and only then they fell.

"The reason that the Rajputs were always so brave in battle was their great piety. Congress takes the country first, and we take religion first. Though I am educated, I think in a different way from Congress: they can deprive me of everything except my blood—it is pure all through; the chastity of blood is there. We have not intermixed anywhere. It is like a pure strain of seed, if you sow it in good ground you cannot fail to get a good crop. The line never goes, if it is pure seed. There are still Rana Partabs surviving, many of them. The fire may seem to burn low, perhaps it is covered with ashes now; but the moment there is a wind, there comes a spark and the whole thing is blazing once more. The purity of blood goes off by intermixture: it is better for everyone to die than lose this chastity of blood—that is why they went to their death in the sack of Chitor."

In our next meeting, the Rao Sahib talked about his own upbringing.

"My earliest memory is of when I was four. My father's real grandmother was alive (you must know he was adopted). She used to obey our slightest command. Sweet days those were—wheat was 10 sers for 1 rupee, and ghi 1½ sers; and 1½ md. barley for 1 rupee, and 1 maund maize. We used to have 100 servants waiting on us, and sixty horses. We had two attendants from the slave class to look after us, and two Rajputs also to attend us. When we slept out in hot weather we had four guards to watch us. When I went to school I had twenty servants with me. We had two elephants in those days. I remember my father riding out every evening with twelve horsemen with him. I saw petromax lamps from my very childhood and I was 5 when we got our Fiat car. And we had four or five very old, experienced shikaris. I used to pray to my father every day for shikar—and if our masters pressed upon our studies, our Rajputs said: 'They are the lords of Mewar, they give food to so many they will never go hungry themselves. Do not make them study.' They used to scold them like that.

"We used to have such wonderful meals—two kinds of meat —we used to have meals thrice a day and milk twice a day.

"I think my father did not love me very much. From the very beginning I knew that he loved my brother better—but he loved my sister best of all. I don't think he liked much to read or write—he never read himself. But he used to pray twice a day—an hour in the morning and twenty minutes in the evening. He was a man of very hot temper—used to turn servants out at every little fault. He liked best to eat, drink and be merry. He loved his children very much—at the slightest illness he called in doctors. He liked parties more than anything and was very friendly to all the European Residents in Udaipur.

" I remember I had a small horse when I was 5—it was pigeon-coloured. I had a sword. I used to go to late Maharana Sahib and pay my respects—he loved me very much.

" When I was 10 or 11, my father wished me to go to Mayo College, and a week before I went to His Highness, and he said: ' You don't need to go to College.' I went home very glad and related all this to my father, but he said: ' You will be a duffer if you do not go.' When I first went, I had seven servants, but when I left I had three, one cook and two servants.

" My mother kept bad health after my brother was born. He is six years younger than me. Before he was born she was quite well, but I could only have milk for one year and a half, then I had cow milk—none of this Cow and Gate or Glaxo, we did not believe in those."

G.M.C. " You said, your earliest memory was of your ' real ' great grandmother. What do you remember about her ? "

R.S. " She used to prepare some wonderful *khana*, I remember it still. It is a custom, the mother always prepares a dish for the son. If my father came late, she would scold him and say: ' Why do you come late, your health will be spoiled.' And of course he could not say anything to us, he could only fold his hands and sit quiet.

" My father had weak eyesight. He used to wear spectacles from a very early age. But he was a very good shikari, better shot even than me. He was a plain good-hearted open man: but strict too. If we went on shikar he sent me with a man to tell us what to do, how to point the gun, where not to fire. He used to rise early at four—earlier than me. He used to go to bed at late hours. He was a stout, well-built man, just as I am. I am not flabby, I am just well-built.

" From very early years I always had Rajputs attending to me. They called me as *Bapji*, or *Bara Bapji*. You know that Rup Singh? His father used to look after me. He was a wonderful rider and a great shot. But we never gave a thought to these men.

"My mother is a very good shot you must know—she has shot panthers. Now I am going to teach my wife to shoot. I'll teach her nothing else, then we shall be two.

"My grandfather's elder brother's son, he was very good to my father: and his son we had with us, brought up just like us. We had competitions of shooting at night and my father said I would be one of the best shots. We had our *khana* separate, but we children always came in ourselves and had a dish with our father.

"We had great times when he had his birthday. There would be a feast with wine and dancing girls. Yes, from 5 to 6 years old I remember that. They were so well-dressed. We admire beauty but we do not touch it. They came from a servant class or from Beragi Saddhu caste, or Mohammedans. If a woman of high caste chose to do this work, I think she would soon be killed. We think it is the lowest work, to be a puppet in another's hands."

G.M.C. "Who was the disciplinarian in your early years?"

R.S. "The Rajput."

G.M.C. "Wasn't he afraid to punish you?"

R.S. "No, he used to slap me. He used to pinch us sometimes. We would pull his nose, and he used to get in a rage and stand at the door, and we would be afraid and run to my mother. Then his rage would subside and we would run out and play again. We were great mischiefs.

"I was a very good tennis player. I still have some master-strokes. I played in All-India tennis tournament— I was beaten by Sohan Lal in the third round. I was very good in doubles also.

"I was at College for seven years. I used to stand first all the times in the studies, that is why they all liked me very much. I was especially good at poetry, and I was an orator and a great debater—that is why I have still got the fluency— otherwise I should have lost it."

Rajendra Singh recited some lines of old Rajput *charans* describing events in the epic history of the Sheshodias. One was about the battle of Haldi Ghati and how the Jhala took the royal umbrella to draw the Mussulman's attack upon himself while Rana Partab was able to escape on his steed, Chetak. The Jhala was killed, but his heroism won lasting fame and advancement for his clan. Another stanza was one of reproach against the Gehlotes for allowing a petty representative of the Moghuls to hold the fortress of Chitor. In these ballads and war-songs there is a stress not merely on the clans, but on their sub-divisions: the effect is one of intimacy, as of a family minstrel singing in praise of his protector's family. One which Rajendra Singh translated for us was the story of the Straw Raja of Bundi.

"My grandmother is a Hada Rajput, of Bundi. It is said of them, if you tease them in the slightest they will kill you at once. Once Udaipur and Bundi were at enmity, the Prince of Udaipur was killed by Bundi and had to be avenged. His successor vowed he would not eat or drink until he had taken his father's vengeance. His Courtiers thought this was not one day or two days' work to be done in a joke. So they planned to burn an effigy of Bundi, and then tell the Maharana, 'Bundi is slain—eat and drink!' The straw Bundi was made near Delhi gate. A Hada Rajput saw this, and heard about it. He said: 'Can a mimic Bundi be burned while a single Hada lives in Mewar?' He drew his sword and fought till he was cut into pieces.

"Recently, the Charan said: 'There was a time when a Hada was cut to pieces for a mimic Bundi: and now you give the real Bundi away without a blow. You do not deserve to survive; die out you devils! Nor meetings can keep you alive, nor gatherings, only the power of the sword will keep you alive. Rise and strike, and stop not till the goal is achieved!' He was bold to say such things to a prince!"

Next day, the conversation turned to the subject of supernatural powers. Rajendra Singh said:

"If five people who have practised the will-power all sit and look at a pot on which has been marked one black spot, if they look at it without blinking for two minutes, then they all think this same thing in their minds then, by the force of their will-power, it will move right round them and come to settle in the same place. But they must be of the same mind.

"If a lifeless thing like this can be moved, no wonder a living person can be moved, because he has a will and you can pull on it. Do not ever look into the eyes of a man who practises yoga, or he may pull on you and make you do what he wants."

This evening, the Rao Sahib was in a high good humour, beaming and cracking rude jokes at which his attendants laughed assiduously. He introduced a thin, gap-toothed middle-aged man, who was sitting cross-legged on the floor:

"You should meet this man. He is even more practised in prayer than me, he has gone a lot farther than me. You might even say he is a saint. Yes, he is a saint. Now he will sing for you, listen."

At his request, the saint (who was further introduced as a Rajput holding a subordinate Jagir within the tikhana of Deoli), began to sing a series of *bhajans*, some of which Rajendra Singh translated for us: in particular, one about the wisdom of knowing that one can do nothing to alter the pre-ordained hour of one's death. "Death is inevitable, so the man who knows this is not afraid of anything. The song says, a saint will clasp the feet of a man who truly knows that death is inevitable, because he is the wise man. This is what we believe."

G.M.C. "Was this a *Bhajan?*"

R.S. "Yes, the Rajputs sing only bhajans, they do not sing anything else."

At this point Devi Singh interrupted the singer to show him an American toy, attached to a key-ring: held to the light it revealed a coloured picture of a nude, lascivious blonde: "Look," he said, "there is a picture of Sri Nathji in this." The saint looked, and burst out with involuntary laughter, which sounded anything but saintly.

Then Rajendra Singh called for another song, singing snatches of it in the pauses between the verses. This, he explained, was not a bhajan but a love-song: a girl writes letters to her lover: she says: "I have golden bangles and all the jewels that I want: all I crave is just one kiss from you." The saint applied himself to singing this song with no less fervour than he had shown in singing bhajans to his lord's command. As he sang, the children ran about and pulled his ears; Rajendra Singh interrupted him from time to time to translate passages to us, to tell his small niece to dance to the bhajan, or to expound a phrase.

On the 18th of February, Rajendra Singh summoned us to see him in his court dress. He wore a long silk coat, with real sovereigns for buttons, and his fingers, ears and turban glittered with gold-set diamonds. The occasion for this magnificence was a party at the Udaipur palace of the heir to the Maharana. Next evening he entertained us to drinks of daru, and it was clear from his expansive good humour that he had already taken one or two glasses before we joined him.

"Last night, I was very drunk, I was nearly insensible. Five of us, we sat down at a small table, and we finished off three bottles of Gilbey's Gin, and two bottles of Scotch Whisky. I think not one of us was in his senses when we were done. When I got home, I was hardly able to pray for more than fifteen minutes—and then I slept like a log until ten minutes before sunrise. Usually, I get up at 5.0; today I got up at 6.30 and I felt very heavy. My wife and my brother, they made fun of me. Then I bathed my head in cold water and then I felt quite all right."

We teased him about his display of jewellery, asked if he was not afraid of the dacoits who were said to haunt the Udaipur road at night. He replied: " Let them only try to attack me! They would not dare. I have only to show my face and they would all run away."

G.M.C. " And you had your sword with you."

R.S. " No need of sword, Sahib. When man has the will-power, no one can stand against him. Besides, I am never unprepared. See, even now. (He produced a miniature automatic, a '25 Walther, in a cloth case, from his coat pocket.) Take a look at that, Sahib. That will do to kill a man. I had that with me last night. Always I have something like that. My mother also has one like this—she is very brave."

He described how necessary it was to be armed during the riots of 1947: " In those days, I always carried my revolver and my gun: then if I am attacked by some mob, I can kill ten, fifteen, and then die. Those were very bad times. Of course, it all began in Pakistan. Those Mahommedans, they taunted our Hindus, they taunted them very much: and then those warlike Hindus, the Sikhs and the Jats, they formed in bands and began to take revenge upon the Moslems. They would stop the train and go through the coaches saying: ' *Pakistani murgi? Pakistani murgi?* ' and then they would kill them, and leave them there.

" One day, Sahib, I was travelling, with my gun with me: and in my compartment there was a Bania from Udaipur— I mention no names, he is of well-known family here. Then they stopped the train and they came along. They asked me: ' Are you Hindu or Mussulman? ' and I said, ' Hindu '. They said: ' Prove it '. So I showed them this (drawing out the triple thread from under his shirt) and they said: ' Yes, the *janoi* '. Then this Mahajan, he had a big beard, and so they thought he was a Mussulman. In those days I had no beard, but only a moustache, up like this—sometimes I keep a moustache, in three or four months I grew it like this, up to the level of the eyes, then I look very fierce, but it is too much trouble stroking it like this all day. So they said: 'You are a Mussulman', but he said 'No, I am Hindu'. But he had no sacred thread—these Jains, they do not wear the triple thread. They said: 'All right, if you are true Hindu, just repeat one *slok*, one Sanskrit verse.' But he, poor fellow, he was so ignorant, he could not even do that. So then they say: 'We shall look to see if you have had phimosis operation'— you know, Sahib, all Mahommedans they have phimosis operation. Then he cried out to me: 'You tell them, you know I am Hindu.' I said, 'I know he says he is Hindu. Perhaps I have seen him somewhere. I am not sure.' I just lay there on my bunk like this (stroking his moustache and concealing his smile with his hand). Then they took his pants right down, right down altogether, and they looked to see if he had phimosis operation (he roars with laughter). And when they were gone, he said: 'I must shave my beard, this very day I shall have it shaved off.' Oh my, he was very much afraid. If I meet him now, I think he will not like me: but what do I care, I hate these Banias. And some of them when they get into positions in the Government, they try and make things difficult for us. I am not afraid of him—if he says anything against me, I will slap his face."

He poured us another drink, and this changed the subject of his conversation:

"There are many poems in Rajasthani about our wine, and about beauty, and of war. Nobody up till now has come to the conclusion exactly as to what is the real beauty. Some say it is fair, some dark. For example, they say that Lord Krishna has a dark skin; but other rulers before him, one had a yellow skin and one had a white skin. People in Arabia say that a woman with big thick hips is very beautiful—they go to that side. And in England they say that a woman with golden hair and black eyes is the most beautiful: and the Japanese like women with small feet, so they bind the feet. So you come to this conclusion—that what you think is most beautiful is best. What your eyes think is most beautiful is best for you. What we say, when we describe our typical Rajput beauty? The poem says (he quotes a Mewari poem and translates it for us): 'The walking of a lady should be with the fragrance of an elephant.'"

G.M.C. "An elephant?"

R.S. "Oh yes, that is the most fragrant animal! Yes, especially in its walk, an elephant is a very delicate animal. Her grace should be like that of a tiger. For a tiger, you know, its waist is so supple that it can bend its head round to the tail end: so should her waist be supple. Her teeth should be like a diamond: the lips should be like the pod of *mung dal*. Her eyebrows should be like the new moon. There are poems about wine too, so many poems. About *daru* they say—everyone says it is bad, it causes harm to the system. But there are two things in its favour. 'As soon as you drink, the pleasure comes out: you are the right lord of all the intoxications, Oh Dobaro.' That is a poem we have. And then it says: 'After drinking you are never miser.' These are the two faculties that wine brings forth from you—bravery in battle and generosity. This is the praise of wine.

"This, I think: if forefathers knew, when dancing girls were heard, if they knew that they would be taken by the sardars into rooms and enjoyed—they would not have encouraged the employment of dancing girls for simple entertainment.

"And if they knew that drinking too much would go to dropsy and sickness they would not have introduced this wine —they only brought in wine in order to make Rajputs brave in battle. Every Rajput has two pegs before going to war, it is a general custom. Still it is the way. Last year, one of the Princes was very drunk, at the Dashera time; and someone was killing a buffalo, but he failed. The Rana taunted this Prince: 'You cannot kill it', and at once he got to his feet, took his sword, and with one stroke he severed its head.

" ' I shall have two sips of wine and then I shall gather the woman into my arms and then '—I forget now how it goes. That is one of the poems composed by Rana Sajjan Singh.

"Red eyes are taken to be very beautiful. They are the sign of lust: those who have the good fortune to have red lines in the eyes, they are thought to be very lusty. Rajputs are very lusty, Sahib. It is because of their food and their drink. It makes them so that they have to have their lust, poor fellows. Wine also makes you lusty. So, now you have another praise of wine. Then she says: 'Oh mighty Lord, my eyes are red —with drink and lust—'. That is another song composed by Sajjan Singh. I cannot remember the whole of it now.

"He was the best ruler ever—he was misled by his courtiers. He was led to drink more. But he was a very wise man. He thought library was very essential in those days. He built the

Victoria Library in Udaipur for everyone to read free—and he built the gardens for the people—and in those hundred years back he started that Gazette. Just imagine, what they consider necessary today, he began already a hundred years back. What a mighty lord he was! But they led him into wrong path—if he could have ruled only twenty years I think Mewar would have gone into a different path: but he died of drink after only ten years. The Resident's doctor said he must stop drinking or it would kill him. But he said: 'What do I care? So let me die.' They could not stop him from drinking. It could not be changed, it was in his fate.

"I'll tell you now about doctors. There was this brother of Sajjan Singh, he had a kidney disease, and the doctor gave him medicine—but he did not like doctors so as soon as he went away he threw the medicine out of the window. Then they brought him those green pills from the bazaar and he swallowed three at once, and his urine was green. When the doctor saw it next day he said: 'Why is this? I did not give you such medicine.' And he said: 'Let me be, doctor. What I choose to urinate, that is my affair.'

"Very mighty people they were: they could cure a man by looking at a man like this. It is not joking, it happens like this—the other night I was coming back from Debari and by bad luck all our petrol ran dry. My driver was very anxious, but I said just wait, God will give us help. So we sat at Ferozeshaw's shop in Udaipur, and after half an hour a man came, and we got four gallons of petrol. You see, I don't believe in all those superstitions like those people in Rudra-prayag.* They believed the panther was the soul of some man. No, Sahib, I believe only these things that I myself know, such as this thing about the will-power."

Without a pause he returned to the theme of the Rajputs' views on physical beauty:

"There are three types of eyes, and all the types, each has a particular effect. One eye is whitish, and these are as if giving beautiful interest—it is as if his eyes are dropping nectar. Such eyes are giving life. And those that have the black lines, that eye is dangerous, it is dropping poison out—dammit, get away. And if he has red eyes, he is full of lust, he is enamoured, gives enamours, gets woman enamoured. These are the three kinds of eyes—one gives life, one gives death, one gets enamoured.

* Referring to Jim Corbett's book *The Man-Eating Leopard of Rudra-prayag*, which I had recently lent to him

"See, such culture, Sahib! These Whitecaps will never learn such culture. The very classical poets and singers, they are to be found in the princely palaces only. Now, Sahib has met about a thousand people in the village by this time, but can any of them tell you all these matters like I have just told?

"Now the art of pleasing people was taught by the dancing-girls, and the princes used to go to learn from them the art to please. The Ruler and the 'pross', they both have the same thing to do, to make people pleased. Yes, they are of one kind.

"When I go away from you, you will talk; my back will be a target. But unless I have been cultured and made you happy, so that you will only speak in my praise, then only will I be pleased."

"God looks at all people with equal eyes, but he treats them all differently. If he treated us all equal, why should Sahib's face be white and my face be like this? If you give a grain of rice to an ant it will be more than enough, but if you give one grain to an elephant, what good will it do? No, Sahib, God does not treat us equally, and that is why some are born to rule, and some are made to be ruled. This Communism will be sure to fail, we shall see it: the rulers will come back into their own."

He discussed next the privileges accorded to senior nobles by the Rana, including exemption from attendance in court. Such privileges are accorded only to those to whom he gives the *tazim*.

"Tazimdar—the way we greet His Highness is like this, with folded hands. And he stands up when we come, and he salutes us like this (right hand across chest, palm upward). And we give the *nazarana*, and then he sits down on a throne and we sit down at his side, but below him. He speaks with folded hands: '*Apro man razi hai?* Are you in happy state?' I reply, with folded hands: '*Hazur i kamun diun*—By your Grace's favour.' Then he asks what my hunting was like, and I tell him, perhaps, that it was not very good. He asks what I have killed, and I tell him such and such: and then I say with deference that His Highness should see that his forests are kept by good men. And he will say: 'I hear your good advice.' Then, we have talked for a little time, he makes a sign like this (raising his chin) and an attendant will bring me the *pan* wrapped in another leaf—it is called the *bira*—and he gives me this. It is a sign that I may take my leave. When we speak, he says '*Hukm*'; and when he speaks, we say: '*Bara hukm*'. But there, you have to be very prompt, because, if not, then his master-of-ceremonies will tell you you have made a mistake, you show want of respect.

"There is so much ceremony, all these things. Now when I am waiting to have audience with His Highness, that attendant comes, and offers me the *bira*, in both hands, like this: that is to show that His Highness is waiting to receive me. And then when I come into the room where he is, another of his Sardars who is always standing there by the door, he calls out loudly to warn His Highness. He says: '*Nazar Apche. Raj Hazir vegia.*' * And as soon as he says this, His Highness will stand up to greet me.

"And another thing, Sahib. If I offer him something, I will offer it like this (holds left hand below right, arms outstretched, palms upward) and he will take it like this, see, I will show you. (Demonstrates how Rana puts right hand over his open palm, left hand under it, then reverses the hand, so that the gift comes to lie in his right hand.) It is held to be bad manners to lift a thing off the hand with the fingers. If he makes to do this, I think I will draw my hand back, and that will show that I think he lacks respect for me."

Rajendra Singh declared his intention of taking an active part in the Rajputs' future political campaign:
"Of course, I am not the same as Churchill, but in my small way I also will serve. I shall, perhaps, make a lot of speeches, go among the Bhils. When I was President before, I used to fire them with one verb—I would say the old Rajasthani saying—' In the time of battle when Bhils die then the sons of Ranis die also.' All Rajputs are sons of Ranis, and when our old allies the Bhils are killed in battle, then we fall fighting also. So then I ask them: ' Do you want the rule of the sons of Ranis, or of these Banias, bloodsuckers?' Of course, they say for us, they hate those greedy Banias. I have decided now that I am ready to accept the Presidentship again."

Of the dispute with Kashmir, which was then being given prominence in the Calcutta *Statesman*, he said:
"Oh no, that will never be settled. Absolutely not. I can tell you, there will be a civil war in India. You may think

* " An audience: the prince is in attendance "

me a war-monger, just like they call Mr. Churchill, but when the time comes they will again turn to us. This is not war-mongering, it is only that I know very well what is going to happen—and they do not like what I say, but it will come to pass just so."

23rd February, 1951

An elderly Brahmin *pujari*, called Udai Lal, visited the Rao Sahib this morning. Rajendra Singh explained that his wife had a half-headache (a common ailment, in this part of India) and that he had come to ask for a *tabiz* to cure it. He invited me to watch while he prepared two pieces of paper, one four inches by two, the other one and a half inches square. " It must be written in special ink ", he said, showing me a pot of dried-up Indian ink and sending it to be mixed with water. Then he lit an incense-stick set in the corner of his desk, and began to write a *jantar* on the larger paper. The smaller paper was divided by two lines, horizontally and vertically, into nine compartments, and in each the same character, representing a name of God, was drawn. I asked if anyone could do this, who knew what to write, but he said: " You can do this only when you have got spiritual rise. He will take these *tabiz* and tie them to his wife's head and in two minutes the headache will be gone—such is the strength of the will-power. Of course, it is God who makes the sickness better, I am only his humble agent. It took me forty days of concentration to achieve the strength of will-power needed for this—and since then I have been practising it for eleven months. Now are you convinced of the power of the will?

" I have a *tabiz* here which cures malaria. Here, take one. When a man has fever I give him a *tabiz* like this, incensed so (waves it in the smoke of a stick of incense) and he wears it round his neck. Then his fever will leave him; either it will leave him at once, or next day he will have a strong fever, and then he will get better. Next time you see a man with fever, give him this. No, don't look at it. It is a secret thing, you must keep it folded like this."

Of the incense-stick he said: " The fragrance pleases your spirit—the angels which are about you." After writing on his two pieces of paper, he folded them and waved them through the smoke, telling me this time: " He will tie these on the side of the head, and in two hours it will not be painful any more." Then he called the Brahmin over and instructed him to tie them to that side of the head which had been aching, and keep them there for four days.

25th February, 1951

On our return from a two-day absence, we were entertained to dinner by Rajendra Singh, who was in very good humour. He explained that a fortunate thing had happened today: a prominent Rajput Prince, the Raja of Jubal, had had a breakdown on the road and asked for the loan of a car. Rajendra Singh insisted on entertaining him, and fairly glowed in his delight at having enjoyed the company of so important a man— a Jagirdar with an income of Rs. 2,500,000. He attributed his good fortune to an act of God, a reward for his spiritual exercises. He quoted much of their conversation to us. He remarked that the Raja ate only two chapattis at lunch, but smoked fifteen cigarettes (for the occasion, Rajendra Singh produced a very special box of gold-tipped ' Carlton Specials ') and enjoyed his gin. " If he had stayed this evening I think he would drink half a bottle of whisky: that would be 16 rupees. And we would have drunk the other half, so 32 rupees —what of it? Get another bottle!"

Rajendra Singh gave us an account of the Rajputs' duty of supporting those whose salt one has eaten. He illustrated it with a story of a former Raj Rana of Sadri, who was at war with the Sheshodia Rajputs. The night before the battle he entertained a travelling Sheshodia in his tents, and next day told him to go on, because a fight was imminent; but his guest insisted on fighting with his host even against his own kin, and was killed in the action. The descendants of this man still hold a Jagir of about Rs. 5,000 under Sadri, in recognition of his gallantry.

28th March, 1951

Rajendra Singh returned from Udaipur late last night. This evening we walked with him in the stables. He introduced a Brahmin from Garhwal, who has a hereditary connection with the Deoli family. His first comment on his stay in Udaipur was: " Such times we had, Madam! Ten days on end I have been drinking and playing. Day before yesterday, my brother-in-law and my sister were to go, but we had such good drinking that he did not go. Each man finished half a bottle of whisky. There was a dancing girl, and we were all drunk. Oh, we did everything with her, Sahib, pulling her this way and that way, making her sit on our laps.

"I have been drinking too much these last few days. Yesterday also, the Maharaj Kumar invited me to play Phag, but I begged to be excused, I knew we should never get away if I went there."

He was not very exuberant in the evening, said he was " feeling heavy, Sahib. One good purgative will make it all right."

On being teased about drinking too much, Rajendra Singh seriously argued that drink does not interfere with " spiritual rise ". In moderation, it may help one attain it as it helps one acquire the necessary concentration. For the last ten days he has had to work very hard to keep from losing his spiritual rise. The best he could do was to hold his own and not lose ground. A man who has achieved great heights of spiritual rise does not need the aid of a picture of God: he can carry that picture about in his mind—wherever he looks he sees it with one part of his mind and is concentrating on it with that part of his mind, while at the same time he talks with people and attends to his affairs.

It is an impediment to spirituality to be involved in business, to regard it as the most important thing—so long as your spiritual rise is the most important thing for you, you can engage in everyday affairs as Rajendra Singh does, without being deflected from the most important purpose.

1st April, 1951

Rajendra Singh returned to a previous theme: that the two greatest things life has to offer are, to take one's ease in the pleasures of the bed with one or two girls of sixteen—" raw girls, who are still virgin "; or else to devote oneself to prayer and spiritual rise. He argued that one should taste experience to the full—if one eats, one should eat until one is replete, and the same with making love. He, himself, as a young man had made love to the limit, attended by two or three girls. So much so, that he had to lie and rest all next day. But after satiating oneself in this way, one comes to appreciate that the satisfaction of bodily appetites is a transitory pleasure: " Soon you want the same again, dammit, silly thing."

A sensible man then turns his endeavours to more lasting satisfactions, the highest of which is " praying God, in order to get a spiritual rise ". He quoted the Bhagavadgita, in which Arjuna asks God what is the use of straining to worship Him, and is reminded that merit is rewarded in one's next incarnation. Rajendra Singh went on to congratulate himself on his good fortune in being born rich and of high caste. " The finest thing ", he said, " is to be born a Rajah." If one is really wealthy, the caste is of less importance. The advantage of wealth is: " I am able to give up four hours every day to these " (shows his string of beads) " to my prayers. But if I am a poor man I must work all the time in order to eat—how then can I say my prayers? "

G.M.C. " You would have to become a *sannyasi?* "

R.S. " That's it: give up all worldly possessions. But I do not have to do that, thank God. I am able to do my prayers and also to pull on in my ordinary affairs."

Rajendra Singh now went on to define three degrees of sexual immorality. The first, a venal offence, is to sleep with a prostitute: " You can afford it, it is her profession—the only crime is that you are giving her something which rightly belongs to your wife. A much more serious crime is to have intercourse with another man's wife, because you are robbing not only your wife, but also that man of their sexual dues. The third, and atrocious crime, is to sleep with someone like your mother's sister's daughter, who is called ' sister ': that is like sleeping with your own sister and for that you will surely die."

G.M.C. " Do you consider women as equal to men? "

R.S. " No, they are inferior to men, for three reasons. One, they are weaker bodily; two, they are less able to stand pain and hardship; three, because they have these periodic ' courses ' for three days in every month when the blood flows. At such times we hold them to be unclean: we do not touch them, and if we are touched by accident we take a bath. At such times they cannot prepare food for us, and they cannot sit with us on the same floor. That is why women are inferior."

Later in the course of this evening I told Singh: " I've noticed that many people here keep asking me for a ' good, strength-giving medicine '."

R.S. " Yes, they will ask you for that: there are so many medicines to keep you strong, to keep from losing the strength of the body."

G.M.C. " And they tell me the strength of the body is lost through the semen. . . ."

R.S. " Exactly so. It says in our Hindu science that one drop of semen is made from forty drops of blood, and it is made with great difficulty. A man who indulges in very much luxury, he loses so much semen that he becomes all weak. Of course, he will not die, but such a man will be less able to resist pain and hardships. Also, he will be liable to get overheated, fever, and get angry too easily. Whereas a strong man, he does not get hot and angry. If things happen to annoy him, he knows that he has only to spend two hours in prayer to God and they will cease to trouble. But a weak man, how is he going to say such prayers? He cannot do it."

4th April, 1951

On our return from an afternoon's shoot at the lake, Rajendra Singh rode alone and told his beads all the way. We were late in getting home, had drinks at 8.30, and dined about 9.0 p.m. Fateh and Prithwi (aged 6 and 3 respectively) were both awake, though in pyjamas. Fateh said they were not ready to sleep because they hadn't yet had their dinner. It seemed that they were obliged to wait until their father had dined before they could eat their meal. I asked Fateh at 8.40 p.m. " Aren't you hungry? " He said: " Not yet. In a little while I'll be hungry."

Almost every evening, the two boys are in attendance on their father, who watches them strictly, uttering sharp, stern commands. Fateh seems absolutely cowed, sitting still beneath his father's gaze with big frightened eyes. Prithwi has far more spontaneity, is aware of his own charm: he is used to his cherubic smile making people respond to him with affectionate indulgence. Prithwi is the more stubborn of the two, and does not always obey his father's gruff commands, though he does sometimes freeze up with fright, and his cherubic face looks uncertain, until his father's attention is distracted from him and then he plays happily and mischievously again with the Rajput who always waits on him.

This evening, he saw his father call a servant to massage his leg, and at once Prithwi began to demand and receive the same attention—nestling in the old Rajput's lap at the same time, like a well-cared for and trusting child.

5th April, 1951

We talked of the local peasants' beliefs in demons and witchcraft, and Rajendra Singh said: " Only one in a thousand of them is the genuine thing. People who are educated do not believe in these ghosts, *dakans, purbaj,* such things. Even if they do exist, such things cannot harm a man who worships God.

"Of course, I believe there are such things as ghosts. Sometimes a man's spirit will stay on in some place: but if you are a man with strong will-power, with a good spiritual rise, then you will not be afraid of them—they cannot do you any harm. I myself have seen a ghost. It was in Gangor House, there in Udaipur. I was sleeping in a room and my wife was sleeping quite near me, when I was awakened, but I did not know by whom. Two other fellows were sleeping in the next room, but I did not see anyone. After wondering what it was that woke me, I drank some water and lay down to sleep again, but very soon I woke, for there was something sitting on my back. It was not heavy, but I felt it there. I gave a kick and it went away. I sat up, thinking, 'What can this thing be, dammit?' Then I went to relieve myself, make water, and as I came back from the bathroom I heard footsteps walking behind me. So I said, 'Come on, if you want to fight, I am ready.' But there was nobody there. After wondering about this for ten minutes, I went to sleep."

13th April, 1951

"Tonight I am very happy, Sahib—so very happy! Last night I had a very beautiful thing happen to me. I dreamt that I saw my Guru. I woke up during the night and I was wondering how Fateh was, because you know sometimes he does not sleep well. Sometimes he cries out in his sleep, and sometimes he gets up and walks about. So my wife got up and went to see, and she came and told me he was sleeping quite quietly. Then I settled myself to sleep again, and I was thinking to myself: 'Why do I have such cares, why is he not better so that I can turn all my thought to higher things?' And then I dreamt that I saw my Guruji himself, and he said to me: 'Rest assured. I know that something very good is about to come your way and that you will be freed from all worry, and your son will be quite well.' Then we talked for a little while, and I had the *darshan* of his presence. Now I know that everything will be quite all right.

"You know, Sahib, when a man has reached a certain stage, a certain level in spiritual rise, he has the power to divide himself into two. One half of him will remain in the body, and the other half will travel anywhere he likes. The Mussulmans call this *diwajir sharir*, and the Hindu words for it are *jis men nura nahin*—It is as if the light which is inside you has gone elsewhere."

G.M.C. " And has your Guruji reached this stage? "

R.S. " Oh yes, of that I am perfectly sure. He has attained such a spiritual rise, Sahib, that he has complete command over matter. He is able to know things that are happening at the same moment, hundreds of miles away. And if, for example, there is an airplane travelling in the sky, and he concentrates his will upon it, it would fall straight away to the ground. Do you not believe that, Sahib? "

G.M.C. " It is very remarkable."

R.S. " I can tell you a very wonderful thing which happened to a relative of mine, my uncle Godha Singh's wife's brother. This was just two years ago. He is a young man, and he was much troubled at that time by pains in the stomach. They thought it was appendix, and Dr. Sharma took out the appendix, but after a little while the pains again returned. Now at that time there was a famous *guru* visiting Udaipur, one of the family of Darunachar, whose far distant ancestors taught Ram Chandarji how to use his bow and arrow. The family is still there in Garhwal and the present *Guru* has a great school in which he teaches Ayurvedic medicine, and the shastars. They still have a very wonderful *mantar* in that family, and the present *guru* knows it. If a man only says this *mantar*, when he goes to shoot an arrow, then the arrow will fly a great distance, and then turn and come back to him, and fall by itself into the quiver he carries on his back. He is a very great Guru, this Darunachar; I went myself to have a *darshan* of him while he was in Udaipur. Well, this young man I was telling you about, he went to ask the *Guru* what he could do to ease the pains in his stomach. And the *Guru* told him: Every day, for forty-one days, you must sit for one hour, promptly at eight o'clock, after going to the bathroom and washing and putting on clean clothes: and you must concentrate to the exclusion of everything else, upon the Guruji, my father. So he did this, he sat with his eyes shut and thought only of that man. And while he was sitting in concentration like that, he used to get shocks running through his body, like when you touch an electric wire—and something used to move his belly inside. He did this for forty-one days, and he was absolutely cured: he had no more pains. He is there in Udaipur still, I think, you can ask him. Was that not a very wonderful thing? "

G.M.C. " Indeed it was—I should like to meet him and ask him about it."

R.S. "Ah, Sahib, I wish if my *Guru* came and simply put his hand on the head of my son—then he would never suffer any more illness the whole of his life—is that not lovely, Sahib? But I know that he will come: when he knows that it is the right time, he will come and tell me how to go on the right path. Even now, Sahib, I know that if I am ever in serious trouble, he will come to help me: all I need do is to sit before his picture and concentrate on him—I do not even need his picture, I can shut my eyes and see his image in my mind. In about ten minutes he will come and appear before me, and talk, and tell me everything that I need to know."

12th August, 1951

"A very holy man is coming to visit me next week, a Mussulman by caste. He is a *chela* of my own *guru*. My *guru* is Hindu; but when you get to a certain spiritual rise you do not give any thought to Hindu or Mussulman or Jew or Christian. If God comes from behind the veil, will not every man of whichever faith see that he is God? The holy man will stay only a day or two and ask what I am doing and how far I have reached in my spiritual rise, and give me some word of teaching and then go on his way.

"The essentials are, to remember God all the time, by making the repeating of his name such a thing of habit that one's heart says *So-han, so-han* with every beat, throughout the twenty-four hours and so that every breath is also a repetition of his name; and also at set times, when one repeats the chosen name of God not aloud, but in one's heart over and over again. Some become *sannyasis*, but others like myself administer the properties with which God has endowed us, and do our duty in the world, as well as pray, and God is doubly pleased because we do both these duties."

G.M.C. "So, I take it the primary thing in this praying, this taking the name of God, is self-forgetfulness?"

R.S. "Oh no, to forget the self, that comes at a much later stage. The first thing is to do everything regularly, every day without fail, and to do it in the proper measure."

G.M.C. "Is that why giving way to anger is so much condemned by Hindus?"

R.S. "The reason for that—you know what causes anger? It is due to excess of sex. Suppose I have sex not according to measure, but every night, or more often: then I become tired, and when it is time for my prayers, at 12.30 at night, or at

5.0 in the morning, I am sleepy and I am not happy, so I do not pray well and so I do not get a good spiritual rise. And that is the thing which is most important to me of all things, so I am out of temper and if anything happens next day at once I fly into a rage. It is all due to excessive indulgence in sex."

G.M.C. "So sex is the chief obstacle to spiritual rise?"

R.S. "Yes, it is the chief obstacle. Of course, if you are a married man you have to have sex, but you should have it according to fixed control—*niyam se*—whether once a week, or twice a week, whatever is your fixed measure. It is the same with everything you do, sleeping or eating or drinking or praying, it should be done according to regulation, that is the essential thing.

"When you get to a certain spiritual rise, you know what is going to come—for example, I am perfectly sure that there will be no elections; that there will be war between India and Pakistan in October. There are other things which cannot be told. Then, they will come to us Rajputs and ask for our help, and we shall say: 'What about our brothers, the Jagirdars? If you do not stop abolishing their rights, we will not help you'. See this village, there are forty Mussulman houses, and they can produce seventy-five fighting men. And out of the 950 other houses in the village, except for us Rajputs, there are scarcely five fighting men. The Rajputs are the real defenders of the country, and of the Hindu religion. Without us they are paralysed."

Rajendra Singh was absent from the village for several days, engaged on political work with the Rajputs' party. On his return I found him despondent and unenthusiastic. He told me that he no longer wished to take part in public life, but instead to concentrate upon his spiritual exercises. He meant to continue with these until he reached that level of insight at which one has clear knowledge of the future—then he would know best when to intervene in worldly affairs: "Strike while the iron is hot, come in on the winning side."

For the meantime, his spiritual advancement was his only concern: "I will talk for them in their meetings only if it does not interrupt my prayers. Must have my tea at 6 a.m., then good clean-out of bowels and bath. Tea at 8.0 will not do. I do not mind giving a lecture for twenty minutes, but I cannot remain for hours listening to all those speeches—I must retire to get on with my prayers.

"That is my nature, Sahib. I know clearly what is right for me to do. It says that in my horoscope, that I will not submit to anyone's bidding."

He then relapsed into a mood of despair—how could a man like him, brought up to princely ways, ever survive in conditions of democracy? It was ruin for the Jagirdars, and the Sardars. All know that if the Jagirdars went, they went—that is why he talked so much of war, not for love of war or that it would be a good thing for the country, but just that he himself and his fellow Rajputs could die and put an end to their misery. He quoted the Jodhpur Rajputs' defiance of Jagirdar Abolition. (They had just written to the Rajasthan Government to say that as they had won their Jagirs, so they would hold or lose them—by the sword.) For himself, he felt like a desperately sick patient who asks the doctor for poison, since there is no way out from his illness—"Only he wants to hasten the end." He refused to consider adapting himself to the new situation—let his sons do that, they would be well educated and would grow up not knowing anything of the princely glory which they had lost.

His mood of despair was evanescent; a moment later he was planning two alternative courses of action; one of devoting himself more and more completely to prayer; the other, of publishing a book of his rare Rajput prints, with his own text, selling it in America and earning at least Rs. 50,000.

During his talk, he referred more than once to a question I had put to him some days before, as to whether drinking wine and eating meat were compatible with spiritual rise: this evidently touched him on a sensitive spot. He said again that he was independent of what other people say—he made his own rules.

1st October, 1951

This evening the Rao Sahib entertained me to *daru*, and spoke with great animation, quoting verses illustrative of Rajput culture.

"—*Mas bina sab ghas rasoi, Daru bina tari shanti na hui*—Lacking meat, all food is as grass: lacking wine, thou hadst no happiness." And then—"*Hun balli hari Ranian*—"—" I must praise all those Rajput wives who teach their sons in their very wombs to seize from the midwife's hand the tube-cutting knife."

"Hear this poem, Sahib, about the marriage: '*Pahahle milanen dhan puchhis*—' It says: 'At the first meeting the wife asks, ' What have you done that your hands are so rough?' The man answering says: " The sword has given me these rough hands.' Let me translate for you this song of a Rajput bride. She says: ' Oh, my bridesmaid, my husband walks in the lanes, like a meek and humble person, but when he hears the songs of war, then he is a Lord. Oh maid, my husband's body looks limber—as soon as he hears the chink of armour every fibre starts to quiver! '

" Similarly I look, Sahib, but when the time comes . . .!

" Today these people came from the school to ask for permission to play inside the palace courtyard. I sent them away—I have nothing to do with them.

" There is another saying of the fight at Komulgarh, Kushal Singh was outnumbered, yet he said: ' If this earth goes under other's rule while I still live, then the sun will rise in the west! ' What a bravery Sahib, eh?

" But another thing you must know is, we Rajputs always remembered: ' Discretion is the better part of valour.' We would not take risks for any worthless cause. If anyone asks me to go and face a tiger on foot, I won't do it. Let some worthless man do that work. But if His Highness of Udaipur is sitting on ground and a tiger attacks him, I will never fly. I will attack it first with my sword. I count it my duty.

" There is a story in our Rajput history—Jamalji of Badnor, coming to Chitor to serve Rana of Mewar, met 200 Bhils. He had twenty-five to fifty Rajputs. The Bhils demanded all his money and some of his weapons. He gave it. He said: ' If I do that, we shall go on all of us to fight gloriously for the Maharana. But who will know I fought these Bhils? That I died fighting these monkeys? But if I fight for Maharana, then I have name in history! ' So he showed discretion. So today, don't die fighting White-caps, what's the good? It's all humbug. Better to fight for religion, then community, then country. If the community is with me, then we can go and grasp any country—China, Burma, anywhere! We should not fight in an unworthy cause. We should not fight the Indian army."

13th October, 1951

Rajendra Singh discussed the coming General Elections. He was very confident that the Rajputs' party would have a sweeping victory in Rajasthan. He described himself as one of the good rulers, in touch with his peasantry: " Out of

35,000 tenants, only some thirty-five dogs of Brahmins and Banias in the village here oppose me, the rest all love me. I am not afraid to take my sword and face them in the bazaar. I shall fight and kill many of them before I die bravely. Dogs bark, the elephant goes his way—what do I care what they say?"

He mentioned the recent *suttee* at Kundela village which he cited as an act of exemplary virtue. The Thakurani sat on her husband's funeral pyre, with a rosary of beads in her fingers while they lit the fire: " Oh, what a fine piety is there, Sahib! She loved her husband so much, she was not afraid to die. People believe that a woman who does this becomes at once very near to God: so when her last moments are come, they ask her questions, believing that she will answer with divine wisdom. She said in reply to one question that Rajput rule will soon come again—and she told people to be true to their religion and stay on the right path."

15th October, 1951

Rajendra Singh quoted songs of the Charans again: recited verses in praise of *suttee*. In one, a Rajput mother hears the news of her daughter's *suttee* and says she is not surprised: " Even as a baby that girl used to leave the breast and gaze entranced if a candle were brought into the room. From that time her mother knew of her love for the consuming flame."

In another, a woman about to commit *suttee* at a time when her husband was killed, calls for the saffron robes appropriate to the suicidal *johar*, and reproves her brother for coming bearing the *chandel* sari instead of the saffron (*keshari*) sari which a woman puts on for the *suttee* fire.

In another verse, a tiger and tigress converse when surrounded by hunters. The tiger is unafraid. The tigress comments on his *keshari* coat: " Rajputs wear this colour for the *johar*, but tigers wear it all the time."

27th October, 1951

Rajendra Singh was on the " moon terrace " when I joined him at 7.30 p.m. on a dark starlit night. He was talking with his lawyer, one Bhamar Lal Vyas, M.A., LL.B., who is also secretary of the Udaipur Hindu Mahasabha, and so a political ally. They talked about the election, the Vakil saying the R.S.S. was in angry mood in the recent Delhi municipal elections—rioted and smashed several ballot-boxes. Rajendra Singh considered this a hopeful sign, and indulged in mockery and abuse of Congress leaders, especially the uneducated ones. He spoke in flattering terms of the learning, administrative skill and integrity of his Rajput friends. He asked me to support his assertion that the peasantry are all in favour of their old Rajput masters. I cautiously said that they made plenty of criticisms of the Congress, and this gratified him.

He noted a blaze in the darkness near the burning-ghat, asked his servants who had died, but they didn't know of any death. The Vakil asked me how I liked the country, and he also tried to draw me on politics. Both he and Rajendra Singh dilated upon the increase in corruption in the last three years. Rajendra Singh said there was corruption in the Jagirdars' rule, but it was restrained by the knowledge that if the Ruler came to hear of it the offender would be summarily punished: " I would put him in my jail, I think. Now, they are not restrained by fear of their superiors, because they too take bribes: everyone has to bribe, rich and poor alike—otherwise their papers get lost or indefinitely delayed."

With a display of nostalgic magnanimity both the lawyer and my host recalled instances of the probity of former British officials. The latter observed that even his fellow-princes used to insist upon a British administrator being the president of any Settlement Commission appointed to arbitrate their territorial disputes because they had faith in his impartiality.

The Vakil quoted, as evidence of the current scarcity of men of integrity, the fact that the Rajputs' Party had recently had a long debate about which candidate they should select for an Udaipur constituency, and found that there was no one in whom they had full confidence. At this Rajendra Singh laughed out loud and said: " We are all like that—I am included in it too."

He listened rather apathetically while the Vakil quoted a much-travelled citizen of Udaipur who said that Mewar had all the natural advantages of Switzerland, Paris and Germany —it only lacked development. Then he took command of the conversation again and told us in a flood of emphatic Mewari about the remarkable properties of a certain holy place near Komulgarh: " If you go to that very spot where Rana Kumbha performed austerities, and dig there, you will find in the earth a substance like quinine. If you eat this and confine your diet to milk and rice only, then in one week you will find that you are having visions of all the Gods at will—Ganesh, Hanuman, Lakshmi, all of them. If you practise *tapassya* * there yourself for only a little while, that spot has such virtue that you will be granted in days what would otherwise take you months to achieve, and in months, the fruit of years. Few people know of this. . . . In Abu, also, there is a holy man, a Sikh, who is 150 years old. He wants none of the rewards of this world. You may think it remarkable that he should be so old and yet so well preserved—yet that is nothing! There are places where you can dig the earth and reveal the body of a man, in perfect physical condition, who took *samadhi* 300 years ago—there are many such in different parts of India. What of that? Doesn't everyone know that these ' risen ' spirits have powers unknown to ordinary men? "

30th October, 1951

Rajendra Singh commented on Churchill's return to power: quoted his paper as saying that now things will heat up in Egypt and in Persia. He said Churchill is pro-Pakistan, and added hopefully that that would increase the likelihood of Indo-Pakistan war. He recalled a prophet's rhyme in Mewari about a world war in Samwat year 2009 (due to begin in March, 1952).

A tipsy servant came up to say something. Rajendra Singh abused him, gave him some orders, shouted after him in Mewari: " Get out, quick—I'll give you such a slap that your faeces will come out." He asked me if I understood what he said, laughed and added: " That is the Rajput way: they are accustomed to command, to have their orders obeyed at once, no argument. Better the rule of one wise man, Sahib, than of a pack of fools—what do you think? " I told him that was what Churchill believed in too, and he agreed. He quoted a Dohita: " This is my land, and I am its master: how dare they take it from me? Let them come and see if they can take the skin from off a tiger while the tiger is still alive! "

When I left Rajasthan several months later, the elections were over, and the Rajputs' party had been defeated (though by a narrow majority). Rajendra Singh remained undecided to the last whether to stand for election or not. In the end,

* *Tapassya:* rigorous exercises of self-mortification

he felt that events were not yet ripe for his intervention, and made a resolve to concentrate still more upon his spiritual rise, so that when the time comes, he will be ready.

RAJENDRA SINGH

Formal Psychological Tests

Rajendra Singh correctly answered 27 out of 60 Ravens Matrices problems in 30 minutes. The scores of the eight other subjects of equivalent educational status who performed this test were: 21, 28, 33, 35, 39, 41, 42 and 45. He was most uncomfortable in the test situation: relieved his feelings by confronting one of his servants with the plates and pointing out, without a pause, that *he* was too ignorant even to attempt to understand it. This uneasiness was still more apparent during his performance of the Rorschach Test: he had to be encouraged more than once to persevere to the end. After this he showed unwillingness to submit to the Word-Association Test. It was suggested on subsequent occasions, but he waved it aside.

Rorschach Test:

RORSCHACH PROTOCOL. RAJENDRA SINGH

Test given 20th February, 1951.

I.

25″ What you see in this, you have got to say?
/Yes, that's it./
For how many minutes?
/For as long as you are interested; then I shall show you the next card./
(Sets card on table, pores over it.)
(Pause, 165″)
I seem to fail in this.
/Just look, and tell me what you see in it./

∧ 1. The whole thing looks to me like a *bat*, that is my first conclusion.
2. This portion (top right corner) is *map of India*: see, this is Rinn of Kutch, this Bombay side.
∧ 3. And this (top left corner) is like South America, like I could draw —nothing special. That's all I can see, nothing else.

Inquiry

/Bat flying or sitting?/ Flying.

/Anything else here?/ And then you must know I am a man who doesn't care about anything. I say a bat, or anything else—what do I care? I don't give much exercise to my brain; I keep my mind for concentration upon God.

TT 4′

II.
(Laughs in an embarrassed tone) I think I'll fail in this.
/Oh no, there's no question of passing or failing: this is not an intelligence test./
15"
∧ 1. They look like bear—two *bears* fighting.
∧ 2. And then as if necks have been cut, and a streak of blood coming from both the heads (top reds).
(Pauses to address some words to a man standing at the back of the room, then remarks):
A Jagirdar has died without heirs—all his property has to be taken into our possession, about Rs. 5,000 worth. (The man goes out.)
∧ (Studies card 20" longer, then turns it over.)
Right: take another one.
TT 2¼'

/How much of it is " bear "?/
All this, the black. And blood streams also this way (red seen beneath the black) and down to here (low centre red).
How could they fight without heads? And I do not think they would let their heads be cut, even with one stroke (laughs nervously). Simply making up! When you don't see something clear, you make up some story.

III.
20"
∧ 1. They look to be like two *skeletons of monkeys* put in some sort of exhibition (laughs).
(Indicates main black forms.)
∧ 2. And the red in between shows some sort of indication of some *heart picture*.
∧ No, I can't do much.
Can you turn this upside down?
/If you like./ (Turns card, then gives up.)
(Subject's six-year-old son stands looking on for one minute.)

/Monkeys doing anything?/ Put in a glass case—dead things, lifeless.
/These things? (outer reds)/ No—simply dots, red dots, that's all. Nothing.

IV.
10"
∧ 1. This looks to me like a trimmed *skin* of some bear (laughs).
∨ 1 ∧ (Mutters: " Eh hamara sala," i.e. " Eh, you bastard "; sits back in chair holding card up to the light. Then speaks with animation):
∧ 2. Now then, Sahib, this time I see something else. This seems to be an *image*, idol-like thing. It is some stone carving. Here I see two eyes and two eyebrows; and this is taken to be the top of the head (details in top centre).

(Image is dimly seen, in a dark shadowy background.)
/Remind you of any special image?/ No Indian God, this: like some Greek God, I have learned in school. Those Greeks had some Gods such as these.

∧   Stone-carving of some old temple: and they have photographed it in the dark, and this portion only got the light.
These notes are very useful, Sahib?
/We'll talk about the test after I have shown you all the cards./
TT ½′

/Made of?/ Dark stone, in a dark place.
What have you seen, Sahib?
/I'll tell you later, what I saw: some the same as you, some different./

V.
10″
∧ 1. This is a *flying-fox* (laughs). A flying-fox-like thing (laughs loudly).
I am taking them all like animals—they might be a man, no?
/Sometimes; it all depends what you see. . . ./
(Pause, 20″)

/Flying-fox doing?/ It is on the alert, standing on its legs and about to start flight—just stretched its wings (waves right hand expansively).
/What are the boys lying on?/ Just guessing, Sahib: I don't make out.

∧ 2. Here I see . . . some *boys*, two boys, lying I feel on both sides with their eyes, small nose, and here are their legs. (Shows silhouette details, upper surfaces of black shape each side.) Nothing else in particular. (Points to rounded prn., upper margin.) He is lying there with his hands like this (folds his hands across his chest, holds chin up).
TT 1½′

I think I shall be the last in this, eh Sahib?
(He is re-assured that there is no question of first or last.)

VI.
⌐ (Sits back, holds card near his face; murmurs in dialect: "What is it?—they are all the same sort.")

10″
< 1. This seems to be a *pelican skin* (laughs).
Nothing I can make out. (Puts card aside.)
TT 1′

/Pelican?/ No, not pelican, penguin, a penguin—found in North Poles.
/Colour or shape?/ Not black and white; they are . . . something like whitish, found on the ice. The skin is stretched out.

I am giving them all the names of different animals (gives a defensive laugh). What were your views, Sahib?
/You are doing perfectly well. I'll tell you what I saw, later on./

VII.

🔲 (Looks at back, reads printed legend there.)

45″
V 1. These seem to be two *legs* with the muscles torn out; just the flesh remaining but the bones taken away: hung up for show (defensive laugh).
V I think I am the worst?
/Not at all, you are doing fine./
TT 1′

V /Animal or human legs?/ I think it is some animal. (Coughs and clears throat noisily, ceasing to take further interest in this card.)

VIII.

∧ (Takes betel-nut in a leaf, chews.) We sent out for panther-news today but we haven't had any reliable news yet.

35″
> 1. Some sort of animal going this way—more or less like a *porcupine* (lateral red forms).
∧ 2. And this looks like a *butterfly*, this portion only; red ones (low centre, red and orange).
∧ 3. Not a butterfly—moth, more like a moth. Not much difference between those two things.
(Pause, 30″.) Nothing.
TT 3′

/Porcupine doing?/ Trying to climb something—but it seems to be made of stone.
/Was it the colour that made you think of porcupine?/ No, no. Porcupines are not of this colour. It is made of some pinkish stone.
/Butterfly?/ It is resting.

You must be laughing, having a joke with Memsahib over this?
/Not at all. We have taken this test too, we don't laugh at it./
I must be showing very dull.
/No, this is not any kind of an intelligence test./
It is a common-sense test? Then you must know, I am not a common-sense man. Hey you—(in dialect, to a young servant)—What do you see in this?
/No, don't let him tell you: this is your turn./

Then it is a test, isn't it Sahib?
What does it matter, what he will
say? What he will say is: "This
is nothing. This is blot of ink."
The one answer he will put
(laughs scornfully).
(Servant waits uncertainly near
his chair.)

IX.

90″ (Calls out to another servant who
looks in the doorway: "What
have you brought?"
Servant: "Nothing." He sig-
nals to the young servant to join
him outside.)

(Pause, 15″ longer.)

1. Heads of two *goats*, or sheep (seen
in green-orange margin).
/Tester says encouragingly:
"Very good."/
Good! I think I will be the
worst (laughs).
(Pause, 40″)
(Puts card away.)

/Goats, or sheep?/ Something
1a. like a small *stag's head*, because of
the horns there: two or three
off-shoots.
/Anything else?/
Oh, yes, yes, yes! This I see
now (points to pink mass).
1b. There I see two *men's heads*—this
is the eye (inner detail). They
are both pictures, only head and
neck. Seem to be made out of
stone, coloured pinkish. Sahib
seems to be laughing at me.
/Not at all. You are doing very
well./

X.

Brain has failed, Sahib.
/Go on, you are doing fine./

15″
1. To me it seems to be different
parts of the body. All the pictures
are different parts of the body,
taken in rough—they are rough
sketches.
2. And this seems to be *skeleton*, a
man's skeleton, this (red masses,
and top centre grey). This is the
waist portion (centre blue
"bridge"), this chest portion
(enclosed white above this blue)
and this neck (top centre grey).
Only the waist and above—nothing below the waist. And
these are the insides, the intestines
laid out on either side. (Indicates all lateral shapes.)
TT 1½′

/Is it a bony skeleton?/ The
bony part has been removed—
only the flesh part has been hung:
dried up and hung up there.
That is all. These inside parts,
they are just laid there.

Is this all very foolish, Sahib?
Tell me now, what did you see in
this one? (Doesn't wait for an
answer.) What is the use of this
test? You see, I have said sometimes animal, sometimes insect—
all different. Tell me now, what
does this tell you about my
psychology?

Notes: Subject is aged 32, is head of his family. Father died when he was 15, mother is still alive. Subject has one younger brother, and one younger sister, both married and normally resident elsewhere. Subject was the preferred child of his father: his younger brother was, and still is preferred by his mother, with whom he does not get on very well. He is married. Three children died, after which he has had two boys and one girl.

Subject had heard of the Rorschach from his younger brother, who had already taken it. He was curious to see the plates, but apprehensive of the test. No amount of reassurance sufficed to convince him that he was not making a fool of himself. He repeatedly made remarks like: " I am the worst " in order to elicit further reassurances. He remained ill at ease throughout the test: at one stage wanted a servant to give some responses, obviously so that he could reassure himself with the spectacle of the uneducated servant's stupidity. At the end of the test, he asked tester to give a brief summary of his personality. When told that his personality could not be understood or expressed in a brief compass, he regained his composure, and read the tester a lecture on the virtue of devoting oneself to the contemplation of God. Those men who neglected religion were worse than beasts. The highest order of men were those who, like himself, devote their efforts towards getting nearer to a knowledge of God, etc., etc.

In this case the test was conducted in English. All cards were presented, and Inquiry then carried out.

Interpretation of Rorschach Test, by Rosemary Gordon, Ph.D.

Rajendra Singh

Rajendra Singh was given a Rorschach Test. The record obtained suggests that he has a predominantly extra-tensive personality structure and is thus more concerned and pre-occupied with events outside himself than with his internal life and activity. In fact, the paucity of human movement responses in his record indicates that his Ego structure lacks the strength and stability necessary to allow free access to phantasy activities. Thus he cannot draw upon the imaginal processes to bridge the gap between the inner world of drives and phantasies and a reality-orientated relationship to outer objects. Consequently his phantasy life has remained childish and dominated by simple and archaic forces, regarding which he tends to lack insight and understanding. He has thus remained a somewhat immature person, who tends to be impulsive and to give in to his need for the immediate gratification of his impulses rather than to direct his activities so as to serve his long term goals.

However, although extra-tensive, Rajendra Singh is by no means at ease in social and emotional situations; rather these tend to provoke a feeling of tension and inner conflict and such aggressive phantasies that his internalised objects—the image of the persons and things that he carries inside him—are liable to be destroyed and broken up into pieces. In order to cope with the difficulty of controlling his emotional reactions he will be tempted either to deny the presence of an affectively charged situation or else to try to control and modify this external situation rather than his reactions to it; at times he does attempt to produce some sort of emotional responsiveness, but as this tends to be rather forced his social relationships are unlikely to be truly free from tension.

Rajendra Singh experiences a good deal of affectional anxiety and is thus concerned with fears and phantasies of being rejected, unloved, unwanted, etc. These anxieties are liable to be felt by him in the form of spasmodic depressive moods and in the longing for a sensuous and close physical contact with others. He attempts to defend himself against such anxiety feelings mainly by trying to avoid entering into unknown and unfamiliar situations, particularly if these are liable to stir up his affectional longings. Yet his defensive system is not very effective and fails to protect him against a certain amount of paranoidal phantasy, such as being watched and exhibited and made fun of.

It would appear that some of his anxiety and general insecurity stems from his level of aspiration, which he seems to have pitched too high for his actual abilities. In order to bridge the aspiration gap he is likely to show a certain amount of intellectual pretentiousness, to pay scant heed to the ordinary details of everyday life and, in spite of the fact that his natural preference would favour the perception and understanding of whole situations, he at times clings unduly to small and limited areas of experience and interest.

In fact his difficulty in responding to emotional situations and stimuli, which has already been discussed, is in part the result of this general underlying feeling of insecurity and diffidence and of his fear of failure and inadequacy. Thus, when on two occasions he had actually achieved an adjusted and well controlled colour reaction, he immediately afterwards felt impelled to retract it, to deny the emotional aspect of the situation and to expect scorn and contempt for his initial responsiveness to it. Thus any effortful attempt to relate himself to emotional situations tends to be followed by suspicion, which leads to the petrification of the impulse, withdrawal and the substitution of impersonal intellectualised and conventional techniques. His emotional responsiveness is thus " tortoise-like "—peeping out occasionally only to retract again quickly into the safety of the protecting shell. Further, his very marked tendency to project his fears, phantasies and anxieties must render his personal relationships particularly difficult, irritating those around him and preventing him from gaining more insight and understanding.

The scarcity of apperceptions of the human person is further and independent evidence that indeed Singh finds it difficult to enter into human relationships and to develop the capacity for empathy. The non-acceptance of his own inner life and phantasy can be expected to interfere with his ability to identify to some extent with the people around him and thus bring to them some understanding, while his wariness concerning his capacity for adjusted and controlled reactions to emotional situations would lead to avoid any true and deep human contact.

An examination of the actual content of his responses suggests that Rajendra Singh's body image is somewhat disturbed, lacking recognisable limits and cohesion; in fact it is not altogether intact. It would appear that it is above all the disturbance he experiences when confronted with emotional situations which provokes phantasies of physical disintegration. It is well possible that his general sensuousness has been developed and encouraged by him as a means of achieving some sort of awareness of himself as a physical entity, a physical whole with actual form and defined limits. Because of this constellation one might suspect that of the various forms of Yoga, Hatha Yoga would attract him most.

It would appear that the internalised figures of both parents are severely damaged and consequently unsatisfactory. The perception on the " Mother card " of—

" Two legs with all the muscles torn out
hung up for show "—

suggests that while the mother has been invested with phallic qualities whose effectiveness, however, is immediately challenged and denied, she yet arouses strong and uncontrollable sensuous longings.

The conflict with the father has been projected for us into the Rorschach responses in much greater detail. Taking sequence and content of his responses to Cards II, III, and IV, it would seem that his phantasy world is pre-occupied with the theme of a violent and bloody battle between father and son in which both die, losing their heads " in a stream of blood ". Thus deprived of life the two carcases are then exhibited in a glass cage; that which could re-infuse life into them—the heart, that is emotional spontaneity—is perceived, but as separate and detached from them. It is not surprising that this phantasied combat should then provoke feelings of guilt, depression and and anxiety in response to the Father card. Here we are presented with the apperception of an idol of " dark " stone, photographed in " the dark " in " an old temple ", belonging to a distant people, the Greeks, in the distant past. Thus it would seem that the aggressive feelings experienced in relation to the father have rendered the latter lifeless and unavailable and separated from the subject by both time and space.

The psychic themes in relation to the parents seem to offer a clue to his feelings of insecurity and diffidence and to the difficulties Singh has in his human relationships.

The record as a whole does suggest that Rajendra Singh has considerable emotional difficulties and that these are responsible for a certain amount of psychological impoverishment. They have not, however, reduced his capacity to relate himself adequately to reality and to maintain thought processes that are orderly and well controlled. Moreover, by escaping from the centre of his anxieties and difficulties and if, as it were, challenged by the danger of a situation (Card V) he then seems capable of drawing on more mature inner resources than are shown in his general level of achievement.

Rajendra Singh possesses an extra-tensive personality structure; yet he finds it difficult to achieve good relationships with the people around him since emotional situations are liable to provoke tension, anxiety and impulsive reactions. He is a very insecure person, afraid of failure, rejection and ridicule. His inner life and phantasy has remained immature, though when challenged he is capable of producing more adult and adjusted responses.

Both parental figures appear to elicit affectional longings, though neither exists in his inner world as a satisfactory and undamaged object. The phantasied unavailability of the father's help and potency may account for Singh's basic diffidence and insecurity.

SUMMARY

In this informant's conversation certain characteristic Rajput values were emphatically asserted: pride of lineage, assertion of authority, exaggeration of his own and his fellow-Rajputs' heroic qualities. He idealised those women of his clan who accepted their traditional role of subservience to their lord, even to entering his funeral pyre. Being well versed in religious teachings he was able to give a highly articulate account of the means of attaining " spiritual rise ". Here, however, his personal limitations were most apparent. He wished to enjoy the supernatural powers attributed to religious devotees, without giving up his princely luxuries: hence his practice and his precepts often differed widely.

Within his family he exercised a tyrannical authority. Towards his children he showed the same pattern of favouritism towards the younger son (the one who would not succeed him) as he described in his own father. Nevertheless, his other references to his father were all in terms of admiration and deference.

In daily affairs he was vacillating and unsure of himself, easily impressed by self-proclaimed holy men. To compensate for this he repeatedly asserted his own profound certainty of purpose. Similarly, he found it necessary to insist upon his own courage and strength of mind.

He differed from other Rajput informants in that, in the recent social reforms, he had been bereft of the wealth and authority to which he had been accustomed. Cast upon his own personal resources of character, he found them unreliable. As a result, he fluctuated from moods of dramatised despair to day-dreams of power and magnificence: these phantasies alternately dwelt upon his triumph through religious " rise ", or through a return to political supremacy. He well exemplified the primary theme of distrust of one's fellow-men, coupled with personal inconsistency against which he struggled unsuccessfully. The inner conflict seemed fated to prevent his turning to full advantage his outstanding gifts of verbal eloquence and quick wit.

The Rorschach report confirms his precarious emotional balance and points out that emotionally, no less than politically, he finds it difficult to meet the challenges which beset him. The heightened tension of the oedipal relationship here exemplified is probably not, however, purely idiosyncratic to his personal history but is rather the inevitable consequence of being born a Rajput elder son.

CHAPTER II

SHRI SHANKAR LAL, BRAHMIN

At the end of May, 1951, a new face appeared in Deoli. It was that of Shankar Lal, a middle-aged school master from the town of Nathdwara who had returned to spend his vacation in his village home. He came to my office in the bazaar, introduced himself in English and asked about my research. After discussing it most intelligently for some time, he volunteered his services as one of my Brahmin informants, and I was glad to accept them. We agreed to meet regularly either in the office or in his house, but preferably not in the palace. "There", he said, soberly but emphatically, "I never go. I do not care a fig for him. I will come to see you with pleasure, but I don't give a fig for him. He is a very foolish man, I think. He is building castles in the air. He thinks that the old rule will return, but that is all nonsense."

Shri Shankar Lal had a quiet voice, and usually spoke deliberately, choosing his words carefully. This tendency was noticeable when he spoke in Mewari, but was more marked in our conversations in English with which he was more familiar as a written than as a spoken language. The deliberation and composure of his speech was repeated in his gestures and bearing. As will be seen, this screen of detachment was sometimes put aside during our interviews; but the lasting impression which remains is of an earnest, thoughtful and serious-minded man.

In spite of his friendliness and good-will, our meetings did not follow the precise schedule which he proposed in the enthusiasm of our first encounter. ("Each day you will come at 3 o'clock, or I shall come here, and we shall have talk for one hour.") Frequently domestic business would delay him, or visitors would appear at his house unannounced; but by this time my own expectations were attuned to the indeterminacy of village arrangements, and I valued each talk the more for its extempore quality.

At our first interview, Shankar Lal embarked upon an account of his career:

Shankar Lal. "I joined primary school here in Deoli, and when I was ten, my father left the world. He was a clerk in the *Tikhana*, when it was in power with all the rights. When he died my study was going to stop but some relations from Udaipur came and took me for further education. I stayed with these distant relatives—he was very friendly to my father. He has one son who was nearly 35 then: the son is still alive but the man and his wife have died. He was a *Vaidya* and I laboured hard. I worked for him, and work was not ordinary. I learned so many prescriptions. For six years I stayed there and had good experience of Indian medicine.

"I had to undergo many difficulties there—sometimes I got shirt and sometimes I had to wear an old worn-out dhoti. Very wretched life I spent, but the motive was before me to pass this examination as I did not care for these hardships and miseries. I passed my High School examination with credit in second division. He treated me more like a servant, not like a son. He was comparatively kind to me, but his wife was very strict—she was harsh in her treatment.

"I always remember my very kind home, where my father and mother treated me so well—they must love me because I was their son. My maternal grandmother also lived in Deoli and she was very kind to me. As a small boy, I used to have a gang of friends: Bheru Lal, and Magan Lal, and Girdar Lalji —those were my playmates.

"I was 16 when I passed the High School examination. After that I realised that I hadn't enough time for study, so I left his house and began to earn my living by tuitions. I could not get money from my mother—though she sold ornaments to give me some money for my further studies. In this way in two years I tried the intermediate exam.—but I had not sufficient time so I plugged history. At that time I left the M.B. college where I had been studying, and entered the teaching profession and studied privately. There, gradually, I progressed. I passed Intermediate, and Hindu exams, and B.A., and M.A. previous, and then I was deputed by the Sri Govardhan High School Nathdwara to Vidya Bhavan Training College for teachers' training, in 1945. In the meantime, I added many Hindi qualifications, passed exams as a private candidate—this is the aim of my life—go on and go on studying.

"At Vidya Bhavan Training College I was prefect of a hostel, and I was appointed as General Secretary to Teachers' Union of that course.

"I will put some questions to you tomorrow on some points pertaining to human psychology.

"The very first job I had was in this same institution in Nathdwara, for twenty years. Till the new Government came in, it was administered by the *Tikhana* of Nathdwara, now it is under Government. The ruler of the Tikhana is a Brahmin by caste, his Holiness of Nathdwara Maharaj Sahib of Nathdwara—but now he has become debauched, he lives in Bombay.

"I have spent my life on thorns: that is why now I am happy. Hard and earnest labour is equally rewarded. When I first came I was well used to hard work, so I could pull on. At first I was drawing only 20 rupees: did teaching work all day and studied at night. . . . Marriage? I did not have to think of these things—mother thought about all those arrangements for me.

"Mother, she was quite a pious lady, always reading Bhagavadgita and hymns of Mirabai, which she knew by heart.

"Up to the age of 10 I was quite happy, but from 10 to 16 I had great troubles. After passing my Matric. my worries and burdens were to some extent lessened—even before then I had done some tuition, enough to pay my expenses. In tenth class I had no money for my exam. fee and I wrote a letter to the Chief Minister Sir Sugdev Prasad. That letter impressed him too much—he read it through two or three times and then he sent his clerk, and he brought me the full fees. I don't exactly remember what I wrote—'You should help me because I am poor, and this help will bring you lasting satisfaction.'

"It is according to our shastars, it is necessary for the rich to help the poor. Sir Sugdev was a moneyed man: he was I.C.S., and he had sold his brain, to be analysed after his death —I'm not sure, I have heard of this. He paid fees for many poor students."

G.M.C. "Can you remember about before you were 10 years old?"

S.L. "I don't remember much of that. I remember that my father brought me up with great care. He engaged a tutor for me, spent money on this beyond his means—he got so little from the Tikhana. As a result of his efforts I have reached this state—had he been alive I should have done much more. He was also a religious-minded man—not so much so as my mother. He was very particular in keeping me quite neat and clean: always checking—'See, there is dirt on your foot'— 'See, you have spoiled your shirt.' He always took his bath at 4 a.m. at the well or at the tank—he was very particular about his appearance. Because he was a clerk and therefore he paid much attention to cleanliness and neatness. He was the more strict: my mother had more affection towards me than my father."

G.M.C. "As a child, were you told anything about sex?"

S.L. "The parents don't like to discuss sex at all. Even now they get confused and do not like to talk. Children learn from their friends, in the gang—nobody teaches them."

G.M.C. "Girls too?"

S.L. "They also learn in the same way, from playmates."

G.M.C. "In this country do girls ever fail to learn about sex?"

S.L. "Not so in India—when a girl reaches the age of 15 she has a perfect knowledge about sex. After marriage, gradually she becomes perfect."

G.M.C. "Do children have sex play?"

S.L. "No, no, they do not understand sexology—they just play, sometimes play at marriages."

G.M.C. "How does a child learn about bodily cleanliness?"

S.L. "He is taught gradually, by the mother. By the age of 2 they have learned—my little boy aged 13 months, he knows to leave the mat and go to the edge of the room—this much he knows that a stiff prohibition is here, not to make water on the durrie. Up to age of 2 he has no sense of bowels and urine. About this age he learns where to make water and where to go to stool—at first, in the yard. If he makes a mess before 2 years, mother and father say: 'What have you done? Why didn't you go outside?' They are not angry—it is meant for instruction only—no, no, she is not angry. Little child is cleaned, washed by mother or sisters—not brothers. At the age of 4 or 5 he can use a water-pot (for cleansing after stool). Lallu (7 years) and my daughter (6 years) take lota and go to latrine by the side of my house.

"Up to age of innocence all the children play together, with no restraint. After 12, there are some restraints from the side of the parents—' Don't go out ', and ' Don't play with them. You are grown-up now, it is not right to play with such boys. They can still play with all their brothers.'"

Shankar Lal describes the customary Hindu bars of consanguinity, against marrying certain categories of cousins. He goes on to say: "Some people go to houses of prostitution, but those who are of good standing in the community would not like to go there. There are these women who became prostitutes for their livelihood: some of them come from the hills in the north, and are very fair-skinned. They say that women are very promiscuous up there, in the hills.

"The caste still has some power: if I do something wrong the others will shun me. There was one, B. N. Sharma, who married in some other caste. He was ousted from his caste, but he was a moneyed man and he cared very little for that. In the Veds there are only four caste distinctions, but now within each caste there are so many distinctions—he can marry so-and-so, and he can do this, and so on. Audich, and Paliwal, Dashora and so on.

G.M.C. "What is taking place of caste-panchayat discipline?"

S.L. "Those bonds are becoming looser and looser: nothing is coming in its place. No new rules, nothing of the kind."

G.M.C. "Gandhi-ism?"

S.L. "It is also a blow to the caste system, although he is an orthodox follower of religion in other ways."

G.M.C. "Most enjoyable memory?"

S.L. "I can't reply in one word. If I remember my hard days, I derive some pleasure in them also: even I derive pleasure from hardship. There should come changes in one's life, and changes give interest, whether it is for comfort or for hardship. Now I look back with equal interest on hard times as well as happy times, because hard days taught me much, taught me how to struggle in the world. If you don't struggle you cannot prosper. I am always prepared for the worst, and I am always more interested in it. Of course, I get dispirited when I meet with hardship, but I don't give up my patience or courage. Yes, yes, I have to struggle hard. There, I have progressed from 20 rupees to 100 rupees a month. I had so many hindrances, I had to struggle hard—they put many obstacles in my path. They wanted that this man should get no increment—because they got none. They were jealous of my qualifications. Still there are some elements who go against me when the question of my increment comes—but now it is a charted increment.

"The school was administered by the Rajah, and these teachers who had no other qualifications they had relatives in positions of authority, and because they were jealous they tried to hinder my promotion. When I was going to pass my B.A. examination there was a question of life and death before me. A case of do or die—I cared very little for my wife and children and myself—if I die, no harm. I worked late at night—when the world was enjoying a sweet sleep, I was poring over the books."

G.M.C. "And you were rewarded with success?"

S.L. "Of course, God helped me: due to his inspiration I came out successful."

G.M.C. "Have you had friends and supporters in Nathdwara also?"

S.L. "There was very little number of such people."

G.M.C. "Any good friends there?"

S.L. "One or two."

G.M.C. "Who have been the best friends in all your life?"

S.L. "What can I say? I think I have never known one who was a perfectly true friend: always there was some percentage of selfishness and self-interest in their friendship."

Early in our acquaintance, Shankar Lal asked a series of questions about my parents, my education, and the time required for each of my professional and academic qualifications. Most of my informants had asked my monthly income and the size of my wife's dowry as a means of assessing my social status: in Shankar Lal's scale of values it seemed that one was measured in respect of his years of undergraduate and post-graduate study. He ended the interview by repeating his desire to ask me some questions next day about human psychology, more particularly about the influence of instinct (and especially the mating instinct) in human behaviour.

At our next interview he reminded me of this topic: "Can you tell me what part is played by instinct in human behaviour?" He did not wait, however, for an answer, but went on to tell me his own observations:

"You must know that dogs are not like men. They have sex in the months of September and October only, whereas men can have mating instinct all the year. Another thing I have remarked. These dogs which you see in the village they are great thieves, but even a young dog will run away as soon as you stoop to pick up a stone—surely that is an remarkable instinct!"

When he asked if I had ever observed this instinct, I replied that I had been accustomed to regard it rather as an example of a conditioned response; but he shook his head: "Oh no, most certainly it is an instinct."

If the opening question was related to some personal cause of disquiet, he was unwilling or unable to bring himself to discuss it explicitly in this interview. When he returned to the theme of instinctual urges, it was only to express the orthodox Brahminical view of how they should be controlled:

"As a general rule, the love-making, the mating instinct should only come in force for the sake of creating offspring, getting an issue. For the sake of getting a son a man should meet with his wife. Of course, they enjoy pleasure but that is not the primary aim, that is secondary thing in Hindu shastras. When a man dies without a son he cannot attain *nirvana* or *mukhti*."

G.M.C. "Why not?"

S.L. "Because when he has no son, after his death there is no one to perform the funeral rites and for lack of these rites he can't get *nirvana:* only the real son can perform these rites. An adopted son may do the rites, but not so well as a true son can do. Another verse from shastras—this is the real definition of a son: ' *Punnamna narakat trayate tat putr*—The son is he who rescues a man from hell.' These are the main principles of Hindu shastras.

"It was my first duty to keep learning the religion. We have to perform sacred-thread ceremony: at that time we appoint a Guru. He taught me the principles of the Vedas. My Guru here, who gave me the sacred thread and spoke the sacred *mantar* in my ear, he was an Udaipur man, and for a few days he taught me—but he hadn't time so I engaged another Guru. From the age of 10 I was studying this Hindu philosophy side by side with school. Always I have liked the study of Hindu religious philosophy, and especially spiritualism, and I have often gone to talk with holy men and learn from them.

"I have heard of this holy man, this Punjabi who is living here. I have the idea to go to him tomorrow to extract something from him."

G.M.C. "What will you extract from him?"

S.L. "These holy men give *gaitri-mantar*—a special mantar which is a prayer to Almighty: ' God throw us knowledge so that we may see you with our eyes: give us such realisation as that we may know and may come to be familiar with you.'

"Right up to this time I have had double instruction. I visited many Sannyasis and Saddhus and Pandits. The Guru taught me for two years. There is one good man in our staff at school, well versed in Vedas and a man of very ripe experience, an older man. The principal of the Sanskrit

College at Nathdwara is also my Guru—he taught me Sanskrit —and all these books on *dharm* are written in Sanskrit."

G.M.C. "Can you tell me what constitutes a Guru?"

S.L. "A man who teaches something new to anybody is called a Guru. There are many kinds of Guru: one is he who educates a young boy up to manhood—but whereas a Master is a paid servant, a Guru is not, he is an honoured teacher. Guru teaches a boy on religious subjects, without any interest in his own reward.

"In ancient time this guru-system prevailed throughout India: students used to go to him and serve him and learn from him, and live in his service for twelve years. Such Gurus hate worldly life, they renounce the world because their inclination is towards leaving the world. Then there are religious Gurus, who instruct others in the beliefs of the different *panths*.

"It is usual first to have a Guru selected at the time of sacred thread—but these times people don't have so much respect and regard for him now. But anyone who teaches me anything new, I call him my Guru—like you, if I learn from you, I will call you Guru also."

G.M.C. "Can you explain about these panth-gurus?"

S.L. "That Guru who gives us sacred thread is also a panth-guru, because he opens the door for us into the Brahminic panth. Brahmins very seldom join other panths, such as you find in the country here, these *bij-marg*, and *kanchli-panth* and so on.

"These panths are for the depressed classes and illiterates —these have nothing to do with religion at all." (He describes the kanchli-panth ritual in which copulation is the central act.) "How can such thing have to do with religion? Only these very lowest castes have to do with that—not Danghis, I think, only Bhils and Khatiks and Chamars. That has nothing to do with Hindu religion.

"Here, you will find so many Vishnu-panthis, and some Shiv-panthis and some worshippers of Devi, and some Kabir-panthis—they do not believe in any idols or temples or mosques or churches, only in the worship of the spirit.

"In the time of Ram Singh, here in Deoli, he was very angry at these low-caste panths, like Kanchli-marg, and he sent spies all round to trace this, where it went on, because such meetings are usually held in some jungle place, secretly. So he heard of such meetings, and caught the people, and scolded them for following this panth."

At the outset of our next meeting, I asked Shankar Lal to continue with the story of his life.

S.L. "As soon as I passed Matric, so many men came to my mother to ask for me to marry their daughters. Before that date I never thought of marriage. I was poor, so I did not think of that at all. It was my fixed opinion that I will not marry until I am able to stand on my two legs. My betrothal was settled that same year, when I passed my Matric. It was when I was 17 years old: but I did not get married until I was 21, nearly 22, and already in this school at Nathdwara."

G.M.C. "You would not have much opportunity to talk with young women?"

S.L. "Oh no, our customs are different: we do not meet with girls. With my sisters of course, I have talked—they are a little educated. They can read and write and do arithmetic but that is all. They can read the Ramayan and the Mahabharat in Hindi—my mother also used to read those books. She was not educated but she taught herself. She once started a girls' school in this village and taught the girls for two months, but contributions were not sufficient so she gave up this work. She was a very religious lady, all day singing hymns and taking the name of God. She was also fond of attending to Saddhus and Sannyasis. In every religious meeting she would sing, or speak."

G.M.C. "Religious meetings?"

S.L. "The women-folk used to meet in our caste temple, the one to Charbhujaji near here—that is for the Audich caste."

G.M.C. "Did she influence you in your interest in religion?"

S.L. "Oh yes, of course she inspired us by saying axioms and so many religious principles. My brother is also influenced to have great interest in religion—but we are not orthodox in a conservative way: we are interested in all the new things, only we are God-fearing men. Nowadays, the majority of young men are godless—atheist, heretics. I see this in our school. They say that Western Education has made them atheistical—but I see many Christians who have full Western education, and still they remain God-fearing, and go to their church every Sunday."

G.M.C. "But there are still many, like you, who hold to the religion?"

S.L. "Even those like me, we are not sufficiently active

in our devotion. We know that we should be paying more attention to it than we do."

G.M.C. " But your ideal is so hard a one—complete renunciation. . . ."

S.L. " There are so many of those Sannyasis and Saddhus who are just beggars, and know nothing of God at all. For my own part I say, living in the world one should live a life of awareness of God. One should make it one's first duty always to remember God. I have ripe experience of this because I have suffered many difficulties. I lost my father in early childhood. I have nobody I can call friend or relative—my only support was the Almighty. When I was in trouble I would always call on His name, and due to His inspiration I have always been able to surmount my troubles, and to do what I have done."

G.M.C. " Your mother had the choice of several girls for you ? "

S.L. " She went this way and that. When she thought that she had found the proper one, she made the betrothal."

G.M.C. " Did it work out all right ? "

S.L. " I may frankly say that I have no complaint; the result has come in my favour. She never stands in my way, she always helps me with my studies, though she has not much education herself, but she can read and write."

G.M.C. " I've been interested to learn this from the Banias: that they consider every act of sex a sacrilege."

S.L. " Sacrilege! " (laughs scornfully). " If you go deep down into the heart of those same Banias you will find only sand and rubbish. They tell you this, but they do something quite different. They always try to cheat, it is in their nature. They may talk like this, that it is sacrilege, but they do not know how to control their passions. They are only pretended ascetic—like our saying: ' *Vrid bharia tapas suni*—As soon as a woman gets too old for it, she becomes a nun.' "

G.M.C. " You yourself, don't hold with that view ? "

S.L. " No, I told you, we believe that the primary purpose of sex is to have children, and the secondary purpose is to have pleasure. Of course, if you have too much, then it is bad for you."

G.M.C. " Do you believe that the man is weakened and woman not ? "

S.L. " No, both are weakened, but their weakness is also compensated by the combination of the man's semen (*viri*) and that of the woman (*raj*). When these combine properly, both of them are benefited: but for this to happen it is necessary that the woman should be young, younger than the man. If she is a year or two older, then it does not matter, but if she is say, 50, and the man is 25, then it will be very harmful for him, because her *raj* is thin and watery so it will not combine well with his semen, so he will get no benefit from intercourse, only loss."

2nd June, 1951

This afternoon Shankar Lal seemed at a loss for a topic. I asked him to tell me about the routine events of his daily life. He replied:

S.L. "The Brahmin's duty is to get up very early in the morning, at the ' Brahmin's *mahurat* '—when the star rises in the east—a hundred minutes before the time of sunrise, that is two and a half *gharis* before sunrise. In our villages night is determined by that star—when they see that star they know it will soon be dawn. Then daily duties are performed—calls of nature, then wash hands, mouth, nose, teeth—we draw water up the nose, then throw it out, and clean the ears with cloth, clean our eyes and have our teeth cleaned with a twig, or with ashes of burnt cowdung, a special black ash. If Brahmin does not bathe in this way, he is not entitled to take food. After taking my bath, I take some physical exercise, some *asan* and *kasrat*, that I do daily according to the permission of my constitution, then walk for fifteen minutes, then sit on that deer-skin and have worship of God. I go through them, and I remember God. We have a process called *Pranayam*, which is a controlling of the breathing by a special method— if you do not know the process you will fall ill. With my eyes shut, I breathe in through the left nostril, hold my breath for a measured interval and then breathe out through the other. Then I do this again, alternating the nostril for breathing in, and so on. And I keep my mind centred here, in the brow and the image is also there (taps his forehead). So I sit with this image before my mind, and I simply take His name."

G.M.C. " Is it some one special image that you see? "

S.L. " Different people have different pictures of God, and I have special picture in my mind: I have special worship of—(here he names one of the great Gods)—and his figure comes before me, because you should have something before you. You may say God is omnipresent, but that is a high thing; for a beginner it is necessary to have some visible thing on which to fix his mind. This is a very private thing I have told you: I would not tell any other person the name of the God whom I see in worshipping. The thing has impressed itself on me, because in every calamity or difficulty, I shut myself in a room and appeal to him, I weep—and in any form he may help, but help surely comes. Even if calamity comes, it is for your good.

"I have fixed number of times to take His name—so many times I take the beads. A hundred and eight beads is a full rosary: the last bead is larger than the others, called *sumeru*. It is a mysterious thing, and not to be explained; because God is so mysterious, He is not to be explained: there are many mysterious matters in this."

G.M.C. "Every Brahmin has a string of beads?"

S.L. "He is expected to have, but there are so many heretic Brahmins now—the majority now neglect the sacred thread. They do not see what they gain by wearing it, so they leave off.

"A Brahmin, according to shastras should complete at least three full rosaries. Some do nothing, while others do more than it is required. When you are finished, you put the sumeru to the two eyes and to the forehead, and to the heart also. After that, I read the Bhagavadgita or some other book like Mahabharat. At the time of my finishing these religious duties, I see the sun has come up, and the last part of these duties is to salute the sun—in our shastras the five principal Gods are Sun, Fire, Water, Earth, Air—Surya, Agni, Jal, Prithwi, Voyu. These are also the five substances of the body. When a man dies, these substances mix into the five Gods—whether he is burned or not, that happens at once. At the evening, when there is light, we salute the main god of the house, and then each other—in some houses, they forget to do this, but not in others."

G.M.C. "I've seen it done in the palace."

S.L. "Yes, they salute the Rao: '*Kama andata*—Hail, giver of bread!' That's what they say, when the lamps are lit. What a slave-mentality! That is the title of God, not of this foolish man. I do not like this custom at all."

G.M.C. "You were telling me about your daily duties——"

S.L. "I have extended my religious duty to some more extent: I do more, some sacred books, some hymns, some mantras, sitting at the same place. I don't take food or drink water before all my religious duties are discharged. So long as I do not have the preliminary bath, I consider my body impure: there is a saying in the shastras—leave 100 jobs of work in order to eat: but leave 1,000 jobs in order to bathe.

G.M.C. " What makes the body so impure? "

S.L. " Because we make water, and we go to latrine—and intercourse also—there are so many sources of impurity; and touching an impure thing. But everything is washed away; and after bath we feel some sort of inspiration and alertness. It is both physical and spiritual cleansing."

" Water must be clean and pure—it must not have been touched by Chamar or Khatik or such person. Their tendency and habit and nature are of such type that they are not considered to be pure: according to our shastras they are depressed, and not to be touched. Some Sudras we can touch, but they are the lowest."

G.M.C. " Who teaches you about this? "

S.L. " These are inherent inspirations in us: when we are small our mother also shows us to do this. Many times when I touched some Chamar or Khatik my mother would not let me enter the room, but make me first take a bath: I remember that often. Even now, because I don't observe these things so strictly, if there was some breach, she felt it very much.

" The father of Himat Lal, who lived in this next house, was quite orthodox. If he were present now he wouldn't allow his son to wear this dress and go this way and that. He would not like to touch Khatik or Chamar—and if he touched by chance, he would have felt very sorry, and had taken his bath. This does not apply to Bhils, they are superior to these. The lowest of all is the sweeper.

" With the morning worship, the duty towards God is finished: then the duty of filling my belly comes, morning meal. At 10.30 I set out for school and work there from 11 to 3.45. As soon as I come from school I go to latrine, and then market work, and then I go for walk with friends. My wife would never go to market—gradually we are trying to shake off this bondage of women—our caste is more advanced in this than Rajputs and Banias, we do not make women keep veils down over face all the time—they simply keep their eyes downwards, in modesty.

" I take two meals, one in morning after worship; the other after sunset, not before it, but there is no hard-and-fast rule. If I am hungry then I can take it earlier. Generally I do not take meals in between times. In winter, when I feel cold, I take tea. My wife is habituated to take tea, having a weak constitution.

"I observe a fast three times in each month—both *pradesh* and *punam*—and on special days in the year, like Shivratri. Pradesh is for Shiv, and punam is sacred to Sath Narayan, who is Lord Vishnu—there are different routes to climb the mountain, but the destination is the same."

G.M.C. "You say it was your mother who taught you not to touch low-caste boys?"

S.L. "If her son is dirty and in filthy clothes, still she will not allow her boy to touch one of the depressed class—that is a different kind of dirt. Khatik is a man of violent profession—*hinsa*—and he is not clean: and in case of Bhangi, it is dirty profession.

"As soon as child grows up he comes to know about food—the main thing to be learned is not to take food or water from one of depressed class: even a child of 6 or 7 knows this well. If someone asks him to take food he says: '*Main chhun jaunga*—I shall become touched.' Specially the mother teaches him this in his first years: the grandmother also gives the same lessons."

G.M.C. "If he breaks these rules, will he feel disturbed?"

S.L. "Of course! He will have to purify himself with bath externally, and with *Ganga-jal* * to drink, and to take names of God. There are special provisions in Shastars to purify a man. Before taking the sacred thread so much stress is not given, but after janoi he has to be very strict with the rules. As he is Brahmin, special responsibilities lie on his shoulders. Other castes don't take these things so much to their hearts. Even now, when people see a man is a Brahmin they bow and salute and pay much respect in comparison to other castes: he is much more closely related to God. The greeting 'Maharaj' used to be a very respected title to be given to Brahmins. It meant 'God-like Man'; because they were perfect persons, discharged their religious duties faithfully. Now, when people say 'Mahraj', it is like an insult, it has gone down, it is used for poor people, cooks and servants and such people.

"In school, the boys are all equal: only if a boy is careful to follow the old rules will he be respected. But times are quite changed; and gradually all the Brahmins will have to cope with the times. Their standard of living and way of life will change, their dress will change, but still the religious duties

* Ganges-water

must be discharged in the old way. A Brahmin will only be recognised as a Brahmin if he performs these duties. A Brahmin who neglects his religion is not a Brahmin, he is a Chandel, a sweeper.

"Nowadays, Brahmins are hankering after money, because this is what is held important. Some have totally left their duties—I see so many among my colleagues have given up the old ways. Himat Lal's father was too conservative. He had money, and he could sit and pray from early morning till 2 p.m., and in the evening he would also pray. He had no job anywhere, he was a man of sound financial position, so he could do this. We often asked him to give up these conservative ideas to some extent—but he would not."

G.M.C. "What about young Kripa Lal?"

S.L. "Kripa Lal! He has got no relation to Brahminical literatures or duties. He has left his wife, and keeps a Daroga concubine. There you have given me the very example of one type of Brahmin."

G.M.C. "But he tells me he has quite a knowledge of the Vedas and of Brahmin *dharm*."

S.L. "That is all lies, he has forgotten all."

G.M.C. "You were proposing to talk to me about *bhakti* today."

S.L. "Bhakti is a very difficult thing. Its first requirement is *shraddha*, which is, ' respect and regard '. For example, I have some respect for you, it is the beginnings of bhakti towards you."

G.M.C. "But can you have bhakti for living people?"

S.L. "Oh yes, it often happens that people have bhakti for one who has attained perfection. There are many examples in our shastars of those perfect souls."

G.M.C. "But aren't they inaccessible to ordinary people, in their meditations?"

S.L. "Such people, after nearing that concentration of the mind of their meditation, they are able to talk very well to their followers. In the meditation, his whole life is withdrawn from his body here, into the head. This spot is called *brahmanand*. That is the perfect concentration. The state of pranayam is a stepping-stone to such concentration. When a man has reached such perfect concentration, his mind moves in the heavens, he leaves the earthly body, and the body is not harmed by physical hurts. If a snake bites, he will not be killed. There was such a sage, Balmukhi, who sank into a deep meditation that went on for years, so that ant-hills grew up round him, and snakes roamed about him, and he had no food or drink for years, but just remained the same.

"As Shraddha increases, it develops into bhakti. Bhakti is generally shown towards God. Prayer is the singing of His peculiar qualities, repeating them. If I praise you, you will have some inclination towards me; so God also, if we remember him he also remembers us. Bhakti is the main way for us to get salvation and release. It has two branches: *yog-marg* and *upasana-marg*, which is also called *puja-marg*, the ways of knowledge and of worship. Worship may be *akarpur* (with images) or *nirakarpur* (with no images, such as the Yogi achieves). The Yogi has no image of God before him, he sees God in each and every thing. You remember the story of Prahalad, whose father said, 'Show me your God!' And he said, 'God is in every single thing'. God has innumerable forms '*anek rup, rup aya*—in forms without number came His form'. He has no specific form.

"I am very fond of these topics about the spiritual life: whenever I go to a Sannyasi or Saddhu I introduce this topic—but I am not a yes-man. I always go against them, I practise *virodh bhakti*—worship of the opposites. I say to them: 'How do you know that God is everywhere?' Or I say that the world of illusion is more pleasing than this state of meditation—then he comes out with his arguments, and I gather them up and store them in my mind.

"Great Indian souls, they ignore the things of this world. A *tyagi*, he is a man who lives in the world, but does not let his spirit become attached to things of the world—if some close relation dies, even a wife or a son, he is not too much distressed, because he knows that this is the rule of the world. He lives in the world like a pearly drop of water on a lotus leaf—it moves about on the leaf but it is not absorbed."

G.M.C. "Doesn't he feel warm love for wife and son, then?"

S.L. "Of course he loves them, but there is some limit to his love. He has affection for them, and he regards it as his duty to bring up his son, and love him, and give him money for his education. He will be dutiful to his wife also, but not so much attached to them as a worldly man, who is affectionate without limits, and who suffers without restraint if they die.

"Now, *shakti*, that means strength, and it may be physical or mental. The mental strength has a wide range: it is the spiritual power, the will-power acquired by the mind, such as Mahatma Gandhi had. He was physically weak, yet his mind influenced so many people. Mental power operates also on the physical world—it guides events like a mahout steers the mighty elephant. In the constant practice of bhakti, a man's spiritual power increases. Mental powers can be cultivated in non-spiritual directions too, as by the training of scientists. Those who have reached a high level in bhakti have increased mental powers—you have this knowledge in English literature also: 'More things are wrought by prayers than the world deems of.'

"A man who has reached a high stage, can do all sorts of things: if he is sitting here, and you ask him what is happening in a distant place he can tell you at once."

G.M.C. "I've heard the Ruler here claim that he had already attained some of these powers."

S.L. "He is all wrong, he is bogus lecher. Always busy with wine and women, how can he ever find his way along this stony and thorny path? Of course, there is one quicker way, and that is the way called Vam-panth, it is the way of contradiction, of virodh-bhakti. By saying the opposite, by blaspheming and denying, and by breaking all the rules, they attain perfection. You see them sometimes on the road, they are always very dirty. People call them Augar-baba. They attain God in no time: all the time this aim is before them. But it is a dangerous way, all the time they are breaking the rules of nature, drink their own urine, live in filth; they use only dirty old broken bits of pots for their utensils. They tell lies all the time, they talk against God and against religion, but in their heart they remember God. I cannot tell you very much about these men, because I have talked very little with them, because we cannot learn anything from what they say to us. Only very ordinary men follow this augar-panth, sensible men never go this way."

G.M.C. "You were saying that a man who practises bhakti increases his will-power. . . ."

S.L. "Of course, he has got a very strong will-power, and due to it he can control a group or a society. Mahatma Gandhi had such will-power, because he was very punctual in his daily prayers, and he read the Bhagavadgita daily."

G.M.C. "You were going to tell me something about the bodily disciplines which control the mind."

S.L. "Yes, the first of these is pranayam, in which the mind is controlled and centred in one place, here (the forehead). That mind sees the very image of God here and at last he becomes infused with so many powers, undefinable powers—this comes only after years of practice, even several incarnations may pass before it is achieved. Such a man, who is coming near to perfection, he is able to see his death before it comes, and tell his family that on such a day, at such a time, he will die: and so it happens. There are others who leave the world of their own will, at a given moment. They tell their followers to bury them alive, at such and such a time, and then they sit in meditation, and so they are buried, without having died: this is *samadhi*.

"The Maharaj of Eklingji,* when he dies he is put in sitting position, and buried in the temple itself, and a *chattri* built over the place, but that is not the same as samadhi. All those who have become Sannyasis, in so doing they become dead to this world—they cut themselves off from their families and their caste. They burn the sacred thread, and swallow the ashes. All such Sannyasis, when they die they are not burned, but are buried."

4th June, 1951

G.M.C. "You may have heard that I'm very interested in hearing about people's dreams."

S.L. "These are all imaginary things, dreams. I very seldom see them being realised—majority are not real. A man does not see any dream when he is in sound sleep: that is the main principle that I hold, and dream is seen concerning only that topic which has some relation with our life. We see people we know, maybe long afterwards. Dream is like a record put on gramophone, moving in our mind. Actual dreams are never seen at dead of midnight, but only near morning."

(Here he briefly outlined a dream in which he was the victim of malicious gossip, then he went on):

"No one dare criticise me, but when I am not there, they criticise me. I am the third senior man in that institution. The first two are liberal, they are not so rigid. It is some of the smaller type, not so qualified, old men who are always criticising good works of others. I am not a yes-man, the old men are always in the opposition. I care a fig for such criticism, I don't care at all. I care for such criticisms as are based on morality, justice, religion.

* Chief priest of a celebrated temple of Shiva, not far from Deoli

"There were only two or three who spoke against me, and I returned their criticism strongly, even though one of them was older than me. Who are they to criticise me in this way? I may live in whatever way I want."

G.M.C. "What were they criticising you about?"

S.L. "On dress, on food, on mixing with other class of people, taking tea with them. I take tea with all, excluding lowest *sudras*.

"Sometimes I enjoy such dream as comes to reality. Once I dreamt that someone was dead: and next morning I came to know that another relative was dead. I also have dreams which give me a picture of God—only once in four or five months that happens—I dream that I see the image of God standing before me. Sometimes I am so much impressed that I weep before the image, and when I awake my eyes are wet with tears.

"Some four or five months before, I saw the face of God, it was just a face and then it disappeared—I wept, and I woke up. Then I closed my eyes and tried to see it again but it did not come. It was a real and living face, very beautiful, with a halo round it, so dazzling that I could not see it clearly. It was the same picture which I have before me when I do pranayam."

G.M.C. "Have you ever talked with God in a dream?"

S.L. "No, no. Up to this time I have never talked, I have simply seen. It is a happy experience: tears of joy came out. When I woke I felt happy, I wished to enjoy the same thing again, but I could not.

"One day I dreamt that somebody has pushed me from the third floor of a building, and my heart palpitated and I woke. Another time I dreamt that I fell by accident in a well, and the palpitations of my heart woke me. Sometimes I have a dream of snakebite also.

"I see one dream three or four times in a year—I see mad elephants, in rut, charging towards me. I am much afraid of *must* elephants—that might be the reason of it. The dream is in different places—in the market or lane or in the street—I don't remember the place exactly. There are other people there, and we all try to run. At once I wake up."

G.M.C. "Have you ever seen such an elephant?"

S.L. "Yes, many times. I think it has left a lasting impression. Many times I saw them in Udaipur, rooting up trees, breaking doors, killing its mahout. In Nathdwara I actually saw, from the roof of a house, where a mad elephant pursued a man and caught him. He put one foot on the man's one leg, and pulled the other with his trunk and tore him into two. When elephant runs mad, it is not controllable."

G.M.C. "Who was killed?"

S.L. "The stable servant who gave him food and water. I saw many times, at 10, and 11, and 18, and 20 and 28 years of age—recently, four years back I saw this man being killed.

"Sometimes dreams come in daytime also, in half-sleep, when I am in subconscious state. I don't care for dreams, because I don't think they are of any importance: but now, when I have some, I shall remember and tell to you."

One morning I started our interview by raising a topic which had been discussed by others of my informants.

G.M.C. "Some of the people I have talked with here have said there was no such thing as a true friend."

S.L. "You will find such friends as are selfish, as are interested. Very difficult to find a real friend."

G.M.C. "What has been your own experience?"

S.L. "All are selfish, selfless friend I have none. Nobody. There is some percentage of selflessness in them, some 60 per cent., some 40 per cent., some 30 per cent. It is very difficult to find selfless friend. Moreover, Nathdwara is a place where people come from every part of India, and stay a short time and then go: so they leave no lasting impression on the people of that place."

G.M.C. "What are Nathdwara people like?"

S.L. "Impression is that the majority of the people in Nathdwara are selfish, are out only to make money from the visitors. There, it is very difficult to find a real friend. It is very difficult to find a real friend who is ready to sacrifice all he has for his friend. I do not know anyone who is a true friend like that.

"The quantity of selfishness is much more at Nathdwara than in Udaipur or here. Many are friends with money, and will pretend to be your friend so long as there is money to be had from you. So I have come to the conclusion that my real friend is God, and no one else."

G.M.C. "Not even one's mother?"

S.L. "In his childhood she is his friend. But later, here in India, because a mother is so illiterate, she cannot advise a man in later life as a friend could do—so her friendship does not go on beyond childhood. The affection remains—but simply affection does not mean friendship: it needs understanding as well."

G.M.C. "What about the custom of making a *dharm-bhai* and *dharm-bahin*?" *

S.L. "This custom does not prevail among educated persons, only among illiterate masses. If you are to make some dharm-bhai, and you are in a position of influence, you can make everyone your dharm-bhai so there is no sense in it. It was the custom in old times, not this time. Its aim has changed—now they appoint a dharm-bahin and have intercourse with her—so what sort of dharm-bahin is she? That is why it has lost its importance: now they talk to her 'bahinji, bahinji'—and still they sleep with her! There are so many examples before me, people of different castes, sleeping together. If a man openly sleeps with another man's wife, society will see it with an angry eye. The very sound 'bahinji' I hate."

G.M.C. "Have you known this happen among your own acquaintances?"

S.L. "It goes on, and it is general custom—'bahinji, bahinji!' I have heard that it is not so in your country, that a man will come into a room and see another man having intercourse with his wife, and he will simply go away again. . . .

"To some extent we can trust, but real friends are few to find: my only real friends are God, and my books.

"I don't believe in these things, dharm-bahin and dharm-bhai—it is an easy way to set up an illicit connection. I am sure your Raoji has that kind of dharm-bahin. In villages you will see that this custom still prevails and still is honoured.

"Ordinary friendships are to some extent limited because I see some defects in them. I have not come across a perfect friend—always I come across the selfish motive. Sometimes I feel this thing too much, when I cannot find a real friend— I am in search still of such a friend, but I don't think I shall find one."

G.M.C. "How about one's wife?"

S.L. "Of course. But wife is not educated like me, so she cannot be the real friend I require. To some extent she is, but not to perfection. Compelled by circumstances you have to set up friendship with your wife; if not, quarrels will go on, and domestic life will be ruined."

Later in this interview I mentioned that I had heard many stories in the village concerning witches and ghosts.

* This is a form of honorary adoption of a blood-brother, or "sister of honour", much esteemed in Rajput history and still observed, particularly among the farming and land-owning castes of Rajasthan

S.L. "You have got this from illiterate persons. I don't believe in any of these things. What is *dakan* and what is *bhut?* People say there is bhut at this well here, but I sleep at the roof here and at midnight I have looked specially and I have never seen such. If I argue with people, they say: 'You are Brahmin and you remember God, so you will not see such things.' I know that the illiterate people in the village think all their illnesses are caused by such witches and ghosts. These Banianis are always generally ill—they take very few baths: they take it as a sin to take bath. Their religion says if they cleanse their bodies and their hair they will kill the insects which live in them. They are smelly and verminous. With them, dirtiness is next to Godliness—I often criticise them. That is why they are often ill. There is much that is senseless in their religion. If we ask them what is the sense, the reality of it, they say: 'It is our rule, it is our shastars.'"

The mention of the Banias' code of behaviour brings him back to the Brahmins' teaching of non-attachment.

S.L. "A man whose mind is devoted to *bhakti* has little time to think over things like personal attachments."

G.M.C. "Do you mean, he cannot love anyone?"

S.L. "The definition of love is quite a different thing: what is called love nowadays is really passion, a physical thing. Love is spiritual thing, and is lasting, while passionate love (*wasna*) is not lasting. *Prem* means affection, if used towards children, but passionate love towards other sex of same age. Many people hold the idea that only physical pleasure matters. When they are young they say like that—but when they are old, they are not able to enjoy passionate love and therefore they are forced to remember God. Even the most passionate man, in his old age his organs will not do the work, and therefore he will now remember God, and cry 'Hai Ram, Hai Ram'.

"There are very few cases of men who renounce these pleasures even in their youth. This pleasure, sexual pleasure, deteriorates our brain and our strength and also it is only momentary: whereas spiritual pleasure benefits the mind, and lasts long. The result of physical pleasure is in the end rather painful, harmful—whereas the other pleasure always brings strength and joy."

During the next few days Shankar Lal was pre-occupied with troubles in his home. Our talks became desultory, and even his dreams reflected his current anxieties.

S.L. " I don't exactly remember. I dreamt that I went somewhere, leaving this place, and there was a great feast—but I could not enjoy that, due to some sort of mental disorder, created by some information. It was not here, it was in some town. I think it was a marriage feast. There were many people there—I couldn't recognise them."

G.M.C. " What was this trouble in your mind? "

S.L. " Some inauspicious news, I don't remember what. There was some happening that took place in my family, some accident. I think somebody fell down from a wall—one of my children fell. I talked with those people, but they were not my close friends."

G.M.C. " Have your children been giving cause for anxiety? "

S.L. " I am anxious for my younger daughter. She is to have treatment soon at the hospital to remedy the disease of her hip.

" Some days ago I dreamt that I received information that I have been transferred to somewhere else. An order was sent to me here, from the school, with reference to the order of the Education Authority."

G.M.C. " Is this likely to happen? "

S.L. " Most probably I may be transferred to somewhere else."

G.M.C. " As headmaster? "

S.L. " No. There is a serious competitive examination for headmaster and I have not applied for it. I intend to appear in this examination—it is nothing, it is a farce only. The man they want to take, they let him pass. But I intend to take it. . . ."

We discussed politics on one of these brief meetings. Preparations were under way for the first popular elections ever to be held in Rajasthan, but Shankar Lal was not enthusiastic. In this respect, he said: " Mewar is most backward place. There is no awakening in the people. Mahatma Gandhi said this Congress had achieved its aim, which was the liberation of the country; so it should be dissolved and in its place another party created with a different aim—to serve the country."

G.M.C. " Do you find yourself involved in politics? "

S.L. " To some extent I am involved, because a teacher is expected to know about these things. . . . I generally attend their meetings but I am not an active member of Congress

Party. The school did not take any part because it was a palace institution and so came under the Mewar Government, which was opposed to Congress."

Shankar Lal reminded me that the town of Nathdwara was a famous pilgrimage centre for worshippers of Vishnu, and listed other shrines which are known all over India.

G.M.C. " Is there much conflict between Shivites and Vaishnavites today? "

S.L. " Each sect has a different view about God. But in the world, where there is such an economic crisis, no cry comes out of them now. Every such conflict is ended now. . . . In the old days the most famous temple of India was in Somnath. It was brought to the ground by Mahommed Gajni in the eleventh century—he was quite against idolatry. Just this year the temple and the idol were rebuilt.

" The image is 6 feet high, the *lingam* of black stone. It is always black—generally black—sometimes it is also white or yellow in colour. The *lingam* is a symbol of God. It has five faces—Agni, Surya, Varuna, Rudra, Brahma.*

" Every *lingam* has a *yoni* round the base, and the water runs away through that *yoni*. People who are learned know that this stands for the *shakti* of the creative act; but people who are unlearned they just have blind faith. They have *darshan* and they don't know its origin and its meaning."

G.M.C. " What exactly does it mean, to have a *darshan?* "

S.L. " Its real meaning is to be inclined to God. When people come to visit an image of God it makes them more inclined toward God."

G.M.C. " But it is used of people, also? "

S.L. " Then it just means that I met you, and I was gladdened by it."

At this moment a Jain teacher joined us. He and Shankar Lal discussed the varieties of *darshans* offered by the images worshipped by different sects of Hindus and Jains. They agreed that the *sidhanth*, or basic truths of each faith were the same.

Our meetings were interrupted for over two weeks. On 22nd June we met again in the bazaar, exchanged news and planned to resume our talks. Next day we found ourselves discussing Madhu Lal, a Brahmin caste fellow and president of the village council, who did not perform any priestly duties.

* The Vedic deities of Fire, Sun, Sky, Storm and Creation

S.L. "This career was closed for him. He is rather inclined towards being a merchant."

G.M.C. "Is that common among Brahmins?"

S.L. "No, no. Brahmins are not generally found to be traders. His father did some trading as a side business. It was not his main support. The Banias are always hankering after money and nothing else. It is not the duty of a Brahmin to be in trade. Not even 5 per cent. of merchants in this country are Brahmins. Vaisyas are generally merchants. Generally, Vaisyas do not wear the *janoi*. Rajputs generally do so, though it is not absolutely necessary for them to do so. Some exceptional Vaisyas may wear it."

G.M.C. "Can a Sudra wear it?"

S.L. "In this age, everybody is free, there is no restriction. But in ancient times it was strictly prohibited. They were not allowed to read Vedas or to hear them chanted. In my own lifetime I remember seeing in Udaipur that Vedas were being chanted and Sudras passed by, and were asked to go away."

G.M.C. "Are they chanted on special occasions?"

S.L. "Who is a learned Brahmin in Vedas, they always recite, and people come to hear. But now there is this economic crisis and they have to earn their bread, so very few do this."

Shankar Lal was absent-minded, and seemed depressed. I remarked on this, he said:

"Yes, these days I feel some sort of mental disorder. There is no rest in my mind to worry over my girl who is sick. I am in a dilemma because she must go with the girl to the hospital and I must stay here to look after the children. Sometimes my Aunt here helps me, but mostly I prepare everything myself. There is one cow also to be looked after."

G.M.C. "You must miss your mother at this time."

S.L. "Yes, of course. Helpless, she has been snatched away."

After this, Shankar Lal devoted two days to telling me some of the village beliefs about bodily functions and disease, and to discussing illnesses which had afflicted his family.

Prominent in his outline of physiology as he understood it, was an account of how *ras* is formed in the stomach, and from ras, blood—" And from every forty drops of blood, one drop of semen is formed. And this gives rise to a glow which comes from the whole body and especially the face. When you see a true *bramchari* there is a shining which comes from his face: it is beaming. The literal meaning of *bramchari* is ' the man full of semen '."

Shankar Lal said that in the event of illness he relied on medical diagnosis and effective drugs—but he added that sometimes spoken charms could also effect cures: " That I do believe, because there is a strength in words."

On the other hand, he despised the villagers' reliance upon *bhopas*, the rustic shamans:

S.L. " There are some educated people also who believe upon the Bhopajis and Bherujis. I have pity on such people. This Bheruji is a degenerated form of Bhatak Bhairav, which means small form of Mahadev. They have added so many things and changed it so that they have become laughing-stock of educated people."

G.M.C. " Have you experienced a lot of anxiety in your life? "

S.L. " I am always prepared for the worst. A man who is always prepared for the worst is not so subject to distress. Due to human weakness I feel some sort of pain and misery—still, after a short time that passes away, because I have resigned myself to the will of God, I do not care. If it comes right or comes wrong, I give it to God. The only thing I care, to fear God and nothing else."

G.M.C. " This is a very Indian practice: we are more concerned with personal affairs."

S.L. " You should also remember we are not idle, we go on working. We do not become inactive or passive. We go on working, and whatever the result of our work, it is all submitted to God. When a man is young, and is attracted by women, he is not able to renounce all that to God. We have a *slok* (he quotes a Sanskrit verse): ' He is only a learned one who takes others' wives as mother; who thinks others' wealth as a clod of earth, and who thinks every living being to be like himself.' "

I had been impressed, in earlier interviews, by the vehemence with which Shankar Lal denounced contemporary standards of sexual morality; so I now offered a cue which might lead him to show on what experience these strong feelings were based.

G.M.C. " Do young people sometimes fall in love here? "
S.L. " Here some people do that because they have come

in contact with Western civilisation. Now, the old principles are observed only in villages in the country. In the towns you will see romance and love, copying the films."

G.M.C. "Here in the villages, not at all?"

S.L. "There are so many stories of Rajputs falling in love with village girls, and they were attracted by their chivalry and bravery also. They cannot marry unless they are of same caste and parents allow them. It is quite different in very big cities like Bombay, Calcutta, Madras, Nagpur, Allahabad, Agra—more advanced cities."

G.M.C. "Are there love-songs?"

S.L. "Only about Rajputs: they were a warrior class and had to face battles, therefore they were allowed to do so. In a Brahmin house it is not possible. If a young Brahmin becomes fond of a girl of other caste, he will be ousted. But nowadays, of course, any such thing may happen."

G.M.C. "Isn't there a natural attraction of young people to each other?"

S.L. "In India there is limitation of attraction. The former Rao here, he was rich and in strong position, so he could be fond of any girl he liked, and he liked many girls. But a Brahmin boy knows there would be trouble if he were fond of the wrong girl.

"There are many who break the rules. If a boy has a friendship in secret with a girl, it is not bad unless they are caught: but then he will be in trouble. There are those also who break the rule openly, like Kripa Lal."

G.M.C. "In mythology, I often read of Gods falling in love with lovely women. . . ."

S.L. "In the early eras, it was different. In those days inter-marriage was allowed, with only the restriction that though Brahmin man might marry low-caste girl, no Brahmin girl could marry low-caste man. But this is now kal-yug and in this yug such inter-marriage is not allowed."

25th June, 1951

This afternoon our interview was delayed because a farmer was talking with Shankar Lal about a loan of money. Although I did not follow the details of their conversation, I could see that the countryman was asking for advice, and expressed fulsomely his faith in Shankar Lal's probity and willingness to help him. When I remarked on this, after the farmer had gone, he replied:

"I am not a man of Bania type. I impart them good advice, and I try to extract them from the clutches of the Banias. They fasten on them by fair means or foul. If he goes to the market he will have to give 100 annas in advance in order to get 100 rupees, in addition to the interest, which is 12 per cent. That is the normal rate—there are some who will take one anna per rupee per month."

G.M.C. "You give them a low rate?"

S.L. "Yes, that is why they have faith in me. That man yesterday borrowed 250 rupees from me, and he gives me one half of the yield of his field. This man today requires money: bazaar rate is very high so he comes to ask me the normal rate of 12 per cent., not charging discount. I have told him to come to Nathdwara in two weeks and I shall lend it to him. There ought to be a co-operative society here, but these are illiterate people. If I remained here I might be able to organise it.

"I do not do this as business: for the sake of help to them and for help to me also I do it. In this way some amount is saved and as soon as hard times come it may be used. Otherwise my financial condition is not well off."

G.M.C. "Do you have fields of your own?"

S.L. "I have some, hereditary lands from the Tikhana—not Jagir. We had a disagreement with the Rao six years ago, and we were not on good terms with him—he is a rogue of the first water. When we had this disagreement we said: 'We shall not give any more services, fix a rent for this land.' Since then, we have been independent. Since that time, there has been a matter of two months' pay which is still owing to my brother. And there was an allowance of one ser of corn a day for a horse which he also stopped giving."

G.M.C. "How did this disagreement arise?"

S.L. "This fellow is encircled by such rascals, and we don't like them. I warned him. I wrote a letter of six pages —I did not particularise, I just said he should get rid of this gang. He is a *gadha, bahinchod*, a duffer. He has got a special gang of rogues like that fat driver. Now what can he do? He is sitting in his palace like a doll in the almira. Formerly these duffers could be a great nuisance, but now they have no longer any power whatever."

26th June, 1951

Knowing that Shankar Lal must soon return to his school in Nathdwara, I was more than usually explicit in my "cue" on this occasion. I asked him to tell me what was the approved Brahmin teaching upon the conduct of a man's sex life.

S.L. "Shastras give no instruction about sex—it is regarded only as a means of having son. We Brahmins also have great shyness of mentioning sex within the family. A child only is able to learn about it from friends of his own age, or older ones. The younger brother ordinarily will not mention his wife to his older brothers. When she is ill he will have to report, but ordinarily he will not report to his older brother. The older brother is like a father, but ordinarily he cannot explain these things to his younger brother."

G.M.C. "After marriage are Indians still shy of discussing sex?"

S.L. "They discuss, but with friends, not with people of superior age—they feel shy. General tendency today is to read novels full of love and romance. Practically, these have replaced the old interest in reading Ramayan and Mahabharat and such classical stories."

G.M.C. "Are they well written, these novels?"

S.L. "No, no, vulgar writers. Illiterate mass who know only reading and writing like worst possible material, written by authors of poor standard. They don't know how to choose good writing. And films also. One picture was brought to Nathdwara, and the women were so anxious to see it that they even sold their saris and household goods in order to see it. In my opinion there should be some restriction. Children should only be allowed to see pictures if they have been approved. Films influence children more than adults, because their knowledge is not so ripe—for example, if they see a pickpocket making money easily, they may think why should we not make money this way also? Of course, there are some good films too; but it is general tendency of man that he picks up from the wrong side earlier.

"Changes are coming gradually in the caste system—many films show that no caste system should be so strict. Congress does not care about caste system, all are on the same platform. The Hindu Mahasabha believes in the continuance of caste system. Formerly, it was only for Caste Hindus—but now I see in one place it has even admitted Moslems."

G.M.C. "What are 'Caste Hindus'?"

S.L. "They are Brahmin, Kshattria, Vaisya—the Sudras are known as Scheduled Castes. They are given more chances than other castes by the Congress—Congress wants to bring them on the same level."

G.M.C. " Not just ' untouchables ' ? "

S.L. " No, there are so many of them who are touchable, such as Dhobie, Nai, Kumbhar, Boi, Danghi, Mali, Teli and so on. There are many divisions also within the Brahmin, as in Paliwals, the Dasse and the Bisse. Among our Audich Brahmins there are the Big and the Little Audich: two divisions. Formerly, there was not intermarriage or eating together between these two divisions, but recently, some ten years back, this was given up. There is one Audich Mahasabha, and it passed this resolution. This Mahasabha met again this May, near Ratlam. Two years before, it met at Jaipur. It has been meeting for about fifty years: people of both divisions of our community meet together in it."

G.M.C. " Can you explain about ' eating together ' ? "

S.L. " Sitting at the same place, side by side, to take food: not out of the same dish."

G.M.C. " Who can eat out of the same dish? "

S.L. " Such as my brother and I, my children and I, but if one of my children has some cough or some disease, I will not allow him."

G.M.C. " Man and wife? "

S.L. " They also, but not daily. It is not customary. If I wish, I may eat with some very close friend. We Brahmins can't eat from others' hands. Other castes also have restriction. We can accept water from other castes, but we cannot accept food."

G.M.C. " What do you think of the future of castes? "

S.L. " Caste is not going to be extinguished in near future —that will take a long time. But its bonds and social limitations will be loosened. It would be a good thing to lose castes to some extent. In time, the restrictions on intermarriage will be relaxed. Up till now, there are no families with relations in different castes."

G.M.C. " How about sitting together to eat? "

S.L. " If a Bania and I each prepare our own food, we may sit together to eat; or if I prepare food we may both sit and eat, but if he prepares the food, I cannot sit to eat with him."

5th July, 1951

My last talk with Shankar Lal took place on the day when all the village was discussing a scandalous event which had occurred in one of the lanes running off the bazaar. A low-caste youth called Mangu had been dared to swallow a small particle of human faeces for a reward of 50 rupees. He had done so, provoking an outcry of indignation and disgust. Shankar Lal's comment was:

"He is bounded by social bondages, so he is not free. It is a melancholy thing which that foolish fellow has done. It is offensive in the society. Police has not the power to interfere in matters of religion."

G.M.C. "Is there special disgust attached to faeces?"

S.L. "Yes, of course! I can't understand what kind of insanity drove him to do this. It is the worst thing. He becomes quite impure; he is considered to be worse than a sweeper. Until he has been purified he is an untouchable. He will have to get himself purified according to the shastras. This is the first time I have heard of such a thing happening.

"If someone kills a dog, or a cow or a man, whether by accident or by design, you need to be purified. That quite often happens. A Brahmin would have to go to Banaras and bathe in Ganga. This boy, I do not know exactly what ceremonies he will have to perform until he is purified. Snuriti is a part of Veda which describes how to do these ceremonies: in one of them a man is asked to sit on the floor, and burning fire is held above his head."

G.M.C. "Himat Lal said he would have to eat the five products of the cow, and bathe ten times."

S.L. "Yes, Panch-gavya—gau-mutra, gobar, dhai, dudh, ghi. (Cow's urine, dung, curds, milk, butter.) Our Hindu shastras hold the opinion that cow's urine has in it such germs as are required to purify a man, as antidote to all the other germs—in both the physical and the spiritual sense. . . . There are so many vulgars in that lane—it is simply a production of vulgarity. You will see, there are no respectable banias' shops on that side."

Shankar Lal was unique among my Deoli informants in this respect: that none of the other informants told me disparaging gossip about him. He was held in very general esteem, and yet if he was not abused, nor was he ever referred to with cordial praise. He remained something of a stranger to his neighbours in the village, an upright, assiduous, but rather unapproachable figure. In my own talks with him I often had the feeling that he wanted to break through the shell of composure and formality within which he lived: but if the urge was there (and not merely in my imagination) it was manifest only in restless gestures, in struggling silences and in sudden impetuous phrases which hinted at depths of feeling which he could not bring himself to expose to me. Here was a man whose personality defences were based upon emotional isolation: how could I expect him to get to know me well enough, in such a short space of time, to enable him to discuss those emotional conflicts at which he hinted, only to conceal them rapidly each time?

SHANKAR LAL

Formal Psychological Tests

In the Ravens Matrices Test, Shankar Lal gave 33 correct answers out of 60 in 20 minutes. This score was just below the mean (34·5) of the scores of the nine informants who had the greatest amount of schooling. It was exceeded by two others who had been educated only up to matriculation standard.

In his replies to the Word-Association Test, he spoke with a slow deliberation which may have concealed possible hesitations. Unusual delays were observed only in response to " Poor " (to which he replied " Weak ") and " Honour " (to which he gave " Your own honour "). Most replies were formal, e.g. " Rajput—the one who gives protection: Vagina— in which a man takes birth: Death—to be quit of this world." Others consisted of a reproduction of the stimulus word in Sanskritised High Hindi. In general the test revealed, but did not penetrate, his customary emotional defence of studious non-involvement.

RORSCHACH PROTOCOL. SHANKAR LAL

Test given 1st June, 1951.

I.
5″

∧ 1. It is *part of the skeleton of a body*—
You put questions and then I may reply.
/Don't wait for me to ask questions—just go ahead and tell me everything you can see in it./

∧ 2. It also looks as though 2 *bats* are flying, one on each side (heads are top outer corners: bats are the lateral black masses, centre structure being excluded).

Inquiry

/A bony skeleton?/
Bones are not visible here, only some portions only (top centre protrusions). Rest is bone and flesh. This is the whole thing (runs finger round entire design).

∧ 3. It also—the centre portion—looks like *a man without a head* with his hands raised (lifts a hand above his head—indicates inner dark shading silhouette). And
>, ∧ you see that it is repeated on each side, like one thing divided into 2 parts.
/Yes, you'll find that all the cards are made like that./
Nothing more.
TT 3′

II.

15″

∧ 1. They look like 2 *men* sitting with their heads bent forward, turban on their head is slightly seen (top margin, blacks) facing away from
∧ 2. us, holding *a torch* up in their hands (this is lateral red, each side).
∧ 3. Very much like 2 *cartoons* (points to blacks) having peculiar sort of heads and mouths (top reds).
∧ 4. As though *two bears* sitting, their backs towards us (outlines black shapes with finger). If you take it in this way you will see that a
∨ 5. *light* is burning (top red, V). The body of the light, the lamp, is here (enclosed white area).
∨ 6. *Two men* holding torches in their hands (torches top centre red) and their inner legs are cut short but are tied together—these are the other legs (lat. reds).
∨ 7. It also looks like *a skin of some animal* put before us—the whole thing (pause) but you will not find such colours (points to 3 reds in turn) in animals—still, it very much looks like that.
< 8. This also looks like *an animal standing* near water (upper ½) and the reflection is seen (lower ½).
/What sort of animal?/
< A strange animal, not found in India, found in Africa.
∧ 9. It looks also like *legs broken* just now and it is bleeding—not like legs of man, more like bears or hogs' legs, some animals (low centre red).

/Bears doing?/ Their paws are joined together.

/Lamp?/ A glass lamp: this is the oil container (enclosed white area) and the flicker of light is coming out (top centre red in V posn.).

/Skin?/ This is a white spot on the back of the skin—white spots are generally found on the back —a kind of deer; hairy.

SHRI SHANKAR LAL, BRAHMIN

∧ 10. There are 2 *persons* who have got their arms chopped off, and other hands bound by rope (black shapes only: top centre black—the bound hands—lat. reds are at the site of the chopped-off hands, which are not shown).

TT 9′

III.

∧ 10″ Similarity with the former figure. This is also very much like the
  1. *thigh* portion of man (clasps his hips). The skeleton only (whole black shapes).
∧ 2. *Two fish* (fish-shaped black segments).
∧ 3. *Two crows* (top lateral reds).
  4. I mean to say *cock*, cock not crows.
∧ 5. This is very like *Buddhist statue face* (low centre black). You may see this picture from any
> direction or any angle of vision? /Yes, you can do./
∨ (points to black) These are like
∨ 6. the *heads of 2 buffalo calves*, which are carved on the sides of a seat (all black shape).
∧ 7. Two *rough sketches of men* (" men " figures).
  (Laughs)—Nothing more.

TT 6′

/Cocks?/ As though they are alive and jumping.
/Why not crows?/ Because the outline is not the right shape, the crow has a longer beak—if you see the shape of this head (outer lower corner of top reds) it is more shape of a cock.
/Buddhist face?/ Mouth, nose, forehead (these are all shown as enclosed white spaces—the nose in centre, totally enclosed, mouth and forehead below and above this, partly enclosed). Eyes are covered with blackish colour. It is made of stone. (Eyes are indicated as under blobs of dense black shading.)
/Seat?/ Whole of this (black shape) is the back portion of
7a. the seat: this is *what that man* sits on (centre red), made of velvet.
/From colour?/ Yes.
/Men doing?/ They are holding something between them.

IV.

∧,∨ 5″
  1. This is also like *a bat* flying in the air, the whole thing.
⌐,∧ 2. Also, very much like *a skin of an animal* (whole of black again).
∧ 3. This is somewhat similar to *a human face*, this upper portion (top centre black inner shading detail).

Human face is statue of wood or stone, not living face.

∧ 4. This figure is very much like *old language* which has been *known through pictures*, in the time of primitive man (whole black, excluding low centre protruding shaft). This upper portion (obscures lower ¼ with hand) looks
∧ 5. very much like the *skin of a deer*: this is the line down the middle of the back.
∧ 6. This is like *head of Ganeshji* (elephant god) with face here and this trunk (seen in upper ½ of form, about midline).
This portion to some extent like
∨ 7. the *head of a horse* (top centre in V).
This and this (top lateral pro-
∨ jections) were united in one, but it has been divided into 2 parts.
∨ 8. These 2 portions are the *foreheads and trunks* bulging out of some building or carved on some seat (top outer corners, grey—in V).
TT 8′

/Does picture language suggest any idea?/

It suggests sadness or gloominess, a melancholy mood—see, the eyes are closed, face is sad (he has reverted to the face). Hairy, hairy skin—hairs are seen on the skin. Ganesh head is made of stone, of very old age, because it is much weathered and dim with wear.

/Horse?/ Is like a dead horse of primitive age, simply a drawing of the horse, as in a picture.

V.
5″
∧ 1. This is the real picture of *a bat*.
∧ 2. Some *bird* is standing on the ground, standing and stretching his wings.
∧ 3. As though the *skin* of an Australian *kangaroo* has been divided into two (puts hand over card to shut off left half).
∨ (20″) < (10″) ∧
∧ 4. As though 2 *animals standing* back to back—*kangaroos*, living, not skins.
> (15″) ∨ < (slowly).
This portion here is like the
∨ 5. *tail and hind leg of a lion* which is jumping on its prey (thick and thin lateral projections, on each side).
This bulged-out portion looks
> 6. very like the *face of a monkey* (projections from black mass, halfway along its upper margin, in ∧).
These 2 portions (top centre) can
∨ 7. be compared with 2 *snakes* with their heads raised high to fight each other.
TT 7′

Bat is alive, very much alive: it is resting on the ground (considers picture, then adds—) When bats are in danger and trying to escape, this way and that—this is a picture of that time.

/Monkey?/ It is jumping—this is its leg and this is its tail (lateral thick and thin projections).
/See the body?/ No, can't see the body: it is in here (describes a vague circle in black shadow, beneath the monkey face profile)

SHRI SHANKAR LAL, BRAHMIN

VI.

20″

∧ 1. 2 kinds of *animals*, one skinned into two (whole of main lower mass of design) and from its
∧ 2. mouth a *flying insect* is coming out. (Insect is top centre black shaft, and lateral projections.)

Insect is a living one, trying to come out of the mouth.

> 3. If we look like this, 2 *birds*, or a reflection on water of a bird with
> beak here (centre line divides bird and reflection: beak is pale indentation in centre black) and wings like this (two uppermost grey projections). This part does not come in (obscures centre projecting part—top centre in ∧ posn.—with his thumb). This whole portion (obscuring protruding shaft) looks like the
< 4. *skin of an animal:* like that (points to a deer skin in his room).
∧ 5. *Two birds* standing and fighting with each other—water birds: we tell by the colour, white and black, that we generally see such birds in water (top centre portion previously excluded). If we ex-
> clude this portion (top centre shaft again) and this portion (entire lowest ⅓ of design, in
> 6. posn.) this part is like the *nose and the horn of a rhinoceros* (nose is grey eminence near centre line: horn the sharp upwards and outwards projecting part).

/Rhinoceros?/ This is the skin of a rhinoceros only, a stuffed head.

> 7. This portion looks very much like *a kangaroo* sitting behind *a rock*.
8. Rock is on the other side. See this is the head (uppermost projection in > posn.). This is the body and tail (quite vague: in grey shading). They are in rather black portion: pale portion is rock.
> (25″) (i.e. Kangaroo is sitting this side of rock but merges against it so that it cannot be clearly seen.)

TT 7′

∧, VII.
∨ 1. Very much like the *middle portion of the skeleton*, this part (runs hand round his belly)
∧ (15″) > (20″) ∨ (15″).

/Skeleton?/ This is the thigh part (lowest ¼″ each side, in ∨) and this is all this hip part (remainder of black).

252 THE TWICE-BORN

V 2. These 2 portions like 2 *ancient statues*, in the dancing pose. Heads (top ⅓, each side) legs (lowest projections) hands (outer projections).

V 3. V (20″) Also very like a *statue cut open into two* (tapping sides of black shape in turn). One dancing statue V (25″).

∧ 4. This portion looks like the *shape of a gaslight* (i.e. pressure lamp, kerosene) (enclosed white area).

∧ 5. Also like *land* and this (all white area, surrounding black " land ") and this one is a straight of water,

∧ 6. *a canal* (low centre midline, pale colour between black lines).

V 7. This portion looks like roughly the *forehead of an elephant* (middle ⅓).

V 8. This whole portion looks like *a butterfly* at rest (top ⅓ of black). This is the body (centre-line dark details) and these are the wings.

V 9. Also these 2 portions (top ¼ each side, excluding centre black detail) look like 2 *rabbits*—the heads here (upper inner angle of black, seen against pale grey, near midline).

Statues are of stone, and not very clear because in those days people were not so advanced in depicting the statues.

/Land and water?/ Like a map, like shown on a map.

/Elephant?/ Carved elephant, carved on stone or wood: because the impression is not so clear.

/Rabbits?/ They are facing each other, sitting.

TT 9′

VIII.

∧ 1. Roughly it is also like the *skeleton* of the middle portion of the body: some quantity of flesh. This is the skeleton (midline, and all blue and grey).

   2. This is some *flesh* (all pink areas and orange).

∧ 3. 2 *animals* climbing up. This portion (centre blue areas) like

∧ 4. *national flags*, 2—having no true colour, but only shape.

< 5. These are 2 *dogs sitting*—heads and this body (head is projecting corner-shape in orange form).

∧ 6. 2 *animals* are creeping up (pink streaks enclosed within blue area).

∧ 7. It also looks like *a decoration* in a house or on some cloth, whole thing.

V 8. Upper portion looks like the *skin of an animal*, coloured skin (top orange and pink, in V). Nothing else in this.

/Animals?/ May be compared to a lion. Shape, not colour.
Flag—not any special flag because there is no symbol or sign, or different colours. Of course they are 2 flags. Dogs are alive, just sitting in an alert position.
/Crawling animal?/ It looks very like a lizard.
/Decoration?/
8a. This part here is a bird in the flying position (centre orange and
V   red area).
/Skin?/ Something like bear, because it is very hairy.

TT 7′

IX.

∧ (3″) ∨ (15″)

∨ 1. Roughly like *the skeleton* of this middle portion (hips and belly) —(indicating green and orange masses).

∨ 2. These are 2 *upper portions of man*— head and neck, with mouth and forehead, these two (top reds in V).

< 3. This portion looks like the mouth of *a crocodile*, on both sides (in green-orange border area).

Crocodile is alive, lying in water —half of the body is seen. There is water here (centre blue). It is not near the crocodile, but at the side of the crocodile.

< 4. These are 2 *rough sketches of men*, here and here (orange details, upright in lower half of card, held <).

∨ This is water (low midline blue area).

∨ 5. This is *a landscape in water*, this (greenish shaft in midline) oblong shape—there is green grass on it.

/Landscape?/ In lakes here we don't have such narrow promontories of land. It is possible in the sea.

< (15″) > (5″) ∧ (5″)

∧ 6. This is also looking like a *man* with comical cap on his head, and a musical instrument at his mouth, this (orange forms). Like a man from Turkestan or Central Asia.

/Men doing?/ They are seen jumping and wrestling, like the funny man in the circus.
/Why Turkestan?/ It is the shape and size of this dress he is wearing, not the colour.
/Elephant?/ Like a circus elephant performing.

> 7. This (upper green mass in >) is *an elephant* standing on its hind legs, with one front leg lifted up and its trunk cut off.

> 8. This portion, with beard (below) and horns (above) is very much like some *deer* found in typical countries (in green-orange border, previously " crocodile ").

/Deer?/ Deer is a live deer, sitting: only see his head.

> 9. This also looks like *a man* sitting by the side of water (man sitting is small detail on inner margin of top orange, with a round mass for body, small round dot for head; water is bluish area in centre).

⌸ ∨ (25″) (shakes head).

∨ 10. It looks like *a decorative thing*, just a print on paper, with these two heads of deers, one looking one way, one the other way (whole form).

TT 11½′

X.

/This is the last card./
∧, ∨ (3″) (Mm-mm)

∨ 1. Roughly, this is also *a skeleton* this portion (low centre area, bounded by red, blue and grey shapes).
∨ 2. A kind of *peculiar type of animal* (top centre green, in V).
∨ 3. These 2 *animals climbing this rod*. These are ears—heads are not visible (low centre grey—" ears " are upper inner projections).
∨ 4. These 2 very much look like *bears* sitting on the ground (rust-coloured shapes).
∧ 5. 2 *human figures* (yellows on inner sides of red shapes). Head (darker spot inside yellow). Leg (lowest end of yellow shape). Hand (downward and inward
∧ 6. projection) sitting on this *mat* (indicates white area).
7. These are 2 *human figures*—not
∧ 8. human—they have *horns* on their heads—have a bag or something in their hands between them (centre blue shape) (" horns " red projections, contiguous with top greys).
∧ 9. These 2 look like *crabs* (lat. blues). This is also a figure of some
∨ 10. *animal* having horns, this (lat. greys—" horns ", 2 top projections). Peculiar type of animal seen in the cartoon: to some extent like an ordinary animal,
∨ but there are specialities—they have horns on their heads: to some extent like monkey—but monkeys have no horns on their heads.
< (10″) ∨ (holds card at arm's length, stretches legs).
∨ 11. This is also like *a painting by a beginner*, when he mixes the colours for experiment he puts some on paper to test the colour (whole card).
∨ (25″) > (2″) ∧ (30″)
No more imaginations.

TT 13′

/Peculiar animal?/
It is a big animal, like some water bird not generally found, with its legs (low centre detail, V) and wings (lateral green masses) and head (centre detail). It is basking in the sun, standing at ease.
/Animals climbing on rod?/
Not like insects, bigger than that: the like of these is not known to me—they look like animals. Climbing a wooden rod.
/Bears?—colour?/ No, no, the shape and size.
/Humans? (7)/ They are jumping and carrying one bag between them.
/Horns?/ Yes, horns on their heads (laughs) this is a wonderful thing: they might be putting on a special dress on festival days to attract the attention of people.
/Crabs?/—are simply lying in water or on the ground: or you could say they are trying to catch this animal in their claws (top green, in shapes).
/What is it?/
It is also a water animal, not a bird, not like a fish.
/Monkey?/ Is jumping: a funny monkey. It is not a real monkey, because of the 2 horns: head looks like a deer's, body looks like a monkey.

Interpretation of Rorschach Test, by Rosemary Gordon, Ph.D.

The Rorschach record of *Shankar Lal* is full and rich and suggests that he is a resourceful intelligent, and perceptive man. His phantasy life is available to him, but the presence of some fabulated and one confabulated responses as well as a few abstract apperceptions indicates that he is liable to excessive phantasying and that his thought processes are not always orderly (the succession is loose) nor firmly and reliably related to reality.

Moreover, the slight predominance of animal movement over human movement responses reveals that immature components figure a little more prominently in his internal world than is desirable in an adjusted adult and these may occasionally stimulate attempt to obtain the immediate gratification of some need or impulse.

As one of his defensive techniques Shankar Lal has developed obsessional, compulsive and over-formalised methods of control, such as intellectualisation, constriction and the use of impersonal and conventional mechanisms. However, even by this means he does not always succeed in relating himself efficiently to reality and with due deference to its demands. The rather high percentage of poor Form responses indicates that indeed his capacity for reality testing is erratic, particularly when his anxieties are evoked, as they tend to be when he is confronted by inter-personal situations, sexual matters or the affectional longing he seems to experience for the father.

Shankar Lal is apparently extra-tensive but his more hidden personality structure tends to be ambi-equal. When confronted with social and emotional stimuli he initially betrays a great deal of anxiety, a feeling of insufficiency and inadequacy and very marked inner tensions. Such emotional situations seem to stimulate intrapsychic drives and phantasies, but these are then experienced as hostile forces, dangerous to the integrity of the Ego structure. When he does react to the external emotional impact, he does so most frequently in an impulsive and rather uncontrolled manner. However, emotional situations evidently also constitute a challenge which he is anxious to take up. This he does by exploring them in greater detail than usual, particularly if they had taken him aback at first and had elicited feelings of anxiety and depression; furthermore, as he continues to draw upon his inner world and phantasy these tend to become more creative and mature. By these introversive techniques he then tends to succeed in re-instituting conventional controls and even to achieve here and there some more less adequate emotional responsiveness. However, both anxiety and impulsive reactions are always liable to recur, and in each instance control depends not on the development of more mature emotional reactions, but on the intervention of phantasy.

The content of the responses indicates that Shankar Lal is very concerned with the theme of personal identity and with the problem of dividing out of the parent figures and assuming an independent existence. This is suggested by his frequent perception—particularly on the Parent cards—of something that is " divided into two " or " cut open into two ". The sequence analysis would lead me to suspect that the idea of cleavage and separation—a necessary development to the process of growth and maturation—fills the subject with fear and apprehension; the phantasy of separation from the mother creates sensuous longings, regret and anxious concern as to what might now be going on inside her, and what might possibly have taken his place. (The several anatomy responses tend to refer to the middle portion of the body, e.g. " a skeleton of the middle portion of the body, ribs and belly ".) Separation from the father, however, evokes aggression and the belief that once divided into two, father and son are bound to engage in combat and hostility, and at the same time some life-giving force escapes them both. (Thus on Card VI, after the percept of " two kinds of animals, one skinned into two " we get " a flying insect coming out of its mouth " (of the skinned animal).)

There is indeed evidence of much phantasy of destruction and mutilation—broken and bleeding legs, " persons with arms chopped off ", " the elephant with his trunk cut off "—which seem to hint at the presence of fears of castration, impotence and hence general sexual difficulties especially if seen in conjunction with the signs of depression, tension, sensuous longings and above all a lowered capacity to perceive and interpret adequately the stimulus material on the phallic card, Card VI.

Shankar Lal is obviously capable of identifying to some extent with the people around him and of showing them some understanding and sympathy; this is evidenced by his many perceptions of human beings. Yet in spite of being generally interested in human relationships he encounters there so many difficulties that he is forced to take some defensive action. This he tends to do by robbing the people around him of a certain amount of value and reality—thus many of the human percepts are changed into skeletons or cartoons or statues, a mode of apperception which would safeguard him from truly entering into a relationship with them. Furthermore the pre-occupation with " eyes " and with figures facing away from one another, suggests that some paranoidal phantasies enter here, thereby increasing his difficulty in social relationships. Nevertheless he has a good capacity to recover and to overcome in the end the various anxieties and the blocking that they have produced.

Moreover, the attitude to " see " and to " being seen " may be rather ambivalent, involving not only paranoidal fears but also depression. This is suggested by Lal's responses to the father card, where the determinants reveal depression and the presence and acceptance of affectional needs, expressed in a desire to be the recipient of approval and of a sense of belongingness. The content of these responses also betrays sadness and melancholy; thus " the face which suggests sadness or gloominess, the melancholy mood; the eyes are closed the face is sad," and there may well be here a symbolic reference to the actual death of the father when Lal was still a child and which, he may feel, has deprived him (Lal) of the knowledge and the magic powers that might otherwise have been passed on to him—" the old language which has been known through pictures in the time of primitive man "; or " Ganesh's head made of stone, of very old age, because it is much weathered and dimmed with wear " and the " head of a horse; like a dead horse of primitive age "; and referring to the top lateral projections this last response is followed by " this and this were united in one but it has been divided into two parts ". Thus it would indeed seem that the father is phantasied as having taken his secrets away with him into death and that now no communication is possible with him. This train of phantasies may have contributed to his sexual fears.

Summary

The record as a whole then would suggest that Shankar Lal has an intelligent, schizoid personality; we have evidence of the presence of a rich phantasy life in which, however, infantile components play somewhat too prominent a role and which at times becomes too lively and autistic, thus interfering with effective reality testing. In social and emotional situations Lal shows himself liable to be either uncontrolled and impulsive or else to experience anxiety and tension. In defence he has developed constricting and compulsive techniques, though a withdrawal into his inner world and the utilisation of its more mature components is also available to him.

Shankar Lal is concerned with the problem of personal identity and with the theme of separating out of the parental body. He fears that this separation will entail depression and anxious longings for the mother and the threat of conflict and combat with the father. The actual death of the father may have further entrenched this psychic theme and led him to feel that this father is now so far removed from him that no communication is possible, and that he has lost the secrets, the power and the knowledge, that the father might otherwise have passed on to him (hence perhaps the continuing search for more and more knowledge " this is the aim in my life to go on and on studying "). The many aggressive and destructive percepts betray his castration phantasies and also his fears concerning the process of separation from the parents, but these aggressive phantasies tend to interfere with his personal and social relationships tempting him to refuse to enter fully into them and to rob the people around him of life and reality, though interest and pre-occupation with them is nevertheless maintained.

Lal has undoubtedly considerable problems but he has also available to him considerable resources: he is intelligent, he is in fairly close contact with himself and can be expected to have a fair degree of insight; he can accept his own affectional needs and in consequence is capable of empathy and a tactful and sensitive appraisal of situations; he is persistent and never perseveres more than if the situation is difficult and challenging. He is also closely related to his culture and seems able to utilise the projective system of his society for his own individual psychological needs.

SUMMARY

In his account of his own life, as in his habitual speech and demeanour, this informant demonstrated the triumph of restraint over emotional spontaneity. All human relationships were described as obligations. Even of his parents, he could only say: " They must love me because I was their son." His attitude towards his wife was no less formal. In describing the pious rules by which he lived he was still capable of the familiar juxtaposition of contradictions: "Brahmins must uphold the old ways—We should not be so conservative."

Like others of his caste he emphasised the importance of non-attachment to things of this world, of spiritual exercises (although in this informant's case study for academic degrees seemed to have acquired quasi-religious merit) and of stoical acceptance of one's fate.

There were, however, indications that Shankar Lal's apparent calm was a precarious one, hardly concealing a recurrent anxiety mounting at times almost to desperation. This was seen in the two contexts in which he involuntarily revealed strong emotions. Firstly, his violent abuse of promiscuity was at variance with the detachment with which he and his fellow informants usually described the moral shortcomings of other people. It could reasonably be inferred that illicit love shocked him because his indifference to sexuality was not as complete as he would have liked. Secondly, hints of real feeling of markedly depressive quality were given in his accounts of how he called upon God's help in times of distress, and of the painful effort required to regain his customary peace of mind.

The analysis of his Rorschach test confirms both his haunting anxieties, and the large degree of success with which he was able to overcome them through recourse to the defence mechanisms of Brahminical religion: it also suggests, more positively than his explicit statements in the interviews would allow, that the early death of his father may have reinforced existing oedipal anxieties in this case.

A striking feature of Shankar Lal's history (which was indeed echoed in those of all the Brahmins except Himat Lal) was the contrast between the reluctance and awkwardness with which deeply personal matters were discussed, and the relief with which he would expatiate upon his religious life. It was quite a different matter in the case of the next informant, Puranmal.

CHAPTER III

SHRI PURANMAL MEHTA, BANIA

NONE of my Bania informants in Deoli spoke English, and so none can be quoted in their own words. Instead, this chapter is devoted to extracts from the autobiography of a young man of a Bania family in Jaipur, the capital of Rajasthan. He chanced to hear of my research and wrote to volunteer his assistance. We were able to meet, and to have a series of interviews, in the course of which he presented me with the manuscript from which the following pages are taken. His story is included here because he has shown himself an eloquent and revealing spokesman for his community. In spite of the fact that he lives in a large and partly modernised town in another part of the state, and that his family, although Banias, are orthodox Hindus and not members of the Jain sect (as are most of the Banias in Deoli) his experiences and attitudes were found to correspond very closely to those of the younger Banias in the village.

Birth and Family History

I was born on Thursday, the 27th August, 1930 (Kartik Krishna II, 1987) in a middle-class merchants' family, in Dr. Vishwamitra Dhanda's house, which was taken on rent by the family. I had not the fortune of seeing my grand-parents. My grandfather, Shri Ramji (popularly called Rambaba), was famous for his vigour, adventures and above all the greatest of all sense—the commonsense. He was famous for good swimming, prescribing medicines, detecting thefts, influence on police and other Government departments, etc. But the worst thing was that he followed the profession of Nilam. In fact he was such a spendthrift that the family used to get flour and vegetables for 1-2 pice many times. My father was the successor of one Great Grand uncle of mine, Shri Sivaji, who was a broker in sugar, and hence we are now called Khandwalas.

My parents were of middle-class standing when I was born, but ill-luck overtook them on the marriage of my brother. My father used to go to Bikaner for monthly Nilam.* When it stopped, he was reluctant to follow the profession here in Jaipur due to the fear of being arrested. But the mother instigated him many times to go to the market and try the luck, which became a fruitful cause of quarrels between the couple. In fact there have always been quarrels between them. Later on they began speculation in gold and silver, which turned out to be a profitable occupation and now we are quite prosperous.

In the year 1933 or so we purchased the house in which we are at present putting up, in about Rs. 1,500 (something we paid from our accumulated cash balance and something we borrowed on the security of ornaments). We incurred about Rs. 400 in the repair of the building.

Yes, here I remember one thing of my childhood. Once we went to Pushkarji in the train and I was very timid. I feared VERY MUCH by the whistle of the train. I thus harassed my parents very much and they decided not to carry me anywhere in the train till I was grown up and in fact there has been no chance as yet of going out for me, except only once, and that to Padampura, a station just 2 hours' journey. This also accounts for my timidness and my being taken by surprise by the firing of guns in the neighbourhood.

Childhood

My mother says that in childhood I was a very naughty child. I used to throw things out of the house very swiftly. Before one thing could be restored I used to throw away another. Once I threw the umbrella on the head of a girl, which caused her nose-bleed, on the one hand, and on the other threw a silver ornament in the refuse pipe.

I was very obstinate in weeping for sitting on the cycle, and my father used to carry me on the cycle in the street, but in it he felt great difficulty as he did not know cycling. Cycle was meant for my elder brother.

The worst habit of mine that embittered our relations with my brother's wife was that I used to pretend spitting on her as she passed by. She created a lot of trouble about this habit of mine. She bathed many times and quarrelled with my mother frequently. Then I used to tease my brother's wife and her only daughter by saying that I do not want them in my house. It was a pure joke and because she was harassing my mother too often and I was pleased to tease them all the more

* Gambling on stock exchange prices

because they took it very very seriously. I have still no sympathy for those wretched creatures, who still hold the same attitude about me and my family. I hate them from the core of my heart and never talk to my brother's wife.

Education

My father was instrumental in putting me to education at a very small age. When I was only 8 years old I was admitted to the IV class in the local Fateh High School (then middle school). Before it I had prepared at home with tutors for only two years. Then a tutor was engaged to me who continued teaching me up to my VIII class in the said school. I never failed in the examinations in my life, but it is a fact that I passed my primary classes (up to VII) due to recommendations and was only promoted.

In the life of my parents there has been a great tragedy. My sister married in a rich family, but her husband has turned out to be a drunkard, gambler, thief and with all the other evils attached to these. He has been to jail many times. My parents have undergone so much troubles on account of him that cannot be described besides spending thousands of rupees over him. He has been asked to settle in business many a times and he has settled but his extravagance knows no bonds. He drinks, keeps lady-loves, purchases cars, radios, fans, tongas and does all other things, with the result that the condition of my sister and his daughter is very pitiable. My niece had the acutest desire for learning, but on account of adverse family circumstances could not pursue her studies. She is so keen that she got herself admitted in the school more than 3-4 times. But unluckily her father is again in the jail on account of theft, with the result that she had to discontinue her studies.

It will not be out of place for me to mention here one event of my life, which goes to prove that from the very beginning, God knows due to what circumstances or influences, I was very timid. When I was in the IV class, one day during the examinations I felt thirsty and also a motion for passing. I sought permission for drinking water. I did not go to urinal because I thought the teachers would think that I have gone without permission with a view to copy. Nor had I the courage of asking for urinal after coming from drinking water. The result it was that urine came out in the examination hall where we were sitting on tat-pattis. This also draws another conclusion, that I had no power of judgment. I could have sought permission for urinal and then could have taken water also as it was just near the way.

I may also mention here that although I had no younger brother or sister, my sister's son, Gopi Goyal used to live with us. We were just of the same age, he being only one and a half years younger than me. We used to quarrel very often and thus caused great trouble and nuisance for the family. Here also I remember of one thing which has taken a deep root in me and which is seen in me since my childhood. My parents used to tell me that I should not tell my nephew about the fruits they give to me and that I should eat them myself, but I one way or the other used to tell him what I received and gladly shared with him. This accounts for the deep root of the habit of being just which is responsible for my good and serene character. But here lurked the habit of disobedience to parents, which is still in me.

Then comes my friendship with Mohan Lal Goyal, a scoundrel of the first class. He used to come to my house for flying kites, etc., as his parents did not allow him to do so at his place. I came in his chakkar and used to pay him for kiting, which amount he was never paid. I used to sell him my kites and thread also under the pretence that they belong to my nephew (thus speaking lies, which I thought were very small, but which I do not like at all now). It goes to explain in me the habit of thrift and saving, for which all the family called me a miser, and that of business—selling one thing and buying another, which continues till now.

Then comes second gentleman, Mr. Chauthmal Jain, who was also a distant relative of ours. We used to study combined at his house. He taught me the lesson of handpractice, I went to such an extremity that for years I wasted my precious semen at least twice a week, and was overtaken by the disease of early-fall at the time of marriage. He was separated from me when he plucked in his VIII class and left his studies. It was with the assistance of Mr. Ram Lal Sharma on the one hand and partly due to my association with wife and my college life that I left this nasty habit of mine.

Further I may mention that in our school games were compulsory and we had to attend the field daily, which would have given me a very good chance of developing my body and association with friends. But as ill luck would have it, my father used to accompany me. This made me of a very shy and coward nature, with poor physique and kept me aloof from society, which habit has become a curse to me in my future life when otherwise I would have done a lot.

Why I am poor in bargaining power is accounted for by another peculiarity of our family, that my parents never allowed me to purchase anything for family or myself. Even when I had to purchase petty requirements like pencil, nib, paper, etc., they used to accompany me and thus I was devoid of the bargaining power. Today also they do not allow me to purchase anything for the family. My father does all this business.

Now to explain why I have grown so careless about things, I may emphasise that my father used to get me a pen and a suit each year, as a matter of routine. But I being a child, other students used to make away with it, and I did not care about it as my parents told me not to worry and they will assure me to bring a new one.

But the events took a different turn when I put my step in the high school. I made friendship with Mr. R. D. Mehta, which continues still; although it was at his initiative. He was in the other section, but he is quite bold in talking to anybody, although I fear in it. I used to go to him for study combined. At last we both of us passed in the II Division in the year 1945.

Marriage

It was when I was reading in the high school that my marriage took place. My betrothal had already taken place when I was in the eighth class. I was married in May, 1944. My wife was a bit tall, and I feared myself what I will be required to do on the honeymoon night. I was quite blank and knew nothing, no-one told me anything. Anyway the chance did not come for a long time for our association, but when it came began the sad tragedies of my life. I trembled to ask her anything as I did not know what to ask and what to talk to her. Only one question I repeated each night. " Why are you sitting? Why not sleep? Is it your daily routine to sit? " and she used to give only one answer: " Yes, I will sleep ", and will wait for some time and then sleep. Mother used to wait eagerly to see us talking but without any result. At last it was through a great determination that I once tried to do intercourse, but I failed and my semen came out before it could go in. This put me in a very pitiable and shameful condition psychological, although now I know that this is only with most people. I worried what my wife would be thinking about me, but now she says she was fearing me more than I did. She says she did not know what I would do with her. Anyway we continued but all the time the semen came out before I could effect penetration. Many times I thrust it but the semen came out just as it entered and one thing which teased me was that Lalita, a friend of mine told me that it should not flow out, although it is natural. This tortured me much and I was under the treatment of Dr, Anthony Rodrigues introduced to me by Lalita. But it was of no use. I may also mention here that after a long time this disease disappeared all at once without any medicine. It took some time before semen came out and now it is perfectly alright.

When my wife, Shrimati Laxmi Rani's first menstruation began, when she was at her father's house I was very much tortured, knowing that it must be due to her corruption although it is not necessary, and I tried to find out from the Ramayan whether she is pure or not, which has testified that she is quite pure. Mr. N. D. Mehta has required me to test her by threatening her to speak the truth or that I will not speak to her; but I have refused his suggestion as it would not create any good.

My attitude towards my father-in-law has been very bad. Firstly they have always sent rotten and useless things to us. Secondly, they have meted out no respect and good language for my family, and lastly, that they used to keep wife for about 16 days in a month, till late years. Statements made by them were most tearing to me as is testified by my diary, where all statements have been recorded datewise.

Wife professes that she is quite pure. She says she feared me much. She says I was very miser and used to hide the hair oil bottle so that she might not use; she is quite correct in this statement of hers. Further that I told Dakhu the wife of my brother all that passed between, which was false.

But one thing which I cannot but regret is that the state of health of my wife is very pitiable as she says. She feels great weakness and is unable to carry out her duties to a satisfactory extent although her weight is 110 lb. Right she has to help the family in domestic affairs, but not quite fully. She is reluctant to cook evening food for me with the result that I have to eat food cooked in the morning. She won't arrange my bedding and all that. She won't wash my clothes and like that. She feels headache daily in her head and could not be cured in spite of our spending Rs. 55 in a lot on the treatment.

Further she does not know any art. She is absolutely ignorant of knitting, embroidery work of good standard, cutting of cloths, making good dishes, etc. She is very keen to read, but I am very sorry I have neglected it due to my being engaged in other activities. I will try to take note of it the next year in winter, as I cannot teach in summers, before everybody. I get time only after we are in our room at night after all have gone to bed.

Then there is a peculiarity in our intercourse. I cannot find out in spite of my best efforts whether or not she is interested in it or not before we do. With her motions I feel that she is, but later she says that " I had only to please you ". At others she is very keen to have it done although I might have done it once before or not. She also acknowledges it. I regret very much that in the winter season of 1949-50 intercourse has been much, on an average about twice or thrice a week.

Further she has no liking for articles of toilet, make-up, dress, etc. She never asks me to bring anything and whenever I ask her to bring some things, she refuses. She does not use cream, powder, vaseline, etc. Also when I bring certain things, whether on her request or not, she will complain about its quality, although this is due to her lack of knowledge.

College Life

After my high school career, I and Rameshwar Das started a very small book shop in a building overlooking the Surajpol Bazar, in front of Saraswati Book Depot. But we did not know what business is; how to get books; from where to get them and so on. We had intended to run a secondhand book shop and had kept our own books only. Then we got a signboard prepared for about 10 annas, which was totally washed away by the rains after 3-4 days; and with it was washed away our shop also.

After this the college reopened after the summer vacations. I did not know what to do; where to serve; how to find out a job and so on and so forth. In the meantime Mr. Mehta instigated me to join the college; my father was also of the opinion that I should join the college. Thus at last I joined the college. Then came the question of selection of optional subjects. I was informed by some of my acquaintances that if I will take shorthand I can be a press reporter and can draw a big salary. While others told that steno is a very difficult subject and as my typing was not good, I should not attempt it. But as I was II class I could get the chance of steno very easily and I availed of it, all through sheer luck. I did not know even what shorthand means. I continued it in spite of Prof. Sharma's repeated warnings that we should leave it as it is very difficult. I also felt, when vowels were being taught, that I could follow nothing, but as good luck would have it, I went on practising without understanding anything, and in the long run I understood all well. I did not work as hard—not even $\frac{1}{4}$ of what was required, but still I could follow it all right. And in the 2nd year I won the FIRST PRIZE in the Shorthand Competition held by the Commerce Association. I lost the prize in the Typing competition, because I typed too swiftly without caring for mistakes. I was much helped by shorthand in the annual examination when I spoiled my typewriting paper. But still due to the help of shorthand I secured Distinction in Steno-typing and came out with flying colours in FIRST DIVISION, the only student from the college, but the most unweary thing was that my friend got plucked and was later on declared compartmental in English, but he left the studies and has started an iron and hardware shop. He is quite well off in it.

One thing which accounted most for my brilliant success in the examination was my habit of note-preparing. I am proud to note that I have never purchased any notes at my own expense and have always prepared notes, rather books of notes, by consulting various notes and class lectures. They have been of immense help to me in the examination. As a matter of fact I depended the whole year on only note-taking, never working for more than $\frac{1}{2}$ hour or so. In the end of the year I would read my notes and pass. This also improved my English very much and thus helped me a lot.

I may also mention here that this habit of mine created an interest in me for writing books. I really attempted to prepare a book of important problems of mathematics, but I firstly being immature in the art at that early hour and then unable to get a publisher, had to discontinue my work, which is still lying with me, but in a useless state.

This passion in me for reading and writing has made me philosophic in my mood since my college life. I do not have any interest in anything of the world else. I would always be thinking about myself only and when somebody tells me I say only " Yes, yes " and later on when a compliance is expected I simply say I did not hear or that you never told me like that. This is bad and I should try to remove absence of mind.

It was during the summer vacation after the 1st year examinations that I joined the Rationing Department as a clerk. Here I was helped by the exaggeration of my age by three years. If my age would not have been exaggerated in the School Certificate, I would not have been a major and thus could not have been allowed to serve. The work was rigorous but I continued without much care. Herein came one event, which is important to be recorded. Once a Muslim Inspector teased me that I did not work hard, although I did, at which I told him that he had no business with me. He reported to the A.R.O. who told me that " Do you know that I can withhold your pay? " At that I told him politely in my view that he should do what he thinks right. But he took it seriously and at the suggestion of my colleagues I had to seek pardon, which I did with tears flowing out of my eyes.

During my 2nd year in the College I was bound in ties of friendship with Mr. Lalita, who initiated it by inquiring about the reasons of my poor physique. I am always in the habit of telling truth and told him about my disease which was eating me viz., early discharge. I am in the habit of disclosing all the secrets, which habit is not appreciable.

This year I with Rameshwar Das started a debating soicety at my residence, but only 2-8 people took interest in it and we were also lacking in knowledge. Hence it came to a close without bearing any fruits.

I may also mention that during the period we initiated certain schemes, but my father curbed them all in the bud with the lion's roar. And I could not dare follow any of my programmes which required me to go out etc. without the permission of my parents.

After passing my Inter Commerce Examination in the First Division I tried much for service. I found one in the S.A.O.'s office and was just appointed when I knew that I had secured First Division in the Examination. It encouraged me to continue my studies further. My acquaintances also advised me to prosecute further studies. I was tired of the work in the S.A.O.'s office after only one day and so intended to join the college. Later on I came to know that I will not get the scholarship, but still I continued the college.

Here I may also mention that still I had not the courage of asking questions and discussing them in the classroom.

During this period I have been maintaining my diary which is a valuable asset to me.

Hobbies

I had no hobby except (i) writing notes, (ii) writing diaries. To be frank I had no such hobby which would cost any money, but only a few papers. I never indulged in photography up to the time I studied in college. It was only after my service in the Rehabilitation Department that I purchased a nice camera and wasted about Rs. 10 on films. Now I fully realise the value of money and will not indulge in reckless expenditure of money on it. Although I will not leave it, but will spend only a very small amount each month, say for 2 photos a month.

Again I am not inclined to see many pictures. I only visit whenever at once I feel a sensation that I should see. And then I will see definitely. I remember to have seen only 20 pictures, which I understood. Besides I had seen Ujala, Tarjem, etc. which I do not remember and when I did not understand the pictures.

All the pictures visited by me were very nice (except 2 which were quite bogus) and created satisfaction.

Tastes

I completely dislike drinking, smoking, betel-chewing (I do indulge at certain times), gambling, adultery, etc. and have never indulged in these nor like others to do so.

Service

During the 3rd year of my college life, I had a plenty of part-time jobs. I had served during my second year at the Prem Prakash Co., which to say, as a matter of fact, was the career-builder for me. At the very first day I was very much discouraged by the foreign addresses and a different atmosphere. But the proprietor encouraged me very sympathetically and it is due to his efforts that today I am a good typist and having experience of business correspondence, etc. It was during this time that I made correspondence as my hobby. This was initiated by some Divine Agency as we began it when some letters on the topic belonging to some other firm were delivered wrong at my house. Although I have lost about Rs. 200 or so in this, but still it has left behind a treasure of information and experience about business affairs. I ordered hair oil, rubber balloons, brass ornaments and radios. I and Rameshwar Das also took agencies of local mail-order businessmen, but in spite of our repeated attempts we could not do business as I am very weak at canvassing. Another conclusion that I have drawn during this period is that one cannot carry on in partnership for long. I had partnerships with about four gentlemen but all turned out complete failures.

To come to our point, I joined the Maheshwari Hosiery, but as the Manager did not like me working small number of hours during the exhibition he discharged me and discharged his firm also as he lost much in the exhibition.

Then I worked with the Quota Cloth Retailers' Association as a clerk, under its Secretary who was a Bania. But he did not like my work as neither was I conversant with the work of such bodies nor could I explain myself well in Hindi. However, I had no more work than 5-6 minutes daily except on month-ends, when meetings took place. There also I used to attend them only and doing nothing, which, of course, I did not like. I was discharged when the control on cloth was taken up. Thus I used to earn nothing short of Rs. 75 per month.

But during the 4th year all was gone. I had not even a single part-time job. Once I worked with the Manager of the Jupiter, but he discharged me when I got typhoid for about one month. He did not even pay my full dues.

Then I came to know that some vacancy of a Stenographer had been in the Inspector General of Prisons' office and I appeared at that office. I was tested for 2-3 days and after the I.G. was satisfied of my worth he took personal interest and got my transfer SPECIALLY sanctioned from the Govt. Although sometimes I had to work hard in this office, but on the whole I have been MUCH better than in the Rehabilitation Department. The only trouble that I have had to face is that one P.A., Mr. Mangilal Aluwala although outwardly he did nothing, perhaps has been tutoring the I.G. and making secret attempts to get me retrenched through some way or other. As yet his attempts have proved futile, but God knows what is my future?

The future has brought out a very different tale. In spite of all that Mr. Aluwala might have done, I.G. loves and respects me like anything—a clear example of this is: (1) he never rebukes me or says a word even when I commit mistakes, when he badly reprimands the other steno, even on slight mistake. (2) When he was seriously ill and did not permit anybody to see him and was completely at rest, still he was constantly enquiring about my health through his P.A. and his peons. He had ordered it, and when he rejoined office it was the first thing he asked me, about my health. (3) He respects my views and invites them in important matters and agrees to them.

A Father

It was during the 2nd year of my college life that a baby was born to my wife. He has been named as Purshottam, as he was born in the Purshottam month. Now he is the object of greatest love for my parents. He is very much attached to his grand-father and neither to his mother or to me. He lives, plays, sleeps, goes to latrine or urinal with grand-father. It is he who feeds him with his own hands and cleans his stool. He cries for him all day and night and does not leave his company. He goes to the bazaar with him and so on. But the worst thing that has happened is that he has cultivated many bad habits such as crying for eatables all day long. It has spoiled his digestive system and he suffers from dysentery so far as I think. He goes to latrine after his meals. He does not love his mother also; he does not go with her to her father's house, nor sleeps with her. She also therefore has not so much attachment for him.

A second child was born. His name as I put it was Jawahar. He was really a jewel. But unluckily he died an untoward (unexpected and unfortunate) death. People (one *dakot*) say that some demon took him the day after he was born, since when he was ill. Wife has once seen him in dream in the life of a lion. God console his soul. But as a result she suffers daily from severe headaches, which in spite of 15 injects and medicine at Rs. 55, has not gone. Wife felt it for a week but not later on. My mind had though no effect of the event. I did not even see his face the last time. He expired and was carried to the burial ground in my absence, when I was in the office. I returned from the office after evening.

Relations with Parents

I have never loved my parents in spite of the fact that they love me more than a God. I hate and do not admire the love bestowed upon me by them. It is too strong to be borne by me. I pass satires on their so much attachment with me, but it pleases them all the more and I am all the more teased. They never leave me alone. They do not allow me to go at night. They go to take me from the office, if I come late, although they know that I generally come late from the office. They would wash my clothes and would never allow me to go out of the city or to the suburbs. Thus they are responsible for my shallow knowledge and helplessness.

I very much regret I could not mete out to them in this small life of mine any tribute. I may do that now. It is due to my parents that one sees me what I am. Their nature and habits and all that have depicted a true picture in me, as if they are seen in a mirror. It is due to their strenuous efforts alone that I have been able to pass the degree examination in such a small age and that also with good marks. It is thanks to them that I have never had any trouble for my eating, clothing, etc. But still there was the inconvenience of shelter. Today also we have to live in a very small space only. However, it matters little.

My Health

Here I am sorry to record a very sorry figure that my health during all these years has been very unsatisfactory. My cheeks are hollow, face pale, chest of poor size and not quite tall structure. My weight has been constant at a very low mark of 88 pounds (with serge suit) during all the four years of my college life. I have to make much efforts in this direction to increase my weight. The greatest reason of this state of affairs is perhaps my nature of being too much sensitive towards petty things in life. I will not allow small things to pass un-noticed, which is very bad. Secondly, I do too much mental work. I take no rest of any kind at any time. I am too much alive, whether at office, home or in work—everywhere.

1. My poor constitution and health is also represented by other general diseases, e.g. I have been suffering from dysentery. I have submitted myself to the treatment of various doctors, allopaths, homeopaths and *vaids*, but of no use.

2. I do not get sound sleep at night. Early in the night I feel Dozy and get sound sleep up to 1 p.m., but after that I do not get sleep (sound). Chains of various unconcerned thoughts come to my mind and disturb my sleep. I previously took medicines for 1-2 days and could get sleep alright for months, but now I do not think it proper to use these

medicines. And the use of other medicines has not proved of any advantage.

3. My eyesight is very weak, the numbering being near — 5. I have submitted myself to various eye-tests, at State Hospital and private doctors, and have taken specs also twice but I am sorry no spec has fitted my eye and this has involved me to a loss of about Rs. 40 without any gain to me. The main reason of my weak eyesight is my excess confinement in the home as I was completely shut out of outside world, etc.

Religious Outlook

My father worships Ram, Krishna, Ganesh and Shiva. He keeps idols of these on a small throne and goes to Govindji to worship them. He always goes to the temple in spite of all his ill health or important work. But as concerns me I am the worst man in this respect. I never pray God with a sincere heart although outwardly I try to do much. I have many times attempted to remember him at the daybreak in the guise of Ramayana and Gita, but have failed in my attempts. I read the holy books, but with little interest. I even do not remember how many chapters I have finished, etc. I am particularly devoted to God Ganesh, who is, as my experience shows me, very very helpful to me at most occasions of my life. He does what I wish at the turn of the eyelid as soon as I remember him. It is through his kind grace that today I am a man with some sense at least, but the unlucky thing is that in spite of the fact, my attachment with him is lessening. I have not paid a single visit for so many months. Still, He is not angry with my behaviours. May God Ganesh give me courage to worship and remember him all the moments of my life.

Pious Ideas

My mother is of very high ideas in this respect. I have her influence. I do not like to touch anybody in the hospital, iron chain in the latrine, sit on the carpet cleaned by the sweeper, or to touch the sweeper, I do not like to get spattered by refuse pipes, but I have to tolerate some of them at times, although I do not like. My mother does not allow me to touch the pots etc. in spite of all this. She would not drink water if I touch the pot, even after washing the hands. This is too much, but I am bearing it like a brave man.

Benevolence or Pity

I have a sufficient degree of pity in my heart towards all men, beasts, plants and other innate objects of Universe, e.g. my heart melts with pity when I see a poor boy who is crying for want of food, or the poor condition of our unlucky brothers. Then I would be very much moved by any harsh treatment with animals—dog, goat, cow, horse and what not. Further I would not like to waste anything. I would not like that electric current is used unnecessarily even though it may not increase the bill. I will feel very much if my treatment just causes pain to anybody.

Cowardice

But still I am a coward of the first class. I would like to die by taking poison rather than at a dagger. I would never like to indulge in violence unless our safety is at stake.

Social Views

I completely hate or dislike the present day social order. I do not like the exorbitant expenditure on marriages, the unequal marriages, early marriage, dowry, absence of education, poverty, drink, gambling and treatment with ladies etc. I have views of complete reformation, e.g. I wish to marry my son in the most reformed way, to educate those around me to marry a widow; if I become a widower, to keep in complete freedom, not to care about social criticism on my personal affairs. I simply dislike the ideas of Rameshwar on these matters who fears the views of others in his personal acts.

Accounts

I have taken birth in a family and at a time when nobody cares or keeps accounts or warns me about the expenditure of mine or the family. Money is put in the room and anybody can utilise without permission. As a result of this I have become very careless about my expenses. I do not realise the value of money, with the result that I always pay more than what I should and not only this, but I become careless in buying useless things and destroying them.

But I have a feeling ruling supreme in me that I want that I should not spend from my parents' pocket and so keep rough accounts of my expenditure, and their expenditure on me. But the method has been very rude and I cannot know what I have spent on and what my parents. I do not pay them openly as they would not accept. Rather I put it in the room to be used by myself and the others, but taking out my responsibility for my expenditure.

During all these years I have been constantly on my guard and have tried to improve myself morally, spiritually, physically and mentally. The worst thing is that I cannot follow upon my programmes and schemes. However, now I will try to practise upon them and see the result very soon.

Another thing that counts for my weakness is that I lose peace of mind very soon. I begin to shiver like anything when any untoward happening takes place. I lose my sense when I get a lot of work.

It is my 19th birthday and the 20th begins. My feelings were that now I am a young man, not only a man but a couple, not only a couple but a part of a family. Thus I should not act as a child now as I have been doing hitherto. I have to be more senseful. I have long visions before me, but I have been unable to do anything worth mentioning by now. Anyway man is a bundle of mistakes and I should not repeat on them. I have to look hopefully towards my future and prepare a plan to achieve this future in its fullness, in its entireness. This is the real thing. May God help me to get my objective as early as possible. May God make me healthy, wealthy and wise, apt to serve the nation in the right earnest right way and at an early moment. Yes, but may I make a beginning now? Is it an auspicious moment? Yes, all moments when a young man prepares such schemes and resolves with a firm mind, become fully auspicious. Time is life and I should not waste a single minute in preparing myself for a soldier, worthy of fighting the battle in a successful manner. God Shrikrishna has also advised us in Gita that one should go on performing his duty without any check. He should never cease to ponder over (without caring for the fruit of) his actions. He should never feel delighted or sorrowful if he has got victory or if a son has been born to his wife, nor should he worry if his only son has expired. It is a man's duty to work, but never to care for its fruit. If work is alright, fruit is bound to follow, sooner or later. But they cannot bluff God, who keeps a big register noting down not only the minutest action of a person, but the least intention or motive behind it. Hence be careful and work, WORK AND WORK, according to the instructions of God and you will be his sincerest friend, servant, devotee, son, and in a general sense HIMSELF.

Relations with Father

It gives me much pain to write this chapter of my life and put before my readers the general view of rebellion held by me towards my father. It is a matter of genuine pleasure and truth that what I am today is solely due to my father—progress as well as shortcomings. I could not have progressed as much had my father not helped me to pursue my studies. He was instrumental in putting me to school early in life and was always encouraging me to continue my studies further in the College. I have only to appreciate this thing. He has been very generously meeting all the expenditure of mine. Even still now when I am earning my own income (1951) he finances me fully and does not want me to pay anything. It is only my pocket expenditure that I meet myself.

But I still regret he has been a great obstacle in my road of progress. It is not that he wanted to be so. But it was purely due to his ignorance. He does not understand the mind of a young man. He thinks I am a doll made of clay or cloth to be treated like an inanimate thing. He does not recognise my feelings, which are very strong to be curbed down.

He would never allow me to go out even in the city for tours which might extend to 3-4 hours. He fears, not that I shall take to bad company, but that I might be overtaken by some vehicles, or might be tired, or that I might be hurt in some other way, as if I am a child. All this is due to their loving me too much. As regards visits to outside places, it is impossible for me to get any permission. It will be strange but it is a fact that he went to the College with me to get me admitted. In my school games were compulsory and so he used to go to school with me. One can very well imagine how one can plan and enjoy when one's parents are with them like shadows!

So all this extreme love which he showers on me appears to me very troublesome. I tease him in all sorts of ways, disobey him, but this all the more pleases him, and I am out of my control—extremely troubled. Still I may say that I am not bold enough to do anything which he forbids me to do because I know that if I do so he will break his own head, which I cannot tolerate.

The clear proof of my apathy towards my father was experienced during his illness. In 1950-51 he became very ill—he was even about to die—but still I did not speak even a word to him when others wept and assured him in every way. I used to sit silent only whenever called by him. I had to play cards with him sometimes to entertain him, but this was very tough job for me and I never felt entertained, rather I was wishing all the time to be rid of the job. It will be a queer thing if I say that I had not even the least agony on the idea that he might die.

But still in the end I pay him a warm tribute that he has taken such great pains to bring me up and has always been trying to do the best for me—as per his own views—May God save him from future troubles.

My Wife

There has been a mingled feeling of pity and complaint against my wife, who is an oasis in the desert of modern life. She has a very peculiar nature, not common to ladies of the time. Till lately I had very bad ideas about her. I had the strong conviction that I cannot carry on my life happily with her. But after I have seen the pictures " Swyamsidha " and " Choti Bhabi " I have realised that the fault is mine; no other. She has old ideas because she is illiterate. Although she is very much willing to study, I have failed in my attempts to do so. Here one might clearly point out me to be the guilty man, that I shirk my responsibility. But no, the fault is mine —it is my surroundings that have foiled my attempts. There is no room or private place where I can teach her. My parents would never like me to engage a tutoress for her. Moreover, now she has much private domestic work and cannot afford to devote any time.

Moreover, she has a strange and at the same time false notion in her mind that I am a miser. Whenever she asks me to bring betel, I do so, but sometimes I forget to bring, she will pass remarks later on. It is all in spite of the fact that I pay her more than what I save myself. I always do what she likes in the matter of her purchases, which are nil.

She treats the children in a most careless manner. She won't care for their food, drink, clothing, etc., and would never follow my instructions to rear them properly, with the result that the elder one has developed many bad habits—e.g., that of eating sweets all the day like a glutton, not eating food, not caring properly for his dress, not taking baths, weeping, etc. Of course, I see that the younger is reared properly and I am constantly caring to do so: whether she cares or not.

All these troubles are due to joint family and absence of private rooms, and this feeling alone has made my mind calm and I think I should set the whole affairs all right if I am given an opportunity to attend to her affairs in a private capacity.

Rameshwar Das Mehta

Man is a social animal. He cannot live without company. I regret I have only a very limited circle of friends. In truth, I have only one friend—Mr. R. D. Mehta, who has been a class-fellow of mine from the year 1935, but with whom my contact developed from 1944, from which year we began to study together. Our friendship has developed so much that I do not feel any doubt in saying that he is my life. I feel that we have two bodies but one soul. Although it is a fact that because of a big difference in our social positions—he being a businessman and uninterested in education, while I being a serviceman and greatly interested in books and advanced life, we cannot participate in everything, but still in cases of entertainment I cannot enjoy anything without him and find that I must get his company. We meet almost daily and keep a good contact.

There have been many quarrels between us—which is the nature of law—but still, with God's grace, we are one and will remain one. All our old quarrels have been washed down and we have—both of us—taken a vow at the temple of Galta, the vow of friendship, which is now unbreakable. We have decided not to feel any difference between us and we have married our vow. The occasion of taking a vow has been a very sacred and unique one. Once when we were going to the Ghat on a Sunday trip R.D.M. told me that he was thinking of asking some high placed man whether or not he could break his oath of not coming to my house, which had taken long ago on a quarrel between us, in which I had slapped him for tearing up my leave application to persuade me to go to college, rather than take leave. I forced him that very moment to go to Galta and we went direct with cycle in spite of my sub-conscious fearing the appearance of a tiger in the way. In fact never before in life had I taken such a hazard, but for this occasion.

He has contributed greatly to my peace of mind and thus has just to a great degree balanced the deficit made by the wife's being illiterate.

It will be of interest as well if it might be said that R.D.M. did not come to my house for 5 years together as he had sweared God. But one day we went to Galta and after taking counsel of the Galta Mahatma he made him break his oath and were again bound in the temple of God for ever.

Before this union of ours, the main point of difference between us two had been the miser nature of Mr. M. I did not like it. But now I promised that I shall not ask him to spend anything for us and if I spend anything I shall not take anything from him—even though I may spend anything. On the other hand if he becomes mean in his behaviour, I shall explain to him the whole situation.

Thus we have quite clear hearts now.

It will also be not out of place for me if I jot down my feelings towards ladies in general. In fact, from the very beginning of my life I have had the least contact with the female sex—just imagine I had no love of aunts, near or distant. I had some of a cousin's wife, but it also was discarded by me due to her bad practices, which are noted somewhere else in this book. As regards my brother's wife, as I have already noted, I did not like her nature and she did not like mine. Further, I was more of a homesick and could not go out anywhere. Thus I have been debarred of the enjoyments of the company of the opposite sex. I rather now feel shy of talking to them—but in truth I have now also no opportunity of contacting them—I have been a Commerce student and there have been no females in the class. My friend Mr. R.D.M. who had been a Science student had also no contact with a lady student and hence I have no contact whatsoever.

But after all human nature is bound to be attracted towards the mysteries of the opposite sex. We do not like to practise adultery, etc., which we think to be the worst crime. But still just to please ourselves—to entertain ourselves—whenever we go out for a walk, we would like to see girls to talk to us. But after all we are always two and no girl can dare talk to two young men. Anyway we enjoy the thing very much.

Another very interesting fact that I am going to record here is that during the period I made two tours—one to Kotah and the other to Bikaner. I shall place my experiences of these two tours in detail here.

Kotah

I, along with the other office staff (Director, Deputy Director, F.A. and the Supt.) left town on the 10.30 a.m. in the red van (bus) of the office for Kotah. Everybody had sufficient bedding, etc., with him. Our van was going at a very fast speed, on an average of 40 miles per hour, reaching to 60 at times. Wind was blowing very hard in our ears and none but the peon with us dared to close the curtains. We made a halt for lunch at a Dak Bungalow, where the A.R.O. received and served lunch to us. The whole of the staff of the dak bungalow was Mohammedan and hence I did not take part in the lunch. I went with the Supt. to his father-in-law's house. It was not very far off, but for saving time we hired a tonga (hire was paid by the superintendent both on going and return; he did not accept anything from me). Tongas there are very dirty and hopeless. They crawl very slowly. There is a straight market from the Clock Tower. There are all sorts of petty traders in this market. There is much Muslim population. Refugees are not to be seen there. I was offered tea and pedas by the Sister-in-law of Shri Bharadwaj. I did not know what to do; the peon had refused pedas. I did not refuse in the beginning but in the end I said that I did not require the same and finished my tea. Later on I was offered betel. I accepted but some juice came out and was dropped on the carpet. I felt very ashamed. She said that the betel-wallas put too much kattha this side. I did not respond.

Then we started from Tonk for Kotah at 2.30. We had asked the Deputy Director Kotah to receive and show us the historical things at Boondi. But as ill luck would have it we searched for him only at the cross-road and did not inquire about him at the dak bungalow, where he was waiting for us. He had arranged passes for showing us all the palaces etc. While going further in the way we saw about half a dozen Europeans with pistols, etc., standing on the way. They stopped our van; we did not know why; then we thought maybe they were expecting smugglers, etc. But it was later on found that they were actors and actresses of the Hollywood (America) who were to have shooting in Boondi, and arrangements were made for our visit to that, but we did not go as said before due to the reason above cited. Anyway one car started before we did and the other followed us.

We reached the Kotah Dak Bungalow at 8.0 in the evening. We unloaded our van and got the same arranged in our rooms. The Director and Deputy Director were allotted separate rooms, while myself, superintendent and the F.A. stayed in two combined rooms. The meals were non-vegetarian and I did not take part in it, but having taken my bread brought with me, went to bed.

Next day morning, I was invited to tea by the Deputy Director. I thought I should take it; there should be no harm in drinking water brought by the Sindhis, etc. But to my great regret with the tea they took eggs and bread with butter. I neither liked the bread with butter, which was of a peculiar type (yellow which is available in hotels everywhere) but took it. I did not like to see others touching my teapot with the hands of eggs but could not help.

Then followed the Conference. It was the first occasion of my taking down notes in a conference. I was successful in my attempt. I very well took down the speech in Hindi of the Director. But later on I found that it was very difficult to note correct figure in view of several changes in the text that they referred to. Hence there was a confusion with regard to figures. Further it has been pointed out to me that I need not write whatever they have spoken, but only a synopsis of the points raised and discussed by them.

As concerns our noon-lunch, I along with the Chief Loans Officer and one other, Mr. Sharma—all vegetarians—took it at one place. It consisted of chapattis, cabbage, tomatoes, curd, lentils, potatoes, etc. I ate quite all right but I did not like the smell of the lentils. There was then chutney with onions which also I ate.

Then again there was a conference.

In the evening we all went to the cinema, and enjoyed it on the box. One-two persons paid their share and I also worried as to will I have to pay an exorbitant charge. But the Superintendent himself did not pay and asked me also to look into the matter later on, with the result that we contributed only Rs. 5 towards our lunch, rent, and cinema, etc. It was taken as our share of the Dearness Allowance.

At night I did not feel hungry and so did not take anything. I had also gone to a certain distance on foot with the superintendent and he asked me to lend him 2 as. for betel, which he returned to me the next day in spite of my denial. I also took one betel but he did not accept anything for it and paid the full amount to me.

Next morning I got up early, took my glass and went out for latrine. First of all I had to cross from over the gate as it was closed, being only 4.30 and a cold night. Then I searched a water tap and went to latrine. My leg went in mud and spoiled my pant. I washed it then and there and went for a walk up to a very far point and returned before the day dawned and sat for writing my notes.

Then again followed the lunch and conference and then we went to a visit at the Motipura Co-operative Farm. We passed through much dust and all our clothing were full of dust; so also my camera as I took my camera with me. I took some poses, out of which only 1-2 are good ones, two were spoiled as the parties moved when I took shots. We ate plums, which were very thick and very nice in the bushes. We then returned to the Narishala, which was very nicely organised. Ladies manufactured good things. It was a beautiful place. Then there was a visit to the Technical Institute, which also was quite a good place. Then followed our lunch and then conference of Assistant Custodians, etc. In the evening we went to attend the programme of the College, arranged by C. B. L. Gupta. It was a hopeless programme consisting of music, mesmerism and jokings, etc.

Next day there was lunch and conference. I did not take part in the lunch. After that I did not take my meals also and started after making small purchases in 5 minutes' time when the motor was taking petrol and started for our home at 1.15 p.m. and reached our home at 8 p.m. when I took my meals and slept.

Bikaner

It was after the cold wind that I had to go to Bikaner to attend the Deputy Director's Conference. I was informed to go on the 13th February by the evening train, but later on when I was about to sit in the train, I received intimation that we will be going after two days. I returned the ticket and came back. After two days, i.e. on the 15th evening by 5.30 p.m. train we started for Bikaner, in the III class. Vans for direct up to Bikaner were all full and I had to change the line at Phulera. Later on from Phulera I sat in the servants' compartment of the Minister for Rehabilitation's saloon. So also

I repeated on my return journey. I thus reached Bikaner at morn at 8.30 after a good sleep during the night. We then went to Bungalow No. 28 and then I left for my lunch in the market, when others were taking it in the bungalow. I had informed them not to make arrangements for me. My watch was rather going wrong those days and when I found myself in the shop with poories before me it was quarter to 10, the time when meeting was to start. I hurried with whatever I had received in the first lot and ran in a tonga, which are very nice in Bikaner, beautiful and clean gharis. But I may mention that it was with great difficulty and at a great distance that I could find a shop (dhaba) where poories were being sold. There the sweetmeat-sellers don't sell poories. However, I reached at 10, but the meeting started at 11 a.m.

Then I attended the conference and after lunch of the other staff we went to attend the tea-party given by the Deputy Director in honour of the Minister. There was a good attending; there were poetries; there were beautiful ladies; there were good bengali sweets, pakodies, oranges and numkeen. But I had doubt from the very beginning if it might not contain eggs, etc., and hence before I could start my bengali sweets were taken away by others and I had to content myself with other things. After this we went in Rolls Royce car of the State Carriage to the temple of Laxminarainji, passing through the lanes of the city, which were not very wide, but rather narrow. The houses were high with underground rooms. The city looked red, it was made of only red stone. There were engravings at each door. The temple was situated on a raised level just like our Deviji's temple with the same kind of curves. The temple was a nice one. There were engravings in a beautiful manner. One road—a long road— from the public garden, was very wide. There were very nice and well furnished shops of all goods.

Then we went to attend the meeting which the Minister was to address. I did not stay there but roamed in the market and when the meeting ended I purchased poories for me and went to the bungalow, where I took my meals. At night I got sound sleep, although I slept just after half an hour after my meals and milk (supplied by the bungalow) but to my wonder when I got up I felt that I have had a very sound sleep. I felt a motion very badly and went to latrine. Then I felt a stomach-ache and did not take anything the whole day. We left very late from the bungalow and the train was just about to start. Our luggage was just thrown in 2-3 compartments and it was fortunate the train did not start till we could arrange our luggage at one place. The next day in the noon I was here at my house.

My experience of this trip has shown that it has been very nice to go to Bikaner and much better than at Kotah.

Just compare here my trip to that of Pushkarji in my childhood. Oh, what a big contrast.

Third thing about which I wish to make a mention here is that I have been teaching shorthand to one student. I started it to 3 students, but one never came except one day; the other having studied for a week left because he changed his mind; while the third is studying but at a *very slow* speed. All this is free and as my social service. One Mannulal offered me his tuition for Rs. 15 but I refused as he wanted me to go to his house; he did not like to come to my house, although he lives near me. I do not think it dignified to go to anyone's, particularly an acquaintance's house, for only Rs. 15. But the worst thing has been that I could not teach my wife in spite of her keen desire. She did not like me to lie down while teaching, but I could not keep sitting on account of my weak physique. It is not that I could not keep sitting, but could not do so idly, while she is reading.

I may also mention here that during these days I have had much interest for reading and writing. I have written an essay on how to improve eyesight without glasses, my own life, hints for expert typists, etc. I am taking sufficient pains to do all this. Further although I have not been successful in maintaining a perfect account of all my transactions yet, still I have evolved a very comprehensive system of keeping family expenditure.

Further to augment the income from the salary I have been engaging myself in typing jobs, from Prof. Vaid. I have purchased a typewriter and can thus do it at my leisure. Similarly recently I undertook to do some work of Prof. M. P. Gopal, but it turned out to be unprofitable although the rate of typing was double that offered by Prof. Vaid, in view of the fact that he called me in the morning and night and took a long time in preparing the manuscript itself, during which I had to sit with him. Furthermore, he required perfect accuracy and I had to waste more than 8 hours in mere corrections. Further, I had not yet received the payment. Not only this he says that he would not pay for typewriter ribbon purchased for his machine, repairs done on his typewriter and carbon papers (costing all Rs. 5). Let me see what he does pay.

There has been a bit changed in my pious ideas, though it is forced. I will have no objection to drink water at Butani's house, because I cannot afford to irritate him by not drinking water, although I have been to his house the whole day. Then supposing some person of high cadre invites me to tea, can I refuse him? Of course, no.

My relations with parents have luckily been not very bad during these days except on the matter of radio. But I have now completely stopped teasing them by various devices, because I now do not get so much time in contact with them so much. Thank God.

During the period I have arranged 1-2 tours to Jhotwara, Motidoongi, Naya Ghat, etc., which have been very much interesting. Once I with R.D.M. went to Naya Ghat and in our way there was a girl. We wanted to talk to her, but on account of R.D.M.'s brother could not and then she also went in tonga. Further we went to Jhotwara and intended to have a talk with about 4 girls and ladies but could not be successful due to one reason or the other. Our intention in doing this was to test the moral characters of the ladies in the villages, we have not immoral intentions whatsoever in this.

Other things continue the same. During this period I have developed an intimacy with my colleague Mr. Bhagwati, an old man of 40, who has put up more than 18 years of service. He is a highly experienced man with good moral character. I have learnt many things from him and have been working according to his guidance. It has only helped me, although I blindly follow his instructions. But he is too much talkative and at times I do feel that he is self-interested. But this view remains only for the short period and disappears in the long run. Our intimacy has been very much, so much that in spite of the best attempts of the Deputy Director it has not been affected at all. Everybody cites that you are very intimate. May God bless him.

Now this for the present. What about the future. Although I have not done much during the period, yet it is nothing if judged in the right perspective. Hence I should try to improve myself in the real sense. To achieve this goal I am making the following scheme—scheme of daily routine, scheme of principles, and above all the budget. May God help me.

This time I am cutting a sorry figure in recording the facts of my life during the month. I had high hopes at the end of the last month, but all those have turned out mere castles in the air. None of them have been satisfied. My programmes, principles, budget, and nothing else could be followed in the least as would be seen from the record in my diary for a few days (I did not write the diary on all the days).

1. There has always been a trouble about the radio. Nobody in the family is interested in it except myself and brother. Mother cannot see the consumption of electricity, wife's curtains of the ear are torn with it as with battle-drums, father seldom begins to rebuke except when he is sad and/or the child is weeping and all that sort of thing. I have decided more than a dozen times both to hear it in spite of the protests of all and also to attempt violence on self and stop hearing it, although it is I who have bought it at a very low price. It actually belonged to Ram Narain Barwala. He pledged it. I got it from there after paying the money, on behalf of my father. Anyway what I decide now, with the concurrence of the mother is as under:

NOTHING

2. I just have to weep about my wife, there is no interest in such a life. I think it is only on account of my parent's presence that I do not feel it. I have never been minding her hopeless nature and habits and dullness and laziness. I have never seen a more hopeless lady than her. But still I do not give her an opportunity to feel anything of this attitude of mine towards her; I do not ask her to do anything for me. There is no use doing this when she would not comply with your orders. She is a disobedient, proudy, and careless lady. She has even passed satires 1-2 times which I understand meant that I love other ladies also, although it is not a deep-rooted one in her heart. She is only doubtful—not even confident of it. I have many a times *shampood* her feet, but she has never even fanned or pressed my hands, even at my request. The worst thing that hurts me most at various occasions is that in spite of the fact that she knows that I am very spend-thrift (luxurious) in my expenditure these days, and that I have paid her Rs. 240 during the year, she would daily pass satires that I am a miser. Here my heart breaks and if I would have dared I would have broken her head on more than one occasion. It is my heart's greatest desire that God forgive her for all this and give me the courage, as given so far, to bear all this patiently till the life of one of us comes to an end—I have been feeling since so many

years that she will die at an early age. Astrologers say at the age of 30. Anyway I am ready to pass the whole of my short life with her and request God with folded hands to excuse me for thinking end about a creature of the same Almighty—May God excuse me and give her long life and all Prosperity.

Contrary to the above, there is one companion—a true companion to a certain extent—say 60 per cent.—but who can be made 100 per cent. with my own endeavours—Mr. R.D.M. It is he with whose help I am getting whatever small amount of interest in life there is. I will here mention an occasion which has been repeated a couple of times, which has given me so much enjoyment as I have never felt, except with 1-2 sorry accompaniments, which is the rule of the universe and hence which I do not mind.

On 15th April I was transferred to the office of the I.G. Jails. The fact that I was with a highly-paid officer and a man with connections who took me boldly with special permission of *the Chief Adviser to the Govt. of Rajasthan* made me very proud—and that I was the highest paid in the ministerial staff. I used to tell everybody about it—of course on request—but proudly.

Anyway it has had a good effect. I have learnt Hindi typing very easily in only 3 hours' time—a wonder of my talents. Here I have been attached only to the I.G. while in my old job I was a wife to everybody. Here, where there is little work and I enjoy a long leisure—of course it is another thing whether or not I can make the best use of this leisure.

I have also started taking shorthand dictations and have begun coaching one more student, who has begun out of 5 who proposed.

I have also prepared a list of words mis-spelt by me and wish to remember them by heart.

I am not yet reading the newspapers regularly.

Monthly Report for the Month of May, 1950

The salient features of the month under review are as under. A perusal of the same shall reveal that I have made no progress in any direction except the greatest success in gaining victory over my habit of " PICK AND EAT ", the worst devil that came in my life a long time ago. This was due to my association with Dr. Surendra Prasad Garg, a doctor practising natural way of cure and an Assistant Revenue Secretary to the Government of Rajasthan. It was only to increase my stock of knowledge on natural cure that I went to him without any introduction from any source, and he was kind enough to extend his hand of co-operation to me. My contact with him made such a lasting impression on me that I have almost completely left this nasty habit of mine, which will be very helpful to me.

Further Dr. Garg has agreed to lend me books for reading and has actually done so. One book on " Practical Nature Cure " has proved of immense value to me; I have taken down exhaustive notes from this book and will try to incorporate them in the form of a book very early.

I have also written to the " AROGYA " to publish this book of mine along with that on " eye sight " and they have informed to send the same to them for their kind consideration. I will be doing so within a fortnight or a month at the latest as I do not want to spoil the beauty of the book by being hasty, as I have been hitherto.

The next salient feature of the period has been the arranging of competition with my friend, Mr. R.D.M. on three points—cards, sexual intercourse, and going to the garden. Now to explain the first I may mention that I keep a fixed level of Rs. 1 over which I do not go in any month and thus this does not become gambling; secondly, it is used as a source of greater enjoyment; thirdly, the stakes which are very low go not to the pocket of any one of us, but to a common fund, which is utilised for common purpose. Thus it is not gambling but a very nice kind of entertainment.

Then about sexual intercourse—we betted that we will not be indulging in it more than once during the month. If we did we will pay Rs. ½ per intercourse. On the other hand if we did not even avail of the one at our disposal, we will be entitled to draw 9 as. from the fund. I have utilised my exception, while Mr. M. has paid a fine of Rs. ½. This does not mean that he is a loser. Not so. He had gained previously when we had arranged the same sort of competition—very much—I had lost as wife was suffering from itch and it being winter I had to do many times, thus paying Rs. 6-7. This time it is summer and I do not get an opportunity to contact wife. The one I utilised on a day when the mother was at my uncle's. I have also reduced the number of funs, etc., which directly lead to craving for sexual contact. Thus we are a gainer in this also.

Thirdly, about the garden, we are regularly going as arranged. I absented myself on four occasions while R.D.M. on only two and thus I had to pay a fine of 8 as. to the fund while R.D.M. only 4 as. But we misused it. We go to the garden and sit and return instead of doing exercise and race as was agreed to. Hence it has turned out to be purely bad.

June 1950

Dr. Garg's promised help was only a show. After reading the first book when I returned it he said he could not lend it because he came to know that I can't purchase books, which he had thought I will do. Hence no more help is expected of him.

Further one day I had just gone to him for seeing him with R.D.M. when he was compelled rather to offer us a mango and a cup of milk, because R.D.M. was his relation, but he felt it very much and passed sarcastic remarks at the very time about that.

As planned during the last month, I have started preparing my book, "Modern Encyclopedia". I am getting extreme success in it—is a matter of great pleasure. I have written, or rather compiled, much.

This month I had intimate talks with Acharya Dabhai, with whom I had only superficial contact. He wanted my help with rooting out sexual corruption and I promised him active help and even tried, but he failed to help me, which was very necessary at the early stage, and also did not tell me his means and hence I did not like to be a tool in his hands without knowing everything. Thanks to God.

I am sorry I followed no progress, etc. to develop my health. I intend to do so from the mid-August definitely.

I was given an idea to start a Typing-Shorthand Institute by Mr. Rathor and I am exerting my best to implement the policy.

August

All this month there has been an inner idea latent in my mind that I shall be a great man—when I read about the lives of great men—thinkers, poets, scientists and what not, I found myself in the same position as they were. All of them were very poor—much more, a 100 times more poor and miserable than me—with poor health and failing eyesight as myself—and yet all these things did not stand in their way of becoming great. Why shall they in my case? I have also the same degree of interest in my work and work very hard to achieve my goal.

You will wonder besides doing the institute work and office work and other engagements as usual, I read one complete book in three days and typed out about 28 double space foolscap sheets—summary of that book. All this means much trouble—but I don't mind.

Further my attention is drawn to the prophecy made by one Mr. Kailash Chand Soyani that some day the initials M.P. will form a suffix to my name—and a second of Mr. Kewal Krish Parti, as a result of my lines of fortune—that I will have a conveyance and will travel foreign countries. I have been striving hard to secure this goal of mine.

As regards my field of action, I am confident it will not be political, as I have not interest in it, but it must be either social or literary. For the latter I have already started working.

For the former, it will not be out of place for me to mention that from the very early years of my life, viz. when we were in college—1st year, we wanted to remove the begging profession, which is a bad thing. We wanted to start some charitable workhouses, etc. for really infirm, but this work being very huge in its dimensions and money being needed in it, we had to leave it, except that we started a charity fund, which will be accelerated till it accumulates in sufficient quantity to help them and other such problems.

Now further, we had a scheme for teaching illiterates in a suburb of the city. But as there is already a scheme under implementation, we left it without anything to fall back upon until recently, when at the initiative of Mr. R.D.M. who has been an associate of mine in this field also and without whose help I would have been able to accomplish nothing, we again wanted to spread learning, knowledge and culture in the villages and the village uplift, through weekly lectures to students of various suburbs and selected Amal Kanta to be our first aim. Through the grace of God we could make beautiful arrangements and now it depends wholly on us as to what we do and how we convince the people. Let the Almighty God help us in that also.

Now about the next important thing to which I devoted my interest during the month. As stated last month, I have started one institute with three persons—myself, Rathi and Brij Mohan as partners. We all have been working very hard to run it and success would have been ours, but for the fact that other partners of mine are taking little interest in organising it in a proper way and Mr. Rathi is absolutely new to the line and cannot convince the people. Nor can he bring money or customers, nor can he give the machine he promised. Thus it is a bitter thing for me to work and get nothing as it is divided in three shares. So we will have to oust him out. Let's see what happens.

As concerns myself, I have come to the clear conclusion that it is impossible for me to work with anybody else, because only exceptional instances are found where people have the same idea of working and cleanliness, order, etc., as I have. They do not care at all about all these petty things, to which I pay the greatest attention. This is the key of my success. I do not like one sitting idle when something can be done. Hence I promise not to take anybody in partnership on any terms in future.

Now about the method of business, I have found that the first thing for a salesman is that he should be confident about what he is doing. Secondly, he should have a complete knowledge of his line. This only will enable him with a little diplomacy to get complete success. Now as I possess mastery over the line, have complete confidence in it, I have been successful in canvassing people about the suitability of our schemes.

Further I have come to certain scientific conclusions, etc., as for example the study of customers, etc., which is just due to experience—only a fortnight running of the institute.

Let's look forward to look for a help.

September 1950

The grass was green, the sand was brown, the sky was blue, people were going from their places of work to their homes and hearths, to meet their husbands, wives, children, sick parents, and all others, to cook their meals, to enjoy dainty dishes, to chat, and for all sorts of other things.

Just on the opposite of all this, we were roaming out in the jungle, passing roads, sand, and lawn and gardens, and enjoying ourselves with all sorts of fun. Now we are chasing some lady, not a beautiful lady, not at all, but a lady—a young lady, a lady with a good-looking nature, a lady with all the qualities of a village maid. We had not bad intention in our minds, but only entertainment, only recreation, and recreation only —to have two minutes of talking, chatting and joking. But still we were careful enough to see that it did not offend the opposite party, and actually it did not. However, there were some who felt some resentment, some felt very much enjoyed and some actually began to talk. Now come along, I will tell you the tale in detail.

1. We met one milk-maid going to sell her milk. She was an old lady, not less than 40. We wanted milk and she gladly offered it, and when we raised the question of sugar, she asked us to go to her house where we could get it and the milk also. We agreed but did not go to her house. Later on we again met her in the way and she led us to her house and we drank pure cow milk. It was served with beautiful love and sympathy or guest-service. We appreciate that. She had no hesitation however, to accept the payment of its price, which she had asked for also indirectly. I may mention that we had every intention of paying the price. We never like to have something without payment.

2. Then we met one lady sitting on the road, while her servant or companion was gone to pass urine nearby. We asked her why she was sitting to which she replied how are you sitting (we riding bicycle) and also said she was sitting quite alright. Later on we took a turn on the road and followed them for a few yards, when they had to go a different route in the sand. We were wonder struck to see her manly motions of walking then. Her age was about 17.

3. We went to one farm and were entertained to see the fields of pepper and maize. Nothing was ready on the farm and we were not offered anything. However, we were told that maize might be ready in other fields but they would not give as it is dear these days. Actually we went to another field and he also said that maize was not ready yet. God knows whether he was correct or wrong. I think he was correct. While returning he offered us by force two-three twigs of small podina as a present and told us that so many college students visit their farm.

4. Then we met one girl of about 13 taking a bundle of sticks on her head to sell in the town. We asked her what shall she charge for it and on her quoting a price, we told her that we would give more than that but that she will have to go to our house, she stopped for a minute or two, gazed at us and looking behind to the back said that her DADA is coming behind and he might settle with you. Hearing this I took my way, really thinking that her dada might be coming and we might have to suffer the consequences. Later on I thought she might have understood our motives and really waited to see if she could go with us. But one day I felt that fearing us she might have

pretended that her dada is coming so that we may not play mischief with her. I can't say which of my beliefs is correct.

5. There were some similar other instances; finally one lady was going to her house in the evening and had a small boy behind her. He was walking briskly and disobeying her. We began talks with her by talking to the child as to why he was naughty and what was his name and why he feared us and all sorts of things and then directly with the lady, who feared us, but was brave enough to step further by answering aptly our questions till she reached her door. On being asked whether she will turn us out blank or will entertain us, she invited us to lunch at her house, which she said she would prepare now and lastly we bade her good bye.

After we bid her good bye we gossiped how beautiful our tour had been and repeated the words: " Would you turn us out blank? " We thought nobody can object, as there was nothing bad in it and she herself might testify to it. In this connection we struck one thought that why not we should attract the children of the village towards us by offering them certain toys or sweets and then I suggested that we might hold weekly meetings of children. The idea was liked by us and the very next Sunday we reached Amalkanta with one illustrated magazine with us and just began to talk to one villager of that place and asked him to help us. He said: What can I do? but in the meanwhile he called one Matric student and he promised us a lot and our scheme began to work.

As settled with the matric student we went the next Sunday at the appointed hour and although quite unprepared, fared very well.

Henceforth the story is in the form of minutes of the organisation.

September, 1950

The month under review was marked out for an all-round busy life—up to the last minute and no rest. Consequently I underwent a radical fall in health although the weight remained constant at 90 lbs. I was very busy in my institution. I am glad to say that I very tactfully was successful in removing all the other partners in the real sense of the term and now I do not worry from that side. I have also been successful in arranging my programmes in such a way that I will have to devote only 2 hours for business daily. But still my mind is constantly labouring under strain and to avoid this I should, in future, not talk too much and do daily prayers and concentration, not worry about anything and playing badminton in the morning. I hope God will give me success. About the progress of my firm, I will write during the next month.

As concerns our social work we have been regularly inside Amalkanta working for the uplift of the people. I am very glad to testify of our grand success, which we have been achieving to now, and last but not least that after a practice of 3-4 lectures, I could very nicely speak at the meeting of about a score village elders and about two scores children combined. Of course I had rehearsed the whole speech beforehand in front of R.D.M. It was also pleasureful indeed that the speech was extempore.

October

The following were the important events of my life during the month under review.

1. I should strike out a note of thanks of the Almighty God that although our neighbouring shop of a sweetmeat-seller fell prey to a thief who took away sugar and cream only, our shop was not even touched although no-one was sleeping to guard it that day.

2. Further I am sorry to record that the students of Amalkanta played a trick on us. As long as we went on helping them economically they continued to do as we wished, while in the background they mis-appropriated the common fund for their private use. Thus was given a complete set-back to our social service programme in the village.

3. It has been a 100 times tested experience of mine that when my mother says to me " Do not do this " and still I do it, I lose badly in 100 per cent. cases. There can't be any exception to it. Hence don't take her permission at all and if you consult her act according to her advice. This time was the case of shop—and I have actually not earned anything although I put my most for it. Secondly was my tour to Delhi for All-India Typing Competition at which also I finally did not appear. To my great pleasure and amazement I have to record that we have been teaching children to salute their parents. One day I thought how dare I advise them and force them, when I myself cannot. As regards my case, I never used to do so even on festive occasions like Deepavali, etc. when everyone does so. Now I have started to practise myself and now their blessings are with me.

21st Birthday Message

WHERE do I stand? To give an accurate idea of my correct position—I am very sorry to say that last year I had made a resolve to build my health and had actually gained 7-8 lbs. in winter, but again in the hurry and bustle of summer, lost 5 of these hard-earned pounds. Again I have resolved to leave no labours to reach this goal. I can sacrifice anything—service, business or money—only if God help me, which I am sure he will. The active steps which I propose to take now to achieve this goal are:

1. Clearing of bowel troubles.
2. Rubbing of oil and exercise regularly.
3. Eye exercise.
4. Avoid things which cause worries, etc.

As regards soul or character, I have done nothing during the period of a year to put a blot on my glaring character, which I have been able to maintain so far. Still now I make the following two resolves:

1. Not to use even a single sheet of the office paper without permission/giving equal remuneration.
2. Try to avoid speaking small lies, which might creep in sometimes.
3. Salute parents and pray God daily to help me keep a good moral life.
4. Obey parents, as far as practicable.

Lastly, as regards wealth, I have been extravagant—to a certain degree as ever—rather it was folly of judgment. In future I will be careful in spending every pie. For this I resolve that:

1. Before incurring any expenditure I will try that it is the cheapest.
2. I will consult parents and/or wife if I should purchase it or not.
3. I will not exceed my budget, which provides for the following:

Board and lodging	Rs. 80
Clothing	10
Savings	15
Miscellaneous	10
	115

November, 1950

This month has been completely new and extraordinary in my life. True as it is that happiness and sorrow go hand to hand or that every cloud has a silver lining over it—during the three first quarters of the month under review, I felt so much depressed that I found myself to be the most miserable man in the world.

I was immensely troubled by the idea that I am a man in the jail. I have no freedom of movement. There is no help, co-operation, or an encouraging hand for any of my actions—however small they may be. There is no one, except one—who is R.D.M.—whom I can call mine. There is not personal attachment with anybody. I cannot expect anything from my wife—she is so sickly—I cannot even see anybody who can rub oil in my back, or stitch buttons to my pant, or just relieve monotony by loving talks.

Truly, it is my duty to create an atmosphere which I like. But conditions are such that I cannot—why say cannot, but at least it is very difficult. Wife wants to learn alphabet—but because there is no separate room I cannot coach her. She may like to go with me to the garden or cinema or exhibition, but the fear of family members, which is quite genuine, closes her mouth. All her intentions have been killed—she has never asked me for anything. It proves sufficiently that it is my family circumstances which have killed all her enthusiasm.

I have no room where I can do what I like—sleep alone, say my prayers, do study, sing, or invite friends to a party. One will even wonder, if he knows that I CANNOT invite anybody to lunch or tea at my house—because who is there to prepare the tea? I have gone so far that once when a friend of mine (D. S. Gupta) came from Ajmer at lunch time and I was asked several times by my mother to take my meals, I could not even ask him to dine with me. Nor did they ask him except only formally when he was going in the staircase.

Anyway—the situation is such that even if I think of it now, my hair stands on end and I think how much God is helpful to me that in spite of such an atmosphere I have been able to mould my life as I wish remaining COMPLETELY free from family influences. None of their influences have affected my life in the least. Had I followed their footpaths there is no doubt that I would have been a man whom society will treat worse than a dog.

Report from last Report's Time up to 31.5.1951

There is nothing particular to mention during this period except that as I had wound up my institutions and students coming to learn shorthand, etc., had also stopped, I was completely free and enjoyed very much.

But in May I took two salaried employments in the evening. There I have to devote 2-2½ hours and get Rs. 45. I think that I had done a mistake in accepting these appointments as they interfere in my programme of evening and hence wish to discontinue them if an occasion arises and not to take any such employment in future. Moreover, I have started taking regular exercise and walking and my health is on an improvement. My weight at present is 92 lbs.

I have written some 4-5 stories during this period. I mean that I have made plots and not written the stories—they depict a view of my life, but seem to be good.

My relations with wife have also been sweet during the period although no sexual satisfaction to any of the parties owing to early ejaculation due to lack of accommodation for doing sexual acts.

I have been on needle's end—i.e., worried over the fact that there is no separate accommodation for us where I could manage my wife.

May to July, 1951

The particular feature of the period under review is that my sexual outlook has changed a great deal. So far I had felt that my sexual disease and early ejaculation are uncurable but after reading a few books on the subject I have been assured that they are neither uncurable nor serious and that there is a need of only change in the psychological outlook. Actually, one day when I had a picture book of various coital positions we enjoyed sexual intercourse to the maximum—unparalleled in our whole life. But after that time again there has been early ejaculation either because there was no full erection due to lack of love-play or because of a greater excitement, etc. It is really very difficult to have an occasion when both have full desire and it was that day I just mentioned.

Next thing is that I am tired of the babies and have decided not to have any more issues—if God permit. To attain this aim I have limited my intercourse to 20 days after menstruation. Let us see the result.

Again these books had to some extent changed my ideas of sexual morality. Firstly, I felt that to practise intercourse with others who love you is not bad and actually one girl invited me to that but could not get an opportunity. Later on, a complete change took place when I studied about the life of Rama. But again that girl appeared in my dreams one day and I saw her again and now I am in a quandary and have not been able to make up my mind on what way should I follow—of morality or immorality. The two things which encourage me to the wrong path are—(1) Intercourse with young maids to help good health; and (2) I am destined to die of worries which must be reduced through joy and recreation. Anyway I request God to guide me on correct lines.

I have read a book of Palmistry and feel that I will die of mind-failure or suicide, etc., if I continue the same mental work that I have been pursuing for the last so many months. Thank God, I have been informed in time and shall be more and more cautious and leave all my present studies. I have finally decided to build a library of good books, instead of compiling good books.

One thing which has been characteristic of my life is SELF-RESPECT. Self-respect is of such an extreme nature that I never thank anybody or say sorry, or ask anybody any favour, or accept an obligation, etc.

Monthly Report for the Month of August 1951 *up to September* 15

The month under review is characterised by some thing higher in my ideals. I have during this month felt that nothing howsoever troubling or annoying or insulting or otherwise can upset my mental balance. I take everything lightly and would not be swayed away by passion. There had been occasions when a peon spoke insulting words, but I passed with a laugh. My wife caused some injury to my heart by telling something about my monetary and financial policy, but I simply heard what she told and did not reply to her. My anger, though it came out, was only momentary and after a minute, it was all gone. I am very much proud of all this.

2. During this month I had an experience of *bhang*. I had gone to a feast and as soon as I reached there I was offered *thandai*. I did not know if it contained *bhang* and took as much as I could. It showed its effect after about an hour when I was sitting under an arch. My head began to be drawn towards the wall and I felt that I am under the influence of

drink. Then I sat on a wall over the bazaar and after some time felt that I was unconscious of all other things and that I might fall. So I went and by this time meals were being served, and I joined, but felt the serving time too much. Then I was feeling that I am too much unconscious of things and was reminding my friend to look after me if I was going wrong, but he was under the same influence and when he came, he was laughed at too much, but I was not as none knew me. I was a stranger to the company. However, came on foot home and my intoxication was not gone till I had to do some typing work the day after in the morning.

3. By now I was labouring under the notion that it is a very bad disease that I go for stools after eating anything, but my study of a few books written by English authors has testified that it is a good habit and in all cases a necessary one and worth cultivating in children. So I do not feel worried about it now. Thank God this disease (worry) will be gone in my 22nd year, as shown in my horoscope, although the habit exists still now.

4. During the month I studied two books on Palmistry written by the well-known Cheiro, and have come to the conclusions that I should do less mental work.

5. During the month I was brave enough to make two new contacts—one was with Mr. Gordhan Das Surana, a local Seth, whom I contacted when he was going in the garden and started the talk by greeting him Namaste. Rest he did.

Second contact was with a girl serving in the P.S.C. I offered her a book " Good Eye for Life " free of charge when she was on her way to home. I had determined to do so and in spite of the fact that one of my neighbours was accompanying me on cycle when I saw her, I carried out my plan. I asked leave of him under the excuse of going to a bookseller and thus was able to talk to the girl. She accepted the offer with a vote of thanks.

6. I note that my English-speaking has been very fluent when I talked to I.G. Sahib on the phone on two occasions. Moreover, when I taught shorthand to the daughter-in-law of the I.G. as well as to other students I was sufficiently fluent, as I had the command of my subject.

7. I feel that my in-laws do not recognise me at a distance unless I look peepingly at them or they happen to look fixedly. This is due to my dress, which is foreign to them.

8. I am much proud of the respect, which is meted out to me by the I.G. Sahib, and his P.A., the D.I.G., and other

clerks of the office. Thanks to God my relations are very very nice with all of them and everyone respects me to the maximum degree. I had never been meted out such a respect. I am never reprimanded over anything. Rather most courteous language is spoken to me. I am taken full care of when I am ill, and all sorts of facilities are always given to me when so required by me.

9. Now I feel the harmonious relations that prevail between me and wife. We had never had any quarrels. Wife might feel certain things about me, but I never.

10. But unfortunately, all these two months, I, as well as my dear friend, Rameshwar Das, have been ill most of the time. I had been overtaken previous month by para-typhoid, and am now suffering from eczema or some such trouble in the feet.

End of September, 1951

All this month my movements were restricted as I had eczema in both my feet and could not walk without the help of cycle. It has been very unfortunate, but no help. One has to endure all that we are entailed upon.

Further, the third week of the month has been very tragic as will be evident from the following facts:

One day I brought 70 sheets of rice paper from the office as I had no rice paper. I had already purchased typewriting paper from the market. It gave me a lot of pain while coming from the office to know that (1) other might know of it; (2) I could not stay although a friend of mine requested me to stay; and (3) that papers were visible to some one when I was riding the cycle. This put me under great mental torture and I could not justify my action of stealing. I decided to return the papers to the office, but later on did not do so.

One day I took away a Rs. 10 note from the cash of my father without telling him as is done usually. He thought it was lost and much search was made. I should not take away cash without permission.

One day my mind was much excited over the offer of a free watch by the Swiss Watch Co., Bombay No. 4. I thought I would sell a large number of coupons and get a decent watch for wife, but as yet my wishes have not matured. It is too difficult to sell them, although that night I could not sleep while thinking of the pleasure which was expected.

In short, to give a short résumé of the history during this period, I may frankly say that I have not been in my best health—it does not mean that I have actually felt weak or lost some weight, but that I felt that I did not increase my health. The main reason has been that I was too busy—firstly with my institution and nextly with domestic affairs like the keeping of children, and playing of cards with father, etc. But now having wound up the shop and having no other part-time job, etc. I have realised that I can arrange my domestic affairs in such a way that they cannot be a hindrance to me. It is on me to do so.

One thing, which I can say very well, that I have been able to acquire during this period, through the help of psychological handbooks is that I have banished WORRY from my head. Now I am perfectly worry-less.

Second thing that I have done during this period is that so far I had been quite unconcerned with my children. But having read some books on child psychology I began to apply them—but I could not because nobody in the family helped me in my executions, but still I now feel concerned about them and try to mend them as much as possible. I have been very successful in gaining their love which was nil before.

Wife is still a problem to me—she could not be attracted to do what I wish. In fact it is not possible so long as my parents live with us. When they are off, I am 100 per cent. confident I can make her do what I like, but in the meantime, I will try to set the things right—but it is a bit difficult job—anyway, I shall try.

As regards parents, now they do not shower that much love on me—Thanks God. But still I am not completely free to do what I like—to go where I like—to get things done in my own way. I doubt the accuracy of the statement—please excuse.

* * * * *

In the intervals of completing three psychological tests, Puranmal further elaborated some of the personal details of his autobiography. A slight, alert-looking young man, he was restless and anxious during our first meetings, so that it was only gradually that I was able to put him sufficiently at his ease to be able to record his words. He spoke softly, responding very eagerly to a friendly approach; but he was evidently unaccustomed to the society of Europeans, and rather afraid of doing or saying the wrong thing.

In his speech, as in his writing, he showed a truly Boswellian candour in the way in which he would blurt out the most intimate self-revelations, only to repudiate them later, as if shocked at his own temerity.

The following notes were made during my subsequent conversations with him:

"My brother is 40 years old, not 35 as I told you. I was born after he was married. I myself was married at 13 or 14."

G.M.C. "He's like a father to you?"

P.M. "Of course. But he is not so interfering, like my father is. We love each other all right: he gives me advice when I ask, but doesn't interfere with me. That is the best relationship. Father used to accompany me all the time, he was very interfering. Only since I joined service did I go out to Bikaner and Kotah. Brother lives in same house, but separately. His wife is very peculiar, cannot get on with my mother. I don't talk to her at all because I think her way of talking is not decent. When one doesn't love or like, there is no pleasure in talking.

"They have one daughter, two years younger than me. She is like her mother, not interested in talking to others—when I was a small boy I'd tease them—they wouldn't come to our rooms, so I'd say they could not come, and then they would be annoyed.

"My sister's son was my only companion: he lived with us. She is about 37, and her husband was often away. He is one and a half years younger. We would play and fight as children. If I got anything I would share it with him—only, he did not like to study and I studied. I was made to enjoy study. I started reading at home, and covered the first and the third forms in one year, at home. In my eighth year I went into fourth form. Until I was in ninth form I didn't really enjoy study: after that I did, and my exams got better. In Matric. I secured 2nd division, in Inter. 1st division, in B.A. 2nd division."

G.M.C. "Brother and brother's wife?"

P.M. "He did not like arguments of his wife, or of his mother. His wife would ask him not to speak to us, or work for us, but he would not do that. She was very hostile: she didn't like that my sister should live with us."

G.M.C. "Sister?"

P.M. "I regarded her as mother, she was good to me. She would help in the household duties."

G.M.C. "Mother?"

P.M. "She was sharing views of father. She is orthodox, she criticises what I do. She would not like me to come to see you. She would not understand—nor radio, nor books.

"The thing is, I tell her everything—I tell everybody everything."

G.M.C. "She is religious?"

P.M. "No, not religious, but she is particular. For example, I go to latrine several times in the day and she would like me to have complete bath every time. It is not possible. Then she would not let me touch food or take water with my hands.

"We should take latrines in early morning and at 4 a.m. before taking food. Not everyone does it, but old especially do this. She will just shut herself in the room and pour a lota of water over her head and then it is all right—I have never seen her taking more than a small lota. In private, ladies remove sari and ghagra to bathe, inside the room."

G.M.C. "Mother's advice——?"

P.M. "Mostly I have acted against her advice, and I have found that it has been to my disadvantage. Even she said 'Don't join the Law College'—I joined it, but then I have to leave it. I have decided that I shall never ask her advice before I do something that I want to do—or else she will say 'No', and then it remains in my mind that she said 'No'. It was always my father who encouraged me to go on with my studies."

G.M.C. "He does so still?"

P.M. "Now he is neutral."

G.M.C. "Is your family engaged in business?"

P.M. "None of our family members do business, only speculation—they all do *fatkya* and *nilam*—it is a form of gambling, which is illegal, prohibited by law. It is all dependent on fluctuations in United States of America. Once when I was young I made predictions for a whole month— I added the numbers and totalled all the figures, down to one figure—I was right every time for a month. But if anyone were to gamble on it, he would lose. Only if he looks on to see, then he would find my figures were correct. Once I did gamble, and lost two annas."

G.M.C. "Why does this happen so?"

P.M. "I think a child's judgment is generally correct, because he is quite innocent."

G.M.C. "Can you tell me a little more about your childhood?"

P.M. "I don't remember anything of when I was a child, not until I was at school. My boy cousin was fond of flying kites and I would only watch: he used to play ball and tip-cat, but I would never play with boys because I did not like to play with low persons."

G.M.C. "Who taught you this?"

P.M. "No one, it was by myself. I did not like to speak with strange people. Still, I want to speak, but I am very shy. My friend Rameshwar Das is not shy at all.

"He is the only companion: I treat him as my only brother, quite inseparable. Whenever I have leisure I go to him. He is three years older, but looks my age. After failing Inter., he gave up studies. He went into business. At first he just did business in the street, but now he has secured a shop in the bazaar and now he is doing well.

"My boy cousin married three years back, and no longer lives with us: but I do not like his company. I tried to teach him, but he said: 'I am hungry, how can I read?'"

G.M.C. "What does he do for a living?"

P.M. "Previously he was doing *nilam:* now I think he sells ornaments. His father is still drinking and gambling—he spends whatever he earns. My sister lives on the lowest standard, by hiring out a room. They don't get on well."

G.M.C. "Have you continued to teach your wife?"

P.M. "If she makes mistakes, I take it as my responsibility to amend her actions, and if I can't I must put up with it."

G.M.C. "Does Rameshwar Das also share your interest in study?"

P.M. "Of course, he has very good relations; because he is quite satisfied with life as it is. But me, if I cannot do something to help society, then I think it is all waste. I am very much annoyed to see people speaking lies for small things, people just caring about making money—people rotting in poverty, if their condition can be improved."

G.M.C. "You have made some efforts, I understand..."

P.M. "I tried to start a debating society in order to improve our speaking powers, but others did not come. Then the beggar problem—we talked to one or two beggars, but they did not want to work. If we did not give them money, they would not want to listen to us.

"For a time some of us went to village and taught boys: 'Don't tell lies', and 'You should keep clean'; and to do exercises, and have good morals. We had five or six meetings with students and with elderly people also: we gave them some little monetary help also but the boys took all the money and spent it at the fair. We said: ' If you repent over it, that's all right '—but they didn't repent, they said: ' We don't want anything from you '; so we did not return there.

"I tried teaching, but my conclusion is that people who don't pay anything, they are not careful—it is just a waste of our time."

G.M.C. "You devote attention to exercise, too?"

P.M. "I have read in books only. I did some parallel bars exercise in college and that also irregularly. I found that when I walked to the Garden every day, the exercise improved my appetite and my health improved—but my Mother was not hopeful of any results, so she was not encouraging me, so that had a bad effect on the mind. The fact is, I don't get good sleep, only for an hour or two. I go to sleep at once at nine, for two or three hours. After twelve or one, I do not sleep well—I keep thinking over what I have done or should do. Even if I go to sleep at seven, I get good sleep, but in the day I can't sleep."

G.M.C. "I noticed that you felt your tiredness might be due to sexual excess?"

P.M. "It was the mental trouble which caused the physical trouble, the tired and weak feeling: because I had set myself a goal."

G.M.C. "You set yourself a rather severe goal, didn't you?"

P.M. "Of course that was severe: It could be done if the wife will not excite me. But if she becomes excited, I feel that I may be injuring her feelings. If she is denied, she may be suffering from hysteria and so on.

"I have never read Shastars, or had any religious teaching: father is not interested. Of course, he worships one deity and used to go to him daily—to the temple of Govindji. People worship all others also, but they think that their *kul dev* will especially watch over them, and be helpful in their lives. I used to believe in God very much, and I believe He did help me: now I try to believe in Him, though I don't believe now in separate deities—I believe that myself, and everything in nature is a god. Once I was going to garden: I was distressed because for some days my mother and self and wife, we were all sleeping in one room, and how can one enjoy the private talk and live with a wife like that? I tried to find out some solution, and that morning I was struck with this idea, that everything, all the flowers, all are God, and so I had the feeling that I was having a *darshan* of God before my eyes, and I felt very happy. That day I felt as if the whole philosophy of the world is clear before my eyes and I can solve any problem: if one doesn't worry, the problem is solved. That was on *Jenam-asthmi*. The very next day my mother took her cot and went outside. We always sleep on the floor, because there is not much space —in the hot weather we sleep on the roof."

G.M.C. " You are distressed by the lack of privacy ? "

P.M. " Yes sir, very much. This is the only trouble that I have at present; without it I cannot carry on. I should like to take her out to walks, but I cannot do that. There was talk that my office should be transferred to Alwar, and I am hoping that will be the case: if I can have one year living with my wife, I can get to know her and teach her things."

G.M.C. " Have you ever thought of living apart from your parents ? "

P.M. " No, because I think my parents' feelings would be very much injured.

" When father is there—and for past two years he has heart trouble and is always at home, and mother is also at home—then I cannot easily talk with my wife. I don't mind, but she and my parents will not like, they will condemn."

G.M.C. " What was your father like when you were a child ? "

P.M. " He was bad-tempered in the early days. Mother would say: ' Why are you troubling this child ? He will learn later on.' Later, father was angry if I asked leave to go out to a fair or somewhere with my friends: he always feared I would get hurt, fall in a lake or a well, or get in a motor accident. He wanted always to accompany me: and then I did not enjoy."

G.M.C. " What was mother's temper like ? "

P.M. " She gets angry only on those small matters: ' You have touched these things ', or ' You have been there, and there—you are doing useless things.' If I go to the cinema she says: ' You are going daily to the cinema ', though I only go once in two or three months. She has been, but she and the other women, they can't understand the Hindi at the cinema or even the radio. . . ."

PURANMAL MEHTA

Formal Psychological Tests

Forty-five out of sixty problems of the Progressive Matrices test were answered correctly in 39 minutes. This was the highest score recorded by any of the subjects tested.

In the Word-Association Test, Puranmal Mehta gave delayed responses to "Vagina", "Anger", "Girl", "Faeces", "Penis", and "In-laws". To three of these words (Vagina, Anger and Penis) he was unable to produce any response, saying: "Nothing comes to my mind", or "Can't decide". In response to Girl he gave "Beauty", to Faeces, "Cleanliness", and to In-laws, "Quarrels". The failures of response can be attributed to his conscious preoccupation with the endeavour to suppress his sexual and aggressive impulses. The relevance of the other sources of delay can be seen in his personal history.

It is interesting that he showed no delay in replying "Healthy Man" when given the stimulus word "Semen". This would suggest that in his pre-occupation with seminal loss and its effects he did not regard himself as peculiarly guilty, but rather as one sharing a widespread disability. Nor was he perturbed by the word "Hinjra", for which he said "Drums". Later he added: "Generally they come when there is a birth in the family. They beat the drums and dance, etc." From this it could be inferred that he viewed the existence of these transvestites as a social phenomenon which did not affect him personally.

RORSCHACH PROTOCOL. PURANMAL MEHTA: AGE 21

Test given 6th October, 1951.

I.
(10″)

∧
∧   Butterfly—the whole thing is a butterfly.
     I think this is a small butterfly sitting on the top of the mount. (This is top left corner, top half inch only.)

TT 1½′

Inquiry

/Doing, those butterflies?/
Small butterfly is sitting, large one looks as though flying.

II. ∧, ∧; 🅂

∧ (45″) There are two cocks (top reds).

I don't find anything else.

TT 1½′

/Can you show me the shape of those cocks?/
> This is the beak (dark red detail adjacent to black mass) and this white one (adjacent pale red area) is the head and these are the legs (inward projections).
/Doing?/ They seem to be walking.
∨ /See this too?—lower red/ I thought they must be arrows, eight arrows.
/And the rest of the card?/
∧ This looks like the end of a pliers (top centre black detail).

III. ∧, ∨; >; ∧, 🅂

∧ (62″) This perhaps a lame dog, both these (Top reds).
This is one leg, dragging (long uppermost red projection) these are other legs (short inward red projections).
∧ These are like cartoons of the heads of two monkeys, just the heads—those ones with the black faces (heads of black figures).
That's all.

TT 3½′

(Unprompted.) Dogs are just sitting and looking back.
/This?—pointing to centre red/
∧,∨ I can't distinguish what it is.

IV. ∧, ∨, ∧

∨ (40″) To me it looks like a fountain, this thing (runs finger up centre line).
∧ And these two, birds (outermost lower corners) the beak, the head and belly (beak and head are small outermost detail, belly the curved adjacent lower margin) but no legs.
(Puts card away.)

TT 1½′

∨ /Can you show me that fountain again?/ Water is not coming, it is just standing there. It is made of stone.
/Colour or shape tells you what it is?/ It is the shape that tells.
/What kind of birds?/ Just some small birds.

V.

(15″)
∨ There are two serpents (top centre projections, in V).
∨ And the whole figure looks like that of a butterfly.
I don't know anything else.

/Serpents doing?/ They are just as if they are listening to the pipe played by the snake-charmer.
∨ Butterfly is flying; this is its head (top centre, same detail as Serpents).

SHRI PURANMAL MEHTA, BANIA

VI. ∧, V; ▣
(30″)

∧   This looks like a statue of stone (top outer corners of main grey mass) and this side also; statue of some God, without limbs (same detail, other side).

∧   These look like serpents, the tails, one, two, three, four, five, six on each side (projections from top centre shaft).

V   The beaks of two birds—only a part of the head is visible (grey claw-shaped top edge details). (Turns card over.)

TT 3′

/Statue, colour or shape told you?/ Colour and shape, both. /Serpents?/ Two are tails (two lowest projections) and the rest are heads—they look like living serpents.

/What bird?/ Birds that are usually found in shallow water, it has a beak like this: a small bird.

VII. ∧, V, ▣
(65″)

∧   There are only a few tower-like things, three towers. Some pillars, like in old places, historical places, ruins of some castles etcetera.

Nothing else.

TT 2½′

/Shape or colour suggests towers?/
White—white colour, like plaster. Plaster pillars.
/Rest of card?/
V This I can say is like a butterfly. (top ¼, in V position). This is the body (dark centre detail). These are the wings (main grey masses). I think it is sitting.

VIII. ∧ ▣
(20″)

∧
V   There are two lions (pink). And here two dogs (outermost parts of orange shapes), only a part of their body and the head.

∧   Some insect that crawls, these two (semi-detached details on outer surfaces of top grey shape).

Nothing else.

TT 2′

∧ /Lions?/ Yes, lions. They look as if they are standing at a high level, on some rock, and they are looking, wanting to go down. There is some water, and they want to go down.
/See the rocks?/ Yes, this and this (all centre-line masses).
/See the water?/ No, it is their pose only makes me think this thing.

IX. ∧, ▣, <; ▣
(55″)

<   Something like a crocodile, the eyes, the mouth, and this is the body (in green-orange margin).

∧   Apples, too (outer rounded pink forms).

∧   And this can be considered to be a fountain (runs finger up centre shaft).
That's all.

TT 3½′

/Apples—colour or shape?/
Shape; colour has also helped to a certain extent.

/That crocodile doing?/ Just relaxing near some grassy bank (points to green-orange area below head). Some of its body

	is in the water (rear portion, vague in outline). This is the water (green area).
∧	Then this is a fountain throwing out water (sweeping gesture of right hand). This water (top centre pale blue).

X. ∧
/This is the last card./
(24″)

∧   This looks like a tube (top centre grey shaft). One only.

∧   Two mangoes (top centre yellow mistletoe shape).

That's all.

TT 2¼′

/Tube?/ A metal tube, of a round shape, with a stand. /Shape or colour?/ I think it is the shape. /And mangoes, colour or shape?/ The shape.

/Anything more to be seen at all?/ Nothing.

(Subject puts card away and tidies up the set of cards.)

Note: This test was carried out in English. Subject is a clerk, son of a small businessman. Married, lives at his parents' house. Has one brother, much older —aged 40. One sister, aged 37. Both are married.

Interpretation of Rorschach Test, by Rosemary Gordon, Ph.D.

Puranmal Mehta

Mr. Mehta, judged by his Rorschach record, is a very constricted and coarted person who had developed obsessional and compulsive defences, and his record is in consequence very meagre and flat. He appears to be so inhibited that he can only react very slowly to new stimuli; he seems to want to avoid concerning himself with general and abstract problems and with attempts to puzzle out the inter-relationship of the parts of a whole situation; he even shows little interest in the usual and everyday details of daily and practical life; instead his attention is riveted to small and limited areas of experience, which are thus capable of providing him with a facile sense of certainty.

Relying mainly on conventional and impersonal mechanisms for the control of his impulses and emotions he is meticulous and hyper-critical and his thought pattern is likely to be rigid and stereotyped.

The record fails to give any evidence that Mr. Mehta might have at his disposal any mature and creative phantasy or the capacity to experience empathy with the people around him; he seems incapable of integrating his impulses with his conscious value system and therefore cannot really accept himself. Yet he has failed in repressing his impulses altogether; instead they have remained childish and immature and he experiences them as urges that are insistent and demand immediate gratification, although he cannot understand them or have insight into them or to perceive their origin and roots within his own personality.

Similarly his reactions to emotional situations—when they do occur in defiance of his defensive techniques—are then impulsive and poorly controlled. Yet it would appear that on the whole his emotional reactions are under better control than are his impulses and phantasies; this is due in part to the fact that he often succeeds in neglecting to attend to or to admit the presence of an emotional situation. Moreover, the impact of such emotional situations is at times capable of stimulating a certain amount of phantasy life and at least some awareness of the divorce that has occurred inside him between his impulse life and his conscious and conventional personality; and with this awareness is mingled regret and a longing to leave the " rocky heights " of aloofness, ambition and independence. When he appears to make contact with his deeper needs and instinctual demands he experiences phantasies of oral satisfaction and an altogether livelier and freer imagination. However, such are only momentary relaxations, for reacting to emotional stimuli also provokes anxiety and sensuous longings and a certain amount of aggression. In consequence the repressive forces quickly re-assert themselves by directing the attention to small and innocuous details and by renewing denial of the presence of an affectively charged situation. Thus after " the lion who stands on a rocky height but looks longingly down at the water below " we return quickly to the " mere insect that crawls up the hill " (responses to Card VIII).

It would appear the Mr. Mehta's problems stem above all from his severe affectional needs and anxieties—possibly caused by some traumatic experience—which have inhibited his capacity to react to other people and to enter into personal relationships with them; for he seems to be oppressed by the fear that he may find himself hurt and repulsed by them. Any demand to relate himself to another person or persons will create inside him tensions from which he will try to escape by a retreat into childish feelings and dull, constricted and conventional modes of apprehending the situation. Moreover, as a result of the combination of fear and aggression which he experiences in his relationships, his inner world is peopled with part objects rather than with whole ones. It is these feelings of anxiety and insecurity and the protective defences that he has developed in order to shield himself from them that seem to have caused him to remain the immature and constricted person that he appears.

It would seem that the principle intra-psychic theme is concerned with the problem of the phallus and its capacity to be functional and life giving. Thus on the Father card Mr. Mehta perceives a fountain, yet no water is coming forth; the serpents on the next card are active only because a snake charmer plays on his pipe to them; while on Card VI, " the Phallic card ", we only meet with incomplete objects—Gods without limbs and snakes that are either just heads or just tails. Thus it would appear that what life force the phallus possesses depends on the presence of an external " charmer ".

Such a phantasy theme would make it extremely difficult for the subject to develop any sort of real independence and self reliance, for he would tend to feel ineffectual and incomplete unless allowed to draw upon the support of some " superior " person. Yet his response to the Father card reveals that the internalised father figure has really been robbed of life and has become " petrified " and rather useless. The subject's relationship to the father can therefore be expected to be very ambivalent, now demanding dependence, now independence, now endowing him with the power to bring forth his—the subject's—own latent forces, only at the next moment to reject him as ineffectual.

The relationship to the mother seems to evoke feelings of depression anxiety and sensuous longings and is perceived as the mere ruin of what was once a splendid, safe and protecting edifice—a castle.

Summing up it may be said that Mr. Mehta has remained an immature and constricted person, exposed to severe affectional longings and anxieties lest he be hurt and rejected by the people around him. He relies upon obsessional and compulsive control mechanisms and is in consequence meticulous, hyper-critical and incapable of entering easily into human relationships or of maintaining an inner world peopled by whole rather than by merely part objects.

His phantasies and needs have remained childish, divorced from his consciously accepted value system and hence not readily susceptible to insight. He tends to deny and overlook the emotional aspect of situations, a method by means of which he often succeeds in suppressing his own emotional reactions which otherwise are likely to betray a good deal of anxiety, sensuous longings and also aggressive and destructive wishes. When the suppressive mechanism fails, his emotional responses are predominantly impulsive and uncontrolled, yet glimpses of the presence of an inner life and phantasy are then made available, which, though consisting of primitive oral wishes, nevertheless are evidence of some inner vitality.

The predominant phantasy theme concerning the father and the phallus suggests that Mr. Mehta is most ambivalent in his relationship to the father and in his attitude to his own dependence and independence.

The relationship to the mother seems to be conceived of as a mere lifeless and hollow relic of what was once magnificent and desirable and in consequence feelings of depression and anxious longings are associated with it.

SUMMARY

This informant would be exceptional in any community for the candour and the disarming naivety with which he tells the most intimate details of his personal life. His account describes all the material inconveniences of life within joint-family household: not least, the difficulties he experiences in his physical and emotional relationships with his wife. His life-story is permeated with the accepted values of his community. Prominence is given to the danger of faecal contamination, and of infringement of his caste's rules on vegetarian and on avoidance of the touch of low-caste members. His frankness enables him to show how, when every possible obstacle is placed in the way of meetings between young people of different sexes, any such encounters become charged with pleasurable, if nervous, excitement.

The influence of his social group is implicit in his attitude to earning money. He tries repeatedly to concentrate upon it with the seriousness which he feels it deserves; but here, as in many instances, his temperament prevents his conforming to the accepted pattern. Again and again he impulsively wastes small sums of money on ill-considered schemes.

He shows clearly that he has repeatedly experienced the short-lived enthusiasms and rapid disillusionments described in Chapter II of this book. His friendships are impulsive, demanding—and unstable. His several business partnerships are disastrous. Even his closest friend is only 80 per cent. reliable, and their friendship suffers violent interruptions. Constantly vacillating in his own purposes, he tries to impose a degree of constancy upon himself by preparing time-tables and lists of resolutions—but to no purpose.

He demonstrates that he shares in the general pre-occupation with fears of impotence and of loss of semen. This gives rise to attempts to impose restraints upon his sexual life; but here again his resolves break down, adding to his anxieties about his failing health and strength. He shares the view of menstruation as a " sign of corruption "; and of intercourse with young virgins as being the least deleterious form of sexual activity.

In his references to his family Puranmal Mehta's unusual insight is apparent. It distresses him to criticise his parents in any way, and yet he rebels impotently against their oppressive over-solicitude, and he is able to admit to himself his feelings of impious rage against his father. In principle, he identifies himself with some of the bolder proposals for social reform (such as widow re-marriage) but in practice he is unable to break away from his upbringing. His naivety in business is perhaps a reflection of his impulsive temperament. His many shortlived enterprises give witness to a fitful enthusiasm for new, idealised projects: but each time his confidence soon falters.

In trying to inspire himself to become constant and assured in what he does, he turns to the Bhagavadgita's teaching of Non-attachment, and intends to make use of prayer and meditation as a soul-fortifying regimen, but to his distress his infirmity of purpose still remains.

The tug-of-war between personal ambition, which is socially disapproved—although professional success leads to a higher social status—and disinterestedness, is still more apparent in Puranmal's history than it is in Shankar Lal's. He is torn between his constant desire to " get on " by winning the favour of influential figures of authority, and his spasmodic, but none the less sincere, resolves to devote part of his time to altruistic public service. In this he resembles many other young followers of Gandhi (and of his disciple, the benign ascetic Acharya Vinoba Bhave) who are unable to commit themselves either to a career of materialistic self-interest, or to its complete renunciation.

This antithesis was described in the majority of the informants' histories. It seemed most acute in the case of the younger Banias, because their traditional " worldly " role was harder to reconcile with the ideal of non-attachment than were those of the Rajputs and the Brahmins. Puranmal is typical of those of his caste (such as Birmal, Chandmal, Bhurmal and Chauthmal) who are turning to careers in politics and in civil administration in the hope of being able to narrow the gulf between their ideal and their actual roles in daily life. Thanks to his gift for self-examination he sees more clearly than the rest that this antinomy has its roots not only in his social predicament but also in the diverse promptings of his own personality.

The lack of mature personality integration is reflected in his Rorschach responses by a turning away from emotional demands which remain infantile and dependent to a would-be isolated and detached position. Once again, relationship towards the father is charged with ambivalent feelings of unmitigated intensity. One cannot help thinking that this may indeed be one of the norms of personality in High-caste Hindus. Towards his mother, on the other hand, the Rorschach elicits feelings of longing and of dereliction which accord well with the general pattern outlined in Chapter X above.

APPENDIX I

CENSUS OF DEOLI, FEBRUARY, 1951

THE following census particulars were derived from the official records of the 1951 census (made available through the courtesy of Sri Yamuna Lal Dashora, M.A., LL.B., Census Commissioner for Rajasthan). The original figures were amended in respect of minor details after a house-by-house check conducted by Vera Carstairs with the assistance of a senior member of the village panchayat.

Total inhabitants	2,417
Households	594

CENSUS ANALYSED BY CASTES

Caste	Households	Persons
Rajput	20	63
Brahmin	36	85
Bania	136	578
Mohammedan	57	228
Daroga (Rajputs' servants)	52	183
Yadows (stone-masons)	45	219
Balahi (weavers)	36	154
Bhil (acculturated tribespeople)	33	157
Bhoi (market gardeners)	23	111
Khatik (butchers)	23	106
Kumbar (potters)	22	78
Nai (barbers)	19	79
Musicians, various sub-castes	9	48
Darzi (tailors)	7	35
Dhobi (washermen)	8	24
Sonar (goldsmiths)	9	46
Lohar (blacksmiths)	5	20
Vairagi (temple attendants)	11	39
Rawat (acculturated tribespeople)	11	45
Harijan (sweepers)	3	22
Sewak (temple attendants)	3	9
Dhabai (cow-herds)	3	8
Halwai (sweetmeat-sellers)	3	7
Teli (oil-pressers)	3	12
Sikh	2	10

CENSUS OF DEOLI, FEBRUARY, 1957

Caste	Households	Persons
Dakot (beggar-caste)	1	9
Bhand (performers)	1	5
Bhat (genealogist)	1	5
Sikligar (swordsmith)	1	5
Suthar (carpenters)	2	6
Kallal (liquor-sellers)	2	5
Vaisye (shopkeepers)	2	8
Christian (the author)	1	2
Hinjra (transvestite)	1	1
Gujar (cow-herd)	1	1
Saddhu	2	4
	594	2,417

APPENDIX II

FORMAL PSYCHOLOGICAL TESTS EMPLOYED

I. *Results of Intelligence Test*

THE test chosen for administration was Raven's Progressive Matrices. This non-verbal test was selected because it was hoped that it might provide a comparative measure of the subjects' intelligence, relatively uncontaminated by their varied degrees of schooling. This hope proved vain.

The number of tests carried out with village Hindu subjects was thirty-seven. Scores ranged from 11 to 45. The mean scores of twelve Rajput subjects was 23; of thirteen Brahmin subjects 27; and of twelve Bania subjects, 26. There was thus no significant difference attributable to membership of one or other caste.

It was a different matter, however, when the subjects were classified into four groups of different levels of schooling. These groups were:

1. Those who had achieved " matric pass ".
2. Those who had attended " middle school ", or who had experienced prolonged instruction along classical Hindu lines.
3. Those who had had elementary school education only.
4. Those whose formal education had been minimal.

All the subjects were literate, but the last group represented those to whom any but the most elementary exercises in reading and writing were unfamiliar if not impossible undertakings. The mean scores of members of these four groups were as follows:

1. Nine members . 35   3. Thirteen members . 22
2. Ten members . 30   4. Five members . 15

There was some overlap between the highest and lowest scores in all groups, with the exception of groups 1 and 4.

The association of schooling and score in the Raven's Test was found to be highly significant, yielding a correlation co-efficient of 0·67 (significant to the 1 per cent. level).

The subjects were also classified in terms of their degrees of familiarity with Western institutions, in order to ascertain whether this might influence the test results also. This classification (which cut across, to some extent, the criterion of formal schooling) was in the following terms:

Group I. Those who had had intimate familiarity with Westernised Institutions (in college, army, or civil administration).

Group II. Those whose business had made them familiar with provincial town life.

Group III. Those who had very little experience of life other than in the village.

The mean scores of members of these three groups were as follows:

Group I. Nine members . . . 36
Group II. Nineteen members . . 25
Group III. Nine members . . . 16

The association of mean scores with these "degrees of exposure to Western influences" was still higher than that with levels of education, yielding a correlation co-efficient of 0·75 (significant to the 0·1 per cent. level).

The conclusion must therefore be drawn that these test scores could be used only to compare the performance of subjects who had enjoyed equivalent amounts of "Westernising" experience; they were not a fair measure of differences in intelligence between members of the population as a whole.

II. *Word-Association Test*

In collaboration with Mrs. G. P. Steed, of Columbia University, a list of eighty stimulus words was prepared and used in field work in Rajasthan in 1950. This list contained a number of words which were believed to be potentially charged with emotional significance and of others whose emotional force was problematical, interspersed among words of a neutral character. During the present study a modification of the former list, containing sixty words, was employed.

The following table shows the words employed, and gives an indication of those which most frequently gave rise to abnormal delays in response, with Rajput, Brahmin, Bania and Moslem subjects respectively. The numbers involved are too small to allow of statistically valid conclusions being drawn; but, nevertheless, certain interesting trends are observable.

WORD-ASSOCIATION TEST

Stimulus word	Rajput	Brahmin	Bania	Moslem
Number of tests completed	9	9	11	8
1. Pani—water		**		*
2. Ghar—house	****	*		**
3. Khet—field			*	
4. Gai—cow		*		*
5. Jalan—envy		**	**	**
6. Shahar—town	*	*	*	*
7. Talwar—sword	****	*	*	**
8. Bachcha—child		**	*	*
9. Talab—lake		*	*	*
10. Jhagra—a fight	****	**	*	**
11. Bap—father	**		*	***
12. Peshi—lawsuit	*	**	**	*
13. Bhangi—sweeper	**		**	**
14. Sharm—modesty	**	*	**	
15. Nasha—intoxication	**	***	***	***
16. Bahin—sister	*	**	**	****
17. Garib—poor	*	**	**	****
18. Gaon—village			*	*
19. Maut—death	*	**	**	****
20. Chutiya—female genitalia	**	***	******	****
21. Parhai—study			***	*
22. Gussa—anger	***	**	*****	*
23. Daru—alcohol	*		**	**
24. Prem—love	**	*	*****	*
25. Jhutha—liar	***			*
26. Larki—girl	**	**	**	*
27. Brahmin		*		**
28. Shadi—wedding			*	
29. Tatti—faeces	**	*	***	
30. Man—mother	*	*	**	*
31. Puja—worship	***		***	*
32. Bhaiband—kinsfolk	**	*		
33. Ling—penis	**	*	******	****
34. Rajput	*			**
35. Biyaj—usury	*	*	*	*
36. Chori—theft	*		**	*
37. Bail—ox				
38. Taqat—strength	**		**	*
39. Bania	*	*	**	*
40. Sasu—wife's mother	**	*	**	***
41. Shastar—Hindu sacred text	***	*	**	

FORMAL PSYCHOLOGICAL TESTS EMPLOYED

	Rajput	Brahmin	Bania	Moslem
42. Barsat—rains		*	*	
43. Susral—in-laws	**		**	***
44. Hinjra—transvestite	****	*	****	*
45. Magra—foothills	*			
46. Bhai—brother	**		*	****
47. Viriya—semen	***	*	**	*
48. Shanti—peace		*	*	**
49. Anyai—immorality		*		
50. Izzat—good name	**	***	**	**
51. Rona—wailing		*		*
52. Guruji—revered teacher		*		**
53. Paisa—money				*
54. Gunghat—woman's veil		*	***	
55. Gobar—cow-dung				
56. Gaddha—ass	***	*	***	*
57. Matki—water-pot				
58. Congress	***	***	*****	**
59. Mussulman	**	*	***	**
60. Mala—garland, or rosary		**	**	*

The suggestive responses are as follows: "House" (2) and "Sword" (7) are especially meaningful to Rajputs, whose role it is to carry arms in defence of the home. "Fight" arrests the attention of Rajputs and Moslems, the two most warlike communities. Frankly (or indirectly) sexual words such as "Vulva" (20), "Love" (24) and "Penis" (33) excite the greatest disturbance among Banias, whose professions of moral rectitude may have been at variance with their private practices. On the other hand, these words were received with equanimity by the acknowledgedly libidinous Rajputs and by the Brahmins (whose sublimation of sexuality may have been more successful than that of most Banias).

A different pattern of response is given to "Transvestite" (44). No community admits to homosexual practices, though each accuses the others. The responses to this word suggests that it is the Rajputs and Banias who are uneasy on this score.

In practice, this test proved most useful in indicating areas of emotional involvement of individual subjects, hence suggesting topics for further talk. Many of the atypical answers revealed interesting associations of ideas. For example, several of the Rajputs seemed to "protest too much". Their defence against uneasy thoughts was one of over-compensation. Thus, Vikram Singh, in whom a naturally belligerent temper was submitting with some difficulty to his application to religion, some responses came very quickly. Among these were " punishment " for both " Immorality " and " Liar ". On the other hand, words at which he paused and gave a more studied reply were, " Sword—it should be for protection ", " Fight—peace ", " Strength—tranquillity " and " Semen—celibacy ".

Nathu Singh, the murderer of his younger brother, showed the defence of over-compensation in high degree. Some of his responses were, " Fight—harmony ", " Kinsfolk—harmony and affection ", " Brother—love ", " Good name—observe decorum ". To " Girl " he gave the unexpected reply " cow ". Later, he explained: " When you said that, I remembered my cow-calf. We have love for calves, as for daughters."

Nathu Singh's surviving brother, Bhagwat Singh, the busy farmer, gave an engaging response with " Ox—comrade ". He added, " He is your friend, he works with you in the fields ". Bhagwat Singh triumphantly over-compensated for the vicissitudes of his family when he replied: " Brother—arm. When you are in trouble, your brother comes and fights for you. He's like your right arm."

This was the first appearance of an association which was echoed by others in all three castes. Several informants also agreed in responding to " Mother " with " fondling ", and to " Father " with " gives instruction ". Bhagwat Singh had been unfortunate in having a mentally unbalanced father, who was no support to his young family. This lent poignancy to his reply: " Father—Guru, one who teaches you." Later, he went on to say: " All he does is he gives you birth, and then he leaves you alone. That's what you find in Mewar. If there's a real good father, such as you very seldom find, he'll teach his sons properly and take good care of them."

Amar Singh showed hesitance in reply to " Poor ", while to " Usury " he said at once: " It oppresses the poor, blast them—it grinds them down. . . . I've always been one to have to borrow rather than to lend money." His response to " Semen ", like that of others, was, " Strength-giving ". He went on to say: " It gives strength to the body. You should not let it become spoiled." In his view, one of the " spoiling " agencies was to surrender to a display of emotion. Thus, " Wailing—never do it. You shouldn't go about being sorrowful and wailing, it does you no good. It dries up all your body. You should pray: God, never let me suffer such a time as will cause me to weep."

Partab Singh singled out " Anger " as a noxious influence. His response was: " Destroys your health. You can't sit down and take things calmly."

The Brahmins' responses were more formal, and introduced mostly accepted idealised values. An interesting variant was in the case of the unlettered, very conservative head of a family, Moti Lal, whose response to " Father " was " Master ", instead of the usual " one who teaches ". Both he and his son emphasised the need to keep the emotions under control. He said: " Peace—keep peace in your heart—one shouldn't become angry "; and Rup Lal said of wailing, with disapproval: " To be rattled by misfortune."

Gopi Lal expressed a private bias when to " Usury " he responded at once " Admirable ". Old Hari Lal gave evidence of the co-existence in his mind of conflicting values, as a result of his travels to big cities, when he gave the response: " Cow-dung—dirty stuff." He qualified this by saying: " It's bad because it's excrement but it's good because it purifies. And it is useful as fuel, too. They give it to you to eat when you undergo a purification. Bullocks' and buffaloes', their dung doesn't purify you. . . . We call cows ' Cow-Mother ', but you don't find us calling oxen or buffaloes ' father '. The Gods themselves consider the cow as sacred."

Puranmal and Daulmal, both Banias, were the only informants to stick completely before a stimulus word. The former was unable to associate to " Anger ". His replies contained echoes of his town upbringing, such as: " Fight—crowd. When there's a quarrel, so many people always assemble," and: " Good name—Business; because generally we hear of business men filing lawsuits for defamation of character ". In keeping with his dual ambitions to achieve material success and to be a philanthropist was his response: " Poor—happy man. Because I think that wealth is a great torment. People lie sleepless, fearing that thieves may break in."

Unlike many of his caste-fellows, Puranmal's response to " Hinjra " was not emotionally charged. He said: " Drums ", and later explained: " Generally they come and play drums and dance when a male child is born in a family."

Daulmal was unable to give any response to this word; a circumstance not unconnected with his private life. Most Banias responded with an abusive rejection of the hinjra, but Bhurmal's response was unusual. He said: " Female penis ". Later he explained: " You have male penis, and female penis and eunuchy. These hinjras often cut their penis short, it's a part of their code. Only those who cut it off are really of that caste."

Several of the Banias showed a hesitance over "Anger", which seemed to imply that their continual profession of non-violence was not sustained without effort. As usual, Rajmal was the most candid, saying: "Anger—assault. Anger, that gives rise to a desperate mood in which you are blind, and not afraid to kill." Bhurmal, a much more circumspect individual, halted for a time at this word, then gave a meaningless clang association: "Gussa-wussa". Later in his test, however, he gave an unusual response in: "Strength—Come on then!" He explained: "When people get angry, they say, 'Come on then, let's see how strong you are'." Much later, in his personal history, Bhurmal revealed that when a cousin tried to appropriate a legacy due to him, he had twice been roused to fight the intruder with a cudgel, in defence of his possessions.

Although the aggressive impulses were there, and related especially to questions of money, they were not consciously recognised. The Banias' idealised outlook was well expressed by two responses of Daulmal, the impoverished rake. Of money, he said: "Bad. It can be good, but it gives rise to all sorts of evil, like stealing, and illness for the want of it. In the eyes of God it is a good thing but among men it gives rise to evil." His response to "Bania" was "Meek", and he later enlarged on this: "However rich a Bania may be, he remains weak at heart. They are never hot-blooded and fierce, like Rajputs. They are ready to swallow insults instead of answering them with more insults and so adding to the quarrel. . . . It is good to be brave in defence of what is holy, and to be steadfast in worshipping God, but not to be quick to get into a rage."

Finally, Birmal, the much-maligned "do-gooder" gave a reply which illustrated a dilemma shared by many others. For "Love" he said: "Wastik (disinterested)", and explained: "There are two kinds of affection, one which is only shown in order to get something out of you, and disinterested affection, which is called 'wastik'."

III. *Rorschach Tests*

The Rorschach "Ink-blot" test was given to all of the principal Deoli informants, and also to nine Moslems in that village and to twenty-two Bhil tribesmen, living in Khajuria and in adjacent hamlets. All but three of these Rorschachs were given in Hindustani, with interpolations in Mewari and in Bhili dialect. It is hoped to make these tests the subject of a separate publication.

Dr. Rosemary Gordon, whose analyses of the Rorschach protocols of Rajendra Singh, Shankar Lal and Puranmal Mehta are given at the end of their respective life histories, made the following observations upon her task:

" The Rorschach records produced by the three Indian men were interpreted by me in much the same way as I would interpret a European record. It is not quite clear to what extent this is a truly legitimate procedure, especially with respect to such scoring categories as animals and animal movements. For it is likely that animals and animals in movement are perceived much more readily by a person living in a rural environment, in a country where animals and fights between animals and between men and animals are daily spectacles and where, moreover, animal figures play a prominent role in mythology and religion. In such a society the culture itself induces the projection of human traits and propensities into the animal kingdom and thus reduces that sense of differentiation between men and beasts current in the western post-Renaissance climate of opinion. Consequently the interpretation of an excess of animal movement over human movement responses as indicative of the predominance of immature and infantile impulses and phantasies, may not really be warranted in a Hindu Rorschach.

" Again, many more Hindu responses would have to be examined before we can really score with confidence the goodness of Form response or Popular and Original responses. Fabulations are also more likely to occur in individuals steeped in a rich and ebullient mythology and surrounded by much baroque statuary and architecture. On the other hand because of the considerable culture contact with the West and coming from a society in transition, a true assessment of each Indian record would have to be preceded by a detailed analysis of the life history of the subject, particularly in terms of the objects and ideas that have surrounded him.

" In the present research, interview material is available as a check on the information provided by the Rorschach; the test can thus be evaluated both as a method of deepening our understanding of the individuals investigated and as a valid tool in cross cultural studies."

APPENDIX III

GLOSSARY OF HINDUSTANI WORDS

Achar-bichar	customary usage, avoidance of lower-caste contamination
Admi	person
Aghori	filthiness
Agni	fire
Agwa	protective escort
Ahinsa	non-violence
Almira	cupboard
Andata	Giver of Grain
Anek	innumerable
Anna	coin, one-sixteenth of one rupee
Arjuna	hero of the Ramayana
Asan	the place where one sits for prayer
Ashram	secluded place of instruction
Asli	genuine
Atma	spirit
Audich	sub-caste of the Brahmins
Augar-Baba	a type of wandering holy men
Ayurvedic	Indian system of medicine
Badparhez	not controlling the passions
Badpheli	unclean leavings of a meal
Badsha	King
Bahin	sister
Balak	infant
Bam-marg	the sect of the left hand (synonym for laja-dharm)
Bania	merchant
Banola	bridegroom's pre-wedding procession and feast
Bāra	twelve
Băra	great
Barabar	equal
Belaiti	foreigner
Bhadarapada	Hindu summer month
Bhagat	devotee
Bhagavadgita	Hindu religious poem

GLOSSARY OF HINDUSTANI WORDS

Bhagwan	God
Bhai	brother
Bhairav	a name of Shiv
Bhajan	hymn
Bhakti	Emotional worship
Bhakti-marg	the way of worship
Bhang	infusion of Indian Hemp leaves (cannabis indica)
Bhangi	sweeper caste
Bhatak	gone astray, erroneous
Bhatak Bhairav	inferior manifestation of Shiv, of a terrible character
Bheruji	local form of Bhairava, the destructive aspect of Shiva
Bhiksha	one who has renounced all worldly goods (cf. sannyasi)
Bhishti	water-carrying caste
Bhopa	priest who becomes possessed by the spirit of his deity
Bhut	bad or evil giant, or ghost
Bidi	leaf-wrapped cigarette
Bij	seed
Bira	betel-leaf containing a spiced chew of betel nut
Brahmacharya	ascetic way of life
Brahmanand	the sacred spot at the vertex of the skull
Brahmin	priest, member of the highest order of castes
Bramchari	student of divinity school
Chakkar	a circle
Chandal	sweeper
Chapatti	unleavened bread
Chaprassi	porter
Charan	member of the minstrel-genealogist caste
Charbuja	" Four-Armed ", a Vaishnavite god
Chattri	canopy
Chela	disciple
Choti	male Hindu's top-knot or pigtail
Dakan	witch
Dak bungalow	bungalow for the use of travellers
Dakot	low-caste temple servant
Dal	lentils

Daroga	servant-caste
Darshan	a vision, revelation
Daru	distilled alcoholic drink
Dashera	Hindu festival
Dashora	Brahmin sub-caste
Daung	fraud
Deepavali	see Divali
Devalo	sorcerer
Devata	small god, ancestor-spirit
Dev-gun	of benign aspect
Devra	shrine
Dhan	wealth
Dhan-teras	festival of the worship of worldly wealth
Dhapa	bride-price
Dharm	faith, rule of conduct
Dharma	duty, right conduct, religious observance
Dharm-bahin	adopted sister-in-honour
Dharm-bhai	blood-brother
Dharm-Raj	Vaishnavite God
Dingal-basha	Rajasthani dialect
Divali	festival of lights
Dobara	" double-distilled ", a form of daru
Dohita	rhymed couplet
Dudh	milk
Durrie	woven cotton carpet
Gaddha	ditch
Gadha	ass
Gaitri-mantar	inspiring religious verse
Galkatia	throat-cutter, butcher
Ganga-jal	Ganges water
Garab	miasma
Gari	a cart, or pony-trap
Garmi	heat; also syphilis
Gau	cow
Gau-mutr	cow's urine
Gawri	Gauri or Parvati; hence, the dance-cycle performed by Bhils in her honour
Gehlotes	Rajput lineage of the Mewar royal line
Ghas	grass
Gher	Bhil stick-dance
Ghi	butter
Ghora	horse
Gis len aya	Bhili for brought by capture

GLOSSARY OF HINDUSTANI WORDS

Gobar	cow-dung
Gopi	girl cow-herd
Gotra	extended lineage—the exogamous fraction of an endogamous sub-caste
Grahasta	one who marries and raises a family
Gur	molasses
Guru	religious teacher
Hada	Rajput lineage
Halki	light-weight; counterfeit
Hanuman	the Monkey-god
Hath	hand
Hau	well
Hindu Mahasabha	Hindu political party
Hinjra	homosexual, institutionalised transvestite
Holi	Spring festival, the Hindu saturnalia
Hukm	an order
Ishwar	God
Jagaran	a wake, an all-night ceremony
Jagir	a grant of land, often held in return for services
Jagirdar	hereditary landlord
Jal	water
Jannu	knowledge
Janoi	the sacred thread
Jantar	amulet
Janwar	animal
Jati	sub-caste
Jenam-asthmi	festival of the birth of Krishna
Jhala	Rajput sub-caste
Jhompri	hut
Jhutha	leavings
Jiman	eating
Jiryan	running, flowing; hence spermatorrhoea
Jogi	an ascetic
Johar	self-immolation in battle
Jot	flame
Jot-marg	secret cult with sexual practices
Jug	era
Kabir-panth	followers of Kabir, a religious teacher
Kaf	phlegm

Kala	black
Kala-nag	black snake
Kali	the black demon-mother Goddess
Kal-yug	era of calamity
Kamand	headless
Kamria-pat	a Bhil god in the form of a brass horse
Kanchli	bodice
Kanchli-panth	secret cult with sexual practices
Karma	pre-ordained fate
Kasrat	exercise
Kattha	chapter
Khadi	coarse hand-woven cloth
Khana	food
Khand-wala	sugar-seller
Khartik	an autumn month
Khatik	Butcher-caste
Ki jai	" victory to . . ."
Krishna	a major Hindu God
Kul-dev	a family or chief deity
Kumhar	a potter
Kunda	basin
Kunda-panth	secret cult which violates normal Hindu rules of sexual and eating behaviour
Laddu	sweetmeat
Laj	shame
Laja-dharm	sect observing sexual rituals
Lota	small metal pot
Magra	foothills
Mahabharata	Hindu religious epic poem
Mahwa	flowering tree (Bassia latifundia)
Makai, makka	Indian corn
Man	a maund (usually equivalent to 40 sers or 82 lbs.)
Mandli	meeting
Mantar	a charm
Mardana	men's section of a Rajput household
Marg	a way, or sect
Mas	flesh
Mast	drunk, frenzied, on heat (of elephants)
Mata	mother
Mataji	revered Mother-Goddess
Maya	illusion

GLOSSARY OF HINDUSTANI WORDS

Mitti	earth, dust, filth
Moksh	deliverance, release, final beatitude
Mukhi	village headman
Mukti	see moksh
Mung	variety of lentil
Murgi	hen
Nahin	no, not
Nai	barber
Namaste	Indian greeting with palms together
Nandi	a bull, the steed of Shiv
Navratri	festival of the nine nights, when offerings are made to the Goddess
Naya	new
Nazarana	ceremonial gift to a superior
Nilam	gambling on stock exchange prices
Nir-akarpur	incorporeal
Nirvana	deliverance, extinction
Niyam	restraining, rule, measure
Niyam-se	in due measure
Nura	brilliance, light
Pakka	complete, ripe. Of houses, soundly built
Pakodi	savoury sweetmeat
Paliwal	Brahmin sub-caste
Pan	leaf flavoured with betel-nut for chewing
Panch	five
Panchayat	council, of caste or village group
Panch-gavya	the five products of the cow
Pandit	learned man
Panth	path or way; a sect
Parmatma	the supreme soul; God
Pat	throne
Pie, pice	small coins
Pi lo	drink up
Podina	mint
Poorie	fried pancake
Pradosh	evening twilight; a fast day
Pranayam	controlled breathing
Prashad	a favour; food which has been offered to a God; food of which one's Guru has partaken
Prem	love, affection
Prithwi	the earth

Puja	respect, worship
Punam	day of the full moon
Purbaj	spirit of a man recently dead
Quam	tribe, sect, or caste
Ragliaji	local deity
Rais	wealthy man, eminent person
Răj	menses
Rāj	rule
Raj-guru	tutor of a prince
Rajput	warrior caste
Rakshas-gun	of demoniac aspect
Ramayana	Hindu religious epic poem
Ras	juice, humour, semen
Rasoi	food
Rawat	tribal community
Rebari	caste of camel-herders
Rohita	red, a kind of deer
Rup	form, appearance
Saddhu	holy man
Safa	turban worn in local fashion
Samadhi	religious vow; act of self-immolation (by burial alive) in achieving nirvana
Samjhana	to instruct
Sandhya	sitting at prayer
Sannyasi	one who had abandoned all worldly possessions
Saran	water-channel
Sardar	headman; polite term of address to a Rajput
Sarhe	prefix meaning " and a half "
Sari	woman's veil
Sath-Narayan	a name of God
Sat-jug	the golden age
Satsang	association with wise men
Ser	a weight (approx. 2 lbs.)
Shakti	power
Shan	nature, disposition
Shanti	peace
Shastar or shastras	Hindu sacred texts
Sheshodia	Rajput lineage
Shikar	hunting

GLOSSARY OF HINDUSTANI WORDS

Shikari	hunter
Shil-vrit	total fast
Shiva	a major Hindu God
Shivratri	festival of the birthday of Shiva
Shraddha	ceremonies observed after a death
Sikotri	Bhili for witch
Sindur	vermilion
Sirauni	food-offering made at the cremation ground
Sirdar	see sardar
Sirpanch	head of the village council
Sita	Goddess, heroine of the Ramayana
Slok	couplet, or text
Sudra	man of the labouring castes
Sujak	penile discharge; gonorrhoea
Sumeru	last bead of a rosary
Suraj, surya	the sun
Tabiz	amulet, charm
Tani layo	Bhili for brought by force
Tapassya	self-mortification
Tat-pattis	rush mats
Tazia	tower of decorated bamboo carried at the Moslem festival of Moharram
Tazim	honour, respect
Teras	thirteenth day of each half-month
Thakur	landlord
Than	breast
Thandai	sweet drink containing hashish
Tikhana	large feudal land grant
Tola	one rupee-weight (180 grains)
Tonga	two-wheeled carriage
Tyagi	an ascetic
Ubo	upright, outstanding
Upasana	worship, reverence
Upasana-marg	the way of devotions
Vaidya	Hindu physician
Vaishnavi	worshippers of Vishnu
Vaisya	Hindu member of the merchant caste
Vakil	lawyer
Vanaprastha	forest-dweller
Vanashrama	place of instruction in the forest

Vayu	vapour
Vedas	ancient Hindu religious epics
Vir	brave
Vir-bhumi	land of the brave
Virodh	opposition, contradiction
Virodh-panth	cult of " the way of opposition "
Virya or viriya	semen
Vrit	abstinence, fast
Wasna	lust
Yogi	see jogi
Yug	see jug
Zai-baraw	marriage by capture (Bhili)

BIBLIOGRAPHY

ANAND, M. R.   Untouchable.   *Hutchinson, London, 1947.*
Coolie.   *Hutchinson, London, 1948.*

BATESON, G. and MEAD, M.   Balinese Character: A Photographic Analysis.   Special publications of the *New York Academy of Sciences*, Vol. II, *1942*.
BENEDICT, R.   Patterns of Culture.   *New York, 1934.*
The Chrysanthemum and the Sword.   *Houghton Mifflin, Boston, 1946.*
BOAS, F.   Introduction to Handbook of American-Indian Languages.   *Washington, 1911.*

CARSTAIRS, G. M.   "The Case of Thakur Khuman Singh: a Culture-conditioned Crime."   Brit. J. Delinquency, **4,** 14-25, *1953.*
"Daru and Bhang: Cultural Factors in the Choice of Intoxicants."   Quart. J. Stud. Alcohol (*Yale, 1954*), **15,** 220-237.
CORBETT, J.   The Man-eating Leopard of Rudraprayag. *Oxford Univ. Press, 1948.*
My India.   *Oxford Univ. Press, 1952.*

DAVIS, A. and DOLLARD, J.   Children of Bondage.   *American Council on Education, Washington, 1940.*
DAVIS, A., GARDNER, B. B. and GARDNER, M. R.   Deep South. *Univ. of Chicago Press, 1941.*
DICKS, H. V.   "Personality Traits and National Socialist Ideology," Human Relations, **3,** 2, 111-154, *1950*.
"Observations on Contemporary Russian Behaviour." Human Relations, **5,** 2, 111-175, *1952.*
DOLLARD, J.   Caste and Class in a Southern Town.   *New Haven: Yale Univ. Press, 1937.*
DOWSON, J.   A Classical Dictionary of Hindu Mythology and Religion.   *Routledge, London, 1950.*
DUBE, S. C.   Indian Village.   *Routledge and Kegan Paul, London, 1954.*

ERIKSON, E. H.   "Childhood and Tradition," in Psychoanalytic Study of the Child, *1945.*
Childhood and Society.   *Norton, New York, 1950.*
EVANS-PRITCHARD, E.   The Nuer.   *Oxford Univ. Press, 1940.*

FENICHEL, O. The Psychoanalytic Theory of Neuroses. *Norton, New York, 1945.*
FORSTER, E. M. A Passage to India. *Arnold, London, 1932.*
  The Hill of Devi. *Arnold, London, 1953.*
FORTES, M. The Dynamics of Clanship among the Tallensi. *Oxford Univ. Press, 1945.*
  The Web of Kinship among the Tallensi. *Oxford Univ. Press, 1949.*

GEDDES, A. "The Social and Psychological Significance of Variability in Population Change, with examples from India, 1871-1941." Human Relations, **1**, *2, 1947.*
GHOSE, S. N. And Gazelles Leaping. *Michael Joseph, London, 1949.*
  The Flame of the Forest. *Michael Joseph, London, 1955.*
GORER, G. The Americans. *Cresset Press, London, 1948* (American edition: The American People. *Norton, New York*).
  Chapter: "National Character: Theory and Practice," in Mead and Métraux, The Study of Culture at a Distance, *1953.*
GORER, G. and RICKMAN, J. The People of Great Russia. *Cresset Press, London, 1949.*

HUXLEY, A. The Doors of Perception. *Chatto and Windus, London, 1954.*

KARDINER, A. The Individual and His Society. *Columbia Univ. Press, New York, 1939.*
  The Psychological Frontiers of Society. *Columbia Univ. Press, New York, 1945.*
KIPLING, R. Letters of Travel, 1892-1913. *Macmillan, London, 1920.*
  Kim. *Macmillan, London, 1950 (new edn.).*
KLEIN, M. Psychoanalysis of Children. *Hogarth, London, 1927.*
  Developments in Psychoanalysis. *Hogarth, London, 1952.*
  New Directions in Psychoanalysis. *Tavistock, London, 1955.*

MALINOWSKI, B. Argonauts of the Western Pacific. *Routledge, London, 1922.*
  The Sexual Life of Savages. *Routledge, London, 1929.*

BIBLIOGRAPHY

MANDELBAUM, D. "On the Study of National Character." American Anthropologist, **55,** 174, *1953.*
MARRIOTT, McK. Editor, Village India. *Chicago Univ. Press, 1955.*
MEAD, M. Coming of Age in Samoa, *1928.*
Growing Up in New Guinea, *1930.*
Sex and Temperament in Three Primitive Societies, *1935.*
From the South Seas. *Norton, New York,* containing the above three studies in one volume, *1939.*
And Keep Your Powder Dry. *Morrow, New York, 1942.*
MEAD, M. and MÉTRAUX, R. The Study of Culture at a Distance. *Chicago Univ. Press, 1953.*
MURPHY, G. and L. B. In the Minds of Men. *Basic Books, New York, 1953.*
MYERS, L. H. The Near and the Far. *Cape, London, 1943.*

NARAYAN, R. K. The Bachelor of Arts. *Eyre & Spottiswoode, London, 1948.*
The English Teacher. *Eyre & Spottiswoode, London, 1948.*
The Financial Expert. *Methuen, London, 1952.*
Waiting for the Mahatma. *Methuen, London, 1955.*
NEHRU, J. Selected Writings. *Probsthain, London, 1950.*

OPLER, M. E. "Themes as Dynamic Forces in Culture". Amer. J. Sociology, **51,** 198-206, *1945.*
OPLER, M. E. and SINGH, R. D. Chapter: "The Division of Labour in an Indian Village," in C. S. Coon's Reader in General Anthropology, *1948.*

RICHARDS, A. I. Land Labour and Diet in Northern Rhodesia. *Routledge, London, 1939.*
RIVERS, W. H. R. Psychology and Ethnology. *Routledge, London, 1926.*
ROHEIM, G. "Psychoanalysis of Primitive Peoples." Int. J. Psychoanalysis, **13,** 2, *1932.*
The Riddle of the Sphinx. *Hogarth, London, 1934.*
Psychoanalysis and Anthropology. *Int. Univ. Press, New York, 1950.*

SCHAFFNER, B. Father Land. *Columbia Univ. Press, New York, 1948.*
SRINIVAS, M. N. Religion and Society among the Coorgs. *Oxford Univ. Press, 1952.*

TAGORE, R. Gitanjali. *Macmillan, London, 1913.*
  Collected Poems and Plays. *Macmillan, London, 1936.*
TAYLOR, W. S. "Basic Personality in Orthodox Hindu Culture Patterns." J. Abn. and Social Psychol., **43,** 3-12, *1948.*
TREVELYAN, G. M. History and the Reader. *National Book League, London, 1945.*

WARNER, W. LLOYD. American Caste and Class. Am. J. Sociol., **42,** 234-237, *1936.*

INDEX

Affection, 45, 157, 159, 161, 235, 237-8, 324
Ahinsa, 98, 119, 166
Alcohol, 97, 109, 136, 164
Ambivalence, 71, 111, 257
Anger, 46, 112, 196, 199, 323-4
Anxiety, 54, 83, 85-7, 107, 109, 114, 166, 168, 212-14, 255-7, 259, 314
Apotheosis, 95, 119 (*see also* " Samadhi ")
Ascetic, 55, 156, 161, 167, 225, 315
Asceticism, 132, 163, 167, 169
Astrology, 33, 52, 71
Atma, 51, 95
Austerities, 97-9, 161, 204
Authority, 19, 25, 112, 128, 140-2, 160, 164, 169, 214-15, 314
Ayurvedic medicine, 15, 82

Bateson, G., 153, 335
Bathing, 66-7, 81-2, 96, 116, 218, 226, 228, 278, 303
Begging, 55-7, 60, 104, 160
Benedict, R., 138, 153, 173, 335
Bhagavadgita, 26, 194, 218, 227, 273, 275, 314
Bhakti, 94, 119, 230-2, 237
Bhang, 116, 118-19, 298
Bhil, 13, 16, 89, 108, 125 ff., 191, 202, 223, 228
Bhopa, 26, 34, 53, 55, 64, 83, 92-4, 105, 131, 135, 149, 165, 241
Blood, formation of, 84, 195-6, 240

Blood, purity of, 181
Blood sacrifice, 93, 135-6, 165
Boas, F., 154-5, 335
British Raj, 13, 15, 41, 142-3
Brother, 69-71, 112-14, 117, 122, 181, 260

Caste organisation, 23-4, 57-9, 145-6
Castration, 47, 159-60, 163, 167-8, 256-8
Celibacy, 73, 84, 87, 96, 132, 145
Child-rearing, 16, 63-4, 66-8, 112, 133, 148-9, 157-8, 181-3
Churchill, W. S., 191, 192, 205
Cleanliness, 63, 66-7, 80-2, 96, 107, 114, 122, 163-4, 219, 228
Cleansing, 80-2, 107
Commensality (*see* " Eating together ")
Communism, 177, 190
Concentration, 98, 101, 192, 194, 198, 230
Congress, 13, 24-5, 30-5, 43, 53, 77, 116, 122, 124, 140-1, 148, 176, 181, 204, 238-40, 244
Constancy, 55, 106, 158, 314
Contamination, 81, 88, 107, 115, 161, 164, 167, 313
Contemplation, 78, 98, 116, 178
Contradictions, 52-4, 91, 104, 106, 111, 232, 259
Cow, 65, 103, 114, 129, 162, 240, 246, 322-3

Darshan, 89, 99, 179, 197, 198, 239, 306

339

Daru, 59, 97, 98, 109, 118-19, 126, 129, 185, 188, 201
Davis, A., 23, 335
Death, 82, 92, 102, 116, 123, 135, 149, 185, 204, 233, 257-8, 271
Defilement, 59, 73, 77, 79-82, 88, 102, 246
Deviant, 123
Dharm, 57, 85, 95, 105, 115, 118, 135, 145, 223
Dharm-bahin, 71, 103, 236
Dicks, H. V., 153, 335
Distrust, 40-3, 45, 55, 89, 106, 215
Dollard, J., 23, 335
Dream, 47, 54, 197, 233-5, 237-8, 271
Drinking, 193, 194
Dube, S. C., 150, 335
Duty, 24, 56-8, 68, 70, 74, 95, 107-9, 115, 133, 147, 177-9, 226-30

Eating together, 24, 59, 75, 85-6, 102-3, 115, 164-5, 234, 245
Elite, 14, 23
Emotion, 49, 94-5, 97-8, 106, 114, 117, 150-1, 211-15, 247, 256-9, 311-13, 315, Ch. 10 *passim*
Emotional deprivation, 38
Empathy, lack of, 49-51, 106, 161, 168
Enthusiasm, 40, 44, 296, 314
Erikson, E., 12, 153, 173, 335
Evans-Pritchard, E., 8, 137, 335
Extended family, 38, 45, 61, 66, 74-5, 146-7, 149, 313

Factions, 43, 46, 113, 121
Faeces, 67, 80-1, 88, 107, 134, 162, 164, 167, 205, 246

Faith, 55, 83, 145, 239
Family relationships, 45, 63 ff., 113-14, 116-17, 122, 124, 133-4, 147, 156 ff., 179, 181-3, 196, 217, 231, 261-4, 271-2, 302-6, 314, Ch. 4 *passim* (*see* " Father-son relations " and " Mother-son relations ")
Famine, 19
Father-son relations, 45, 67-70, 75-6, 113-14, 116-17, 122, 133-4, 147, 159-67, 181-2, 196, 213-15, 256-7, 276-7, 312-15
Forde, D., 173
Formality, 27, 46, 48, 106, 116
Forster, E. M., 10, 44
Fortes, M., 8, 137, 335
Freud, S., 139
Friend, 41-2, 44-5, 216, 221, 231, 235-6, 278, 314
Friendship, 221, 235-6, 278, 314

Gandhi, 10, 33-4, 37, 42, 116, 121, 141, 180, 232, 238, 315
Geddes, A., 38, 336
Ghosts, 53, 78, 89, 92, 94, 197
Goddess, 55, 91, 120, 126, 130, 135 (*see* " *Mataji* ")
Goodwill, 40-1, 44
Gorer, G., 138, 153, 171, 173, 336
Gotra, 24, 70, 75, 128
Gough, K., 72, 80
Guilt, 86, 115, 160, 307
Guru, 44-6, 71, 96, 98, 103-5, 106, 160-1, 178, 197-9, 222-3

Homosexuality, 60, 72, 113, 148, 161, 163, 167, 321
Hospitality, 50, 89, 180, 193
Huxley, A., 118-19, 336

INDEX

Ideal, 55, 57, 71, 84, 86, 87, 96-9, 107, 113, 119, 122, 139, 156
Idealism, 44
Impatience, 85, 132, 167, 314
Incest, 70, 104-5, 118, 195
Intoxication, 110, 118, 165, 188

Jagir, 21, 113, 185, 193, 201
Jagirdar, 21, 24, 176-7, 200-1, 204
Jain, 16, 25, 26, 35-6, 121, 239
Janoi, 102, 186, 229, 240 (*see also* " Sacred Thread ")
Jiryan, 85, 87
Johar, 111
Joint family (*see* " Extended family ")
Jutha, 80, 162, 164

Kal-yug, 142, 242
Kardiner, A., 8, 153, 336
Karma, 57, 95, 145, 180
Klein, M., 155-6, 336
Krishna, 163, 273

Laja-dharm, 102-4, 118, 164
Leighton, A., 8
Lineage (*see* " *Gotra* ")
Lingam, 163, 166, 239
Lorenz, K., 112

Magic, 86, 89, 90, 104, 130-1, 149, 155, 161
Mahabharat, 26, 100, 142, 144, 227, 244
Malinowski, B., 137, 337
Mandelbaum, D., 138, 337
Mantar, 116, 131, 198, 222, 227

Marriage, 12, 24, 45, 70, 130-2, 135-6, 150, 218-19, 224, 242, 264
Marriott, M., 150, 337
Masturbation, 72, 263
Mataji, 55, 65, 131, 135, 157, 159-60, 163, 165
Maya, 48, 92, 145, 158
Mead, M., 8, 12, 137, 138, 153, 171, 173, 335, 337
Measure, 87, 96-8, 109-11, 199-200
Meat, 84, 87, 93, 96-8, 109-10, 118, 124, 135-6, 165-6, 181, 201
Mediator, 47, 121, 130
Meditation, 100, 105, 116, 230-1, 314
Métraux, R., 153, 171, 337
Meyer, A., 11, 170
Miracles, 99-101, 107
Mistrust, 56, 158
Mohammedan (or Moslem), 25, 26, 39, 85, 89-90, 120, 127, 186-7, 200, 244
Moksh, 95, 101, 102, 105, 116-17, 124, 145, 161, 180, 222
Money-lending, 20, 114, 120, 243
Mother-child relationship, 63 ff., 70, 75-6, 133, 155 ff., 256, 312-13, 315
Mother-goddess (*see* " *Mataji* ")
Mother-in-law, 66-7
Murder, 30, 108, 112, 120, 127, 132
Murphy, G., and L. B., 67, 147, 337
Myths, 48, 91

National character, 3-4, 10-15, 138, 172-3
Nehru, J., 10, 53, 337

Neurosis, 10, 86, 87
Niyam (see "Measure")
Non-attachment, 97, 124, 156, 231, 237, 252, 314-15
Non-violence, 16, 46, 112, 121, 169, 324

Obligations, 57, 68, 75, 76, 115, 120, 124, 133, 149-50, 160, 168, 180
Obsessional traits, 107, 163-4, 310
Oedipal situation, 159, 161, 165, 166, 215, 259
Oedipus complex, 86, 168, 259
Omens, 51
Opler, M. E., 8, 138, 150, 337
Optimism, 54, 106, 157
Outcast, 60-1, 115, 145

Paranoid reactions, 15, 82, 83, 106, 125, 127, 161, 163, 213, 257
Peacemaker, 47
Phantasy, 44, 45, 55, 78, 83, 111, 127, 139, 151, 152, 154, 156, 157, 158, 159, 172, 211-15, 255-7, 311-13
Philosophy, 10, 11, 113, 138-9, 144
Phoneme, 154-6
Piaget, J., 152
Possession, 83, 92-4, 131, 135, 149
Prashad, 80, 103
Prayer, 99-100, 105, 116, 177-80, 182, 185, 195-6, 200-1, 222, 230, 232
Primal scene, 66, 134
Psychoanalysis, 11, 125, 139-40, 151, 154, 164, 167-8, 171-3
Psychobiology, 11, 170

Psychology, 10-11, 110, 137-8, 153, 176, 217, 221
Purbaj, 92-3, 197
Purdah, 14, 70, 112, 122
Purification, 63, 115, 229, 246, 323

Quarrel, 30, 33, 46-7, 74, 79, 106, 114, 121, 236, 261, 263, 278

Rajah, 12, 13, 41, 49, 50, 108, 110, 142-3, 195, 220
Ramayana, 26, 100, 114, 142, 144, 224, 244, 265, 273
Release (see "*Moksh*")
Reliability, 52
Renunciation, 56, 62, 102, 225, 315
Restraint (of emotional display), 60, 61, 66, 68-9, 72, 76, 106-7, 117, 147, 159, 231, 258
Richards, A. I., 137, 337
Roheim, G., 12, 153, 337
Role, 57-8, 60-2, 109, 115, 146-7, 150

Sacred thread, 14, 81, 150, 177, 180, 186-7, 222, 223, 227, 233
Saddhu, 51, 55, 78, 86, 89, 96, 100, 118, 121, 224, 322
Samadhi, 101, 102, 119, 161, 205, 233
Sannyasi, 55, 97, 102, 111, 195, 199, 222, 224-5, 231, 233
Saturnalia, 72
Secret cults (see "*Lajadharm*"), 102-5, 223
Self-control, 46, 72, 156
Self-discipline (mortification), 79, 100, 107, 111

INDEX

Self-repression, 134
Self-restraint, 47, 124
Semen, 72, 83-8, 98, 103, 109, 117, 132, 159, 195-6, 240-1, 263, 265, 307, 314, 322
Sensuality, 72, 106, 107, 110, 145, 163, 169
Serenity, 56, 168, 263
Sexual intercourse, 64-6, 72-4, 81, 84-7, 96, 103, 104, 110, 117-18, 134, 148, 159, 166, 195, 222, 225-6, 228, 236-7, 265-6, 288, 297-8, 314
Sexuality, 105, 160-1, 163, 166-7, 259
Shakti, 231, 239
Shastras, 218, 228, 230, 237, 246, 305
Shikar, 179, 181-2
Shiva, 48, 80, 93, 102, 118, 159, 163, 165-6, 177, 223, 229, 273
Sister, 70-1, 75, 181, 224
Social mobility, 23-4, 142, 147
Social structure, 137, 150, 153
Spontaneity, 40, 44, 57, 61, 68, 86, 113, 136, 147, 152, 156, 160, 168, 258
Srinivas, M. N., 24, 150, 337
Status, 23-4
Steed, G. P., 8, 17
Suckling, 63, 157, 162
Suspicion, 40-2, 212
Suttee, 74, 91, 203

Tapassya, 100, 163, 205
Taylor, W. S., 150, 338
Toilet training, 66-7, 134, 149, 164, 219
Tolerance, 148, 174

Transvestism, 59-62, 133, 307
Trevelyan, G. M., 173, 338
Trust, 44, 56, 83, 178

Untouchable, 25, 59, 82, 134, 162, 228-9, 245-6
Upbringing (*see* " Child-rearing ")

Vedas, 102, 220, 222, 240
Violence, 13, 47, 65, 109, 111-12, 129, 132, 274
Virya (*see* " Semen ")
Virility, 109, 166-7
Vishnu, 48, 93, 163, 165, 229, 239

Warner, W. L., 23, 338
Weaning, 63-4, 133, 150, 158
Western influences, 20, 141-2, 144, 148, 224, 242
Whitecaps (Congress supporters), 190, 202
Wife, 45, 68, 84, 96, 277, 286
Will-power, 99-100, 184, 189, 192, 232
Wine, 84, 87, 93, 96, 118, 179, 187-8, 201
Witch, 56-7, 73, 83, 93-4, 157
Witchcraft, 26, 56-7, 89, 90, 105, 130-1, 196
Women, inferiority of, 195
Women, phantasies concerning, 56-7, 157-9, 167-8

Yoga, 95-6, 184, 213
Yogi, 86, 180, 231

MADE AND PRINTED IN GREAT BRITAIN
BY MORRISON AND GIBB LIMITED
LONDON AND EDINBURGH

RET'D NOV 4 1986